Learning Languages in Early Modern England

John Gallagher was educated at Trinity College Dublin and Emmanuel College, Cambridge. After holding a Research Fellowship in History at Gonville & Caius College, Cambridge, he joined the University of Leeds, where he is now Associate Professor in Early Modern History.

Learning Languages in Early Modern England

JOHN GALLAGHER

OXFORD
UNIVERSITY PRESS

OXFORD
UNIVERSITY PRESS

Great Clarendon Street, Oxford, OX2 6DP,
United Kingdom

Oxford University Press is a department of the University of Oxford.
It furthers the University's objective of excellence in research, scholarship,
and education by publishing worldwide. Oxford is a registered trade mark of
Oxford University Press in the UK and in certain other countries

First published 2019
First published in paperback 2022

Published in the United States of America by Oxford University Press
198 Madison Avenue, New York, NY 10016, United States of America

British Library Cataloguing in Publication Data
Data available

Library of Congress Cataloging in Publication Data
Data available

ISBN 978–0–19–883790–9 (Hbk.)
ISBN 978–0–19–286515–1 (Pbk.)

Acknowledgements

This book would not exist were it not for the kindness, generosity, and support of my colleagues, teachers, and friends. My first thanks go to Phil Withington. I owe more than I can say to his interest, patience, and encouragement at every stage of research and writing. Alex Walsham and Warren Boutcher examined the dissertation from which this book emerged: I would like to thank them for their careful and generous reading, and for their advice and support ever since. I am also grateful to Stephen Alford and Ciarán Brady, with whom I first began to explore the questions that animate this book.

I have been lucky to work on this book in a series of happy academic homes. Emmanuel College, Cambridge, was a supportive and friendly environment in which to write a PhD. It was a privilege to spend nearly three years as a Research Fellow at Gonville and Caius College, Cambridge. Caius is home to an extraordinary community of historians, and I am grateful to them and to the fellowship as a whole for everything I learnt there. Since moving to the University of Leeds, I have benefited from the collegiality and kindness of my colleagues and friends in the School of History and beyond, and been continually inspired by our brilliant students. Support from the Arts and Humanities Research Council, the Robert Gardiner Memorial Scholarship, and all three of these institutions allowed the book to be researched and written.

Thank you to everyone at Oxford University Press, in particular to Cathryn Steele, Christina Wipf-Perry, John Smallman, Gayathri Manoharan, and the two anonymous readers of the book manuscript.

No good history book can be written without the help of librarians and archivists, and I am grateful to the staff at Cambridge University Library and to individual Cambridge college and faculty libraries, the Bodleian Library, the British Library, the National Archives, the London Metropolitan Archives, Lambeth Palace Library, West Yorkshire Archive Service, Longleat House, and the Brotherton Library at the University of Leeds.

One of the great pleasures of research and writing has been the opportunity to travel and to discuss these questions among communities of scholars in the UK and beyond. My thanks go to audiences in Cambridge, Oxford, London, Leeds, Sheffield, Plymouth, Nottingham, Glasgow, Dublin, Galway, Helsinki, Tours, Florence, Boston, and Toronto (among others) who offered their own criticisms and perspectives on the work. The time I spent as a fellow of the Academy for Advanced Study of the Renaissance in the spring of 2013 was transformative for me and for this project: I would like to thank the whole group of fellows for thoughtful and inspiring discussions and for their scholarly friendship, and Ed Muir and Regina Schwartz for bringing us together.

This is a book about conversation, and it owes an incalculable amount to those who were generous with their thoughts, time, attention, and help. Any errors are, of course, mine. My thanks to Simon Abernethy, who helped create the graphs in Chapter 2, Alex Bamji, Sara Barker, Laura Beardshall, Jennifer Bishop, Richard Blakemore, Abigail Brundin, Peter Burke, Melissa Calaresu, Alex Campbell, Matthew Champion, Tom Charlton, Darragh Coffey, Paul Cohen, Liesbeth Corens, Caroline Cullen, Bronwen Everill, Andy Fleck, James Fox, Heather Froehlich, Caoilfhionn Gallagher, Tom Hamilton, Eva Johanna Holmberg, Lisa Jardine, Samuli Kaislaniemi, Lauren Kassell, Andrew Keener, Laura Kilbride and Brendan McCormick, Olivia Laing, Mélanie Lamotte, Mary Laven, Elisabeth Leake, Diane Leblond, Sjoerd Levelt, Aislinn Lucheroni, Helen Macdonald, Katherine McDonald, Christina McLeish, Peter Mandler, Andrea Mulligan, Emilie Murphy, Hannah Murphy, William O'Reilly, Danika Parikh, Ian Patterson, Helen Pfeifer, Sophie Pitman, James Purdon, Susan Raich, Virginia Reinburg, Jennifer Richards, Fern Riddell, Dunstan Roberts, Kirsty Rolfe, Ulinka Rublack, Jordan Savage, Jason Scott-Warren, Cathy Shrank, Sujit Sivasundaram, Edmond Smith, Ralph Stevens and Julie Maher, Matt Symonds, Kristen Treen, Kate Wiles, Mark Williams, Rachel Willie, and Richard Wistreich for their kindness and for their help. My thanks, too, to the online community of early modernists and #twitterstorians who made writing and researching a less lonely experience. Great friends in Dublin make me feel as if I never left: I am grateful to every one of them. Special thanks go to Aaron Alexander-Bloch, Kim Roper, Rob Tetley, and Helen Woodfield. To Chris Kissane, a brilliant scholar and endlessly generous friend, thank you.

In a book about language-learning, it feels right to thank my own language teachers. There are too many to name individually, but I will always be grateful to Louise Curtin, who taught me French for six years. Her commitment to teaching, arguing, and living multilingually continues to inspire me.

· Fletch Williams has lived with this book—and with me—in Cambridge, New York, and Leeds. Her belief in the book and its author sustained me even at the most difficult moments. I am very lucky to have someone so brilliant, determined, and loving in my life: thank you.

I come from a family where language and talk are at the centre of everything. Growing up with two languages—Irish and English—set me on the path towards writing this book. More than anything, the support and love of my family have made this journey possible. To my sisters Niamh and Aifric and my brother Hugh, go raibh maith agaibh. And to my parents, Noëlle and Seán, who have always said that education is the most important thing: thank you. This book is dedicated to you.

John Gallagher

Leeds,
November 2018

Contents

List of Illustrations

Introduction

In 1578, the Anglo-Italian author, teacher, translator, and lexicographer John Florio wrote of English that it was 'a language that wyl do you good in England, but passe Dover, it is woorth nothing'.[1] The most mobile of Englishmen, Florio went on, had no use for their native language beyond their own borders: 'English marchantes, when they are out of England, it liketh them not, and they doo not speake it.'[2] Florio's statement highlights a simple fact that is missing from our understanding of the history of early modern England. For all that the modern popular image of the period is of a literary-linguistic golden age, English in the early modern period was the little-known and little-regarded language of a small island out on the edge of Europe. Incomprehension was a constant risk for anglophone travellers and traders on the continent and farther afield. This basic feature of early modern life had practical consequences for any English-speaker who wished to venture past Dover, as well as for the many who craved the cultural capital represented by competence in a fashionable vernacular like Italian or French. For many people born in England in the early modern period, a monoglot existence was not an option. These English-speakers had to become language-learners.

That the English learnt foreign languages should be no surprise—English archives reveal language-learning as a crucial concern for individuals at many levels of the social scale. We find a penniless priest scribbling down the phrases he uses to beg for bread in Spanish, and a wealthy tourist making notes on beggars' cries in Italian and French.[3] A parliamentarian diplomat travels to Sweden with a trilingual manuscript phrasebook in his pocket, while a Royalist émigré packs his saddlebags with a grammar alongside maps and a prayer book for his journey southwards through France to Italy.[4] A lady-in-waiting attends her mistress at a Saumur church, hoping to learn some of the local language, and an English scientist pens a critique of a Paris sermon.[5] Children and young adults are sent

---

[1] John Florio, *Florio His firste Fruites which yeelde familiar speech* (London, 1578), p. 50.

[2] Ibid.

[3] Fr Daniel O'Bryen, letter from Oviedo, 16 November 1641, Parliamentary Archives: Main Papers HL/PO/JO/10/1/73, fol. 87r. William Bromley made notes on beggars' words: William Bromley, *Remarks made in travels through France & Italy. With many Publick Inscriptions. Lately taken by a Person of Quality* (London, 1693), pp. 12, 73–4, 195.

[4] Bulstrode Whitelocke, manuscript phrasebook, British Library, RP 209; Richard Symonds, travel journal, British Library, Harleian MS 943, fol. 42r.

[5] Deborah Fowler to Helena Southwell, 10 November 1677, British Library, Add. MS 46954 B, fol. 198r; Martin Lister, *A Journey to Paris in the Year 1698* (London, 1698), p. 174.

abroad to learn the languages that will allow them to participate in England's burgeoning continental and global trade.[6] At the oars of a north African galley, newly captured Englishmen pick up the basics of the Mediterranean's pidgin lingua franca from more seasoned captives, while from the Arctic Circle to the Americas, English explorers and traders compile rudimentary wordlists of unfamiliar tongues.[7] Crossing the Channel and the continent are servants acquiring foreign languages, formally and informally, in the entourages of their masters; a soldier using his 'spared houres' to write a French grammar; and immigrants to England teaching their native tongues and working to pick up the language of their new home.[8] As speakers of a practically unknown (and wholly unprestigious) vernacular, the English abroad had to become language-learners.

The idea of England as a monoglot nation is a modern one.[9] Not only did its kings and queens rule over speakers of Irish, Welsh, Scots, Gaelic, and others, but England itself was also abuzz with a veritable Babel of tongues—French, Dutch, Spanish, Italian, German, Persian, Japanese, Algonquian, Arabic, Ottoman Turkish, and many more—spoken by the migrants, refugees, exiles, slaves, and visitors who found themselves in England's ports, cities, and towns.[10] In urban environments like Norwich and Canterbury, French- and Dutch-speaking migrant communities rubbed shoulders with their English counterparts, while at the Royal Exchange in London buyers and sellers talked 'in severall Languages, And (like the murmuring fall of Waters) in the Hum of severall businesses: insomuch that the

---

[6] This practice is mentioned in Robert Southwell's travel notebook, British Library, Add. MS 58219, fol. 4r; for an account by a young Englishman who experienced it, see E. H. W. Meyerstein (ed.), *Adventures by Sea of Edward Coxere* (Oxford: Clarendon, 1945), pp. 3–4.

[7] William Okely, *Ebenezer; or, A Small Monument of Great Mercy, Appearing in the Miraculous Deliverance of William Okely* (1675), quoted in Daniel J. Vitkus (ed.), *Piracy, Slavery, and Redemption: Barbary Captivity Narratives from Early Modern England* (New York: Columbia University Press, 2001), p. 48. See also John Gallagher, 'Language-Learning, Orality, and Multilingualism in Early Modern Anglophone Narratives of Mediterranean Captivity', *Renaissance Studies* (forthcoming, 2019). For a wordlist of this kind, see 'The voyage of the foresaid M. Stephen Burrough, An. 1557. from Colmogro to Wardhouse, which was sent to seeke the Bona Esperanza, the Bona Confidentia, and the Philip and Mary, which were not heard of the yeere before', in Richard Hakluyt, *The principal navigations, voiages, traffiques and discoveries of the English nation* (London, 1598–1600), vol. 1, p. 293.

[8] While resident at Saumur, the grand tourist Philip Perceval was 'att the charges of having his man Thomas taught the language': Jean Gailhard to Robert Southwell, 3 January 1677, British Library, Add. MS 46953, fol. 218r. The soldier is John Wodroephe, author of *The spared houres of a souldier in his travels. Or The True Marrowe of the French Tongue, wherein is truely treated (by ordre) the Nine Parts of Speech. Together, with two rare, and excellent Bookes of Dialogues . . .* (Dordrecht, 1623). On immigrant teachers, see Chapter 1.

[9] On the late emergence of the idea of the monolingual nation state, see Eric Hobsbawm, 'Language, Culture, and National Identity', *Social Research* 63:4 (1996), pp. 1065–80.

[10] On the linguistic situation in early modern Britain and Ireland, see Paula Blank, *Broken English: Dialects and the Politics of Language in Renaissance Writings* (London and New York: Routledge, 1996); Tony Crowley, *Wars of Words: The Politics of Language in Ireland 1537–2004* (Oxford: Oxford University Press, 2005); Felicity Heal, 'Mediating the Word: Language and Dialects in the British and Irish Reformations', *Journal of Ecclesiastical History* 56 (2005), pp. 261–86.

place seemes Babell, (a Confusion of Tongues.)'.[11] Some artisanal workplaces, like the mixed English-Italian glassworks of sixteenth- and seventeenth-century London, were as international and multilingual as the royal courts, where multilingual musicians rubbed shoulders with visiting diplomats.[12] English-speakers lurked in the congregations of the city's Italian and French churches in order to practise their foreign languages, while civil and ecclesiastical authorities dealt with the disagreements and disorders of multilingual populations.[13] Interpreters found work at the Old Bailey, and there was a system in place whereby native speakers of French or Dutch could opt to be tried by a mixed jury of English-speakers and speakers of their mother tongue.[14] It was not necessary to venture beyond Dover to find oneself in Babel.

Historians have been slow to consider language-learning and linguistic competence from a historical perspective. The study of foreign languages has received

[11] Peter Trudgill, *Investigations in Sociohistorical Linguistics: Stories of Colonisation and Contact* (Cambridge: Cambridge University Press, 2010), p. 49; Christopher Joby, 'Trilingualism in Early Modern Norwich', *Journal of Historical Sociolinguistics* 2:2 (2016), pp. 211–234. Dekker quoted in Julia Gasper, 'The Literary Legend of Sir Thomas Gresham', in Ann Saunders (ed.), *The Royal Exchange* (London: London Topographical Society, 1997), p. 101. For a detailed recent exploration of how one foreign language was used in early modern England, see Christopher Joby, *The Dutch Language in Britain (1550–1702): A Social History of the Use of Dutch in Early Modern Britain* (Leiden and Boston, MA: Brill, 2015).

[12] For language-mixing in glassworks, see James Howell, *Epistolae Ho-Elianae: Familiar Letters Domestic & Forren* (London, 1645), section I, p. 5; for multilingual musicians, see John Gallagher, 'The Italian London of John North: Cultural Contact and Linguistic Encounter in Early Modern England', *Renaissance Quarterly*, 70 (2017), pp. 88–131. French at court is considered in Kathleen Lambley, *The Teaching and Cultivation of the French Language in England during Tudor and Stuart Times* (Manchester: Manchester University Press, 1920); for Italian, see R. C. Simonini, *Italian Scholarship in Renaissance England* (Chapel Hill, NC: The University of North Carolina Studies in Comparative Literature, 1952). For French at the Henrician court, see Gabriele Stein, *John Palsgrave as Renaissance Linguist: A Pioneer in Vernacular Language Description* (Oxford: Oxford University Press, 1997). For Italian under Elizabeth, see Michael Wyatt, *The Italian Encounter with Tudor England: A Cultural Politics of Translation* (Cambridge: Cambridge University Press, 2005), pp. 6, 125, 128. On Prince Henry's court, see 'Humanism and the Education of Henry, Prince of Wales', in Timothy Wilks (ed.), *Prince Henry Revived: Image and Exemplarity in Early Modern England* (Southampton: Paul Holberton, 2007), pp. 22–64. On French culture at the courts of Charles I and II, see Gesa Stedman, *Cultural Exchange in Seventeenth-Century France and England* (Aldershot: Ashgate, 2013), pp. 32–107.

[13] Roger Ascham criticized those English-speakers who attended the Italian church in Mercers' Hall 'to heare the Italian tonge naturally spoken, not to heare Gods doctrine trewly preached': Roger Ascham, *The Scholemaster* (London, 1570), fol. 28v. For English-speakers at the French church in the Savoy, see E. S. de Beer (ed.), *The Diary of John Evelyn, Selected and Introduced by Roy Strong* (London: Everyman, 2006), p. 766; Robert Latham and William Matthews (eds.), *The Diary of Samuel Pepys* (London: G. Bell and Sons, 1970), vol. 3, p. 207; Travel journal of Edward Browne (France), British Library, Sloane MS 1906, fol. 37r. The congregation of the Italian church in later sixteenth-century London was international and multilingual: see O. Boersma and A. J. Jelsma, *Unity in Multiformity: The Minutes of the Coetus of London, 1575 and the Consistory Minutes of the Italian Church of London, 1570–91* (London: Huguenot Society, 1997).

[14] See, for instance, the trial for murder of John Martyn, who 'could speak no English, and therefore had an Interpreter, as likewise a Jury for the purpose being half English and half French': *Old Bailey Proceedings Online* (www.oldbaileyonline.org, version 7.0, accessed 23 August 2014), August 1681, trial of John Martyn (t16810831–3). On these trials 'de medietate linguae', see Matthew Lockwood, ' "Love ye therefore the strangers": Immigration and the Criminal Law in Early Modern England', *Continuity and Change* 29:3 (2014), pp. 349–71.

only patchy attention from historians of early modern England: what remains the best work on the topic, Kathleen Lambley's *The Teaching and Cultivation of the French Language in England during Tudor and Stuart Times*, was published almost a century ago in 1920.[15] Historians, most influentially Peter Burke, have argued for the importance of a 'social history of language' and for historical approaches to multilingualism and translation, but the history of language (as written by historians, rather than scholars of language) has remained a relatively niche field.[16] Recent and forthcoming work on language-learning, multilingualism, and linguistic ecologies—not to mention the appearance of transformative studies in the history of communication—suggests that this neglect may be witnessing a reversal.[17] More broadly, literary scholars have been quicker than historians to consider the importance of multilingualism, translation, and codeswitching in the early modern period, and much of the best work on the language-learning texts of the sixteenth and seventeenth centuries has come from literary studies.[18] The literary cultures of early modern England have been portrayed as

---

[15] Other essential works include Frances Yates, *John Florio: The life of an Italian in Shakespeare's England* (Cambridge: Cambridge University Press, 1934), and Vivian Salmon, *Language and Society in Early Modern England: Selected Essays, 1981–1994* (Amsterdam and Philadelphia, PA: Rodopi, 1996).

[16] Burke's contributions are too numerous to list here, but key works include Peter Burke, *Languages and Communities in Early Modern Europe* (Cambridge: Cambridge University Press, 2004); Peter Burke, *The Art of Conversation* (Cambridge: Polity, 1993); Peter Burke and Roy Porter (eds.), *The Social History of Language* (Cambridge: Cambridge University Press, 1987); Peter Burke and Roy Porter (eds.), *Language, Self, and Society: A Social History of Language* (Cambridge: Polity, 1991); Peter Burke and Roy Porter (eds.), *Languages and Jargons: Contributions to a Social History of Language* (Cambridge: Polity, 1995); Peter Burke and R. Po-Chi Hsia (eds.), *Cultural Translation in Early Modern Europe* (Cambridge: Cambridge University Press, 2007).

[17] On language-learning, see Jean-Antoine Caravolas, *La Didactique des langues: précis d'histoire I, 1450–1700* (Montreal: Les Presses de l'Université de Montréal, 1994); Konrad Schröder (ed.), *Fremdsprachenunterricht 1500–1800* (Wiesbaden: Harrassowitz, 1992); Helmut Glück, *Deutsch als Fremdsprache in Europa vom Mittelalter bis zur Barockzeit* (Berlin: W. de Gruyter, 2002). In England, see Jason Lawrence, *'Who the devil taught thee so much Italian?' Italian Language Learning and Literary Imitation in Early Modern England* (Manchester and New York: Manchester University Press, 2005); Wyatt, *Italian Encounter*; Emilie K. M. Murphy, 'Language and Power in an English Convent in Exile, c.1621—c.1631', *Historical Journal* (forthcoming, early view available at https://doi.org/10.1017/S0018246X17000437). Eric Dursteler has set out some important questions for thinking historically about linguistic ecologies: Eric Dursteler, 'Speaking in Tongues: Language and Communication in the Early Modern Mediterranean', *Past & Present* 217:1 (2012), pp. 47–77; on interpreters and communication across languages, see E. Natalie Rothman, 'Interpreting Dragomans: Boundaries and Crossings in the Early Modern Mediterranean', *Comparative Studies in Society and History* 51 (2009), pp. 771–800; for multilingualism in the context of slavery and empire, see Natalie Zemon Davis, 'Creole Languages and their Uses: The Example of Colonial Suriname', *Historical Research* 82 (2009), pp. 268–84. On language and communication, see Filippo de Vivo, *Information and Communication in Venice: Rethinking Early Modern Politics* (Oxford: Oxford University Press, 2007); Elizabeth Horodowich, *Language and Statecraft in Early Modern Venice* (Cambridge: Cambridge University Press, 2008); John-Paul Ghobrial, *The Whispers of Cities: Information Flows in Istanbul, Paris, and London in the Age of William Trumbull* (Oxford: Oxford University Press, 2013); Alejandra Dubcovsky, *Informed Power: Communication in the Early American South* (Cambridge, MA: Harvard University Press, 2016). For a new perspective on multilingualism and mediation, see Paul Cohen, 'Torture and Translation in the Multilingual Courtrooms of Early Modern France', *Renaissance Quarterly* 69 (2016), pp. 899–939.

[18] See, for instance, Susan E. Phillips, 'Schoolmasters, Seduction, and Slavery: Polyglot Dictionaries in Pre-Modern England', *Medievalia et Humanistica* 34 (2008), pp. 129–58; Juliet Fleming, 'The French

profoundly multilingual and international, importing and adapting language, texts, and techniques from continental vernaculars as well as classical antecedents.[19] The work of linguists, literary scholars, and historians working on the medieval period offer models for thinking about a multilingual England: one different in character from the early modern nation, but where questions of language, power, and identity were as potent as they would be in the centuries to come.[20] Viewed through the polyglot perspectives of recent work, the importance of understanding early modern English history as multilingual and contingent on language-learning and linguistic mediation becomes clear.

Learning Languages in Early Modern England is a book about language-learning as a set of practices that were central to the English encounter with the wider world. Amidst discussions of translations and ideas about language in the early modern period, the day-to-day practices and processes by which people learnt to speak to one another across language barriers have been obscured. Thus, the focus here is on language-learning not as a silent, scholarly activity, but as an endeavour that was oral, aural, and sociable: a kind of everyday work that made communication and conversation possible.[21] This was a period when conversation manuals, which taught socially appropriate language through situational dialogues, became increasingly popular in English print. In the hands of early modern language-learners, they became 'speaking books', animated by the voices of their readers and in polyglot aural contexts. It was a period when a printed grammar of Italian could also contain advice on the appropriate gestures to

Garden: An Introduction to Women's French', *ELH: English Literary History* 56 (1989), pp. 19–51; John Considine, 'Narrative and Persuasion in Early Modern English Dictionaries and Phrasebooks', *Review of English Studies* 52 (2001), pp. 195–206; Lisa H. Cooper, 'Urban Utterances: Merchants, Artisans, and the Alphabet in Caxton's *Dialogues in French and English*', *New Medieval Literatures* 7 (2005), pp. 127–62; Christine Cooper-Rompato, 'Traveling Tongues: Foreign-Language Phrase Lists in Wynkyn de Worde and William Wey', *The Chaucer Review* 46 (2011), pp. 223–36.

---

[19] Ann Coldiron, *Printers without Borders: Translation and Textuality in the Renaissance* (Cambridge: Cambridge University Press, 2015).

[20] The medieval scholarship is too rich to survey in full here, but some very useful works include Ardis Butterfield, *The Familiar Enemy: Chaucer, Language, and Nation in the Hundred Years War* (Oxford: Oxford University Press, 2009), Jonathan Hsy, *Trading Tongues: Merchants, Multilingualism, and Medieval Literature* (Columbus, OH: The Ohio State University Press, 2013), Jocelyn Wogan-Browne (ed.), *Language and Culture in Medieval Britain: The French of England c.1100—c.1500* (York: York Medieval Press, 2009), D. A. Trotter (ed.), *Multilingualism in Later Medieval Britain* (Cambridge: D. S. Brewer, 2000).

[21] The classic and still essential work on orality in early modern England is Adam Fox, *Oral and Literate Culture in England 1500-1700* (Oxford: Clarendon, 2000). On early modern oralities more broadly, see the essays in Elizabeth Horodowich (ed.), *Speech and Oral Culture in Early Modern Europe and Beyond*, special issue of *Journal of Early Modern History* 16 (2012); Virginia Reinburg, *French Books of Hours: Making an Archive of Prayer* (Cambridge: Cambridge University Press, 2012); Tom Cohen and Lesley Twomey (eds.), *Spoken Word and Social Practice: Orality (1400–1700)* (Leiden: Brill, 2015); Stefano Dall'Aglio, Brian Richardson, and Massimo Rospocher (eds.), *Voices and Texts in Early Modern Italian Society* (London and New York: Routledge, 2017); Adam Fox and Daniel Woolf (eds.), *The Spoken Word: Oral Culture in Britain 1500-1850* (Manchester and New York: Manchester University Press, 2002).

accompany everyday phrases, and students of Dutch learnt the translations of English interjections like 'Oh me' ('ogh my'), 'Ha, ha, ha, he' ('Ha, ha, ha, he'), and 'Woo, O God!' ('Wee, o Godt!'), alongside the language necessary for a bargain or an introduction.[22] As today, language-learners toiled over grammar and syntax, and kept careful lists of vocabulary, but they also worked to understand codes of gesture and behaviour that animated foreign conversations. They took multilingual notes on what they heard, turning travel diaries into records of jokes shared, ballads heard, and advice received. They frequented teachers who could instruct them in the finest and most fashionable accents and varieties of prestige languages like Italian and French. The question of language-learning brings together the histories of reading, speaking, and hearing—indeed, the everyday experiences of early modern men and women—alongside those of education and communication.

Learning to speak in another language is a social skill, which is why this is also a book about the idea of linguistic competence: something early modern people thought and wrote about at great length. It was understood that to be able to speak and be heard in a foreign language required far more than a grasp of grammar, syntax, and vocabulary. Linguistic competence was social: it meant being able to choose between languages, registers, vocabularies, and tones according to one's own social situation, occupation, and gender, and those of the company. Early modern people displayed a keen ear for language used successfully and unsuccessfully.[23] Returned travellers were mocked for their affected use of 'oversea language', and judged little better than those who had travelled for months or years and come home with little more than a smattering.[24] Grand tourists were expected to work diligently on their French in the provinces before being allowed to enter Parisian society as fluent speakers and social performers, while would-be merchants were tested on their linguistic abilities before they were employed.[25]

[22] Giovanni Torriano, *Della lingua toscana-romana* (London, 1657), p. 231 explains that the expression 'Zítto, whosht, not a word' should be accompanied by 'Putting the forefinger across ones mouth'. Dutch interjections are taught in J. G. van Heldoren, *An English and Nether-Dutch Dictionary/ Een Engels en Nederduits Woortboek* (Amsterdam, 1675), pp. 80–2.

[23] On 'failures' in language use, see Carla Mazzio, *The Inarticulate Renaissance: Language Trouble in an Age of Eloquence* (Philadelphia, PA: University of Pennsylvania Press, 2008). See also Hillary Taylor, '"Branded on the Tongue": Rethinking Plebeian Inarticulacy in Early Modern England', *Radical History Review* 121 (2015), pp. 91–105.

[24] Thomas Wilson, *The Arte of Rhetorique, for the use of all suche as are studious of Eloquence, sette forth in English, by Thomas Wilson* (London, 1553), fol. 86r.

[25] One influential author of grand tour advice argued that 'one must have learned the Language, some customs of the Nation, and gotten some experience before he be ripe for Paris': there, '[the] people of Quality have not the patience to hear a Gentleman unable to speak two words together of good sense, but in other Towns it is otherwise': Jean Gailhard, *The Compleat Gentleman: or Directions For the Education of Youth As to their Breeding at Home And Travelling Abroad. In Two Treatises* (London, 1678), pp. 34–5. For trading companies testing potential factors' language skills, see Alison Games, *The Web of Empire: English Cosmopolitans in an Age of Expansion 1560–1660* (Oxford: Oxford University Press, 2008), pp. 94–5; see also Meyerstein (ed.), *Adventures by Sea*, p. 4 for the teenage Edward Coxere, who returned home after eleven months in France around 1647 and 'was examined by a French merchant in the French tongue, who gave my father an account that I spoke it as well as if I had been born in France'.

Teachers were judged on their competence to teach and their knowledge of a prestige accent and prestige variety.[26] But in spite of the importance with which it was viewed by people in the early modern period—not only by theorists and teachers, but by those who interacted in polyglot contexts and judged the speech of others—linguistic competence remains a concept without a history.[27] *Learning Languages in Early Modern England* offers a history of linguistic competences in a polyglot context, investigating the methods by which they were acquired, used, tested, and judged.

In order to understand how linguistic competence was imagined, acquired, and perceived in the past, *Learning Languages* draws on work from sociolinguistics and the sociology and social history of language. Central to this understanding of the social nature of historical linguistic competences is the idea of 'communicative competence' first put forward by Dell Hymes in a critique of Noam Chomsky. Where Chomsky's work on competence had worked from the idea of 'an ideal speaker-listener in a completely homogeneous speech-community, who knows its language perfectly', Hymes argued for a 'socially constituted linguistics' which would recognize that 'communities may hold differing ideals of speaking for different statuses and roles and situations'.[28] There is no one 'ideal speaker', since individuals must constantly modify their speech according to variables of company and context.[29] As Pierre Bourdieu argued, the ability to form grammatical sentences is only the beginning of linguistic competence, since '[t]he competence adequate to produce sentences that are likely to be understood may be quite inadequate to produce sentences that are likely to be *listened to*, likely to be recognized as *acceptable* in all the situations in which there is occasion to speak'. Speakers who lack the 'legitimate competence'—the ability to speak in a

---

[26] See Chapter 1.

[27] For one recent attempt to trace an early modern individual's polyglot existence, see Christopher Joby, *The Multilingualism of Constantijn Huygens (1596–1687)* (Amsterdam: Amsterdam University Press, 2014).

[28] Noam Chomsky, *Aspects of the Theory of Syntax* (Cambridge, MA: MIT Press, 1965), p. 3; Dell Hymes, *Foundations in Sociolinguistics: An Ethnographic Approach* (Philadelphia, PA: University of Pennsylvania Press, 1974), pp. 196–7, 46.

[29] This is a fundamental tenet of sociolinguistics: for a historian's view on the relevance of these concepts in historical research, see Peter Burke, 'Introduction', Burke and Porter, *Social History of Language*, pp. 1–17. There are many helpful introductions to sociolinguistics; two helpful texts are Suzanne Romaine, *Language in Society: An Introduction to Sociolinguistics* (Oxford: Oxford University Press, 2000), and Nikolas Coupland and Adam Jaworski (eds.), *Sociolinguistics: A Reader and Coursebook* (Basingstoke: Palgrave, 1997). Work in historical sociolinguistics has explored these questions in relation to the languages of the past: some key examples include Suzanne Romaine, *Socio-Historical Linguistics: its Status And Methodology* (Cambridge: Cambridge University Press, 1982) and Terttu Nevalainen and Helena Raumolin-Brunberg, *Historical Sociolinguistics: Language Change in Tudor and Stuart England* (Harlow: Longman, 2003), particularly the introduction, pp. 1–15; Nevalainen and Raumolin-Brunberg, *Sociolinguistics and Language History: Studies Based on the Corpus of Early English Correspondence* (Amsterdam and Atlanta, GA: Rodopi, 1996); Wendy Ayres-Bennett, *Sociolinguistic Variation in Seventeenth-Century France: Methodology and Case Studies* (Cambridge: Cambridge University Press, 2004).

register, tone, and variety (whether dialect, slang, or polished rhetoric) appropriate to the situation—are 'condemned to silence'.[30]

Early modern language-learners knew that linguistic competence meant more
than just the knowledge of an abstract system of signs. Social linguistic competence lies, as early modern authors on behaviour and speech understood, in
decorum: the ability to produce speech appropriate to one's social situation.[31]
Early modern writings on civility, politeness, and sociability share many concerns
of modern work on sociolinguistics and the social history of language.[32] Authors
then, as now, were concerned with the social functions of accent, tone, and
gesture; the relative prestige of dialects, varieties, and emergent 'national' or
proto-national vernaculars; the ways that certain words and vocabularies could
draw admiration or calumny. Learning a language was a way of training the body:
it was no coincidence that programmes of linguistic education often went hand in
hand with an education in bodily comportment. When Europeans encountered
peoples whose languages were utterly strange to them, the body's role in communication was foregrounded: cross-cultural communications were performed by
hand.[33] Histories of language which focus only on words and not on how they
sounded, the bodies that produced them, and the spaces and contexts in which
they were spoken can only tell part of the story. The social history of language-
learning draws us into the question of who got to speak (and be heard) in the early
modern world. By investigating the ways in which early modern speakers learnt,
taught, and used foreign languages, and the ways they ranked their abilities and
those of others, *Learning Languages* makes the case for thinking about linguistic
competence as a useful and important category of historical analysis.

This history of language-learning matters, too, because questions of language
were of real importance in early modern England. This was a period of intense
linguistic consciousness—a consciousness perhaps jolted by the fact that the
English language was undergoing an unprecedentedly rapid lexical expansion.[34]
Debates over 'inkhorn terms' were about much more than abstruse academic
terminology in print: they responded to the experience of hearing and experiencing

---

[30] Pierre Bourdieu, *Language and Symbolic Power*, ed. John B. Thompson (Cambridge: Polity, 1992),
p. 55. See also Phil Withington, *Society in Early Modern England: The Vernacular Origins of Some
Powerful Ideas* (Cambridge: Polity, 2010), pp. 183–85.

[31] On decorum, see Jennifer Richards, *Rhetoric and Courtliness in Early Modern Literature*
(Cambridge: Cambridge University Press, 2003), pp. 24–6, 66–85; Withington, *Society in Early Modern
England*, pp. 169–201.

[32] On conduct manuals, see Anna Bryson, *From Courtesy to Civility: Changing Codes of Conduct in
Early Modern England* (Oxford: Clarendon, 1998).

[33] On the history of gesture, see Jan Bremmer and Herman Roodenburg (eds.), *A Cultural History of
Gesture: From Antiquity to the Present Day* (Cambridge: Polity, 1991); Michael J. Braddick (ed.) *The
Politics of Gesture: Historical Perspectives* (*Past & Present* 203, supplement 4, 2009).

[34] Terttu Nevalainen, 'Early Modern English Lexis and Semantics', in Roger Lass (ed.), *The
Cambridge History of the English Language, vol. 3: 1476–1776* (Cambridge: Cambridge University
Press, 2000), p. 332.

language contact and language change.[35] Political centralization went hand in hand with linguistic standardization, as the use of English became more common in official settings throughout Britain and Ireland.[36] English authors of the sixteenth and seventeenth centuries were conscious that the Anglophone world was small and marginal, and that the English language was needy and porous. Even in England, speakers of the 'same' language could suffer incomprehension; in many places throughout the three kingdoms, language barriers were more of a reality than political borders.[37] They collected 'hard words' and dialect terms in an attempt to fix the boundaries and write the history of 'English'.[38] They toyed with universal language schemes in response to the difficulties of international communication at a time when Latin's role as a learned lingua franca was gradually diminishing.[39] England's culture of translation touched worlds beyond the literary canon: news was translated in manuscript, in print, and in coffee-houses; secretaries summarized and paraphrased documents in Latin and a wide variety of vernaculars; migrants and refugees brought skills, knowledge, and foreign terminology from continental Europe; and scientists and scholars participated in multilingual communication networks that stretched across Europe.[40] In early modern England, linguistic difference was part of the fabric of everyday life.

Questions of language became increasingly relevant, too, as England's overseas relationships developed in this period. With the expansion of the English Mediterranean trade, Italian became an important language for English commerce, from the Italian peninsula to the Barbary States and the Ottoman Empire.[41] Less

[35] See Gallagher, 'The Italian London of John North'.
[36] Crowley, Wars of Words, chapter 1.
[37] William Caxton offers an anecdote about a dialect-based misunderstanding in William Caxton, Here fynyssheth the boke yf Eneydos (London, 1490), sig. A1v. See also Blank, Broken English; Crowley, Wars of Words; Heal, 'Mediating the Word'.
[38] See, for instance, Robert Cawdrey, A Table Alphabeticall, conteyning and teaching the true writing, and understanding of hard usuall English wordes, borrowed from the Hebrew, Greeke, Latine, or French. &c. With the interpretation thereof by plaine English words, gathered for the benefit & helpe of Ladies, Gentlewomen, or any other unskilfull persons (London, 1604); Terttu Nevalainen, An Introduction to Early Modern English (Oxford: Oxford University Press, 2006), p. 50.
[39] On universal languages, see James Knowlson, Universal Language Schemes in England and France 1600-1800 (Toronto and Buffalo, NY: University of Toronto Press, 1975); Rhodri Lewis, Language, Mind and Nature: Artificial Languages in England from Bacon to Locke (Cambridge: Cambridge University Press, 2012). On the complex roles played by Latin in early modern Europe, see Jürgen Leonhardt, Latin: Story of a World Language (Cambridge, MA: Harvard University Press, 2013), trans. Kenneth Kronenberg, pp. 122–244; and Françoise Waquet, Latin, or the Empire of a Sign (London: Verso, 2001), trans. John Howe, passim.
[40] For the translation of news, see S. K. Barker, '"Newes lately come": European News Books in English Translation', in S. K. Barker and Brenda M. Hosington (eds.), Renaissance Cultural Crossroads: Translation, Print and Culture in Britain, 1473-1640 (Leiden and Boston, MA: Brill, 2013), pp. 227–44; for coffee-house translation, see the 1702 advertisement for Grigsby's in Threadneedle Street, where 'all Foreign News is taken in, and translated into English, immediately after the arrival of any Mail': Flying Post or The Post Master, issue 1162 (15 October 1702—17 October 1702).
[41] J. Cremona, '"Accioché ognuno le possa intendere": The Use of Italian as a Lingua Franca on the Barbary Coast of the Seventeenth Century. Evidence from the English', in Journal of Anglo-Italian Studies 5 (1997), pp. 52–69. This context saw the emergence of texts like Giovanni Torriano, The Italian Tutor, or

fortunate anglophone slaves in the Mediterranean encountered the Romance pidgin known variously as 'Lingofrank', 'Moresco', and 'the common language', as well as Ottoman Turkish and Arabic.[42] In North America, English-speakers at first relied on native interpreters (both willing and forced) and linguists like John Eliot and Roger Williams who worked to understand both the grammar and the social underpinnings of Native American languages for their own reasons.[43] In Muscovy, in Persia, along the coast of Africa and in India, English traders, soldiers, and explorers encountered languages unknown to them: travel writing and traders' records show the place of incomprehension in English encounters with the wider world.[44] Chinese and Arabic made their appearance in English print, university chairs in 'oriental' languages were established, and manuscripts were among the cargo of Levant Company ships returning from the Ottoman Empire.[45] These expansions all took place at the same time as that great lingua franca of the medieval period, Latin, was undergoing a slow decline as a language of spoken communication: even while Fynes Moryson could marvel at how '[t]he very Artificers of Polonia can speake Latin, but most rudely and falsly', Latin's everyday utility was increasingly threatened by divergent regional pronunciations, the impact of the Reformation, and the growing numbers of non-Latinate travellers.[46] Close to home, the French state's burgeoning military might and cultural

---

a new and most compleat Italian Grammer. Containing above others a most compendious way to learne the Verbs, and rules of Syntax. To which is annexed a display of the monasillable particles of the Language, with the English to them (London, 1640), which was addressed 'To the Right Worshipfull and now most flourishing Company of Turkey Marchants', for whom knowledge of Italian was essential.

[42] On the Mediterranean lingua franca, see Jocelyne Dakhlia, *Lingua franca: histoire d'une langue métisse en Méditerranée* (Paris: Actes Sud, 2008); Dursteler, 'Speaking in Tongues', pp. 67–74; Karla Mallette, 'Lingua Franca', in Peregrine Horden and Sharon Kinoshita (eds.), *A Companion to Mediterranean History* (Chichester: Wiley Blackwell, 2014), pp. 330–44; Rachel Selbach, 'On a Famous Lacuna: Lingua Franca the Mediterranean Trade Pidgin?', in Esther-Miriam Wagner, Bettina Beinhoff, and Ben Outhwaite (eds.), *Merchants of Innovation: The Languages of Traders* (Berlin: De Gruyter Mouton, 2017), pp. 252–71; Gallagher, 'Language-Learning, Orality, and Multilingualism in Early Modern Anglophone Narratives of Mediterranean Captivity'.

[43] J. Frederick Fausz, 'Middlemen in Peace and War: Virginia's Earliest Indian Interpreters, 1608–1632', *The Virginia Magazine of History and Biography* 95 (1987), pp. 41–64; John Eliot, *The Indian Grammar Begun: Or, an Essay to Bring the Indian Language into Rules* (Cambridge, 1666); Roger Williams, *A Key into the Language of America: or, An help to the Language of the Natives in that part of America, called New-England* (London, 1643).

[44] Collections like Richard Hakluyt's *Principal Navigations* and Samuel Purchas's *Pilgrimes* are treasure houses of material for the history of global linguistic encounters in the early modern period, and have yet to be studied closely as such by historians.

[45] G. J. Toomer, *Eastern Wisedome and Learning: The Study of Arabic in Seventeenth-Century England* (Oxford: Clarendon, 1996); Vivian Salmon, 'Arabists and Linguists in Seventeenth-Century England', in G. A. Russell (ed.), *The 'Arabick' Interest of the Natural Philosophers in Seventeenth-Century England* (Leiden: Brill, 1994), pp. 54–69; Simon Mills, 'Learning Arabic in the Overseas Factories: The Case of the English', in Jan Loop, Alastair Hamilton, and Charles Burnett (eds.), *The Teaching and Learning of Arabic in Early Modern Europe* (Leiden: Brill, 2017), pp. 272–93.

[46] Fynes Moryson, *An Itinerary written by Fynes Moryson Gent. First in the latine Tongue, and then translated By him into English: containing his ten yeeres travell through the twelve dominions of Germany, Bohmerland, Switzerland, Netherland, Denmarke, Poland, Italy, Turky, France, England,*

prestige turned it into a linguistic superpower, and French into the language of the seventeenth- and eighteenth-century European elites.

The 'questions of language' debated in early modern England and Europe were where everyday speech met broader narratives of nation, reformation, political power, and social stratification. In a landmark volume of essays on the social history of language, co-edited with Peter Burke, Roy Porter wrote that:

> [l]anguage is so intimate to living that it has long been overlooked by historians, rather in the way that little historical attention has been paid to such other home truths as the body, its gestures and clothing, and the everyday objects with which people surround themselves.[47]

Like the histories of the body, of clothing, and of material objects, the history of language and linguistic encounters speaks to broader questions of cultural, social, and political change in the early modern period. 'Questions of language' addressed the great issues of the time, but all were grounded in the everyday experiences of speaking and hearing, often in multilingual contexts, and in a world where 'national' and 'standard' languages remained fluid and debatable. These are the questions addressed by this book.

Learning Languages in Early Modern England is divided into four chapters. Chapter 1 considers language-learning in the context of the culture of extracurricular and extrainstitutional education that became increasingly important during this period. It argues that early modern England did witness an educational revolution, but that it did not happen solely, or even primarily, in universities and grammar schools. Instead, it took place in private homes and ad hoc schools, and at the coffee-houses and bookstalls where new subjects, new groups of teachers, and new kinds of teaching emerged and adapted to reflect new concerns and new relationships between England, English, and the continent. Linguistic and pedagogical authority were up for debate in an increasingly crowded market. By tracing the careers of language teachers, their relationships with students, and the market for language-teaching in early modern England, this chapter builds a picture of a thriving and innovative educational economy that equipped English-speakers for the encounter with other vernacular cultures.

Scotland, and Ireland (London, 1617), part III, book I, p. 15. Peter Burke, '"Heu Domine, Adsunt Turcae": A Sketch for a Social History of Post-Medieval Latin', in Burke, *The Art of Conversation* (Cambridge: Polity, 1993), pp. 34–65; Burke, 'Latin: A Language in Search of a Community', in Burke, *Languages and Communities in Early Modern Europe* (Cambridge: Cambridge University Press, 2004), pp. 43–60; James W. Binns, *Intellectual Culture in Elizabethan and Jacobean England: The Latin Writings of the Age* (Leeds: Francis Cairns, 1990). On Greek in early modern England, see Mischa Lazarus, 'Greek Literacy in Sixteenth-Century England', *Renaissance Studies* 29:3 (2015), pp. 433–58.

[47] Roy Porter, 'Introduction', in Peter Burke and Roy Porter (eds.), *Language, Self, and Society: A Social History of Language* (Cambridge: Polity, 1991), p. 1.

Chapter 2 considers an important but underappreciated genre of early modern print: the multilingual conversation manual. Affordable and portable, these printed books contained phrases and dialogues in English and at least one foreign language (some editions offered material in up to eight languages), often alongside information on grammar, vocabulary, and pronunciation. Working from a corpus of over 300 unique editions, Chapter 2 charts the changing place of these texts in the early modern print market from their beginnings in the late fifteenth century to the early eighteenth. It traces the languages they offered, who wrote them, how much they cost, how many were printed, and how they developed as a physical object that could be carried in the hand or stowed in a pocket during travel. This chapter asks what these texts were meant to do, and how their readers read them, showing how by teaching skills from correct pronunciation to social interaction, these manuals demanded that their readers read in conversation with the oral and sociable world beyond. The relationship between speech, print, and sound in these manuals was unique to this genre and offers a new way of understanding both linguistic education and shifting ideals of linguistic competence. The early modern conversation manual offers new perspectives on the histories of reading, education, travel, the book, and the English encounter with continental Europe in the early modern period.

Chapter 3 turns to the question of linguistic competence, asking what it meant to be able to speak another language in early modern England. Linguistic competence was more complicated than a simple binary between fluent and not. Just as historians have argued for the existence of multiple literacies in early modern England, so too were there multiple linguistic competences, depending on the speaker's status, age, gender, origin, occupation, and ability. Learners of different languages had to master different ways of expressing superiority or deference and of managing ritual situations where competent speech and acceptable behaviour overlapped. Immigrants to England in the sixteenth and seventeenth centuries had to learn a new vernacular while accommodating themselves to new rituals, fashions, and rules of conversation: texts directed at these new arrivals show language-learning as a process of adaptation and assimilation. Reading the corpus of conversation manuals alongside broader discourses of civility, speech, and behaviour, this chapter uncovers the dynamics of multilingual speech and silence in an age of encounter.

Chapter 4, the final chapter, turns to the experiences of English-speakers who did venture beyond Dover, in order to understand the oral and aural practices that were so central to early modern language-learning. The study of vernacular languages was an inescapable aspect of continental travel. This was particularly true for the educational travellers who went to the continent in growing numbers from the latter half of the sixteenth century onwards. This chapter uses a rich set of manuscript source materials (including travellers' polyglot diaries, letters, and notebooks) to address and remedy the absence of actual educational practices from most histories of educational travel. It argues that linguistic concerns helped to shape everything from the routes that travellers followed to the company they kept and the notes they wrote. Attention to the everyday pedagogies of language-learning in travel illuminates the oral and face-to-face realities of the English encounter with continental cultures and languages, and sheds new light on England's place in early modern Europe.

The idea of the monoglot nation-state is a recent one. Early modern states were commonly multilingual: their rulers and elites were increasingly convinced of the usefulness of a shared language in this period, but cultural pressure and legislative action would take centuries to bring about 'national langues' as we think of them today. Even so, our understanding of the history of early modern England is plagued by modern monoglot assumptions. It takes, I think, a genuine mental effort to imagine a world where English—now a global lingua franca—was practically useless outside the island of Britain, and even in many places within it. Narratives of the 'triumph of English' do not reflect the situation on the ground: in the early modern period, English often proved impractical and unprestigious.[48] A polyglot perspective is necessary in order to allow us to remarginalize the early modern histories of English (and, perhaps, of England), and to understand how ideas of language and nation were shaped through international and multilingual encounters, and in the rush to translate, to adapt, to borrow and steal from other vernacular cultures. The polyglot perspective reveals the importance of multilingual competences to the practice of politics, trade, print, travel, sociability, religion, warfare, cultural production, and migration. It also allows us to understand early modern England as a multilingual country, reliant at many different levels on language-learning, linguistic mediation, and polyglot conversation.

[48] Richard Foster Jones, *The Triumph of the English Language: A Survey of Opinions Concerning the Vernacular from the Introduction of Printing to the Restoration* (London: Oxford University Press, 1953).

1

Extracurricular Economy

Language Teachers and Language Schools in Early Modern England

Introduction

In the midst of the upheavals of the 1640s, two Huguenot immigrants to England saw an educational opportunity. Hugh l'Amy and Peter le Pruvost wrote to the educational reformer Samuel Hartlib to propose the establishment of an 'Academie a la francoise'—an academy, based in London or an appropriated university college, at which a reformed curriculum would be taught through French.[1] Their proposal was one of many in the sixteenth and seventeenth century that aimed to remedy the lack of institutional provision for the formal study of modern foreign languages. In 1573, Humphrey Gilbert had plotted a curriculum for 'Queene Elizabethes Achademy' which would go beyond mere 'schole learninges' in order to teach 'matters of accion meet for present practize, both of peace and warre'. At Gilbert's proposed academy, Italian, French, Spanish, and 'the highe duche toung' would be taught alongside Latin, Greek, Hebrew, and English.[2] In the 1630s, Francis Kynaston's short-lived 'Musaeum Minervae' promised to eliminate the need for Englishmen to travel abroad in search of an education, providing instruction in vernacular languages and all necessary accomplishments in London, while John Milton's idealized Puritan academy aimed to correct the deficiencies of the university curriculum and help to shape a reformed—and multilingual—English ruling class.[3] Private ventures and public-spirited proposals alike attempted to capitalize on the failings of the universities and ambivalent attitudes to educational travel, and to establish environments where continental

---

[1] Proposals of Hugh l'Amy and Peter le Pruvost, Hartlib Papers, 12/101A-102B: Mark Greengrass, M. Leslie, and M. Hannon (eds.), *The Hartlib Papers* (HRI Online Publications, Sheffield), https://www.dhi.ac.uk/hartlib/view?docset=main&docname=12B_101, accessed 5 February 2019. Charles Webster, *The Great Instauration: Science, Medicine and Reform, 1626–1660* (London: Duckworth, 1975), p. 217; see ibid., *passim*, for a general discussion of Puritan proposals for educational reform in the mid-seventeenth century.
[2] Humphrey Gilbert, *Queene Elizabethes Achademy, A Booke of Precedence, &c., with Essays on Italian and German Books of Courtesy* (London: Early English Text Society, 1869), pp. 1–12.
[3] For Kynaston's 'Musaeum Minervae', see Richard Cust, 'Charles I's Noble Academy', *The Seventeenth Century* 29:4 (2014), pp. 346–53. On Milton's proposals, see Timothy Raylor, 'Milton, the Hartlib Circle, and the Education of the Aristocracy', in Nicholas McDowell and Nigel Smith (eds.), *The Oxford Handbook of Milton* (Oxford: Oxford University Press, 2009), pp. 382–406.

vernaculars could be formally studied.[4] They sought to harness and exploit the thriving educational economy that had grown up outside and alongside England's traditional institutions of teaching and learning.

Grand proposals of this kind rarely got far beyond the drawing board, but they attest to a pervasive sense that England's interests—educational, economic, and cultural—were not being adequately served by the established institutions and the curriculums of the period. They also reflect a new educational reality that was taking hold in early modern England, as the period witnessed a boom in both autodidacticism and private educational provision. Traditional histories of education have been slow to grasp the importance of these phenomena, and the extent to which changes in educational culture were happening outside traditional institutions.[5] The vibrancy of early modern England's educational economy could be seen in the scientific lectures given in coffee-houses, the private schools springing up and offering instruction in handwriting and arithmetic, and the growing number of women's boarding schools teaching pastrywork or needlework alongside music, deportment, and languages.[6] Language-learning was central to this changing educational culture: it brought vernacular teaching to new audiences in new spaces, and relied on the labour of those often excluded from more prestigious educational environments, such as immigrants and women. Over the course of the seventeenth century, extracurricular education moved from the margins to a situation where the teaching of languages was carried on in dedicated schools and academies, and had begun to penetrate even older institutions like the universities. At the same time, the debates over language pedagogy—who was best qualified to teach, which methods were preferable, who was capable of language

---

[4] See, for instance, Balthazar Gerbier, *The Interpreter of the Academie for Forrain Languages, and all Noble Sciences, and Exercises* (London, 1649); the advertisment concerning the proposed 'Royal Academies' in *Collection for Improvement of Husbandry and Trade* (London, England), Friday, February 22, 1695; Issue 134; in 1676, Edward Panton published his proposals for a 'Royal Academy' in *A Publick and Pious Design for the Preserving the Generous Youth, and Consequently the Nation from Ruine* (London, 1676). On the dissenting academies that emerged after 1662, see *Dissenting Academies Online* at http://dissacad.english.qmul.ac.uk/, accessed 5 February 2019.

[5] Secular education in early modern England has been an understudied subject in recent years. Important contributions include Helen M. Jewell, *Education in Early Modern England* (Basingstoke: Macmillan, 1998); Rosemary O'Day, *Education and Society 1500–1800* (London and New York: Longman, 1982); Kenneth Charlton, *Education in Renaissance England* (London: Routledge & Kegan Paul, 1965); Margaret Spufford, *Contrasting Communities: English Villagers in the Sixteenth and Seventeenth Centuries* (London: Cambridge University Press, 1974), pp. 173–205; Natasha Glaisyer and Sara Pennell (eds.), *Didactic Literature in England, 1500–1800: Expertise Constructed* (Aldershot: Ashgate, 2003). See also Jennifer Richards, *Voices and Books in the English Renaissance: A New History of Reading* (Oxford: Oxford University Press, forthcoming). There have also been exciting advancements in the history of Catholic education (particularly that of women) in England and abroad: see, for instance, Caroline Bowden, '"For the Glory of God": A Study of the Education of English Catholic Women in Convents in Flanders and France in the First Half of the Seventeenth Century', *Paedagogica Historica: International Journal for the History of Education* 35 (1999), pp. 77–95; Emilie K. M. Murphy, 'Language and Power in an English Convent in Exile, *c.*1621–*c.*1631', *Historical Journal* (forthcoming, early view available at https://doi.org/10.1017/S0018246X17000437).

[6] For advertisements for each of these respectively, see *Post Boy (1695)*, issue 2807 (5 May 1713–7 May 1713); *Daily Courant*, issue 428 (31 August 1703); *Spectator*, issue 342 (2 April 1712).

education, and what language or languages should be taught—helped to shape early modern ideas about language and education more broadly. This chapter traces the history of language schools and language teachers in the sixteenth and seventeenth centuries and uses the story of foreign-language learning as a way of rethinking the history of education in early modern England.

Educational Environments: Where Language-Learning Happened

The early seventeenth-century writer George Buck argued that London could be described as England's 'third universitie' because all subjects could be studied there, from law and theology to fencing and dancing. As well as Greek and Latin, he wrote, '[t]here be also in this Cittie Teachers and Professors of the holy or Hebrew Language, of the Caldean, Syriak, & Arabike, or Larbey Languages, of the Italian, Spanish, French, Dutch, and Polish Tongues', alongside 'the Persian and the Morisco, and the Turkish, & the Muscovian language, and also the Sclavonian tongue, which passeth through 17. Nations'. Not only these, there were also teachers offering 'divers other Languages fit for Embassadors and Orators, and Agents for Marchants, and for Travaylors, and necessarie for all Commerce or Negotiation whatsoever'.[7] In Buck's telling, London offered a rich and vibrant educational environment in which languages far beyond those on the curriculum at grammar schools or universities could be learnt for a fee. Most of the languages Buck mentioned—as well as the many other subjects he claimed could be studied in the city—were taught outside traditional educational institutions. Language-learning in early modern England was not bounded by the walls of the school-room or the lecture hall. It happened in churchyards and coffee-houses, at court and in private homes, and this variety of educational environments offered homes to diverse students and pedagogical approaches.

The household was, for many, a centre of language teaching. Teachers commonly offered tuition at home, particularly for wealthier students who may have wanted to be taught separately from those of lower status. Language instruction at home could be preparatory to travel: in a 1639 letter, Frances Lady Pelham commented to her brother that 'I hear *your Lordship's* sonnes have a good tutor therfore I beleve they learne the frinch Language well in ingland and then *you* have time enough to send them in to france.'[8] Domestic teaching was often considered particularly suitable for female students, with some families engaging resident language tutors. The French exercise book kept by the 10-year-old Barbara

---

[7] George Buck, *The Third Universitie of England* (London, 1615), p. 965.

[8] Frances Lady Pelham to Edward Viscount Conway and Killultagh, 16 January 1638/9, National Archives, SP 16/409, fol. 229v.

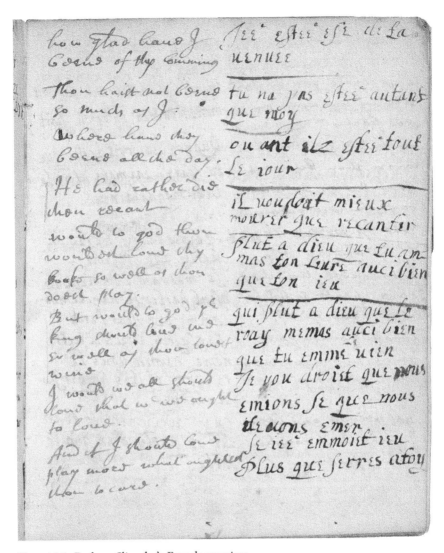

Figure 1.1 Barbara Slingsby's French exercises

Source: Folger Shakespeare Library, V.a.596, fol. 10r. Used by permission of the Folger Shakespeare Library.

Slingsby (see Figure 1.1) is one record of this kind of domestic French education—Slingsby's age and her family's location in rural Yorkshire clearly made the engagement of an (unnammed) domestic language tutor the best option.[9] John Harington of Exton retained Catherin le Doux (also known as Catharinus Dulcis) as a tutor in

---

[9] Slingsby's exercise book is Folger Library, Washington DC, V.a.596. See also Jerome de Groot, 'Every one teacheth after thyr owne fantasie: French Language Instruction', in Kathryn M. Moncrief

languages to his polyglot household during the 1590s.[10] Le Doux, who brought with him a sophisticated library of works on grammar and language, contributed to the multilingual education of Lucy Harington, to whom John Florio would dedicate his first dictionary, with praise for her skill in languages.[11] Throughout this period, wealthy households appear as sophisticated educational hubs: the Duke of Gloucester's accounts for 1697 record the presence of 'Mr. Persode French Master' among a number of other educators, including another unnamed French teacher, a governor, sub-governors, preceptors and sub-preceptors, and an '[a]lmoner or Latin Master'.[12] The later seventeenth century saw the appearance of printed advertisements placed by multilingual women seeking employment as governesses or household tutors, like the French-speaking 'Gentlewoman that has lived well, and brought up several Children', who 'desires to be Tutoress to some young Gentlewomen', or another 'that has waited on Persons of Quality' and sought 'to be Governess to some young Lady', each suggesting a potential overlap between educational labour and women's household employment.[13]

The story of domestic language-learning is not simply the story of teachers and tutors. It was not for nothing that humanist writers on education were so concerned with the impact of nurses on a child's linguistic education.[14] Even leaving aside families where the parents spoke different native languages (far from uncommon in places like London and Norwich), there were households that became multilingual through employing foreign or multilingual servants and

and Kathryn R. McPherson (eds.), *Performing Pedagogy in Early Modern England: Gender, Instruction, and Performance* (Surrey: Ashgate, 2011), 33–51.

[10]   On le Doux, see Warren Boutcher, 'A French Dexterity, & an Italian Confidence: New Documents on John Florio, Learned strangers and Protestant Humanist Study of Modern Languages in Renaissance England from *c.*1547 to *c.*1625', *Reformation* 2 (1997), p. 97; and le Doux's own Latin biography, Catharinus Dulcis, *Catharini Dulcis linguarum exoticarum in Academia Marpurgensi Professoris Vitae Curriculi Breviarium* (Marburg, 1622), pp. 18–19. A helpful biographical sketch (in German) is provided by Isabel Zolina and Gabriele Beck-Busse at http://www.dulcis-info.de/vita.html, accessed 5 February 2019.

[11]   The inventory of le Doux's library is London, Lambeth Palace Library MS 654, fols. 185r–86v. Florio's dedication is John Florio, *A Worlde of Wordes, Or, Most copious, and exact Dictionarie in Italian and English, collected by John Florio* (London, 1598), sig. A3r-A5r. On Lucy Harington, see Helen Payne, 'Russell [née Harington], Lucy, countess of Bedford (bap. 1581, d. 1627)', *Oxford Dictionary of National Biography*, Oxford University Press, 2004; online edn, May 2014 (https://doi. org/10.1093/ref:odnb/24330). Harington was also the dedicatee of Claudius Hollyband, *Campo de fior, or, The Flowrie Field of Foure Languages* (London, 1583), and a manuscript copy of Giacomo Castelvetro, *The Fruit, Herbs and Vegetables of Italy: An Offering to Lucy, Countess of Bedford*, trans. Gillian Riley (Totnes: Prospect, 2012).

[12]   'Establishment of the Duke of Gloucester's family', [August?] 1697, National Archives, SP 32/7, fols. 309r–310r. For a spat between Persode and Abel Boyer, see Rex A. Barrell, *The Correspondence of Abel Boyer, Huguenot Refugee 1667–1729* (Lewiston, NY, Queenston, Ont., and Lampeter: Edwin Mellen, 1992), pp. 78–80.

[13]   *Collection for Improvement of Husbandry and Trade*, issue 206 (10 July 1696); *Collection for Improvement of Husbandry and Trade*, issue 223 (6 November 1696).

[14]   See, for instance, Thomas Elyot, *The boke named the Governour, devised by Thomas Elyot knight* (London, 1531), fols. 16v–17v.

staff. The records of the Sidney household in 1572–3 recorded a payment to 'Mistress Maria, the Italian': it cannot be known for certain whether she was employed as a formal teacher, but the presence of multilingual members of the household could allow for language practice, particularly in a family as determinedly polyglot as the Sidneys.[15] Servants' knowledge of other languages could make them more employable: *The Gentlewomans Companion* (1683) urged the study of French or Italian to those who would serve elite women, 'insomuch that a Court-Lady will not be induced to esteem a friend, or entertain a Servant who cannot speak one of them at the least'.[16] A contemporary market for the skills of multilingual servants can be seen in advertisements of the period, such as that placed in 1696 by 'a genteel Valet de Chambre, that can trim and look to a Peruke, write, cast Accompt, receive and pay money, speaks Dutch and understands French'.[17] The early modern English household could be made into a multilingual space.[18]

The university towns of Oxford and Cambridge were fertile grounds for language-learning, though modern languages were not a part of the established curriculum but rather an extracurricular accretion. Tutors recognized the existence of a substantial constituency of wealthy students who 'come to the university not with intention to make scholarship their profession, but only to get such learning as may serve for delight and ornament and such as the want whereof would speak a defect in breeding rather than scholarship'.[19] Modern languages were important to this 'gentleman's curriculum', and private tutors offered their services to the students who followed it: John Florio accompanied Emmanuel Barnes to Magdalen College, Oxford, in the 1570s, where he also taught others and made the acquaintance of men like Samuel Daniel and Richard Hakluyt who would be valuable contacts as Florio made his career in print.[20] At Cambridge in the 1580s, Gabriel Harvey mentioned an 'Italian maister' who taught him and his brother; Harvey also owned a copy of the third edition of Pierre du Ploiche's

[15] Jason Lawrence, '*Who the devil taught thee so much Italian?*' *Italian Language Learning and Literary Imitation in Early Modern England* (Manchester and New York: Manchester University Press, 2005), p. 14.
[16] Anon. ['Hannah Woolley'], *The Gentlewomans Companion; or, a guide to the female sex* (London, 1683), pp. 11–13, 30–2.
[17] *Collection for Improvement of Husbandry and Trade*, issue 186 (21 February 1696).
[18] A dialogue from a 1646 Dutch conversation manual depicts the household as a carefully delineated multilingual pedagogical space, in which the children 'have alwayes a pedagogue at home, who is both learned and diligent, he teacheth us alwayes to speak Latin, and speaketh nothing in our mothers tongue except to expound somthing', where the children speak Latin with their father, and their mother tongue with their mother: Anon., *Den Engelschen School-Meester &c. The English Schole-Master &c.* (Amsterdam, 1646), p. 148.
[19] From Richard Holdsworth's 'Directions for a student in the university', quoted in Mark H. Curtis, *Oxford and Cambridge in Transition, 1558–1642: An Essay on Changing Relations between the English Universities and English Society* (Oxford: Clarendon, 1959), p. 131.
[20] For Florio and Barnes, see Frances Yates, *John Florio: The life of an Italian in Shakespeare's England* (Cambridge: Cambridge University Press, 1934), p. 27; for Florio and Daniel, see Lawrence, *Who the devil*, pp. 9–10; for Florio and Hakluyt, see James McConica, 'Elizabethan Oxford: The Collegiate Society', in James McConica (ed.), *The History of the University of Oxford, volume III: The Collegiate University* (Oxford: Clarendon, 1986), p. 710.

A treatise in Englishe and Frenche with the inscription '[e]x dono Autoris, Monsieur du Ploiche'.[21] Du Ploiche was associated with Oxford, where he had lived in the 1550s; it is likely that he came into contact with Harvey through university networks.[22] Another teacher who tied his work to a university context was Gabriel du Grès, whose *Dialogi Gallico-Anglico-Latini* went into at least three editions in the middle of the seventeenth century (otherwise a relatively slow period for language publishing). The books were printed and sold in Oxford and clearly aimed at a university audience, not least in their assumption of Latin competence on the part of the reader.[23] The first bilingual English-German textbook was published in 1680 by Martin Aedler, a migrant language teacher who had sought to supplement his income by appealing for university employment.[24] Language teachers operating at the universities, as Warren Boutcher argues, 'contributed to the unofficial development of the arts curriculum in the area of modern languages', forming 'a tutorial subspecies answering...the need for a personally directed course of cultural education broader than that expected in the university statutes'.[25] During the seventeenth century, the English universities also established themselves as centres for the formal and informal study of 'oriental languages', catering for a growing interest in non-European languages.[26]

The presence of foreign-born scholars at the universities allowed students and scholars to build multilingual pedagogical relationships. For the young Henry Wotton, a friendship with Alberico Gentili—then professor of civil law at Oxford—offered a means of improving his Italian.[27] But for a window onto the relationships between a university language teacher and his students we can turn to the manuscripts made by Giacomo Castelvetro, who was in Cambridge

---

[21] Lawrence, *Who the devil*, p. 9; Pierre du Ploiche, *A treatise in English and Frenche, right necessarie, and profitable for all young children* (London, 1578); the edition with Harvey's inscription is held at the Huntington Library. Caroline Brown Bourland, 'Gabriel Harvey and the Modern Languages', *Huntington Library Quarterly* 4 (1940), p. 87; for more on Harvey's reading of modern language materials, see Virginia F. Stern, *Gabriel Harvey: His Life, Marginalia and Library* (Oxford: Clarendon, 1979), pp. 156–8.

[22] Lambley, *Teaching and Cultivation of the French Language*, p. 200.

[23] Gabriel du Grès, *Dialogi Gallico-Anglico-Latini per Gabrielem Dugres linguam Gallicam in illustrissima, et famosissima, Oxoniensi Academia edocentem.* (Oxford, 1639); du Grès, *Dialogi Gallico-Anglico-Latini per Gabrielem Dugres linguam Gallicam in illustrissima & famosissima Oxoniensi academia haud ita pridem privatim edocentem* (Oxford, 1652); du Grès, *Dialogi Gallico-Anglico-Latini. Per Gabrielem Dugres, linguæ Gallicæ in illustrissima & famosissima Oxoniensi Academia haud ita pridem privato munere prælectorem* (Oxford, 1660). A comparable work for learners of Italian—printed in Latin at Oxford—was Carolus Mulerius, *Linguae Italicae, compendiosa institutio* (Oxford, 1667), first published in the Low Countries in 1631.

[24] Fredericka van der Lubbe, *Martin Aedler and the High Dutch Minerva: The First German Grammar for the English* (Frankfurt am Main: Peter Lang, 2007), pp. 76–7.

[25] Boutcher, 'A French Dexterity, & an Italian Confidence', p. 49.

[26] See G. J. Toomer, *Eastern Wisedome and Learning: The Study of Arabic in Seventeenth-Century England* (Oxford: Clarendon, 1996), *passim*; Vivian Salmon, 'Arabists and Linguists in 17th-Century England', in G. A. Russell (ed.), *The 'Arabick' Interest of the Natural Philosophers in Seventeenth-Century England* (Leiden, New York, and Cologne: Brill, 1994), pp. 54–69.

[27] Logan Pearsall Smith, *The Life and Letters of Sir Henry Wotton*, vol. 1 (Oxford: Clarendon, 1907), pp. 5–6.

in 1613/14, teaching Italian (and possibly other languages) to a group of students and fellows. Castelvetro was nearing the end of his life—he would die in England in 1616—and seems to have been hoping to acquire some kind of official position at the university, albeit without any success.[28] The kind of work Castelvetro was doing at Cambridge can be seen in a manuscript found in the library of Trinity College (see Figure 1.2). Dating from 1613, it announces itself as a 'Libretto De varie maniere di parlare della Italica Lingua'.[29] It is a notebook filled with dialogues in Italian, mostly written only on the verso of each folio, allowing the student to use the recto to practice translating the Italian text.[30] A student's attempts at translation have been carefully corrected: the text contains multiple crossings-out and superscripts and, on at least one occasion, another hand correcting his turn of phrase.[31] Castelvetro's labour in composing the dialogues and, presumably, guiding his pupil through them—correcting his translations orally and in writing—gives some sense of the personal pedagogical relationships that were formed at the edges of the traditional university curriculum.

It is rare to be able to reconstruct an individual teacher's circle of students, but the survival of Castelvetro's album amicorum offers a window onto his contacts in Oxford and Cambridge in these years shortly before his death in England in 1616.[32] The inscriptions left by his pupils and friends in the album amicorum show these acquaintances giving testimonies of their respect and admiration for Castelvetro, frequently drawing attention to his great age. Several write in multiple languages, including Greek, Latin, English, Spanish, Italian, and French. The inscription of George Stanhope, a fellow of Trinity, is entirely in Italian: the album amicorum offered an opportunity for a pupil to demonstrate their progress to the teacher, their writing standing as a testament to shared experiences and to the master's abilities.[33] Others shared literary tags, quoting sixteenth-century Italian authors including Guidobaldo Bonarelli and Torquato Tasso, while one writer included a quotation from Spenser's *Shepheardes Calender* alongside his tag from Luigi Groto's tragedy *La Dalida* (1572): since none of the authors is identified in the text, it is reasonable to infer that the people who copied them out could assume Castelvetro's familiarity with the works.[34] The shared

[28] Kathleen Butler, 'Giacomo Castelvetro, 1546–1616', *Italian Studies* 5 (1950), pp. 32–42.
[29] Trinity College, Cambridge, MS. R.10.6.
[30] Castelvetro prepared teaching materials for William Waller of St John's and William Woodford of King's; Kathleen Butler argues that Castelvetro had probably planned to have those found in Trinity College, Cambridge, MS. R.10.7 printed: Butler, 'Giacomo Castelvetro', pp. 34–7.
[31] Trinity College, Cambridge, MS. R.10.6, fol. 9r.
[32] Giacomo Castelvetro, journal and album amicorum, British Library, Harleian MS 3344. For the identities of many of the contributors, see Butler, 'Giacomo Castelvetro', pp. 32–4.
[33] BL, Harleian MS 3344, fol. 63r.
[34] BL, Harleian MS 3344, fol. 63r contains a tag from Guidobaldo de'Bonarelli, *Filli di Sciro* (Paris, 1786), p. 227. BL Harleian MS 3344, fol. 63v contains tags from the *Shepheardes Calender* and from Luigi Groto, *La Dalida* (Venice, 1572). A transcription of the 1572 edition has been made available online by Dana F. Sutton at http://www.philological.bham.ac.uk/groto/, accessed 17 June 2014.

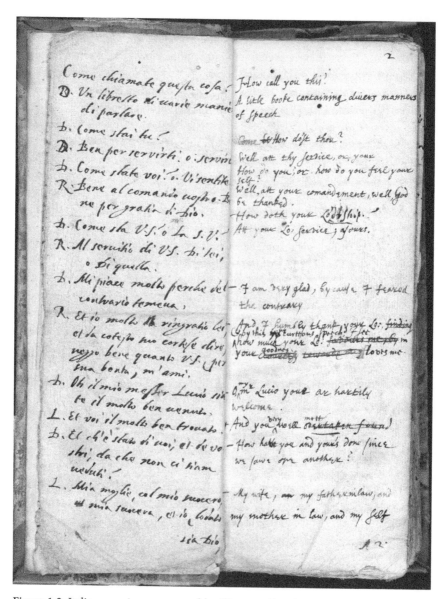

Figure 1.2 Italian exercises, composed by Giacomo Castelvetro, 1613

Source: Trinity College, Cambridge, MS. R.10.6, fols. 1v–2r. Courtesy of the Master and Fellows of Trinity College Cambridge.

knowledge of these works demonstrated by his grateful teachers and friends could suggest that they were read or studied together: they certainly show that Castelvetro found a place in Cambridge's Italophile literary circles towards the end of his life. Other inscriptions include proverbs in Italian: these students and friends used foreign-language proverbs to establish solidarity between students and teacher.[35] Lastly, it is worth noting that there is a palpable sense of affection and admiration in the messages written by these acquaintances of Castelvetro: respect for his skill in languages and in teaching, for his uncle, the famous humanist, and for his piety.[36] It is uncommon for documents which record teaching to give much insight into the emotional aspects of pedagogy, but the Castelvetro album amicorum offers a rare portrait of the intense relationships which animated one community of university linguists, as well as a glimpse into the informal vernacular pedagogies which flourished at Cambridge and Oxford long before modern languages took their place on the university curriculum.

The court and the royal household were other environments which merged formal language-learning and opportunities for practice. Language teachers could thrive in the multilingual environment of the court, where skill in the most fashionable language of the day was sought by aspiring courtiers. Elizabeth delighted in practising Italian with her musicians and addressing foreign diplomats in their native languages; courtiers welcomed foreign visitors in many tongues.[37] The multilingualism of the court, and its suitability as a language-learning space, was a fact from the beginning of the period to its end. John Palsgrave, who wrote the first major early modern grammar of French, was employed at and around the Henrician court.[38] Giacomo Castelvetro pursued a position as tutor to James VI and Anne of Denmark—one he ultimately attained—while John Florio served as Anne's tutor and Italian secretary on the pair's coming south to London.[39] Florio ultimately dedicated the second edition of his great Italian dictionary to the queen, and was himself rewarded for his service by becoming a gentleman of the privy chamber, though the fact that Florio died penniless and practically forgotten by his former patrons suggests that patronage was no less precarious than the rest of the extracurricular economy. Pierre Massonnet appears in the record as the holder of a comfortable position in

[35] Proverbs can be seen at BL Harleian MS 3344, fols. 58r, 64r, 101r; compare with the alphabetized *Giardino di Ricreatione* which was published as a supplement to John Florio, *Second Frutes* (London, 1591); on Florio and proverbs, see Michael Wyatt, *The Italian Encounter with Tudor England: A Cultural Politics of Translation* (Cambridge: Cambridge University Press, 2005), pp. 175–80, 183–4.

[36] On Castelvetro's piety and its relationship with his teaching, see Paola Ottolenghi, *Giacopo Castelvetro: esule modenese nell'Inghilterra di Shakespeare: spiritualità riformata e orientamenti di cultura nella sua opera* (Pisa: ETS, 1982), pp. 53–4.

[37] John Florio, *Florio His firste Fruites* (London, 1578), fol. 18r; Wyatt, *Italian Encounter*, pp. 128–35.

[38] Gabriele Stein, 'Palsgrave, John (d. 1554), teacher and scholar of languages', in *Oxford Dictionary of National Biography* (https://doi.org/10.1093/ref:odnb/21227); Stein, *John Palsgrave as Renaissance Linguist: A Pioneer in Vernacular Language Description* (Oxford: Oxford University Press, 1997).

[39] Butler, 'Giacomo Castelvetro', pp. 14–15; Desmond O'Connor, 'Florio, John (1553–1625), Author and Teacher of Languages', in *Oxford Dictionary of National Biography* (https://doi.org/10.1093/ref: odnb/9758).

1638, and as an abject petitioner for payment of a pension in both 1664 and 1668.[40] Florio's own father, Michelangelo, had experienced another kind of precariousness in elite employment, having been tutor to Lady Jane Grey (and author of a manuscript grammar of Italian for her use); during Mary's reign, Elizabeth's Italian tutor would find himself in hot water and subject to interrogation about his movements and the company he kept.[41]

Michelangelo Florio's son was not the only author to attempt to turn court employment into print success: Giles du Wès advertised his *Introductorie for to lerne to rede, to pronounce, and to speake Frenche trewly* (1546?) as having been 'compyled for the ryghte hygh, excellent, moste vertuous lady, the lady Mary of Englande, doughter to our mooste gracious soverayne lorde kynge Henry the eight'. Mary herself featured as a character in several of du Wès's dialogues. A concomitant fault of the text was its lack of concessions to the linguistic needs of non-royal readers: there can have been few readers who were in need of instruction in how to address 'A Messanger commyng from themperour, the french kyng, or any other prynce'.[42] In Pierre Lainé, we see how the acquisition of royal patronage could allow a teacher to change his public self-presentation: his first primer was published in 1655 as *A Compendious Introduction to the French Tongue*, with the author identifying himself on the title page as 'Peter Lainé, a Teacher of the said Tongue, now in London', but in 1667, and after a period in the royal service, his work appeared under the significantly different title *The Princely Way to the French Tongue. Or, a new and easie method to bring Her Highness, the Lady Mary, to the true and exact knowledge of that language*. Not only had the work's title been changed, but so too had its author's: now calling himself 'P.D.L. Tutor for the French to both Their Highnesses', Lainé had become de Lainé, presumably adding the nobiliary particle to match his new role as gentleman usher.[43] When he reissued the work in 1677, Lainé would point to his

---

[40] Warrant to Sir David Cunningham to pay to Peter Massonett appointed to instruct the Prince in the French tongue 60*l.* per annum, December 20th 1638, *CSP Dom.* Charles I, 1638–1639, vol. 13, p. 182. Petition of Peter Massonett to the King, to confirm the allowances made him by the late King, of 170*l.* 13*s.* 4*d.* a year, for attendance on himself, and 52*l.* for the Duke of York, February 28th 1662, National Archives, SP 29/51, fol. 98r. Petition of Peter Massonnet to the King, for one year's payment of his pension, the arrears now amounting to 668*l.*, for want of which he is outlawed for debt, [March?] 1664, National Archives, SP 29/95 fol. 32r. Peter Massonnet to Lord Arlington, [undated] 1668, National Archives, SP 29/251, fol. 144r.

[41] For Michelangelo Florio and his manuscript grammar, see Giuliano Pellegrini, 'Michelangelo Florio e le sue regole de la lingua thoscana', *Studi di filologia italiana* 12 (1954), pp. 72–201. For Castiglione, see Interrogatories to [Giovanni] Battista [Castiglione], [Italian tutor to Princess Elizabeth], with his deposition in answer, 31 May 1556, National Archives, SP 11/8, fol. 132r–v. See also Wyatt, *Italian Encounter*, p. 125, which describes Castiglione as Italian tutor and 'a sort of bodyguard', as well as Elizabeth's link to the outside during her time in the Tower.

[42] Giles Du Wès, *An introductorie for to lerne to rede, to pronounce, and to speake Frenche trewly: compyled for the ryghte hygh, excellent, & moste vertuous lady, the lady Mary of Englande, doughter to our mooste gracious souerayne lorde kynge Henry the eight* (London, 1546?), sig. [T4v].

[43] Peter de Lainé, *The Princely Way to the French Tongue. Or, a new and easie method to bring Her Highness, the Lady Mary, to the true and exact knowledge of that language* (London, 1667). Compare

continued work in the royal service, adding to his title that the text 'was first compiled for the use of her Highness the Lady Mary, and since taught her Royal Sister the Lady Anne'.[44] Lainé's contribution was noticed by Daniel Defoe in his printed elegy for Mary: he described her as 'that absolute Mistriss of the French Tongue', and added the opinion of 'her French Tutor, the famous Peter de Laine', indicating that the 'de' had caught on, and that Lainé's reputation had spread somewhat over time.[45] What we know of Lainé's career suggests that he realized that the court could provide patronage, and the canny teacher could translate that into prestige—and perhaps profit. With monarchs and courtiers hungry for foreign languages, the court would remain a crucial venue for language teaching.

The home, the university, and the court were all rich language-learning environments, but as Buck's *Third Universitie* had made clear, it was in the early modern city that vernacular educational offerings were truly booming. The period saw growing numbers of private schools operated by individual teachers in metropolitan areas, like the one operated by Claudius Hollyband in St Paul's Churchyard in the final decades of the sixteenth century. From at least 1575, Hollyband taught in the churchyard, 'by the signe of the Lucrece', moving only within the yard to 'the signe of the golden Balle' in 1581, remaining there at least until 1597.[46] Hollyband's inclusion of his location on the title pages of his manuals can be read as a canny advertisement for his services: copies of the title pages nailed up in public spaces could direct readers straight to his school.[47] Hollyband's books also advertised the service he provided, their dialogues dramatizing the activity found in his classrooms and his characters praising his skill as a pedagogue.[48] He seems to have provided private or one-to-one teaching (probably in French and Italian) to elite students too: in 1577–8, the returned traveller John North recorded buying a book from Hollyband and engaging him as a French

---

Guy Miège, who described himself as 'le Sieur Guy Miege' in Guy Miège, *Methode Abbregee pour Apprendre l'Anglois* (London, 1698), and as a 'Gent.' in Miège, *Miege's Last and Best French Grammar* (London, 1698).

[44] Peter de Lainé, *The Princely Way to the French Tongue, as it was first compiled for the use of her Highness the Lady Mary, and since taught her Royal Sister the Lady Anne* (London, 1677).
[45] Daniel Defoe, *The Life of that incomparable princess, Mary, our late sovereign lady, of ever blessed memory* (London, 1695), p. 8.
[46] Claudius Hollyband, *The Pretie and Wittie Historie of Arnalt & Lucenda* (London, 1575); Hollyband, *French Littelton* (London, 1578); Hollyband, *French Littelton* (London, 1581). Laurent Berec, 'L'École de Claude de Sainliens', in Anne Dunan-Page and Marie-Christine Munoz-Teulié, *Les Huguenots dans les Îles britanniques de la Renaissance aux Lumières: Écrits religieux et représentations* (Paris: Honoré Champion, 2008), pp. 89–99. An edition of Hollyband's *Frenche Littelton* is dated 1566 by its title page and the ESTC, but this is a misprint for 1576: see A. W. Pollard, 'Claudius Hollyband and his French Schoolmaster and French Littelton,' *The Library*, 3rd series, no. 21, vol. 6 (1915) pp. 77–93. I am grateful to Andrew Keener for drawing my attention to this fact.
[47] For this practice, see J. Voss, 'Books for Sale: Advertising and Patronage in Late Elizabethan England', *Sixteenth Century Journal* 29 (1998), p. 737.
[48] Hollyband, *French Littelton* (1578), pp. 10–13.

teacher at a rate of fourteen shillings a month.[49] Another pedagogical presence in the Elizabethan churchyard was G. de la Mothe, author of the *French Alphabet*, who wrote that if anyone wished to enquire after him or to engage his services, 'you shall heare of him, in Fleetstreet beneath the conduit, at the signe of S. John th'Evangelist, where this booke is to be sold: or els in Paules Churchyard, at the signe of the Helmet'.[50] A few minutes' walk away, the London-born French teacher Robert Sherwood operated a school at the churchyard of St Sepulchre's in 1625.[51] The area around St Paul's was the beating heart of early modern London's international, multilingual print trade—it made an ideal home for teachers of languages throughout our period.[52]

Some teachers' advertisements and book prefaces made little reference to their owning premises or schools of their own, but still directed their readers as to where they could be found, either at their lodgings or those of their friends or through the capital's booksellers. As the seventeenth century wore on, some French teachers began to move to the increasingly fashionable West End, with Guy Miège to be found in Panton Street near Leicester Fields, Paul Festeau on the Strand and on Clare Market, and Claude Mauger on Long Acre.[53] Festeau, Mauger, and Peter Berault also used their books to advertise their connections with the French booksellers of the West End, highlighting the close personal relationships that linked the educational economy and the book trade.[54] Meanwhile, teachers like Pietro Paravicino, Peter Berault, Francesco Colsoni, and Marten le Mayre clustered in the eastern half of the city at various points during

---

[49] Travel journal of Sir John North, 1575–7, Bodleian Library, MS Add. C. 193, fols. 26r, 47r.

[50] G. de la Mothe, *The French Alphabeth* (London, 1592), sig. Br.

[51] Robert Sherwood, *The French Tutour* (London, 1634), sig. A4v.

[52] Later teachers with a presence in Paul's Churchyard included Claude Mauger, the several editions of whose French grammar could be bought at the sign of the Bell, and Paul Festeau, whose *Nouvelle Grammaire Angloise* (London, 1675) was for sale at the sign of the Sun 'au Cymitiere de Saint Paul'. On the yard as a centre of the book trade, see Peter W. M. Blayney, *The Bookshops in Paul's Cross Churchyard* (London: Bibliographical Society, 1990); Michael Saenger, *The Commodification of Textual Engagements in the English Renaissance* (Aldershot: Ashgate, 2006), pp. 10, 148. On the international and multilingual nature of the early modern English book trade, see A. E. B. Coldiron, *Printers Without Borders: Translation and Textuality in the Renaissance* (Cambridge: Cambridge University Press, 2015).

[53] Guy Miège, *A New French Grammar; or, a New Method for Learning of the French Tongue* (London, 1678), sig. [A6v]; Paul Festeau, *Paul Festeau's French Grammar* (London, 1675), sig. [A6v]; Claude Mauger, *Claudius Mauger's French Grammar* (London, 1662), sig. [A8v]. Teachers were not necessarily resident at the places where their title pages or prefatory material said they could be found (though many were), but their changing associations with particular places and areas are revealing.

[54] See, for instance, Paul Festeau, who could be found 'at Mr. Lowndes, Book-Seller, over against Exeter-House in the Strand': Paul Festeau, *Paul Festeau's French Grammar* (London, 1675), sig. [A6v]. For a close relationship with a bookseller, see the prefatory material to Festeau, *Nouvelle Grammaire Angloise, Enrichie de Dialogues curieux touchant l'Estat, & la Cour d'Angleterre* (1675), [263], sigs. [A5v–A6r], which advertised the French books sold by Mr Thornicroft at the sign of the Sun in Paul's Churchyard, including Racine and Molière, and included a preface written by Thornicroft himself, '[l]e Libraire aux Etrangers', who also advertised his shop, 'where you may have most sorts of new French Books that come forth'.

the seventeenth century.[55] There, they could benefit from their proximity to the polyglot world of the Royal Exchange and the local coffee-houses, at least one of which (Grigsby's of Threadneedle Street) promised translations of all foreign news to its customers in 1702.[56] Just around the corner, at the Blue-Coat coffee-house in 1711, 'the French Tongue is taught Gratis publickly, by a French Gentleman; who teaches the said Language, Greek, Latin and English to Gentlemen, Ladies and others, at their Habitations or elsewhere'.[57] In 1707–8, Lorenzo Casotti, an Italian teacher and preacher (who advertised his printed sermons as pious language-learning materials) could be found at Jacob's coffee-house by the Royal Exchange in the mornings, and in the evenings at Paris's near Charing Cross; he also advertised his sermons (delivered near Leicester Fields) to learners of Italian.[58] Teachers of foreign languages could be found in spaces private and public throughout early modern London.

The seventeenth century, and particularly the Restoration, saw the emergence of private schools (some residential, some not) where French was an important aspect of the curriculum or, in some cases, the language of instruction. Early in the eighteenth century, French author Maximilien Misson praised the French-run schools in and around London, writing that they offered the 'particular Advantage...that besides all the Things that are taught in other Schools, [pupils] here learn the French Tongue'.[59] The newspaper press was abuzz with advertisements for schools of this kind, often operated by French émigrés like the Monsieur Meure who advertised in the London Gazette in December 1685. Coming originally from 'Saumur in France, where he hath had several English Gentlemen under his Care and Education', Meure now kept 'a Boarding School in London', where he taught 'French, Latin, Greek, Geography, Mathematicks, &c. Also Writing, Fencing, and Dancing'.[60] Meure's school was located in the heart of

---

[55] In 1660, Pietro Paravicino was 'dwelling in the Old-Jury, at the Wind-mill': Pietro Paravicino, *The true idioma of the Italian Tongue* (London, 1660), title page. In 1688, Peter Berault gave his address as 'Coleman-street, in Gleyn-Alley, next door to the White-Heart Inn': Peter Berault, *A New, Plain, Short, and Compleat French and English Grammar: Whereby the Learner may attain in few Months to Speak and Write French Correctly, as they do now in the Court of France. And Wherein all that is Dark, Superfluous, and Deficient in other Grammars, is Plain, Short, and Methodically supplied. Also very useful to Strangers, that are desirous to learn the English Tongue: for whose sake is added a Short, but very Exact English Grammar.* (London, 1688), p. [334]. In 1688, Colsoni described himself as 'Maestro di Lingue Habitante Vicino alla Borsa Reggia, in St. Christopher's-Alley in Thread-Needle-Street': Francesco Colsoni, *Il Nuovo Trismegiste, overo Il maestro di tre lingue* (London, 1688), title page. Marten le Mayre was 'dwelling in Abchurch lane' in 1606: Marten le Mayre, *The Dutch Schoole Master* (London, 1606), title page.

[56] *Flying Post or The Post Master*, issue 1162 (15 October 1702–17 October 1702).

[57] *Spectator*, issue 241 (6 December 1711).

[58] *Post Man and the Historical Account*, issue 1732 (30 January 1707–1 February 1707); *Post Man and the Historical Account*, issue 1921 (6 July 1708–8 July 1708).

[59] Maximilien Misson, *M. Misson's Memoirs and Observations in his Travels over England. With some Account of Scotland and Ireland* (London, 1709), p. 285.

[60] *London Gazette*, issue 2102 (7 January 1685).

fashionable London, next door to the White Hart inn on Long Acre, next to Covent Garden—the same area that was welcoming a growing number of teachers of French at this time. Schools like Meure's were frequently run by Frenchmen and their families, offered boarding to some or all of their pupils, and an education in languages and some combination of gentlemanly and practical skills. Another was that of Mr Vaslet, who taught 'French, Latin, Greek, Geography; and keeps Masters for other Exercises, as Writing, Arithmetick, Dancing, Drawing, &c.'; there was also Mr Robert in Greenwich, who ran 'a French Boarding School for Boys only, and teacheth them Latin, French, Geography and Manners; as also Writing and to cast Accounts upon very reasonable terms'.[61] Not all were in London: a 1705 advertisement gave notice of a French master operating a boarding establishment 'in Hatter-street in St Edmund Bury in Suffolk over against the Angel and Crown'.[62]

While competence in French remained an accomplishment which carried significant social prestige, some schools and teachers addressed the fact that it had practical value to those outside elite circles. The school by Somerset House seemed to be addressing a less refined clientele than its competitors by offering education in 'the Rudiments of the Latin, French and English Tongues, Writing and Arithmetick' at ten shillings a quarter, or twelve pence a week; while '[a]pprentices, and such as are grown to maturity, may be instructed in Arithmetic, &c. Suitable to their Trades and Employments, between 5 and 8 these Winter Evenings'.[63] The Holborn writing school operated by Charles Snell catered for students with commercial ambitions, teaching several hands, merchants' methods, and 'the true practice of Foreign Exchange', but also took in boarders and taught the same curriculum through French.[64] A 1707 advertisement for a boarding school promised '[e]xperienc'd Masters' who would teach 'whatever is usual in other Boarding-Schools, to fit Youth either for the University or for Common Business'.[65] In 1701, one Lewis Maidwell sought and received royal support for opening a '[p]ublick Schoole' in the parish of St James's Westminster, 'for the Instruction of Youths, Gratis, in Greek, Latin, & the Mathematicks, as also for learning the French, Italian and Spanish Tongues'. The aim of such schooling was to qualify the pupils 'not only for Our Universities, but likewise to prepare them for Our Sea Service': this was free education with modern languages at its heart, and the service of the state as its aim.[66] Any suggestion of socially mixed

---

[61] *London Gazette*, issue 3689 (17 March 1701–20 March 1701); *Post Man and the Historical Account*, issue 1071 (5 January 1703–7 January 1703).

[62] *Post Man and the Historical Account*, issue 1447 (15 September 1705–18 September 1705).

[63] *Post Boy*, issue 853 (24 September 1700–26 September 1700).

[64] *Daily Courant*, issue 1235 (30 March 1706).

[65] *Daily Courant*, issue 1658 (6 June 1707).

[66] Bill for Lewis Maidwell, esq., to found a school for the instruction of 40 youths *gratis*, February 16th 1702, National Archives, SP 44/348, fol. 340r. Around the turn of the century, Maidwell also produced handbills advertising his proposals: Lewis Maidwell, *Proposals reviv'd, of establishing, and supporting a public schole* (1699), EEBO Tract Supplement/C8:1[66].

education could be the source of tensions, as one teacher, Christopher Switerda, understood. Advertising his educational services to individuals at different points along the social spectrum, he wrote that 'every [student] is to pay according to their Quality', but assured status-conscious clients that 'every Gentleman and Ladies is Instructed in a room privately, if they will not be in Company'.[67]

A significant change that occurred in the educational economy of seventeenth-century England was the growth in professional private schooling offered to women. This period has been characterized as 'a turning point when the informal method of schooling girls that had dominated since 1500 was replaced to some extent by a more formal tripartite system of education at home, in charity schools and in private boarding schools'.[68] Among the most important arguments for the education of women came in Bathsua Makin's *Essay to revive the antient education of gentlewomen* (1673), in which Makin—herself an experienced teacher, former royal tutor, and prodigious polyglot—argued for women's capacity to learn, mocking the insecurity of men who sought to resist their access to schooling.[69] Writing that '[a] Learned Woman is thought to be a Comet, that bodes Mischief, when ever it appears', Makin mused that '[w]ere a competent number of Schools erected to Educate Ladies ingenuously, methinks I see how ashamed Men would be of their Ignorance, and how industrious the next Generation would be to wipe off their Reproach'. Putting her money where her mouth was, Makin concluded the *Essay* with an advertisement for a school in Tottenham to be run by Makin herself, where half the pupils' time would be spent studying '[w]orks of all sorts, Dancing, Music, Singing, Writing, Keeping Accompts', and the other half devoted to 'gaining the Latin and French Tongues; and those that please, may learn Greek and Hebrew, the Italian and Spanish: In all which this Gentlewoman has a competent knowledge'.[70] Even if Makin's school did not flourish, her principles did, at least to some extent, with women's academies and boarding schools becoming an established element of the educational economy in the later seventeenth century.[71]

---

[67] *English Post with News Foreign and Domestick*, issue 151 (26 September 1701–29 September 1701).

[68] Amanda L. Capern, *The Historical Study of Women: England 1500–1700* (Basingstoke and New York: Palsgrave Macmillan, 2008), p. 280.

[69] On Bathsua Makin, see Frances Teague, *Bathsua Makin, Woman of Learning* (London: Associated University Presses, 1998); Jean R. Brink, 'Bathsua Makin: "Most learned matron"', *Huntington Library Quarterly* 54 (1991), pp. 313–26; Vivian Salmon, 'Bathsua Makin (1600–c.1673): A Pioneer Linguist and Feminist', in Vivian Salmon, *Language and Society in Early Modern England: Selected Essays 1981–1994* (Amsterdam and Philadelphia, PA: Rodopi, 1996), pp. 239–60.

[70] Bathsua Makin, *Essay to revive the antient education of gentlewomen* (London, 1673), pp. 42–3.

[71] Boarding schools also commonly featured on the Restoration stage, for instance in Thomas d'Urfey's *Love for Money: or, The Boarding School* (London, 1691). On one London academy, see Richard Ansell, 'Foubert's Academy: British and Irish Elite Formation in Seventeenth- and Eighteenth-Century Paris and London', in Rosemary Sweet, Gerrit Verhoeven, and Sarah Goldsmith (eds.), *Beyond the Grand Tour: Northern Metropolises and Early Modern Travel Behaviour* (London, 2017), pp. 46–64.

The commitment to foreign-language teaching in these establishments often went beyond making French central to the curriculum: a number seem to have offered an immersive language experience, with French as the working language of the school. A notice printed in 1661 announced that in Long Acre next to Covent Garden 'a French School for young Gentlewomen, hath been kept these four yeers', where alongside writing, dancing, and music, '[pupils] are taught the French Tongue with great advantage, every one in the house speaking that language'.[72] French was the everyday language spoken in this academy, just as it was at a nearby 'French Boarding-School' advertised in 1682, where 'Young Gentlewomen are taught to Read, Write, and Speak French, to dance, to Sing, and to Work all sorts of Work'.[73] Claude Mauger's '[d]ialogue betweene a Gentleman and his daughter, that is newly come from Schoole' gives a sense of the centrality of French language education to an establishment of this kind:

Have you not forgot your English quite?
No, sir.
I suppose you speak French excellently well by this time.
I understand it better than I can speak it.[74]

Many of these academies were either French-run or employed French teachers. Francesco (sometimes François) Colsoni's *English Ladies New French Grammar* (1699) began with a prefatory address '[a]ux Dames et Demoiselles Francoises d'Angleterre', praising the Frenchwomen who 'take a particular care in raising the young daughters of the English in your schools'.[75] Particularly after the revocation of the Edict of Nantes in 1685, there was no shortage in London of educated French-speaking women with the skills necessary to run an establishment of this kind, nor of families keen to educate their daughters in a fashionable tongue which was increasingly seen as a desirable accomplishment for young women.[76]

The French competence of the female academy student was coloured by the environment in which it was learnt. Colsoni's later text includes a French master (standing for the author) explaining his method, and is followed by a series of

---

[72] *Kingdomes Intelligencer*, issue 14 (1 April 1661–8 April 1661).
[73] *Loyal Protestant and True Domestick Intelligence*, issue 154 (13 May 1682); see also the advertisement for Mrs Elizabeth Tutchin's school, which was visited twice weekly by masters of French and other subjects, in the *British Mercury*, issue 280 (4 January 1712–7 January 1712).
[74] Claude Mauger, *The True Advancement of the French Tongue* (London, 1653), p. 211.
[75] 'Vous qui jouissez librement de la conversation des Angloises, & qui prenez un soin particulier d'elever leurs Jeunes Filles dans vos Ecoles': François Colsoni, *The English Ladies New French Grammar* (London, 1699), sig. [A2v].
[76] On the rise of French as a gendered social accomplishment, see Michèle Cohen, 'French Conversation or "Glittering Gibberish"? Learning French in Eighteenth-Century England', in Natasha Glaisyer and Sara Pennell (eds.), *Didactic Literature in England 1500–1800: Expertise Constructed* (Aldershot: Ashgate, 2003), pp. 99–117.

bilingual English-French dialogues 'entre la Maitresse et ses Ecolieres Pensionnaires'. These cover some of the things women in these academies were meant to learn: from a discussion of table manners to a dialogue concerning the obedience due to one's teacher: 'You know, my Children, that obedience is more agreable than sacrifice; I do bid you nothing, but it is for your good; do think on't well.'[77] Colsoni's final dialogue treats of the Sabbath and of the pupils' attendance at the sermon of a new French preacher (a language-learning tool roughly a century and a half old in London at this point).[78] Pious behaviour is enjoined—'prepare your self to receive devoutly the Sacrament of the holy Supper'—along with an urge to more general virtue: 'Take care to keep your heart as clean as your body; let your cloaths be the Looking glass of your virtues; give a good example to all the world.'[79] Propriety, obedience, and piety: this text reflects the enclosed environment of the female academy, being as much about reinforcing the ideals of female virtue and restricting women's movement and expression to a limited, controlled, private, female-dominated space as it is about teaching French.[80] Here, the argument made by Mary Astell for a kind of Protestant female convent met its pedagogical counterpart in a multilingual pedagogy grounded in seclusion and piety.[81]

By the end of the seventeenth century, academies for women were a relatively unremarkable part of the London metropolitan educational scene, but they have yet to receive substantial historical attention, not least because surviving records are few and far between.[82] One early academy was that of Margaret Kilvert, to whom Claude Mauger dedicated his first French grammar in 1653, having taught there since moving to London from Blois (see Figure 1.3). He wrote in praise of '[t]he most Worthy, most Vertuous, and most Religious Gentlewoman, Mrs Margaret Kilvert', saying that 'I have now a good while since had the happinesse to be called by you, to teach those many gallant young Gentlewomen, who are of the most Noble Families of England, that are committed to your sage, prudent, & religious Education.'[83] The only surviving source referring to the

[77] Colsoni, *English Ladies New French Grammar*, p. 78.
[78] Roger Ascham attacked those who attended the Italian church 'to heare the Italian tonge naturally spoken, not to heare Gods doctrine trewly preached': Roger Ascham, *The Scholemaster* (London, 1570), p. 28.
[79] Mauger, *True Advancement*, pp. 79–80.
[80] On ideals of women's linguistic competence, see Chapter 3.
[81] Mary Astell, *A Serious Proposal to the Ladies for the Advancement of their True and Greatest Interest. In Two parts* (London, 1697). Gilbert Burnet suggested that female academies could be 'something like Monasteries without Vows': Gilbert Burnet, *History of His Own Time* (London, 1734), vol. 2, p. 653. I would like to thank Liesbeth Corens for drawing my attention to this reference. See also Bridget Hill, 'A Refuge from Men: The Idea of a Protestant Nunnery', *Past & Present* 117 (1987), pp. 107–130.
[82] There are some exceptions, such as the probate lawsuit concerning the late Elizabeth Hoskins, who died in a boarding school in Hampstead and was 'very much addicted to the drinking of strong liquors to excess': London, The National Archives, PROB 18/39/28.
[83] Mauger, *True Advancement*, sig. A2v.

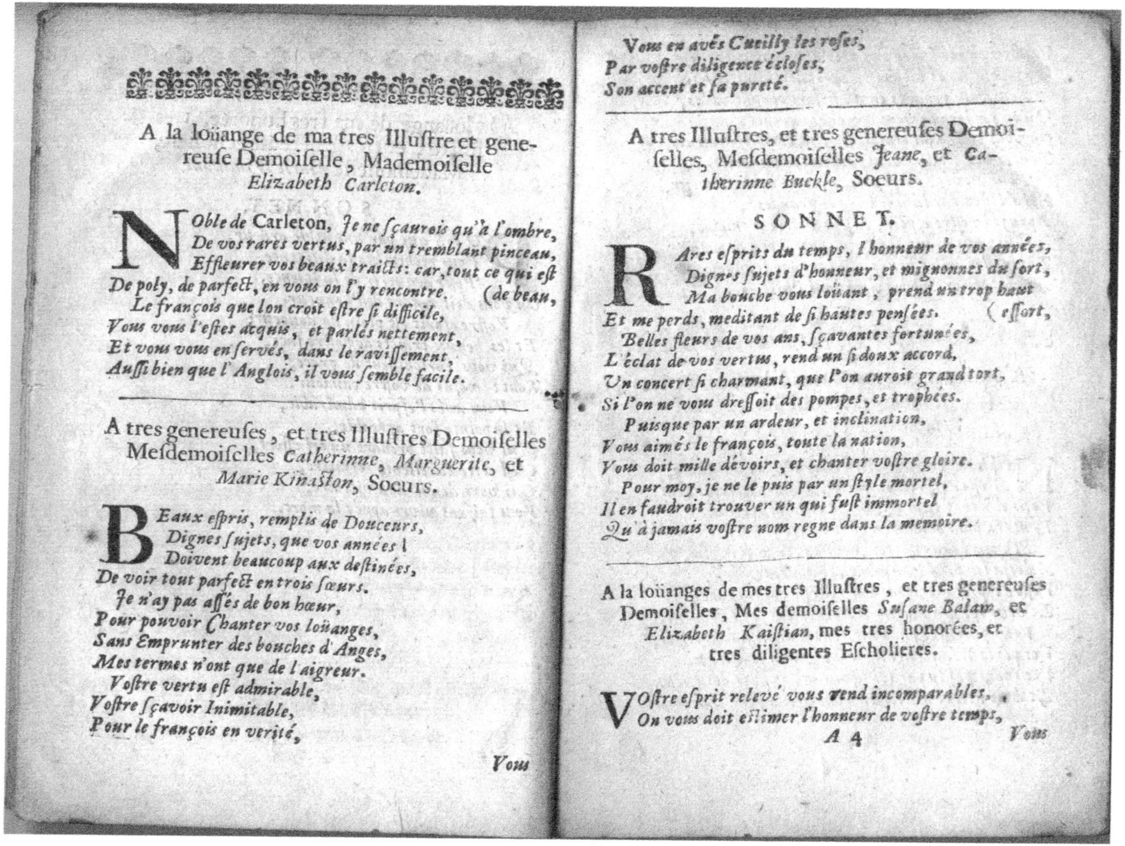
A la loüange de ma tres Illuſtre et genereuſe Demoiſelle, Mademoiſelle *Elizabeth Carleton.*

*N*Oble de Carleton, *Je ne ſçaurois qu'à l'ombre,*
De vos rares vertus, par un tremblant pinceau,
Effleurer vos beaux traicts: car, tout ce qui eſt
De poly, de parfect, en vous on l'y rencontre. (*de beau,*
Le françois que lon croit eſtre ſi difficile,
Vous vous l'eſtes acquis, et parlés nettement,
Et vous vous en ſervés, dans le raviſſement,
Auſſi bien que l'Anglois, il vous ſemble facile.

A tres genereuſes, et tres Illuſtres Demoiſelles Meſdemoiſelles *Catherinne, Marguerite,* et *Marie Kinaſton,* Soeurs.

*B*Eaux eſpris, remplis de Douceurs,
Dignes ſujets, que vos années!
Doivent beaucoup aux deſtinées,
De voir tout parfect en trois ſœurs.
Je n'ay pas aſſés de bon hœur,
Pour pouvoir Chanter vos loüanges,
Sans Emprunter des bouches d'Anges,
Mes termes n'ont que de l'aigreur.
Voſtre vertu eſt admirable,
Voſtre ſçavoir Inimitable,
Pour le françois en verité,

Vous

Vous en avés Cueilly les roſes,
Par voſtre diligence écloſes,
Son accent et ſa pureté.

A tres Illuſtres, et tres genereuſes Demoiſelles, Meſdemoiſelles *Jeane,* et *Catherinne Buckle,* Soeurs.

SONNET.

*R*Ares eſprits du temps, l'honneur de vos années,
Dignes ſujets d'honneur, et mignonnes du ſort,
Ma bouche vous loüant, prend un trop haut
Et me perds, meditant de ſi hautes penſées. (*effort,*
Belles fleurs de vos ans, ſçavantes fortunées,
L'éclat de vos vertus, rend un ſi doux accord,
Un concert ſi charmant, que l'on auroit grand tort,
Si l'on ne vous dreſſoit des pompes, et trophées.
Puisque par un ardeur, et inclination,
Vous aimés le françois, toute la nation,
Vous doit mille dévoirs, et chanter voſtre gloire.
Pour moy, je ne le puis par un ſtyle mortel,
Il en faudroit trouver un qui fuſt immortel
Qu'à jamais voſtre nom regne dans la memoire.

A la loüanges de mes tres Illuſtres, et tres genereuſes Demoiſelles, Mes demoiſelles *Suſane Balam,* et *Elizabeth Kaiſtian,* mes tres honorées, et tres diligentes Eſcholieres.

*V*Oſtre eſprit relevé vous rend incomparables,
On vous doit eſtimer l'honneur de voſtre temps,

A 4 *Vous*

Figure 1.3 Claude Mauger, *The True Advancement of the French Tongue* (London, 1653)

Source: Westminster Abbey Library Gal. I. 1.44, sig. A3v–A4r. Copyright: Dean and Chapter of Westminster.

academy is Mauger's manual, but Kilvert's background can be discerned in archival documents. In April 1655, she was part of a group petitioning the Council of State who described themselves as 'antient servantes to the late kinges Children [who] attended upon them from time to time under severall Governors . . . untill they came to be setled under the Countess of Leicester' after the execution of Charles I in 1649, at which point they had been dismissed.[84] For Kilvert, the private academy seems to have been a way to make money after she was forced out of a place in the royal household. Mauger's manual is also a rare source in that it lists the academy's pupils by name—class lists of this kind generally do not survive. The teacher addressed prefatory verses to over thirty of his female pupils by name: 'Mademoiselle Marie Windham', 'Mademoiselle Elizabeth Carleton', and the Kinaston sisters—'Catherinne, Marguerite, et Marie'—among others.[85] One student, 'Jeane Thornehill', might be the Dame Jane Thornhill who married Sir Thomas Peyton in February 1667, while Benedicta Drake is very likely the daughter of Joseph Drake of Kingston upon Hull, for whom a record of her 1652 marriage settlement survives, detailing the substantial Yorkshire properties that she and her prospective husband would bring to their union—including a signifi-cant mansion house on the Drake side.[86] Mauger expected that the book could derive some prestige and perhaps some future employment from linking his name to those of his high-status pupils; his strategy allows us to glimpse inside one elite female academy.

Women like Kilvert are important and underappreciated figures in the history of early modern English education. They established new institutions of private education, developing and advertising a curriculum aimed at young women of middling and high status. Education in foreign languages was at the heart of this new educational movement, and it would remain a mainstay of women's educa-tion beyond the early modern period. As female proprietors of schools, they were visible: they advertised in print and made themselves accessible in public—anyone interested in Bathsua Makin's academy was encouraged to seek out one of her representatives at an appointed hour in a London coffee-house.[87] Other female teachers advertised their services, like the 'Italian Gentlewoman [who] designs to teach both the Italian and French Tongues' and could be contacted 'at

---

[84] Petition of Margaret Kilvert et al., servants of the late king's children, to council, 19 April 1655, National Archives, SP 18/96, fol. 80r.

[85] Mauger, *True Advancement*, sigs. [A3r–A6v].

[86] Marriage allegation, 1667, Dame Jane Thornhill & Sir Thomas Peyton, Baronet. London, Lam-beth Palace Library, FM I/6 (Thornhill is described as a widow, which makes it possible that this is not the same woman). Marriage settlement, 17 April 1652, '[b]etween Thomas Stockdale of Bilton Park and Joseph Drake of Kingston upon Hull, gent., concerning the marriage settlement of Benedicta Drake, Joseph's daughter, who is to marry William Stockdale, son and heir apparent of Thomas Stockdale'. Leeds, West Yorkshire Archive Service, WYL132/257.

[87] Makin, *Essay to revive the antient education of gentlewomen*, p. 43.

Mrs Guedon's in St. Andrew's-street, by the Seven Dyals, at the Sign of the Barbers Pole'.[88] These women were pioneers—but the role of women and of women's labour in the educational economy of early modern England goes deeper and is insufficiently represented in our histories of education in this period.[89]

To get closer to the nature of women's labour in the early modern educational economy, we should first return to the 1661 advertisement for the young women's French school on Long Acre (discussed above), where we read that 'besides all fitting accommodations they are taught the French Tongue with great advantage, *every one in the house speaking that language*' (my emphasis).[90] The immersive language-learning environment promised by the emergent French schools relied on the capacity not only of French masters to speak French, but of the servants and staff of the establishment more generally. This shared educational labour is made explicit in a 1695 advertisement for the free school at Keldon operated by 'Mr Peter Noblet, a French Gentleman', where 'this Schoolmaster's Mother, Wife and Servants speak French mostly, and he does very advantageously teach the French by Conversation, with great ease'.[91] These women, like the unnamed 'Servants', were 'invisible educators' in the sense that Steven Shapin talks about 'invisible technicians'. Shapin shows how the name of the gentleman scientist generally obscured the crucial work done by technicians, who generally went unnamed and underappreciated—their knowledge, skill, and labour carefully concealed behind a figure whose social status allowed him to advance greater truth claims.[92] In essence, '[t]he philosopher has a name and an individual identity: the technician does not'.[93] Similarly, in the educational economy of early modern England, women worked in schools and classrooms, performing what is unquestionably educational labour, speaking French with pupils and creating the immersive linguistic environment that was the main selling point of this new kind of schooling. Wives, daughters, and servants rarely appear in discussions of historical teachers, except as exceptions or where—as in the case of Makin—theirs was the name above the door. Still, the story of women's role in English education is not simply one of pioneers and innovators. To take one important group as an example, later seventeenth-century England hosted growing numbers of French migrants of both sexes who, uprooted from their homes

---

[88] *Post Man and the Historical Account*, issue 1747 (13 March 1707–15 March 1707).

[89] New directions are considered by Rosemary O'Day, *Women's Agency in Early Modern Britain and the American Colonies: Patriarchy, Partnership and Patronage* (Harlow: Pearson Longman, 2007), pp. 320–37.

[90] *Kingdomes Intelligencer*, issue 14 (1 April 1661–8 April 1661).

[91] *Collection for Improvement of Husbandry and Trade*, issue 148 (31 May 1695).

[92] For the concept of 'invisible technicians', see Steven Shapin, *A Social History of Truth: Civility and Science in Seventeenth-Century England* (Chicago and London: University of Chicago Press, 1994), pp. 355–408.

[93] Ibid., p. 359.

and professions, could turn their knowledge of the French language into gainful employment.[94] Not all became well-known teachers or the proprietors of schools, but the educational economy that allowed men like Claude Mauger to rise to fame was built on the educational labour of countless other unnamed women and men—invisible educators underpinning an early modern educational revolution.

Language Teachers: Community, Competence, and Authority

Claude Mauger was the most famous French teacher in Restoration England. Having established himself as a language tutor to northern European travellers in the fashionable Loire valley town of Blois, he moved to England around the middle of the century, where—as we have seen—he took a job teaching French at Margaret Kilvert's academy for young women.[95] This was the base from which he established himself in print, producing a French grammar which would ultimately go into tens of editions in England, the Low Countries, and even France itself.[96] Mauger was keen to portray himself as a teacher of the very best variety of French, and someone with elite contacts and students on both sides of the Channel. He wrote that his method had the approval of 'the other masters of the Languages' active in London (although there were exceptions), and seems to have collaborated with at least one of them on a 'double grammar'.[97] New editions of his works came with revised prefaces and fresh dedications to the great and the good, as well as biographical updates which confirmed their author's commitment to top-flight pedagogy: readers learnt of Mauger's correspondence with figures at the French court, of the esteem in which he was held by the grammarians of Port-Royal, and of his removing himself to Paris in order to ensure his grammar contained nothing but the most up-to-date and fashionable French. Mauger was more prolific and better known than any of his other competitors, at a time when the study of French was booming in England. He came highly recommended: the author of the popular *Gentlewoman's Companion* praised him as 'that unimitable

---

[94] For perspectives on French migrants as teachers, see Geraldine Sheridan and Viviane Prest (eds.), *Les Huguenots éducateurs dans l'espace européen à l'époque moderne* (Paris: Honoré Champion, 2011), and Susanne Lachenicht, 'Les Éducateurs huguenots dans les Îles britanniques (XVIe–XVIIIe siècles)', in Vladislav Rjéoutski and Alexander Tchoudinov (eds.), *Le Précepteur francophone en Europe* (Paris: L'Harmattan, 2013), pp. 53–63.

[95] Mauger appears in the Verney correspondence, teaching French at Blois in the 1640s: Mark Motley, 'Educating the English Gentleman Abroad: The Verney Family in Seventeenth-Century France and Holland', *History of Education: Journal of the History of Education Society*, 23 (1994), pp. 243–56.

[96] See the Supplementary Bibliography of conversation manuals for a list of Mauger's many editions.

[97] This was Paul Festeau, whom Mauger also recommended as 'a good and excellent Writer' in 1653: Mauger, *True Advancement*, p. 187. The publication that brought them together was Claude Mauger and Paul Festeau, *Nouvelle double grammaire francoise-angloise et angloise-francoise par Messrs. Claude Mauger et Paul Festeau* (The Hague, 1693).

Master of the French Tongue'.[98] Mauger's fame was such that, when Winlove in John Lacy's play *Sauny the Scot* disguised himself as 'an ordinary French master about the Town' (complete with a comic French accent), he took the name 'Mr. Mawgier'.[99]

Mauger was not a typical teacher—certainly, the amount we can learn about him is unusual, since many teachers appear only fleetingly in the historical record. Even though early modern language-learning was vocal and even noisy, language masters remain frustratingly silent. Mauger's career, however, introduces some key themes in the history of foreign-language teaching in early modern England. Like his contemporaries, he understood that he was working in an economy of reputation, skill, and prestige—one which bears comparison with the early modern 'medical marketplace', described by Mark Jenner and Patrick Wallis as 'an emergent diverse, plural and commercial pre-professional system of health care'.[100] Mauger carved out a place as London's most prominent teacher of French by using his presence in print, his networks of contacts, and his claims to pedagogical skill and linguistic prestige. Mauger's career stretched over half a century or more, against the backdrop of an increasingly crowded and competitive market for language teaching, particularly in London. A central problem faced by teachers and learners operating in this environment was the lack of any overarching institution which could confer legitimacy or authority on a particular teacher, text, or method. Instead, linguistic prestige and pedagogical authority were debated and defined by teachers and learners. Language masters had to develop means of assuring potential pupils of their competence to teach an approved variety of the language, and of persuading a public with good reason to be sceptical that they possessed more authority and a closer link to 'pure' language than their competitors. It is possible to use archival traces and printed texts to reconstruct teachers' careers, their professional networks, and the ways in which they advertised their abilities and argued for their superior skills. By approaching their story in a broadly chronological way, we can see how the profession of a language master developed alongside new debates about prestigious language and pedagogical skill, and how debates about and between teachers helped to shape early modern English ideas about vernacular languages.

---

[98] Anon. ['Hannah Woolley'], *The Gentlewomans Companion*, p. 32. The author also recommended Giovanni Torriano as a teacher of Italian.

[99] John Lacy, *Sauny the Scot. Or, the Taming of the Shrew* (London, 1698). The play was first performed at the Theatre Royal in 1667: Julie Sanders, 'Lacy, John (c.1615–1681)', *Oxford Dictionary of National Biography*, Oxford University Press, 2004 (https://doi.org/10.1093/ref:odnb/15856).

[100] Mark S. R. Jenner and Patrick Wallis, 'The Medical Marketplace' in Jenner and Wallis (eds.), *Medicine and the Market in England and its Colonies, c.1450–c.1850* (Basingstoke: Palgrave Macmillan, 2007), p. 1. The essays in *Medicine and the Market* offer a helpful overview of the historiography on the 'medical marketplace' alongside a rigorous reassessment: particularly relevant are the essays by Patrick Wallis, Mary E. Fissell, and Elaine Leong and Sara Pennell.

In September 1613, Pierre Erondell wrote to Elizabeth, Lady Hicks to apologize for his inability to continue teaching French to her daughters, by reason of the family's departure from London. To make up for this, he sent the letter by a bearer whom he recommended as a replacement teacher, explaining that

> [t]o the ende that the Gentlewomen doo not over muche neglect their frenche, I have thought good to recommend this bearer unto Lad*yship*, for whose honest behaviour, and diligence in teaching, I will be answerable, w*hich* I wold not doo, unles I had certen knowledge of his sound religion and Conscience[101]

Erondell's recommendation worked on several levels. He offered his own personal guarantee, presumably drawing on his own credit with the addressee, and he made explicit reference to the candidate's skill as a pedagogue, his general honesty, and his religious conformity: all important criteria for someone who would spend a significant amount of time in close contact with young women in a household environment. Erondell's addressee also had the opportunity to test the teacher's competence herself, a postscript adding that the teacher 'intendeth to tarye w*ith* you some fortnight, upon triall of your liking'.[102] Letters like Erondell's rarely survive, but they offer some insight into how a domestic language teacher might have been chosen, and how teachers operated within the educational economy of reputation and recommendation. As in a 1562 letter from Edward Horsey to William Cecil which mentions the sender's attempts to find 'some grave french woma*n* to wayte upon y*our* dowghter & to teache her the fre*n*che tongue', the importance of personal recommendation and reputation were clear.[103] Scribal remnants like these show an educational economy in which face-to-face relationships were crucial.

Other teachers made their reputations in print. As we saw above, Claudius Hollyband, as an immigrant teacher in late sixteenth-century London, employed his many language-learning texts as paper representatives of his person and his pedagogy. His main innovation in print was his appeal to the purity of the variety of French he taught. In his *French Littelton* (first published in 1578), he boasted that

> after that my scholers have framed their tongue by this booke, they are so far off to pronounce such letters which ought not, that when they heare anie new scholar coming to me from other Fre*n*ch schooles, and pronouncing any letter otherwise then it should be, they spie the fault as soone as I, yea they cannot abide

---

[101] Erondell to Elizabeth, Lady Hicks, 1 September 1613, British Library, Lansdowne MS 93, fol. 29r.

[102] Ibid. On domestic teaching for women, see also de Groot, 'Every one teacheth after thyr owne fantasie'.

[103] Edward Horsey to Cecil, 22 December 1562, National Archives, SP 70/47, fol. 113r.

it: & which is more, they will discerne whether the maister which taught them first, was a Burgonion, a Norman, or a Houyvet.[104]

Hollyband's warning established three things: that there was a prestige variety of French, that Hollyband spoke it, and that to speak differently was cause for disdain by those in the know. Crucially, he also established that to speak a variety of French that was not socially approved could be cause for ridicule or embarrassment: not to speak the same French as Hollyband, the 'gentleman of Bourbon', was a 'fault', something his students 'cannot abide'. By insisting that inappropriate speech was a sure recipe for social embarrassment, teachers could commodify the variety of French that they spoke and devalue that of their rivals: it was another element of social or communicative competence in which they could corner the market (as well as being one which could only be learnt in person). The threat of social exclusion for speakers of non-standard varieties became a key weapon in the arsenal of the language teacher: in 1623, Juan de Luna offered the cautionary tale of the Duc de Maine and his entourage, who had studied Spanish for six months at Paris before departing on an embassy, only to find on their arrival in Spain that 'in stead of admiring, every one laught at them, hearing their bad accent, worse pronunciation, and worst phrase'.[105] Even in German—a language with its own inferiority complex in relation to the southern European vernaculars—a teacher could write in 1680 that the speaker who did not know how to pronounce the language correctly would be 'disgraced'.[106] The need to speak a socially acceptable variety of one's new language became a pressing concern for learners, and one that was carefully manipulated by their teachers.

Claudius Hollyband's dismissive attitude towards other teachers signalled the potential for conflict in a competitive educational economy. In the vituperative preface to his *Ortho-Epia Gallica* (1593), John Eliot addressed himself to 'the gentle doctors of Gaule', 'the learned professors of the French tongue, in the

---

[104] Hollyband, *French Littelton*, p. 6. For debates about the best variety of spoken French in the sixteenth and seventeenth century, see Paul Cohen, 'Courtly French, Learned Latin, and Peasant Patois: The Making of a National Language in Early Modern France' (unpublished PhD thesis, Princeton University, 2001); Peter Rickard, *A History of the French Language* (London and New York: Routledge, 1989), pp. 81–119 Rickard, *La langue française au seizième siècle: étude suivie de textes* (Cambridge: Cambridge University Press, 1968), pp. 18–24.

[105] Juan de Luna, *A short and compendious art for to learne to reade, write, pronounce and speake the Spanish Tongue. Composed by John de Luna of Castile, Interpreter of the Spanish Tongue in London* (London: William Jones, 1623), B2r. For the growing attention given to accent in early modern linguistic thought, see Peter Burke, 'A Civil Tongue: Language and Politeness in Early Modern Europe', in Peter Burke, Brian Harrison, and Paul Slack (eds.), *Civil Histories: Essays Presented to Sir Keith Thomas* (Oxford: Oxford University Press, 2000), p. 40.

[106] Martin Aedler, *The High Dutch Minerva A-La-Mode or A Perfect Grammar never extant before, whereby the English may both easily and exactly learne the Neatest Dialect of the German Mother-Language used throughout All Europe* (London, 1680), p. 24; for Aedler on German dialects, see ibid., pp. 3, 11; see also Offelen, *Double Grammar*, p. 133. It is worth noting, however, that Aedler and Offelen seem to differ on which dialects are inappropriate.

famous cittie of London', begging them to deride his work: 'I pray you be readie quickely to cavill at my booke...I request you humbly controll my method as soone as you may, I earnestly entreat you hisse at mine inventions.' Eliot sarcastically begged these critical Frenchmen to

> persuade every one that you meet, that my booke is a false, fained, slight, confused, absurd, barbarous, lame, unperfect, single, uncertaine, childish peece of worke, and not able to teach, and why so? Forsooth because it is not your owne, but an Englishmans doing.[107]

Eliot's overblown rhetoric addressed an audience of French-born teachers in London who presumed that no Englishman could teach French: quite a change from the earlier sixteenth century, when John Palsgrave's stock was high as a teacher and grammarian both at the Henrician court and in France.[108] Among the period's last English-French conversation manuals to be written by an Englishman was Robert Sherwood's *French Tutour*, which appeared in two editions in 1625 and 1634. Sherwood identified himself as a Londoner, and the second edition advertised his school in St Sepulchre's churchyard. Even so, he clearly understood the increasingly dominant opinion that Loire valley French was the best, writing that

> [t]his Grammar I have compiled and gathered, partly out of my long experience of Teaching, and partly by following in many things Monsieur Maupas of Blois, a man well knowne to some of the greatest of this Kingdome (who have travelled) to bee the learnedest and most expert Teacher of this tongue.[109]

By the middle of the seventeenth century, English-born authors had effectively disappeared from the market for printed English-French conversation manuals, ending a process which may already have been under way when John Eliot addressed the carping French teachers of London in 1593. In 1679, Paul Festeau described himself as '[n]ative of Blois, a City in France where the true tone of the French Tongue is found by the Unanimous consent of all French-Men': the teachers of his generation had made it their business to leverage that 'unanimous consent' into commercial advantage.[110] There is a palpable defensiveness in an advertisement for an Englishman's language school in 1680, which announces

---

[107] John Eliot, *Ortho-Epia Gallica. Eliots Fruits for the French* (London, 1593), sig. A4r.

[108] For Palsgrave's reputation in France, see Stein, *John Palsgrave as Renaissance Linguist*, p. 38.

[109] Robert Sherwood, *The French Tutour* (London, 1625), sig. A2r. Maupas's grammar was published in English in 1634, the same year that Sherwood's *French Tutour* went into its second edition. Charles Maupas, *A French grammar and syntaxe contayning most exact and certaine rule, for the pronunciation, orthography, construction, and use of the French language* (London, 1634).

[110] Paul Festeau, *Nouvelle Grammaire Françoise* (London, 1679), title page.

that 'he doth not onely teach [pupils] the Latin Tongue, but also instructeth them in all Civilities, as well as them which are born at Paris'.[111]

Language teaching was a social business: teachers relied not just on their profile in print, but on networks of students and patrons, to secure ongoing employment. The printed language text offered the ability to mobilize one's social networks, to draw attention to the social quality or linguistic excellence of one's students, and thus to burnish one's reputation as a language master. The prefatory spaces of conversation manuals came to resemble multilingual social spaces, crowded with patrons, dedicatees, pupils, and sponsors.[112] Language teachers used the paratextual materials in their teaching texts to situate themselves in contexts which would cause readers to value their work and esteem their reputation—and, by extension, their competence as teachers. These contexts could be institutional, as in the case of John Minsheu's 1599 dedication of a Spanish grammar 'to the right worshipfull gentlemen students of Grayes Inne health and happines, and to the affected to languages there', Paul Festeau's claim that the 'Nomenclature' contained in his *New and Easie French Grammar* (1667) was the same one used 'in the famous school of Westminster', or the appeals of Giovanni Torriano and others to the patronage of the Levant Company as a centre of Italian language-learning.[113] Authors also sought to tie their texts and their teaching to exalted social circles. In the preface to his 1591 English-Spanish manual, William Stepney defended his capacity to teach Spanish, but also sought to justify the study of the language at all (in the light of continuing Anglo-Spanish tensions) by referring to the many 'very noble persons in our England who are very fond of the Castilian language'; his qualifications were established by reference to 'diverse gentlemen my good friends, unto whom I do reade the sayd tongue'.[114] Stepney's appeal to a gentle readership and an elite pedagogical community established his social credentials and his ability to teach prestigious language.

Teachers used the prefatory spaces of their books to claim well-known pupils as their own. Teachers invoked their students (actual or potential) in the knowledge that a skilled student was a walking advertisement for their teacher's abilities: their reputations were intertwined. Skilled polyglots could be identified with their teachers: in his copy of John Florio's *Firste Fruites*, Gabriel Harvey bemoaned his own difficulties in learning Italian with reference to those who had flourished under Florio's care. 'How the Earl of Leicester, Master Hatton,

---

[111] *True Domestick Intelligence or News Both from City and Country* (London, England), issue 84 (20 April 1680–23 April 1680).

[112] On the 'sociability of print', see Michelle O'Callaghan, *The English Wits: Literature and Sociability in Early Modern England* (Cambridge: Cambridge University Press, 2007).

[113] John Minsheu and Richard Perceval, *A Spanish Grammar* (London, 1599), sig. I2r; Paul Festeau, *New and Easie French Grammar* (London, 1667), sig. [A5v]; Giovanni Torriano, *The Italian Tutor or a new and most compleat Italian Grammer* (London, 1640).

[114] 'personas muy nobles en nuestra Inglatierra que son muy afficionadas a la lengua Castillana': William Stepney, *The Spanish Schoole-master* (London, 1591), sig. A2v.

Sir Philip Sidney, and many of our outstanding courtiers, speak the Italian tongue most fluently...Florio, how often have you instantaneously created blossoming Italians?'[115] Authors commonly praised their students' diligence or skill in their dedications, allowing the reader a glimpse of a successful pedagogical relationship. Henry Grantham dedicated his English translation of Scipio Lentulo's Italian grammar to 'the right vertuous mystres Mary and mysres Francys Berkeley daughters to the Right honourable Henry Lord Berkeley', for the instruction of whom he had originally made the translation. He praised 'the good inclinations you have, and the great endevours you use towards th'atteining of the Italian tonge'.[116] A dedication of this kind attested to the teacher's service in a network of patronage and to the quality of his students. The prefatory material of a printed book could also be a performative space in which the virtuosity of the author's friends and pupils, or the approbation of fellow teachers, was on display.[117] Heinrich Offelen, who advertised himself as '[p]rofessor of Seven Languages, (viz.) English, French, Spanish, latine, Italian, and High- and Low-dutch', included prefatory verses in German, English, Latin, Spanish, Italian, Dutch, and French, written by writers in England and beyond.[118] Multilingual prefatory spaces established the author of a grammar or conversational manual as the centre of a network of polyglot speech, writing, and learning; they reproduced the classroom—and its successes—in print.

Claude Mauger was one teacher who turned the 'sociability of print' to spectacular advantage, working hard to derive credit from his pupils' social status and their skill in the language. He published two bilingual volumes of his letters, often addressed to those who had been his students. They included a fawning address to Gustavus Adolphus, in which Mauger recalled 'the honour which you did me in choosing me at Blois, to teach you the French tongue', and announced 'the just desire which I have to exercise you in it' by means of a French-language letter.[119] Mauger also wrote to members of the French court, bolstering his claim to be in touch with those who spoke the most up-to-date and fashionable French.[120] Other recipients included various members of the northern European noble classes,

---

[115] Lawrence, *Who the devil*, p. 28.

[116] Henry Grantham, *An Italian Grammer; written in Latin by Scipio Lentulo a Neapolitane: and turned in English: by H. G.* (London, 1587), sig. A2r.

[117] A French language master named Penson contributed a verse to the 1656 edition of Mauger's grammar, while Giovanni Torriano contributed a verse to the 1658 printing: Claude Mauger, *Mr Mauger's French Grammar* (London, 1656), sig. [A6r]; Mauger, *Claudius Maugers French Grammar* (London, 1658), sig. [A8v].

[118] Heinrich Offelen, *A Double Grammar for Germans To Learn English; and for English-Men To Learn the German-Tongue* (London, 1687).

[119] Claude Mauger, *Mauger's Letters written upon Several Subjects: Faithfully Translated into English, for the great facility of those, who have a desire to learn the French Tongue* (London, 1671), sig. B2r.

[120] For instance, he wrote to M. de Barrière, formerly the agent of the Prince de Condé in England: ibid., p. 79.

ambassadors both English and foreign, Edward Colman (the secretary to the Duchess of York, later executed during the Popish Plot), artists, teachers, scholars, and the daughters of an MP.[121] Writing to a student who was himself an MP, Mauger rejoiced that 'the improvement which you have made in [the French language], doth much contribute to my credit, since all England looks on you as one of her wisest Senatours'; to another, serjeant-at-arms to Charles II, he wrote that 'I should lose my Credit, if God should not raise me from time to time, some persons like you, who by their diligence and capacity, with the help of my method, sustain it.'[122] The relation of Mauger's printed letters to any he might have originally written is unclear, not least because some change their details and contents between the two printed editions.[123] Nonetheless, his two volumes of *Letters* were a masterclass in how to leverage the reputations of one's pupils (or those one claimed as pupils) to one's own advantage as a teacher. Mauger—for decades the best-known French teacher in England—understood the value of well-known and well-spoken students to spread the teacher's fame. He understood, too, that educational print was sociable and conversational, and that it could be turned to great advantage by the savvy teacher.

The emergence of the newspaper as a forum for advertising services helped to transform how teachers established and defended their reputations in the public eye. Cities—London in particular—were expanding, as was the extracurricular economy, and urban education was undergoing a transformation. By the mid-seventeenth century, Samuel Hartlib could dream up an Office of Public Advice which would provide information about '[p]rofessors of Sciences, Teachers of Hebrew, Greek, Latin, English, French, Italian, Dutch, or any other Languages...Tutors or Governors for Noblemen or Gentlemens Children... School-Masters, or School Mistresses of the better sort'.[124] Newsprint allowed teachers and the proprietors of schools to advertise their services publicly without printing a book of their own or relying on a personal network. The reader of a Restoration newspaper could read of the services offered by 'Christianus Gravius, a Gentleman that formerly taught the French, Italian and Spanish Languages in the famous University of Heidelberg' and who was newly arrived in London, or consider attending the multilingual lectures of Mr Caffarelli, an Italian Minister who taught 'Geography, History, Chronology, and the use of the Terrestrial Globe'

---

[121] For Colman, see Claude Mauger, *Claudius Mauger's French and English Letters, upon All Subjects, mean and sublime... The Second Edition* (London, 1676), pp. 111–113; for the MP's daughters, see ibid., pp. 245–51.

[122] Ibid., pp. 57–9.

[123] The title page of the second edition describes the letters as 'All much Amended and Refined according to the most quaint and Courtly mode; wherein yet the Idiom and Elegancy of both Tongues, are far more exactly suited then formerly': Mauger, *Claudius Mauger's French and English Letters*, title page.

[124] *The Office of Publick Advice, Newly set up in several places in and about London and Westminster* (London, 1657).

at Cole's coffee-house at five in the evenings—'On Monday in Latin, Wednesday in Italian, and Friday in French'.[125] They could ponder sending their children to the school run by the French minister John Cairon, to learn 'French, Latin, Greek, Hebrew, Geography, Writidg [sic], Arithmetick, and how to keep Merchants Accounts'; or perhaps choose 'the Accademy in Chancery-lane, [where] is carefully and perfectly Taught, either French to the English, or English to the French: With all Parts of Philosophy; Mathematicks, Astronomy and Geography, by two University-Scholars of each Country'.[126] Newspaper advertisements reflected the booming educational marketplace of early modern London and England.

The rise of newsprint did not entirely displace the face-to-face educational economy of the earlier period: in a newspaper like John Houghton's *Collection for Improvement of Husbandry and Trade*, one could read in 1695 of '[a] Gentleman of Sober Life and Conversation, well qualified Grammatically, to teach the Greek, Latin, French, and Italian Tongues' who sought employment 'as Usher to a School or Tutor to any Gentleman's Children'. Houghton added that the man in question 'is known by me and well recommended by several persons of eminent Learning and Quality'.[127] Through the *Collection*, Houghton had used print to create a role for himself as a mediator in property deals and in the engagement of servants.[128] He commonly matched educators with employers, seeking and advertising the services of French-speakers for employment at schools and in private homes.[129] It was implied that Houghton himself (or someone trusted by him) would be the judge of an applicant's skill in French and in English, as well as of his references; as a mediator, he tested the quality of the service offered and, if he found it good, commended it to potential buyers. Newspaper advertising, rather than representing a wholly new departure, combined the developing medium of the print advertisement with the age-old economy of personal reputation.

For an example of one teacher who sought to exploit the potential of newsprint, we can turn to Christopher Switerda, whose name and claims to pedagogical excellence can be found scattered throughout the periodicals and trade cards of the last decade of the seventeenth century. Taken together, his advertisements—which

[125] *Mercurius Publicus Comprising the Sum of Forraign Intelligence*, issue 39 (20 September 1660–27 September 1660); *Post Man and the Historical Account*, issue 881 (30 September 1701–2 October 1701).
[126] *Post Man and the Historical Account*, issue 239 (17 November 1696–19 November 1696); *New State of Europe Both As to Publick Transactions and Learning*, issue 9 (8 July 1701–12 July 1701).
[127] *Collection for Improvement of Husbandry and Trade*, issue 148 (31 May 1695).
[128] On Houghton's *Collection*, see Natasha Glaisyer, 'Readers, Correspondents and Communities: John Houghton's *A Collection for Improvement of Husbandry and Trade* (1692–1703)', in Alexandra Shepard and Phil Withington (eds.), *Communities in Early Modern England: Networks, Place, Rhetoric* (Manchester: Manchester University Press, 2000), pp. 235–51.
[129] In 1695, Houghton wrote that '[i]f I can meet with a Frenchman that is a good Scholar and speaks the French language well, with its best Accent and Propriety, I can help him to an Usher's Place': *Collection for Improvement of Husbandry and Trade*, issue 164 (20 September 1695). In 1696, he carried an advertisement on behalf of '[a] French-Man about 26 Years old' who, Houghton assured his readers, 'speaks English as well as ever I heard a French-Man', adding that '[h]e can be well recommended': *Collection for Improvement of Husbandry and Trade*, issue 207 (17 July 1696).

appeared in English, French, and Latin—offer the fragments of a biography (though, as so often, the veracity of the information is impossible to determine). He declared himself an 'Equite Brandenburgico' and the brother to a late colonel who had served in the wars against the Turks.[130] This brother had left Switerda a comfortable inheritance that allowed him to teach languages merely—or so he claimed—as 'a Diversion to him'.[131] He insisted on his elevated social status, saying that he had been persuaded to teach languages even 'tho' it is below him'; as his students he favoured 'chiefly such persons as may be any way serviceable to the publick in Divinity, Law and Physick, or teaching of School'.[132] He claimed variously to have been recommended by William III, to have received a valuable gift when he was presented to the queen, to be an intimate of William Dockwra (promoter of the penny post), and to have taught the son of John Methuen, the Lord Chancellor of Ireland.[133] Switerda made grand claims for his skill as a teacher, telling readers how he had taught Latin and French to 'several Tradesmen... who have so well improv'd that they have leaved their Trade, and are esteemed great School-masters'.[134] To the sceptical, he offered proof, boasting that '[h]e is Confident that none can produce one Boy, that has so good Foundation of the Latin Tongue, as he has Taught a little Girl 8 Years of Age'.[135]

Switerda's argument for his own skill as a teacher was hedged about with what seems like a deep insecurity about his place in the English educational market. He wrote in 1693 of his surprise that 'no Noblemen nor Ladies have taken Notice of his Proposals', when they would surely have been greeted with enthusiasm in Germany, Sweden, or Denmark.[136] Over time, he became increasingly exasperated with what he saw as English indifference to his services, accusing 'the Virulent Temper of some Envious Men' for slandering him by saying he taught without rules.[137] In an attempt to prove his abilities, he began to propose increasingly elaborate wagers, once putting up £100 to be forfeited if one of his students was not superior in Latin to a returned educational traveller after a year's study.[138] Later, he offered to take '2 Ingenious Youth of a good Carriage' as his boarders, whom he promised to teach so well that 'they shall be able in a Year to make a

---

[130] 'Equite Brandenburgico' comes from a Latin trade card issued by Switerda, beginning 'Si quis Linguas' EEBO Tract Supplement E4:2[26e], http://gateway.proquest.com/openurl?ctx_ver=Z39.88-2003&res_id=xri:eebo&rft_id=xri:eebo:image:195504, accessed 5 February 2019; on his brother, see *Athenian Gazette or Casuistical Mercury*, issue 26 (7 October 1693).

[131] *Athenian Gazette or Casuistical Mercury*, issue 26 (7 October 1693).

[132] *English Post with News Foreign and Domestick*, issue 356 (18 January 1703–20 January 1703); *Post Man and the Historical Account*, issue 733 (2 April 1700–4 April 1700).

[133] *Post Man and the Historical Account*, issue 733 (2 April 1700–4 April 1700); *Athenian Gazette or Casuistical Mercury*, issue 26 (7 October 1693); *English Post with News Foreign and Domestick*, issue 356 (18 January 1703–20 January 1703).

[134] *Post Boy*, issue 456 (5 April 1698–7 April 1698).

[135] *Athenian Gazette or Casuistical Mercury*, issue 26 (7 October 1693).

[136] *Athenian Gazette or Casuistical Mercury*, issue 10 (12 August 1693).

[137] *Athenian Gazette or Casuistical Mercury*, issue 26 (7 October 1693).

[138] *Post Man and the Historical Account*, issue 733 (2 April 1700–4 April 1700).

Latin Speech before His Majesty on his Birth-day'.[139] While his proposals and protestations can read as hyperbolic, Switerda was a creature of the educational economy of his time. A surviving letter in his hand, addressed to the Archbishop of Canterbury, is a plea for a licence to teach languages. Switerda wrote that he had suffered 'affronts and injuries, chifly [sic] in Pall-mall—where all my windows were broken, and so abused, that I was obliged to leave that place, and to goe in the City in Bishops-gate street, where every one asketh me about a License'.[140] Schoolmasters generally required licences in order to teach, though the application of these rules to private teaching seems to have been lax, if it was ever seriously enforced (and was challenged and defeated later in the seventeenth century).[141] Even so, the pressure faced by Switerda to acquire and produce a licence is a reminder of the ways in which authority to teach was uncertain and contested, and required teachers to assert their skill and qualification in ways both traditional and innovative—sometimes while seeking to sow doubts about their competitors' competence. Switerda's pugnacious self-presentation and his proposed challenges reflected the ways that teachers used newsprint to trial new ways of debating and communicating pedagogical authority in a changing economy of recommendation and reputation.

Switerda's advertisements were the product of an increasingly crowded educational economy, and one in which teachers strove to differentiate themselves from one another. A rueful dialogue in a 1660 French-English text by the Flemish-born religious author William Herbert dramatized the process of choosing a teacher. In the dialogue, a friend of Herbert's asks '[w]hy doth [Herbert] not call himself Professor of the French tongue, since he doth teach it at home and abroad?' The friend responds that Herbert is loath 'to see himself reduc'd to the necessity of embracing a profession, which so many servants, ignorant and mecanick persons make daily contemptible', arguing that many teachers lack the competence they claim to have:

> I know many of these ranks which pass for great masters; yea there are some who take upon them to correct and make Books, who yet would perhaps find it a hard task to write 7 or 8 lines in French, of any solid, and not ordinary discourse, without committing many faults.

---

[139] *English Post with News Foreign and Domestick*, issue 151 (26 September 1701–29 September 1701).

[140] Christopher Switerda to William Sancroft, 31 March 1686: Bodleian Library, Oxford, MS Tanner 30, fols. 1r–2v.

[141] W. E. Tate, 'The Episcopal Licensing of Schoolmasters in England', *Church Quarterly Review* 157 (1956), pp. 426–32. Language teaching is mentioned in an episcopal licence granted in 1683, which describes the bearer, Joseph Povey, as 'very servisable in instructing Children in *the* Languages as alsoe in *the* Tenents of *the* aforesaid church', though it is unclear whether this refers to classical or modern languages: Licence for Joseph Povey, Schoolmaster, All Hallows Lombard Street, 1683, Lambeth Palace Library, London, VH 33/6. So far I have been unsuccessful in finding licences granted to private teachers of modern languages.

The fundamental problem facing the educational economy, argues the stranger, is that '[a]ll Gentlemen are not wise, to examine judiciously the capacity or the ignorance of their Master': students lack the knowledge necessary to tell the difference between a good teacher and a bad teacher. A possible solution is suggested—why not have the teacher perform a translation test, to judge of their skill?—but '[a]n English man that will begin to learn to speak French, cannot make this trial, because he understands not this last tongue'.[142] On top of this, a test based on reading and writing would give no indication of the teacher's skill in speech. Herbert is sharp-eyed about what might cause a poor teacher to be mistaken for a good one: their attendance on the great, their fine clothing, their knowledge of elite culture and sociability; the learner might also make the mistake of paying for the cheapest teacher rather than the best.

From about 1650 onwards, this crowded and competitive educational market saw the emergence of a group of French teachers in London who emphasized their qualifications as native speakers of prestige varieties of French. Claude Mauger explained to an Englishman that he could learn French at home, asking '[i]f your affairs permit you not to go to Paris, to give your self to it, what need you care if you have Blois at London, which is its source?'[143] The teachers of London's 'little Blois', to use Kathleen Lambley's memorable phrase—most notably Mauger, Guy Miège (who was Swiss), Paul Festeau, Peter Berault, and Abel Boyer—competed with each other over the efficacy of their pedagogical methods, the quality of the texts they wrote, and their linguistic authority.[144] These teachers drew attention to the dangers of engaging a teacher who did not speak 'good' French. Claude Mauger insisted to his readers that 'you must have a speciall care, that you have not to do with those that are not true French men, as your Gascons, and Normans'. Grudgingly, he accepted that 'a Norman, that is a man of some quality, or one that hath seen the world, or that is a good Scholler, may possibly have the right Accent: but any other, that hath not such parts, can never give the true Accent'.[145] A rival of Mauger's warned that the ability to teach 'the true modern French' was 'a Thing few people can boast of, besides Courtiers and Scholars, so nice a language it is'; undiscerning learners risked losing 'their time, pains, and mony amongst the common Sort of Teachers, who speak for the most part but a corrupt and Provincial French'.[146] Tracing these Restoration discussions of pedagogical and linguistic competence reveals the role of teachers in shaping ideas about language. New approaches to language emerged from the educational

---

[142] William Herbert, *Herberts French and English Dialogues. In a more Exact and Delightful Method then any yet Extant* (London, 1660), p. 10.

[143] Mauger, *Claudius Mauger's French and English Letters*, p. 117.

[144] Kathleen Lambley, *The Teaching and Cultivation of the French Language in England during Tudor and Stuart Times* (Manchester: Manchester University Press, 1920), pp. 301–18.

[145] Mauger, *True Advancement*, p. 6.

[146] Guy Miège, *A New French Grammar; or a New Method for Learning of the French Tongue* (London, 1678), sig. [A5r].

economy, and from the collaboration and criticism in which teachers publicly engaged: this tight-knit pedagogical community helped transform English thinking about vernacular languages both foreign and native.

Teachers' appeals to their origins were nothing new: as we have seen, Claudius Hollyband was using his to commercial advantage nearly a century earlier. But after 1650, this group of French teachers began to lay increasing stress on their closeness to the 'best' French as it was currently spoken and written. Mauger insisted that, even though he was resident in London, he was still in close contact with the finest French, writing that 'though I be in this Countrey, I am daily with Courtiers as well Ambassadours as other great Lords and Gentlemen of the Court of France, whom I teach the English Tongue'. People were one source of linguistic information, and books were another, so Mauger informed his audience that 'since I am curious to read all our new Books, and that I keep a correspondence with our best Authors, none need wonder if I make use always of good language'.[147] Being up to date was an increasingly pressing concern: in a 1667 edition of his grammar, Paul Festeau drew readers' attention to his recent 'journey to my birthplace of Blois'.[148] In the tenth edition of Mauger's grammar, published in 1682, Mauger drew attention to his recent departure from London for France, the title page describing him as 'the Author, Now Professor of the Languages at Paris'. He explained that he had 'neglected Blois' and headed for the capital, where 'I frequented that Court, and those Courtiers whose Meen and Language is the Standard of all the politer part of Europe'. French was now the courtly language of all Europe, and Mauger's travels and encounters had placed him in close contact with 'the best Flowers of Eloquence', which he could now distribute to his readers.[149] Mauger characterized his move to Paris as part of a linguistic fact-finding mission: a means of ensuring that the French he taught was of the finest and—crucially—the most up-to-date variety. He assured readers that he had incorporated this modish language into his grammar, and signalled a shift towards the French of Paris (as distinct from that of the Loire valley) as the standard for imitation by English learners:

> I being at Paris, that is the Center of the purity of our French Tongue, where the true Phrase is to be found, having corrected it all exactly, all my Dialogues are Modish, there is not a word in them but Elegant.[150]

In 1689, Mauger augmented his pitch by arguing that the 'very Modish' quality of his French was proven by the fact that 'I was every day with some of the Ablest

---

[147] Mauger, *Claudius Mauger's French and English letters*, sig. A8r.
[148] Festeau, *New and Easie French Grammar* (1667), sig. [A5v].
[149] Claude Mauger, *Claudius Mauger's French Grammar* (London, 1682), sig. [A4v].
[150] Claude Mauger, *Claudius Mauger's French Grammar* (London, 1686), sig. [A4v].

Gentlemen of the Port-Royal, who assured me that my Grammar is in their Library, and my French Letters Translated into English also.'[151]

Mauger's appeal to fashionable French was taken up by other teachers. Abel Boyer advertised the first edition of his *Compleat French-Master* as '[a] New Method, to Learn with ease and delight the French Tongue, as it is now spoken in the Court of France'.[152] The French of Paris and Versailles had become, by the end of the seventeenth century, the yardstick against which English-speakers' competence would be judged, and the standard which teachers were expected to supply. Boyer reassured his readers that 'in the Spelling and Expressions, my chief business has been, to follow those Authors who are now in the highest Reputation in the Court of France'.[153] Boyer and Mauger appealed to the fact that fashion was mercurial: what it meant to be 'modish' in speech was constantly changing. John Dryden's *Marriage à-la-mode* (1671) satirized a character's obsession with 'new' French words: '[n]o lady can be so curious of a new fashion, as she is of a new French word. She's the very mint of the nation; and as fast as any bullion comes out of France, coins it immediately into our language.' The character— Melantha—spends time studying and learning new French words, discarding them as soon as they lose their sheen. Her servant uses the word 'intrigue', to which Melantha responds '[t]hat's an old phrase; I have laid that word by. *Amour* sounds better. But thou art heir to all my cast words, as thou art to my old wardrobe.'[154] Language, like clothing, was subject to fashion, and words could become gauche in just the same way as garments did. A keen sense of the modish was necessary to make sure that one's French remained up to the minute. Mastery of the latest vocabulary—and rejection of any words that had entered common usage—carried the mark of distinction, and it was a commodity that teachers could sell.

With teaching ability and linguistic prestige up for debate, the relationships between teachers—in print, at least—grew increasingly fraught, with growing numbers of Restoration teachers criticizing the works of their rivals. Guy Miège took aim at his competitors in 1682, writing that

Of Three French Grammars that have had hitherto the Vogue, I find amongst the Criticks and Observators, that Maugers Grammar is lookt upon as fit only for those who desire to get a little smattering of French at random: Mr. Festeau's, for

[151] Claude Mauger, *Claudius Mauger's French Grammar* (London, 1689), sig. [A4r–A4v].
[152] Abel Boyer, *The Compleat French-master, for ladies and gentlemen* (London, 1694), title page.
[153] ibid., sig. [A7r].
[154] Quoted in Stedman, *Cultural Exchange in Seventeenth-Century France and England* (Aldershot: Ashgate, 2013), pp. 145–51. For the growing Restoration interest in French civility (and critiques of the same), see Lawrence E. Klein, 'The Figure of France: The Politics of Sociability in England, 1660–1715', *Yale French Studies* 92, *Exploring the Conversible World: Text and Sociability from the Classical Age to the Enlightenment* (1997), pp. 30–45.

such as are inclined to some Grammatical Learning; and my former Grammar, for the most exquisite Learners.

With characteristic modesty, Miège conceded that 'I confess the Observation is not altogether ill-grounded', and hoped that his public would agree of his grammar 'that I have not only out-done others in it, but my self; and that this is the Truest, Shortest, and Easiest Grammar, and consequently of a most general Use'.[155] Later, seeking to challenge Mauger's overwhelming popularity in the print market, Abel Boyer took aim at his grammar—not mentioning him by name but referring to the book 'which Fifteen Editions have proclaim'd the best'. Boyer complained that

> if any Understanding Reader does but examine it without partiality, he will soon be convinced, that it is but a confused heap of fragments, and scraps of other Grammars shuffled and jumbled together without Method.[156]

By this time, it was not enough for a French manual to be confident of its own appeal: teachers needed to show where it fitted in a competitive market, and to persuade teachers as well as students to adopt it. Miège commented elsewhere on this tendency, writing that '[w]e have had of late a Swarm of Grammars to learn the French Tongue, each forsooth with a Pretence of Out-doing the Rest, right or wrong'.[157] Pedagogical print became more reactive and critical as teachers adapted to succeed in a competitive reputational economy.

These questions of fashion and pedagogy contributed to a broader change in ideas about French and English in the later seventeenth century. The distaste for arcane and unfashionable terms described above was on show in the lexicographical work of Guy Miège, who set out to supplant the standard *Dictionary French and English* (the first edition of which was published in 1611) compiled by Randle Cotgrave and subsequently updated by James Howell. Miège argued that Cotgrave was not 'accommodated to our present Age', regardless of what its printers might claim.[158] Where the French author of a preface to Cotgrave's dictionary had

---

[155] Guy Miège, *A Short and Easie French Grammar, Fitted For All Sorts of Learners* (London, 1682), 'The Author to the Reader'.

[156] Boyer, *Compleat French-master*, sig. [A5v–A6r].

[157] Guy Miège, *Miège's Last and Best French Grammar* (London, 1698), sig. A2r.

[158] On Miège as lexicographer, see Janet Bately, 'Miège and the Development of the English Dictionary', in John Considine (ed.), *Ashgate Critical Essays on Early English Lexicographers, Vol. 4: The Seventeenth Century* (Aldershot: Ashgate, 2012), pp. 453–62. On Cotgrave, see Peter Rickard, 'The French-English *Dictionarie* of Cotgrave (1611)', in ibid., pp. 377–85. See also Monique C. Cormier and Herberto Fernandez, 'Standing on the Shoulders of Giants: Abel Boyer's Innovations in English-French Lexicography', in ibid., pp. 463–93; and Cormier and Fernandez, 'A Study of the Outside Matter in 17th-Century French-English Dictionaries', in Elisa Corino, Carla Morello, and Cristina Onesti (eds.), *Atti del XII Congresso Internazionale di Lessicografia, vol. 1* (Alessandria: Edizioni dell'Orso, 2006), pp. 49–59.

praised its compiler for his reading of 'every kind of books, old and new, of all our dialects', Miège complained that

> the Book is so far from being refined according to Cardinall Richelieu's Academy, as is pretended in the Title, that it swarms every where with Rank Words and Obsolete Phrases, savouring more of King Pharamonds Reign than that of Lewis XIV.[159]

Miège envisaged his new dictionary not as a reading aid for 'old French Books', but as a text which would reflect as closely as possible the prestigious speech of its time. As such, he was all for the wholesale exclusion of more archaic words, regardless of their utility to the reader of older texts, asking 'what are those Antiquated and Cramp't Words which make up a great part of Cotgrave, Words that offend the eyes and grate the ears, but the Rubbish of the French Tongue?'[160] Miège was concerned with the French language as a social accomplishment, and designed his dictionary to aid those who sought to speak well in fashionable company. It seems, however, that Miège was too modern for readers' tastes, since in 1679, with extreme bad grace, he issued *A dictionary of barbarous French. Or, a collection, by way of alphabet, of obsolete, provincial, mis-spelt, and made words in French*, which he had compiled '[f]or the Satisfaction of such as Read Old French'.[161] When his *Great French Dictionary* appeared in 1688, it included terms not approved by the Académie, though these were clearly marked in order to warn the reader that they were 'only used in a burlesk, jocose, or comical Sense; or else, that it is not current in any Style, but is either forced, or Provincial, or such that grows out of date'; other marked words were those that were 'obsolete, or antiquated... hardly fit to be used in any manner of Style'.[162] 'Old words' might have been out of fashion, but they still had their place in the market: a mastery of the modish was clearly not enough for some English francophones.

---

[159] Guy Miège, *A new dictionary French and English, with another English and French; According to the Present Use, and Modern Orthography of the French* (London, 1679), sig. [A3v].

[160] Miège, *New dictionary French and English* (1689), 'The Preface to the Reader'. For debates over vocabulary and archaisms in sixteenth-century French, see Douglas A. Kibbee, *For to speke Frenche trewely: The French Language in England, 1000–1600: Its Status, Description and Instruction* (Amsterdam and Philadelphia, PA: John Benjamins, 1991), pp. 121–3; see also Ayres-Bennett, *History of the French language*, pp. 140–77.

[161] Guy Miège, *A dictionary of barbarous French. Or, a collection, by way of alphabet, of obsolete, provincial, mis-spelt, and made words in French* (London, 1679). For Peter Rickard, this title is a reminder of 'the gulf which had opened up between the language of the sixteenth century and that of the 1670s': Rickard, 'French-English *Dictionarie* of Cotgrave', p. 385.

[162] Guy Miège, *The Great French Dictionary* (London, 1688), A2v. A comparable, though more sophisticated technique would be used by Abel Boyer in his 1699 dictionary: see Cormier and Fernandez, 'Standing on the Shoulders of Giants', p. 474. On style labels in dictionaries, see Wendy Ayres-Bennett, *Sociolinguistic Variation in Seventeenth-Century France* (Cambridge: Cambridge University Press, 2004), pp. 64–72.

Debates among teachers contributed to thinking about English as well as French. Throughout our period, debates about foreign vernaculars were an arena in which ideas about the fast-changing English vernacular were worked out. English interest in the Académie Française—founded in 1635—pivoted quickly to the question of whether English was in need of a comparable linguistic academy of its own. Seventeenth-century learners of French were increasingly aware of the work of the Académie: in 1676, Jacques d'Abbadie's French grammar had advertised itself as containing French 'as the Witts, or the Gentlemen of the french Academy, speak and pronounce it at this present time', while in 1703, one could see advertisements for 'Grammatical Tables, Entituled, The Building of the French Academy, or the most Modish Construction of the French Tongue'.[163] Pellisson's *History of the French Academy* appeared in English translation in 1657, and the question of an English academy along the same lines seems to have struck writers in English, most notably Thomas Sprat, whose *History of the Royal-Society of London* (1667) is barely under way before it takes a linguistic detour.[164] Sprat noted that both Italy and France had academies concerned with language, and that the French had seen 'the French Tongue abundantly purifi'd, and beginning to take place in the Western World, almost as much, as the Greek did of old, when it was the Language of Merchants, Souldiers, courtiers, and Travellers'.[165] Sprat proposed the establishment of an English academy which could 'make a great Reformation in the manner of our Speaking, and Writing', arguing that linguistic and imperial ascendancy have historically been intimately linked: 'the purity of Speech, and greatness of Empire have in all Countries, still met together'.[166] Similarly, in 1665, John Evelyn called for a Royal Society dictionary, which would contain 'all pure English words', and to regulate the entry of 'exotic words' into the language.[167] Claude Mauger praised English for being 'so rich, so copious, and so eloquent, especially since the Gentlemen of the Royal Society have given it its utmost lustre'.[168] With one eye firmly on the institutions that defined and regulated continental vernaculars, English ideas about the English language emerged from a multilingual pedagogical context.

It was not only in the teaching of French that English linguistic neuroses worked themselves out: Martin Aedler's *High-Dutch Minerva* (1680) echoed many of the arguments about English in its treatment of German, most notably in its voluble denunciation of the borrowing of foreign terms: the language had been 'defiled' by 'this bastard way of enriching our toung'. Aedler's polemic

---

[163] J. G. d'Abbadie, *A new French grammar* (Oxford, 1676); *Post Man and the Historical Account*, issue 1218 (14 December 1703–16 December 1703).
[164] Paul Pellisson, *A history of the French Academy, Erected at Paris by the late Famous Cardinal de Richelieu, and consisting of the most refined Wits of that Nation* (London, 1657); Thomas Sprat, *The History of the Royal-Society of London, For the Improving of Natural Knowledge* (London, 1667).
[165] Sprat, *History of the Royal-Society*, pp. 39–40.   [166] Ibid., p. 41.
[167] Blank, *Broken English*, p. 52.
[168] Mauger, *Claudius Mauger's French and English Letters*, p. 77.

elided the difference between English and German, accusing 'half-learned Latin smatterers, pettifoggers and ignorant travellers' of 'underlining almost each nativ word with a parole a-la-mode from France, or a motto maraviglioso from Italy, or a Rodomontado spaventoso that is in plain English an horrible spanish ly'.[169] Teachers like Aedler, d'Abbadie, and Miège were central to the development of English ideas of prestigious or reprehensible speech in foreign vernaculars, and of changing ideas about the English vernacular itself. These ideas were not abstractions: worked out at the intersection between a community of teachers and a competitive educational market, they reflected the changing concerns of teachers, learners, thinkers, and speakers. The educational economy was a crucible in which ideas about teaching, learning, and language that were central to the cultural and social history of early modern England were shaped.

Conclusion

If an educational revolution did happen in early modern England, it was not bounded by the walls of established institutions, nor restricted to traditional curriculums.[170] The study of continental vernaculars was at the heart of proposals for the reform of English education—its utility for the commonwealth, its importance for trade, and its status as a social accomplishment were clear to those who criticized the deficiencies of English education. Crucially, this theoretical enthusiasm for language education reflected what was happening on the ground. Even where grand schemes and national educational projects came to nothing, there were schools and teachers working to make a multilingual education available to a growing (and increasingly diverse) public. But the history of language-learning and its place in the early modern English educational economy does not end with the people, places, and pedagogies considered in this chapter. The teaching and learning of foreign languages did not happen only in classrooms or within student-teacher relationships. Understanding domestic teaching, the extracurricular communities of the universities, and the growth of private schooling and academies gives some sense of the expansion of language education, but there remained a world of interactions and activities that complemented formal practices of language acquisition. Language-learners sought out native speakers with whom they could practice their language; they attended the stranger churches and language clubs in order to hear other tongues spoken or to participate in multilingual

---

[169] Aedler, *High Dutch Minerva*, p. 34. On debates over borrowed words and purism in German, see C. J. Wells, *German: A Linguistic History to 1945* (Oxford: Clarendon, 1985), pp. 263–300.

[170] For the 'educational revolution' debate, see Lawrence Stone, 'The Educational Revolution in England, 1560–1640', *Past & Present* 28 (1964), pp. 41–80, and J. H. Hexter, 'The Education of the Aristocracy in the Renaissance', in Hexter, *Reappraisals in History* (London: Longmans, 1961), pp. 45–70.

conversation.[171] Multilingual workplaces—from ships to workshops—were places where language-learning took place, while polyglot households are easily found in the records of England's cities.[172] The study of foreign languages was a practice, and one which could thrive in the polyglot surroundings of the early modern city: formal relationships of teaching and learning are only one part of the story. The history of language-learning is not simply the history of teachers and schools, even if they are the best place to start.

At the same time, the concept of 'teacher' as a profession was an elastic one in the early modern period. As we have seen, the idea of a fixed vocation of 'teacher' can obscure the educational labour of many who do not easily fit a modern conception of the professional educator.[173] Furthermore, for many early modern language masters, teaching was just one element of a constellation of activities that made up a precarious career. Many were immigrants or the children of immigrants who sought to carve out a living as jobbing linguists or, to use Michael Wyatt's memorable phrase, 'language merchants'.[174] And since even royal tutors found themselves pleading poverty when work dried up, it was important to have other strings to one's bow. Many of these individuals taught other subjects, from Latin and Greek to mathematics and geography.[175] The most prominent language teachers of the late sixteenth century—John Florio, Claudius Hollyband, Jacques Bellot, Giacomo Castelvetro—had close ties to the book trade, fulfilling the need of England's polyglot print culture for multilingual authors, editors, and translators. Those who travelled abroad as tutors could also double as political informants, sending dispatches on continental events, just as Jean Gailhard reported the

---

[171] A speaker in a 1689 work by Giovanni Torriano mentioned that among clubs 'for Musick, and for News', London had clubs 'for Language', where language practice and clubbable conversation went hand in hand: Giovanni Torriano, *Mescolanza dolce di varie historiette, favole morali & politiche, facetie, motti & burle di diversi scrittori Italiani; raccolta & cappata per uso, commodità & ricreatione, della Gioventù Inglese* (London, 1688), p. 98.

[172] See Introduction.

[173] Rosemary O'Day has asked whether early modern England had a teaching profession, concluding that it is unclear whether early modern teachers conceived of themselves as a distinct group with a distinct vocation, though Jean-Antoine Caravolas has argued that both England and the continent saw a professionalization of the teaching of languages during the Renaissance: O'Day, *Education and Society*, pp. 167–77; Jean-Antoine Caravolas, *La Didactique des langues: précis d'histoire I, 1450–1700* (Montreal: Les Presses de l'Université de Montréal, 1994), p. 100. See also David Cressy, 'A Drudgery of Schoolmasters: The Teaching Profession in Elizabethan and Stuart England', in Wilfrid Prest (ed.), *The Professions in Early Modern England* (London: Croom Helm, 1987), pp. 129–53; Richard L. DeMolen, 'Richard Mulcaster and the Profession of Teaching in Sixteenth-Century England', *Journal of the History of Ideas* 35 (1974), pp. 121–9; Jean Boutier, 'Compétence internationale, émergence d'une 'profession' et circulation des savoirs: le tuteur aristocratique dans l'Angleterre du XVIIe siècle', in Maria-Pia Paoli (ed.), *Saperi in Movimento* (Pisa: Edizioni della Normale, 2009), pp. 149–77.

[174] Michael Wyatt, *The Italian Encounter with Tudor England: A Cultural Politics of Translation* (Cambridge: Cambridge University Press, 2005), p. 3.

[175] Paul Festeau offered his services to 'Gentlemen curious to exercise or practise Arithmetick' and other mathematical subjects: Paul Festeau, *Nouvelle Grammaire Françoise* (London, 1679), sig. [A7v–A8r]. Guy Miège taught geography: see Guy Miège, *A New French Grammar; or, a New Method for Learning of the French Tongue* (London, 1678), title page and sig. [A3v].

revocation of the Edict of Nantes in a letter to William Wharton.[176] Advertisments placed by women hoping to be employed as governesses went on to say that, should such a position not be available, they were also qualified to work as housekeepers.[177] Tracing the careers of those who taught foreign languages in early modern England shows that a more expansive understanding of what constituted teaching—of the nature of educational labour—is required. Almost nobody in early modern England was 'just' a language teacher, but teaching was a central activity for the men and women who served England's polyglot economies of skill, service, knowledge, and information.

[176] Jean Gailhard to William Wharton, 1 August 1685, Bodleian Library, MS Carte 80, fols. 825r–6v.
[177] See, for instance, *Collection for Improvement of Husbandry and Trade*, issue 206 (10 July 1696).

2

Speaking Books

The Early Modern Conversation Manual

Introduction: 'A Book for the Language'

On his arrival in Rotterdam in July 1678, the young Ralph Thoresby wasted little time getting to grips with his surroundings. Thoresby had been sent to the Low Countries by his father, a Leeds merchant dealing in wool and cotton, in order to learn French and Dutch and to study the trade. He took lodgings with a Dutch-speaking family, enrolled in a school 'in order to my learning the Dutch lingua' alongside 'their way of cyphering', and made a point of 'observing the customs, &c.' of Rotterdam's urban and commercial life. In his diary, he recorded that he had spent his first week 'walking about the city, observing their customs, which at first seemed mighty strange, differing so very much from my own country's'. Thoresby wrote that he had spent this valuable time 'not neglecting to look into a book for the language, and being very intent upon it', and noted with some pride that the family with whom he lodged had praised his 'considerable progress' in Dutch.[1] He gives no indication of which 'book for the language' he was using in Rotterdam, though one strong candidate is Edward Richardson's *Anglo-Belgica*, subtitled *The English and Netherdutch Academy*, which had been published in Amsterdam in 1677.[2] Richardson's manual was designed to appeal to a learner like Thoresby, who would benefit from its collection of 'Dialogues, Letters, Bills of Exchange, and other things relating to Merchandise: whereby men may in a short time attain to the perfect knowledge of the Dutch Language'.[3] *Anglo-Belgica* assumed that the audience for an English-Dutch manual was primarily mercantile, and sought to provide materials that would be of particular use to those involved in trade and finance. Among its dialogues, it offered an in-depth conversation (in Dutch and English) in which speakers navigated the complexities of bills of exchange and trade between European cities, as well as a bilingual set of sample merchants' letters, accounts, bills, and bonds in the Dutch style.[4] A list of 'Words of most use amongst the Merchants' included commercially useful

---

[1] Joseph Hunter (ed.), *The Diary of Ralph Thoresby, F.R.S. Author of the Topography of Leeds (1677–1724)*, online edition courtesy of the Thoresby Society and the Leeds Library, at http://www.thoresby.org.uk/diary/1678.html, accessed 12 Mar. 2019.

[2] Edward Richardson, *Anglo-Belgica, The English and Netherdutch Academy* (Amsterdam, 1676/7).

[3] Ibid., part II, title page.   [4] Ibid., part II, pp. 74–83, 116–161.

vocabulary from 'Arbeytsloon. Labourage', 'Factuur. Invoice', and 'Loots-gelt. Pilot-money', to 'Wissel. Change, Exchange'.[5] A book like Richardson's would have suited a traveller and merchant-in-training for whom linguistic competence needed to consist not just in a knowledge of grammar and syntax, but in the mastery of technical vocabulary and foreign ways of writing and drafting documents.

Anglo-Belgica was, in many ways, a typical early modern 'book for the language'. It was what I will call a 'conversation manual': a bi- or multilingual text which usually included some material on pronunciation, orthography, vocabulary, and grammar, and which had at its heart material that mimicked speech and could be employed in conversation by the reader. In early modern conversation manuals, phrases, proverbs, and situational dialogues taught situationally appropriate language to a variety of audiences, ranging from artisans to elite travellers. The conversation manual was a popular genre of early modern print: polyglot manuals offering dialogues in up to eight languages were printed, reprinted, and plagiarized throughout Europe, while in England books offered instruction in languages from French, German, and Italian to Malay and Narragansett.[6] Popular authors like Claudius Hollyband and Claude Mauger shaped language-teaching practice in print and saw their works go into multiple editions, with some especially popular texts long outliving their authors. Conversation manuals were used as textbooks in language schools or as private aids to learning; men and women made multilingual notes in their margins; and travellers bought and packed them when departing for the continent. Usually pocket-sized, affordable, and concerned with teaching useful speech for everyday situations, these books represent a culture of language-learning which was oral and sociable. They engaged their readers in the overlapping activities of reading, writing, speaking, and listening in a way that has been underappreciated: these were speaking books.

---

[5] Ibid., part II, p. 162.

[6] On polyglot manuals, see Susan E. Phillips, 'Schoolmasters, Seduction, and Slavery: Polyglot Dictionaries in Pre-Modern England' in *Medievalia et Humanistica* 34 (2008), pp. 129–58; Werner Hüllen, 'Textbook-Families for the Learning Of Vernaculars between 1450 and 1700', in Sylvain Auroux (ed.), *History of Linguistics 1999: Selected Papers from the Eighth International Conference on the History of the Language Sciences* (Amsterdam and Philadelphia: John Benjamins, 1999), pp. 97–107. See also Alda Rossebastiano, 'La Tradition des manuels polyglottes dans l'enseignement des langues', in Sylvain Auroux, E. F. K. Koerner, Hans-Josef Niderehe, and Kees Versteegh (eds.), *History of the Language Sciences*, vol. 1 (Berlin and New York: de Gruyter, 2000), pp. 688–95; Rossebastiano, 'Prefazione' to *'Introito e Porta': vocabolario italiano-tedesco compiuto per Meistro Adamo de Roduila, 1477 adi 12 Augusto* (Turin: Edizioni dell'Orso, 1971); Rossebastiano, *Antichi vocabolari plurilingui d'uso popolare: la tradizione del 'Solenissimo Vochabuolista'* (Turin: Edizioni dell'Orso, 1984); Maria Colombo Timelli, 'Dictionnaires pour voyageurs, dictionnaires pour marchands ou la polyglossie au quotidien aux XVIe et XVIIe siècles', *Linguisticae Investigationes* 16 (1992), pp. 395–421; Gabriele Stein, 'The Emerging Role of English in the Dictionaries of Renaissance Europe', reprinted in Roderick McConchie (ed.), *Ashgate Critical Essays on Early English Lexicographers, Volume 3: The Sixteenth Century* (Aldershot: Ashgate, 2012), pp. 87–120.

Scholarly treatments of the conversation manual can be broadly divided into four approaches. First, work in literary studies and book history on particular editions or texts has argued for the popularity and cultural importance of these materials, and traced the transmission of particular texts across political and linguistic borders.[7] Second, research in linguistics—particularly historical socio-linguistics and historical pragmatics—has attempted to use these manuals as the basis for analysis of speech in the past, examining the rules and norms governing early modern speech situations.[8] Third, literary scholars have used critical readings to explore representations of gender, race, and international politics in the manuals.[9] Fourth, work by historians and literary scholars has related the manuals to broader questions of foreign-language study, though this remains a relatively uncrowded field.[10] But while conversation manuals have not been ignored by scholars, their role in multilingual encounters, their importance in histories of education, reading, and the book, and their unique place at the intersection of oral, aural, and textual cultures remain to be explored. This chapter begins by defining

[7] See, for instance, Lisa H. Cooper, 'Urban Utterances: Merchants, Artisans, and the Alphabet in Caxton's *Dialogues in French and English*', *New Medieval Literatures* 7 (2005), pp. 127–62; William Edward Engel, 'Knowledge that Counted: Italian Phrase-Books and Dictionaries in Elizabethan England', *Annali d'Italianistica* 14 (1996), pp. 507–22; William F. J. DeJongh, *Western Language Manuals of the Renaissance* (Albuquerque, NM: University of New Mexico Press, 1949).

[8] Jonathan Culpeper and Merja Kytö, *Early Modern English Dialogues: Spoken Interaction as Writing* (Cambridge: Cambridge University Press, 2010), pp. 21–60. For linguists working with conversation manuals, see Monika Becker, '"Yf ye wyll bergayne wullen cloth or othir merchandise…" Bargaining in Early Modern Language Teaching Textbooks', *Journal of Historical Pragmatics* 3 (2002), pp. 273–97; Birte Bös, 'What do you lacke? what is it you buy? Early Modern English Service Encounters', in Susan Fitzmaurice and Irma Taavitsainen (eds.), *Methods in Historical Pragmatics* (Berlin and New York: de Gruyter, 2007), pp. 219–40; Richard J. Watts, 'Refugiate in a strange countrey: Learning English through Dialogues in the 16th Century', in Andreas H. Jucker, Gerd Fritz, and Franz Lebsanft (eds.), *Historical Dialogue Analysis* (Amsterdam and Philadelphia, PA: John Benjamins, 1999), pp. 215–41.

[9] Juliet Fleming, 'The French Garden: An Introduction to Women's French', *English Literary History* 56 (1989), pp. 19–51; Fleming, 'Dictionary English and the Female Tongue', in Richard Burt and John Michael Archer (eds.), *Enclosure Acts: Sexuality, Property, and Culture in Early Modern England* (Ithaca, NY, and London: Cornell University Press, 1994); John Considine, 'Narrative and Persuasion in Early Modern English Dictionaries and Phrasebooks', *Review of English Studies* 52 (2001), pp. 195–206; Phillips, 'Schoolmasters, seduction, and slavery'.

[10] The outstanding work here remains Kathleen Lambley, *The Teaching and Cultivation of the French Language in England during Tudor and Stuart Times* (Manchester: Manchester University Press, 1920). See also A. P. R. Howatt, *A History of English Language Teaching* (Oxford: Oxford University Press, 1984); Douglas A. Kibbee, *For to speke Frenche trewely: The French Language in England, 1000–1600: Its Status, Description and Instruction* (Amsterdam and Philadelphia, PA: John Benjamins, 1991); N. E. Osselton, *The Dumb Linguists: A Study of the Earliest English and Dutch Dictionaries* (Leiden and London, 1973); P. L. M. Loonen, *For to learne to buye and sell: Learning English in the Low Dutch Area between 1500 and 1800. A Critical Survey* (Amsterdam and Maarssen: APA-Holland University Press, 1991); Jason Lawrence, 'Who the devil taught thee so much Italian?' *Italian Language Learning and Literary Imitation in Early Modern England* (Manchester and New York: Manchester University Press, 2005); R. C. Simonini, 'The Genesis of Modern Foreign Language Teaching', *The Modern Language Journal* 35 (1951), pp. 179–86; Simonini, 'The Italian Pedagogy of Claudius Hollyband', *Studies in Philology* 49 (1952), pp. 144–54; Simonini, *Italian Scholarship in Renaissance England* (Chapel Hill, NC: The University of North Carolina Studies in Comparative Literature, 1952).

the conversation manual as a genre, tracking the numbers of texts and the languages on offer from the late fifteenth to the early eighteenth century, and tracing the development of the conversation manual as a textual genre: from questions of size, price, and print runs to those of layout and content. It then turns to questions of practice, asking how different kinds of conversation manuals were read, and drawing together teachers' injunctions and educational developments with textual cues and readers' responses. It ties developments in form and format with the practical and pedagogical concerns of teachers and learners, and argues that these texts model unique interactions between the worlds of print, speech, and hearing. These 'books for the language' allow us to understand early modern language-learning as it was experienced by individual language-learners and as it related to the broader cultural and social changes shaping England and Europe in the early modern period.

Conversation Manuals: Tracing an
Early Modern Print Phenomenon

What was a 'conversation manual'? These texts, which prefigure in a number of ways the modern phrasebook, developed gradually in dialogue with early modern Europe's cultures of print and education. Different from stand-alone grammars and dictionaries (though conversation manuals commonly contained grammatical and/or lexicographical material), these were texts which aimed to inculcate competence in reading, writing, and—crucially—speech. I use 'conversation manual' to mean any text which offered dialogues or collections of conversational phrases (which I define as 'speech-oriented' material) in English and at least one other language. Historical linguists Jonathan Culpeper and Merja Kytö, in their study of early modern English dialogues, suggest three kinds of 'speech-related' texts: 'speech-like', meaning texts such as personal correspondence which share features with oral speech; 'speech-based', meaning writing based on actual observed speech events, such as depositions or records of sermons and orations; and 'speech-purposed', meaning that the text at least attempts to be mimetic of spoken interaction.[11] Culpeper and Kytö place conversation manuals in this third category, but I would argue that the conversation manuals are more than simply 'speech-purposed'. Their authors did not aim simply to imitate speech in their

---

[11] Culpeper and Kytö, *Early Modern English Dialogues*, p. 13. On other kinds of text—such as early modern letter-writing—which contain features considered characteristic of orality, see Andreas H. Jucker, Gerd Fritz, and Franz Lebsanft, 'Historical Dialogue Analysis: Roots and Traditions in the Study of the Romance Languages, German and English', in Jucker et al., *Historical Dialogue Analysis*, pp. 5–6; Fitzmaurice and Taavitsainen, *Methods in Historical Pragmatics*, pp. 19–20; Suzanne Romaine, *Socio-Historical Linguistics: Its Status and Methodology* (Cambridge: Cambridge University Press, 1982), pp. 17–18. On 'oral residue' in sixteenth-century English, see Walter J. Ong, *Orality and Literacy: The Technologizing of the Word* (London and New York, 1982), p. 115.

phrases and dialogues: they expected that their printed materials would make the jump from text to speech, and be used in conversation and in the classroom. These are texts which trumpet their practical usefulness and even contain embedded instructions for speaking and performing their pedagogical materials aloud. The term I use for outward-facing texts like these is 'speech-oriented'. Culpeper and Kytö recognize that language-learning dialogues could be used in classroom situations, for performance and practice between students and teachers, but neglect the role they played in the wider social world. The authors of conversation manuals, by and large, attempted to model their dialogues and phrases on language which would be socially acceptable and useful in a variety of interpersonal situations, and as such the aim of the conversation manual was not just to represent effective speech, but to allow for its redeployment in conversation. It reflected social realities but also was intended to act within them. In this—as this chapter shows—the conversation manual models a unique and underappreciated model of reading and its relationship to speech and hearing.

Having established a definition of the conversation manual as containing speech-oriented material in English and at least one other language, the next step is to work out the number of these texts which were printed across our period, from the beginning of printing in England until 1715. Using the English Short Title Catalogue, the bibliographical work of R. C. Alston, and works on the study of different languages, I have compiled a bibliography of conversation manuals published between 1480 and 1715, counting each edition of each manual separately.[12] Three caveats, before we look at the data: firstly, while every effort has been made to make this list exhaustive, there is no doubt that some editions have escaped my notice. I am confident, however, that this is the most comprehensive bibliography of its kind so far created. Secondly, this bibliography only lists texts which have survived. Some texts listed by other authors have been difficult to identify with any certainty, while others are known to have disappeared relatively recently, such as the last known copy of Gabriel Meurier's *Traité pour apprendre a parler Francois et Anglois* (Rouen, 1553), which was destroyed during the Second World War.[13] Some early language-learning texts like *A lytell treatyse for to lerne*

---

[12] The full list of manuals, including those not referenced directly in the text, is included as a supplementary bibliography. In assembling this bibliography, I drew on texts including R. C. Alston, *A Bibliography of the English Language from the Invention of Printing to the Year 1800, Vol. 2: Polyglot Dictionaries and Grammars* (Ilkley: Janus, 1967); Loonen, *For to learne to buye and sell*; Rossebastiano, *Antichi vocabolari plurilingui*; Spartaco Gamberini, *Lo studio dell'italiano in Inghilterra nel '500 e nel '600* (Florence: G. D'Anna, 1970); Edward Gray, *New World Babel: Languages and Nations in Early America* (Princeton, NJ: Princeton University Press, 1999); Lambley, *Teaching and Cultivation of the French Language*; Helmut Glück, *Deutsch als Fremdsprache in Europa vom Mittelalter bis zur Barockzeit* (Berlin and New York: de Gruyter, 2002). The English Short Title Catalogue online—estc. bl.uk—was also a crucial tool in locating obscure manuals and confirming details of editions and physical characteristics.

[13] Nigel Stoughton, '"His hatband is made of diamonds": France's First English Textbook', *The Book Collector* 60 (2011), p. 63.

Englysshe and Frensshe (Antwerp, 1530?) survive only in fragments. Further to texts like these, there are also texts whose absence we are unaware of: smaller, cheaper, and unbound texts may have been less likely to survive.[14] Relevant to questions of textual survival, recent work at Belton House by Abigail Brundin and Dunstan Roberts suggests that in at least one case, more utilitarian books purchased during travel were stored and kept separately from more prestigious texts, not being bound or kept in the family's library.[15] This type of behaviour has obvious implications for survival rates. The final caveat is to remind the reader that what follows is based on a bibliography of speech-oriented conversation manuals, meaning that stand-alone grammars and dictionaries which contained no speech-oriented materials are not included in the graphs below.[16]

With these caveats in mind, we can turn to the data on the publication of conversation manuals between 1480 and 1715. The number of conversation manuals published for each language across the period can be seen in Figure 2.1. By far the most popular language of bilingual manuals was French, with 146 separate editions published across the period (many of them new editions or reprints of work by popular teachers like Claudius Hollyband and Claude Mauger). Italian texts appeared in twenty-two separate editions, Dutch twenty, and German eleven. Twelve Spanish manuals appeared irregularly across the period, and two manuals for Portuguese (still regarded by some as simply a dialect of Spanish) appeared near the end of the period.[17] Eighty-five separate editions of polyglot manuals (those containing more than one language besides English)

[14] As examples of these more ephemeral texts, see François Cheneau, *The shortest way to write and speak Latin, by numbers and rules, hereto unknown to masters* (London, 1710?); Anon., *Phrases Françoises fort necessaires pour ceux qui apprennent à parler françois, en forme de question* (London, 1624)—a small (sixty pages) monolingual French text containing correct French phrases for learners who already knew their French verbs and some of the language but wanted to correct their speech.
[15] Abigail Brundin and Dunstan Roberts, 'Book Buying and the Grand Tour: The Italian Books at Belton House in Lincolnshire', *The Library* 16 (2015), pp. 61–79.
[16] The scholarship on early modern grammars and dictionaries is far too broad to summarize here. On grammars of Italian, see Lucilla Pizzoli, *Le grammatiche di italiano per inglesi (1550–1776): un'analisi linguistica* (Florence: Accademia della Crusca, 2004); for Dutch, see Osselton, *Dumb Linguists*; on French, see the essays in Jan de Clercq, Nico Lioce, and Pierre Swiggers (eds.), *Grammaire et enseignement du français, 1500–1700* (Leuven: Peeters, 2000); and Douglas A. Kibbee, 'French Grammarians and Grammars of French in the 16th Century', in Hans-Josef Niederehe and Konrad Koerner (eds.), *History and Historiography of Linguistics: Papers from the Fourth International Conference on the History of the Language Sciences (ICHoLS IV), Trier, 24–8 August 1987*, Vol. 1 (Amsterdam and Philadelphia: John Benjamins, 1990), pp. 301–14. On dictionaries, the work of John Considine is indispensable: John Considine, *Dictionaries in Early Modern Europe: Lexicography and the Making of Heritage* (Cambridge: Cambridge University Press, 2008); Considine, *Academy Dictionaries 1600–1800* (Cambridge: Cambridge University Press, 2014); Considine, *Small Dictionaries and Curiosity: Lexicography and Fieldwork in Post-Medieval Europe* (Oxford: Oxford University Press, 2017). See also Werner Hüllen, *English Dictionaries, 800–1700: The Topical Tradition* (Oxford: Oxford University Press, 1999).
[17] James Howell, *A new English Grammar* (London, 1662) contained a 'Grammar of the Spanish or Castilian Toung', to which was appended 'som special remarks upon the Portugues Dialect'. See also Francisco Javier Sánchez Escribano, 'Portuguese in England in the Sixteenth and Seventeenth Centuries', *Sederi* 16 (2006), pp. 109–32.

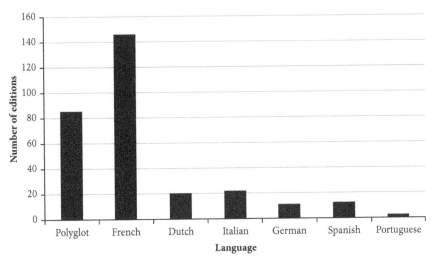

Figure 2.1 Conversation manuals featuring English by language, 1480–1715

were counted.[18] Not included in this graph are the rare manuals which attempted to provide instruction in non-European languages, like Roger Williams's famous *Key into the Language of America* (London, 1643), and Augustine Spalding's translation of Arthus Gotthard's *Dialogues in the English and Malaiane languages* (London, 1614), written at the behest of Thomas Smith, governor of (among others) the fledgling East India Company. Other kinds of text boasted wordlists or vocabularies of non-European languages—one example is Thomas Gage's *The English-American his Travail by Sea and Land: Or, A New Survey of the West-India's* (London, 1648), which boasted among its contents 'a Grammar, or some few Rudiments of the Indian Tongue, called, Poconchi, or Pocoman', compiled on the basis of Gage's study of the language.[19] The focus here, however, is on texts whose primary aim was the teaching of a continental European vernacular language. With at least 294 editions of conversation manuals featuring continental vernaculars published across a 235-year period—so, just over 1.25 editions a year—the market was a vibrant one. (It should be noted that some manuals have probably been lost, and also that these conversation manuals could be supplemented by the stand-alone grammars, verb tables, and dictionaries also

[18] On the polyglot manual tradition, see Hüllen, 'Textbook-Families for the Learning of Vernaculars between 1450 and 1700'; Rossebastiano, 'La tradition des manuels polyglottes dans l'enseignement des langues'; Rossebastiano, 'Prefazione' to '*Introito e Porta*'; Rossebastiano, *Antichi vocabolari plurilingui d'uso popolare*; Timelli, 'Dictionnaires pour voyageurs, dictionnaires pour marchands'; Phillips, 'Schoolmasters, Seduction, and Slavery'; and Stein, 'The Emerging Role of English in the Dictionaries of Renaissance Europe'.
[19] Thomas Gage, *The English-American his Travail by Sea and Land: Or, A New Survey of the West-India's… With a Grammar, or some few Rudiments of the Indian Tongue, called, Poconchi, or Pocoman* (London, 1648), pp. 213–20.

published during the period).[20] By way of comparison, in his study of vernacular medical literature, Paul Slack found 153 medical titles published in the period c.1486–1605, a figure which accounts for roughly 3 per cent of the total number of books published.[21] In the same period, my own research finds eighty-eight conversation manuals: more than half the number of vernacular medical texts, so (following Slack) around 1.5 per cent of the total number of texts published in the same period. A further 206 were published in the period 1606–1715. Conversation manuals came nowhere near genres of print like almanacs or popular religious literature in their numbers, but innovations and reprintings ensured that the would-be language-learner rarely lacked for printed materials throughout our period.[22]

It is difficult to be certain how many copies of each edition were printed, and this definitely varied depending on factors like projected demand for the book. In September 1578, the Court of the Stationers' Company ordered that Thomas Vautrollier, the printer of Hollyband's *French Littelton*, deliver 100 copies of every edition of the text to Abraham Veale, 'whereof there shalbe printed twelfe hundred & an half of an ympression'.[23] That year, Vautrollier would print the second edition of what became an extremely popular text: if we assume that 1,250 copies were printed of every edition of the *French Littelton*, then 17,500 copies of this text alone had been printed by 1639. John Palsgrave agreed with his printer that 750 copies of his *Lesclarcissement* (1530) would be produced, but this was an enormous book, with the attendant commercial risks, as well as one whose sale was restricted by its author.[24] Paul Slack, following H. S. Bennett and Lucien

[20] On the different types of text produced for early modern European language-learners, and the difficulties in establishing a strict typology, see Barbara Kaltz, 'L'enseignement des langues étrangères au XVIe siècle. Structure globale et typologie des textes destinés à l'apprentissage des vernaculaires', *Beiträge zur Geschichte der Sprachwissenschaft* 5:1 (1995), pp. 79–106.

[21] Paul Slack, 'Mirrors of Health and Treasures of Poor Men: The Uses of the Vernacular Medical Literature of Tudor England', in Charles Webster (ed.), *Health, Medicine and Mortality in the Sixteenth Century* (Cambridge: Cambridge University Press, 1979), pp. 237–73.

[22] For almanacs, see Bernard Capp, *English Almanacs, 1500–1800: Astrology and the Popular Press* (Ithaca, NY: Cornell University Press, 1979); for popular religious print, see Tessa Watt, *Cheap Print and Popular Piety, 1550–1640* (Cambridge: Cambridge University Press, 1991); and Margaret Spufford, *Small Books and Pleasant Histories: Popular Fiction and its Readership in Seventeenth-Century England* (London: Methuen, 1981); for an in-depth consideration of one genre of religious print, see Ian Green, *The Christian's ABC: Catechisms and Catechizing in England c.1530–1740* (Oxford: Clarendon, 1996). The question of popularity in early modern print has been heavily debated and will not be considered in detail here; see the essays in Andy Kesson and Emma Smith (eds.), *The Elizabethan Top Ten: Defining Print Popularity in Early Modern England* (Farnham: Ashgate, 2013).

[23] W. W. Greg and E. Boswell (eds.), *Records of the Court of the Stationers' Company 1576 to 1602: From Register B* (London: The Bibliographical Society, 1930), pp. 7–8; *English Short Title Catalogue* (2nd edn), 6739, at http://estc.bl.uk/S108253, accessed 12 Mar. 2018.

[24] H. S. Bennett, *English Books and Readers, 1475 to 1557: Being a Study in the History of the Book Trade from Caxton to the Incorporation of the Stationers' Company* (Cambridge: Cambridge University Press, 1952), p. 226; Stein, 'Emerging Role of English', p. 93. Palsgrave's *Lesclarcissement* is not strictly speaking a conversation manual by the definition given above, but it is included and discussed here for two reasons: firstly, it was one of the most important and accomplished manuals for the study of French published in the period and, secondly, the extent and detail of its pronunciation instruction means that, even if it does not contain conversational material, it is very clearly a text with the teaching of correct speech at its heart.

Febvre and Henri-Jean Martin, argues that an average print run for the medical texts he looks at in the period 1486–1605 would have been around 1,000 copies.[25] The maximum permitted print run after 1587 was 1,500 copies, though this was relaxed in 1635 to between 1,500 and 2,000.[26] In 1679, Paul Festeau boasted that 2,000 copies of the third and fourth editions of his French grammar had been printed, 'whereas they use to draw but one thousand'.[27] If we assume an average print run of 1,000 for these conversation manuals, then we are left with a very rough figure of around 300,000 copies printed across just over two centuries.

How did different languages fare in the conversation manual market across the period? Figure 2.2 offers an answer to this question, showing the publication of editions of conversation manuals, divided by language, at ten-year intervals. Some trends in provision responded to their immediate political contexts, while others reflected the rise and fall in popularity and prestige experienced by specific languages.

French is the first foreign vernacular language to appear in the corpus of conversation manuals: at the end of the fifteenth century, a generation of printers (often themselves with strong connections to French- and Dutch-speaking communities on the continent) saw a market in England for bilingual texts offering instruction in French conversation.[28] Early manuals published by William Caxton, Richard Pynson, and Wynkyn de Worde were followed by, among others, John Palsgrave's monumental *Lesclarcissement de la langue francoyse* (1530). Palsgrave's work treated pronunciation in great detail, acting (as Gabriele Stein has argued) 'not [as] a help to read French texts, but to produce correct French, in a spoken or a written form'.[29] French would remain the most popular vernacular foreign language in print across our period, as—with the decline of Latin as a spoken European lingua franca—it became the working language of international politics, and competence in it became a prestige accomplishment for both men and women.[30] The only significant negative fluctuation in the popularity of French conversation manuals also hit other languages: this was the general slump in the

---

[25] Slack, 'Mirrors of Health', p. 239.

[26] Joad Raymond, *Pamphlets and Pamphleteering in Early Modern Britain* (Cambridge: Cambridge University Press, 2003), p. 80.

[27] Paul Festeau, *Nouvelle Grammaire Françoise* (London, 1679).

[28] On French, see Lambley, *Teaching and Cultivation of the French Language* and Kibbee, *For to speke Frenche trewely*. On the international nature of England's early print culture, see A. E. B. Coldiron, *Printers without Borders: Translation and Textuality in the Renaissance* (Cambridge: Cambridge University Press, 2015).

[29] Gabriele Stein, *John Palsgrave as Renaissance Linguist: A Pioneer in Vernacular Language Description* (Oxford: Clarendon, 1997), p. 45.

[30] On gender and competence in French, see Michèle Cohen, 'French Conversation or "Glittering Gibberish"? Learning French in Eighteenth-Century England', in Natasha Glaisyer and Sara Pennell, *Didactic Literature in England 1500–1800: Expertise Constructed* (Aldershot: Ashgate, 2003), pp. 99–117; see also Gabriele Beck-Busse, 'À propos d'une histoire des "Grammaires des Dames". Réflexions théoriques et approches empiriques', *Documents pour l'histoire du français langue étrangère ou seconde* 47–8 (2012), at https://journals.openedition.org/dhfles/3121, accessed 12 Mar. 2019.

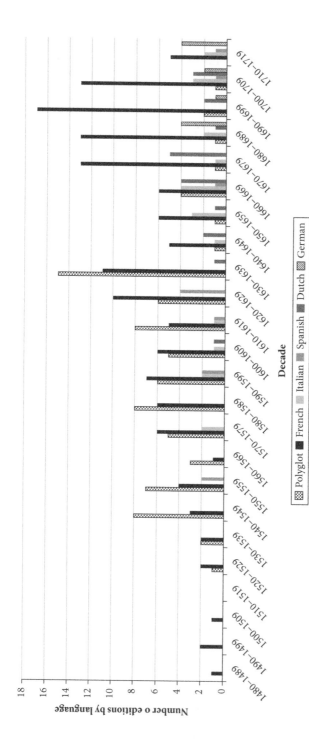

Figure 2.2 Conversation manuals by language per decade, 1480–1719

[1] Portuguese is omitted here to avoid crowding the graph: the bilingual English-Portuguese conversation manuals published in this period were A. J., *Grammatica Anglo-Lusitanica: or a short and compendious system of an English and Portugueze grammar* (London, 1702), and a second edition of the same text published in Lisbon in 1705. On these, see Rolf Kemmler, 'The *Grammatica Anglo-Lusitanica* (London, 1701), a translation of Bento Pereira's *Ars grammaticae pro lingua Lusitana addiscenda Latino idiomate* (Lyons, 1672)?', *Beiträge zur Geschichte der Sprachwissenschaft* 23:1 (2013), pp. 87–102.

production of conversation manuals during the period 1640–60. This is particularly noticeable in the case of manuals for French, with eleven texts in 1630–9 shrinking to five, seven, and six in the succeeding decades, before climbing to an unprecedented high of thirteen editions in 1670–9, a figure which was maintained in the decade that followed. The slump in the years of the civil wars and Interregnum is difficult to peg to any particular factor, especially as the breakdown of censorship in the early 1640s saw a rapid increase in the numbers of texts of other kinds being printed; however, this was a period in which significant numbers of people (including many Royalists) travelled to the continent and learnt languages abroad.[31] It seems likely that a series of factors, including the cultural prestige granted to French by the Francophile court of Charles II, the growth of what would become the 'grand tour', and the increasing numbers of French Protestant immigrants coming to England in the two decades surrounding the revocation of the Edict of Nantes, may together have helped to push up provision for students of that language during the Restoration.[32] By the final decade of the seventeenth century, Abel Boyer could write with only some exaggeration that French had become 'the General language of all Courts, and one of the chiefest Qualifications of accomplisht Persons in Europe', and that 'there is scarce any thing to be seen every where, but French-Grammars'.[33]

Italian-English conversation manuals first appeared in the final quarter of the sixteenth century, beginning with the work of Claudius Hollyband, who first published a manual for the language to accompany an Italian edition of Diego de San Pedro's *Tractado de Amores de Arnalte y Lucenda* in 1575.[34] When a

[31] Joad Raymond, *The Invention of the Newspaper: English Newsbooks 1641–1649* (Oxford: Clarendon, 1996), pp. 85–6; Raymond, *Pamphlets and pamphleteering*, pp. 202–75. On travel during the Interregnum, see Timothy Raylor, 'Exiles, Expatriates and Travellers: Towards a Cultural and Intellectual History of the English Abroad, 1640–1660', in Philip Major (ed.), *Literatures of Exile in the English Revolution and its Aftermath, 1640–1690* (Farnham and Burlington, VT: Ashgate, 2010), pp. 15–43.

[32] On Restoration Francophilia, see Gesa Stedman, *Cultural Exchange in Seventeenth-Century France and England* (Aldershot: Ashgate, 2013), pp. 63–107; Lawrence E. Klein, 'The Figure of France: The Politics of Sociability in England, 1660–1715', *Yale French Studies* 92, *Exploring the Conversible World: Text and Sociability from the Classical Age to the Enlightenment* (1997), pp. 30–45; Michael G. Brennan (ed.), *The Origins of the Grand Tour: The Travels of Robert Montagu, Lord Mandeville (1649–1654), William Hammond (1655–1658), and Banaster Maynard (1660–1663)* (London: Hakluyt Society, 2004), p. 231. On French-speakers' immigration to England, see Robin D. Gwynn, *Huguenot Heritage: The History and Contribution of the Huguenots in Britain* (London: Routledge and Kegan Paul, 1985); Susanne Lachenicht, 'Huguenot Immigrants and the Formation of National Identities, 1548–1787', *Historical Journal* 50 (2007), pp. 309–331; Bernard Cottret, *The Huguenots in England: Immigration and Settlement c.1550–1700*, trans. Peregrine and Adriana Stevenson (Cambridge: Cambridge University Press, 1991); Randolph Vigne and Charles Littleton (eds.), *From Strangers to Citizens: the integration of immigrant communities in Britain, Ireland and colonial America, 1550–1750* (Brighton & Portland: Sussex Academic Press, 2001).

[33] Abel Boyer, *The Compleat French-Master, for Ladies and Gentlemen* (London, 1694), sig. A5v.

[34] Claudius Hollyband, *The pretie and wittie historie of Arnalt & Lucenda: with certen rules and dialogues set foorth for the learner of th'Italian tong: and dedicated vnto the Worshipfull, Sir Hierom Bowes Knight* (London, 1575); Ivy A. Corfis, *Diego de San Pedro's Tractado de Amores de Arnalte y Lucenda* (London: Tamesis, 1985).

second edition appeared in 1597, the novella had been relegated in importance and the text bore the title *The Italian Schoole-maister*. This period also saw the publication of John Florio's two Italian conversation manuals, the *Firste Fruites* (1578) and the *Second Frutes* (1593), both texts which appealed to a literate elite readership seeking to access the literature and culture of the Italian Renaissance at a moment of English Italophilia.[35] Florio's texts were literary, but they were also written with an eye for the everyday, containing dialogues that featured shopping, eating, and drinking in company. These were not the first or only texts available to learners of Italian: William Thomas's *Principal Rules of the Italian Grammer*, first published in 1550, went through two further editions during the 1560s, while readers could also consult grammars by Scipione Lentulo (translated into English by Henry Grantham) and John Sanford.[36] The popularity of Italian was commented on by William Stepney in his English-Spanish manual (1591), where he argued that 'in my simple judgement, [Spanish] is farre more necessary for our countrey-men then the Italian tongue is'.[37] In spite of the prestige status of Italian in the latter half of the sixteenth century, there was only one English-Italian conversation manual published in the decade 1600–9, and one more in 1610–19, with the language disappearing entirely from the bilingual market in the 1620s and 1630s.

Italian only reappeared on the conversation manual market with the efforts of Giovanni Torriano, who cast himself as a successor to John Florio, and had inherited some of Florio's papers.[38] Where Florio's flowery language was often suited to courtly speech and writing, and to those who sought to read Italian literature, Torriano addressed himself to 'the good of all the English Nation', but aimed his work more 'espetially' towards 'you who are in a continuall commerce with most parts of Italy, as well as Turkey, where the Italian Tongue is all in all'.[39] The expansion of English Mediterranean trade replaced cultural prestige as the main reason for the study of Italian: it was a language which could serve as a lingua franca throughout the Mediterranean, from the Italian peninsula to the Barbary Coast, and to Istanbul,

---

[35] See John Gallagher, 'The Italian London of John North: Cultural Contact and Linguistic Encounter in Early Modern England', *Renaissance Quarterly* 70 (2017), pp. 88–131; Michael Wyatt, *The Italian Encounter with Tudor England: A Cultural Politics of Translation* (Cambridge: Cambridge University Press, 2005); Jason Lawrence, *'Who the devil taught thee so much Italian?' Italian language Learning and Literary Imitation in Early Modern England* (Manchester and New York: Manchester University Press, 2005).

[36] For a more detailed discussion of trends in Italian language-learning in this period, see John Gallagher, '"Ungratefull Tuscans": Teaching Italian in Early Modern England', *The Italianist* 36:3 (2016), pp. 392–413.

[37] Stepney, *Spanish Schoole-master*, A4v.

[38] Frances Yates, 'An Italian in Restoration England', *Journal of the Warburg and Courtauld Institutes* 6 (1943), p. 220.

[39] Giovanni Torriano, *The Italian Tutor or a new and most compleat Italian grammer* (London, 1640), 'To the right worshipfull and now most flourishing Company of Turkey Marchants'.

Izmir, and beyond.[40] Writing in 1660, Pietro Paravicino noted that his readers were more likely to be using their Italian in 'the piazzas of merchants than in the courts of princes'.[41] From this period there survives a manuscript fair copy with the title 'Raccolta di Frasi Italiane. A collection of Italian Phrases. Taken out of the best Authors, and Orderly Disposed under their Alphabetical Heads in English ... For the use of such as desire to write and speak Italian'. The manuscript was evidently drawn up for the press, though no printed text matching it survives; its author, who signs themselves 'B.S.', dedicated the text to senior figures in the Levant Company, since they 'have always here been justly esteemed the proper Patrons of the Italian Language which is soe useful to their Factorys in the Levant', Italian being 'more currant than any other' in the company's factories abroad.[42] The manuscript aimed to serve a wider audience but left no doubt that its composition, much of which had been undertaken under the roof of the Levant merchant Dudley North in Istanbul, owed much to the linguistic opportunities and activities associated with the Levant Company and with England's Mediterranean trade.[43]

The figures for conversation manuals bear out contemporary teachers' impression that Italian language-learning had suffered a mid-century slump. In 1657's *Della Lingua Toscana-Romana*, Torriano wrote that, after a period of decline, the study of the language had been made popular again amongst women by 'several Ladies of qualitie', a formulation which suggests that he may have been disregarding the language-learning efforts of less socially distinguished students, such as those involved in commerce.[44] The view of Italian as a language which had fallen into disuse for a time before regaining its prestige was encapsulated in the title of Torriano's *The Italian Reviv'd* (1673). A further blow to the study of the language, according to Torriano, was the destruction by the Great Fire of London in 1666 of stocks of Italian books. 'Had not the late dismal Fire destroyed all the Printed Books which concern the Italian', he wrote, 'there would have been no need for one while of more Books of that nature; but for want of them, the Italian declining, and almost expiring, I thought it necessary to revive it in time.'[45] The market for Italian books does seem to have picked up somewhat in the 1650s and

---

[40] For Italian's use as a lingua franca, see Joseph Cremona, ' "Accioché ognuno le possa intendere": The Use of Italian as a Lingua Franca on the Barbary Coast of the Seventeenth Century. Evidence from the English', *Journal of Anglo-Italian Studies* 5 (1997), pp. 52–69. Note that this usage of Italian is not to be confused with the Mediterranean Lingua Franca, a spoken Romance-based pidgin: see Jocelyne Dakhlia, *Lingua Franca: histoire d'une language métisse en Méditerranée* (Paris: Actes Sud, 2008); Hugo Schuchardt, *Pidgin and Creole Languages: Selected Essays*, trans. Glenn G. Gilbert (Cambridge: Cambridge University Press, 1980), pp. 66–87.

[41] Pietro Paravicino, *Choice Proverbs and Dialogues, in Italian and English* (London, 1660), sig. A4r.

[42] British Library, London, Harleian MS 3492, 'Raccolta di Frasi Italiane', fols. 4r, 3r.

[43] Ibid., fols. 5v–6r.

[44] Giovanni Torriano, *Della Lingua Toscana-Romana* (London, 1657), 'To the Reader'.

[45] Giovanni Torriano, *The Italian Reviv'd: Or, the Introduction to the Italian Tongue* (London, 1673), sig. A2r; see also Adrian Johns, *The Nature of the Book* (Chicago: University of Chicago Press, 1998), p. 68.

1660s, broadly in line with Torriano's implication that it was undergoing a revival as a prestigious cultural attainment, though its popularity dipped again in the 1670s.[46] The end of our period witnessed the beginnings of a new revival of Italian, with a manual like Giacomo Rossi's *Le maître aisé & rejouissant; Ou nouvelle methode agreable pour apprendre sans peine la langue italienne* (London, 1710?) reflecting the new taste for things Italian that went hand in hand with the beginnings of opera performance in England—fittingly enough, Rossi was to write libretti for some of Handel's works.[47]

The appearance of occasional Spanish-language material often seems to have been tied to political factors: two texts were printed under the Marian regime, while a flurry of texts appeared when the Spanish Match was a serious prospect.[48] When the political situation was less favourable, authors had to explain their motives carefully, as we can see in the preface to William Stepney's *Spanish schoole-master*, published just three years after the Armada, though reprinted in 1619 and 1620.[49] This work was at pains to stress its author's loyalty and the suitability of its subject, knowing the potential for accusations of disloyalty associated with Spanish print.[50] As Christopher Highley argues, '[the] prejudice

---

[46] Stephen Parkin's account of Italian printing in early modern London broadly reflects these conclusions, seeing it as episodic and recognizing the slump in Italophile sentiment around the mid-century: Stephen Parkin, 'Italian Printing in London, 1553–1900', in Barry Taylor (ed.), *Foreign-Language Printing in London 1500–1900* (Boston Spa and London: The British Library, 2002), pp. 133–174. On Italian printing in England until the middle of the seventeenth century, see Soko Tomita, *A Bibliographical Catalogue of Italian Books Printed in England 1558–1603* (Farnham: Ashgate, 2009), and Soko Tomita and Masahiko Tomita, *A Bibliographical Catalogue of Italian Books Printed in England 1603–1642* (Farnham: Ashgate, 2014).

[47] Donald Burrows, 'George Frideric Handel, 1685–1759' in *Oxford Dictionary of National Biography* online (https://doi.org/10.1093/ref:odnb/12192). Rossi's manual, published in London but written in Italian and French, neatly illustrates the point that Italian was often at least the second 'foreign' language studied by any given learner—they would likely have had French (as assumed by Rossi's text) or Latin, as assumed by a text like Francesco di Gregorio, *Discepulo instrutto nelli Principij della Lingua Latina, spiegati per la Volgare & Inglese a modo di Dialogo* (London, 1643).

[48] Anon., *The boke of Englysshe, and Spanysshe*; Anon., *A very profitable boke*; William Stepney, *The Spanish schoole-maister* (London, 1619), and reprinted in 1620; César Oudin, *A grammar Spanish and English: or A briefe and compendious method, teaching to reade, write, speake, and pronounce the Spanish tongue* (London, 1622); Juan de Luna, *A short and compendiovs art for to learne to reade, write, pronounce and speake the Spanish tongue* (London, 1623); Richard Perceval/John Minsheu, *A dictionary in Spanish and English: first published into the English tongue by Ric. Perciuale Gent* (London, 1623). On the beginnings of the study of Spanish in England and on the continent, and on trading contexts for Spanish study, see Hans-Josef Niederehe, 'Die Geschichte des Spanischunterrichts von den Anfängen bis zum Ausgang des 17. Jahrhunderts', in Konrad Schröder, *Fremdsprachenunterricht 1500–1800* (Wiesbaden: Harrassowitz, 1992), pp. 135–55; and Jean-Antoine Caravolas, *La Didactique des langues: précis d'histoire I, 1450–1700* (Montreal: Les Presses de l'Université de Montréal, 1994), pp. 114–16.

[49] The earliest edition is William Stepney, *The Spanish schoole-master* (London, 1591).

[50] On the circumstances surrounding the early history of Spanish printing in England, see Gustav Ungerer, 'The Printing of Spanish Books in Elizabethan England', *The Library* 20 (1965), pp. 177–229. For contemporary English attitudes to the Spanish, see Patricia Shaw, 'Sensual, Solemn, Sober, Slow and Secret: The English View of the Spaniard, 1590–1700', in C. C. Barfoot (ed.), *Beyond Pug's Tour: National and Ethnic Stereotyping in Theory and Literary Practice* (Amsterdam and Atlanta, GA: Rodopi, 1997), pp. 99–113.

of the English toward the Spanish was equalled only by the English fear of becoming like the Spanish': language education, with its potential for personal transformation, was fraught with danger for the English reader's identity.[51] William Stepney played it safe by addressing his manual to 'all those which are desirous to learne the said tongue *within* this our Realme of England' (my emphasis), potentially covering himself from the charge that his book might encourage or facilitate travel to Spain.[52] Stepney's epistle to the reader further emphasized his loyalty, citing his motivation for writing as 'my duetie, and the good will which I do beare unto my countrey'.[53] Dialogues set at Paul's Cross, a humble dedication to Robert Cecil, and a bawdy joke about a friar reminded any reader of the author's English political loyalties, while the distinctly Protestant tenor of the prayers with which the book closed left no doubt as to his religious orthodoxy.[54] This wariness about providing materials for learning Spanish—and for travel in Spain—had its roots in anxieties about Spanish power, English national security, and Catholicism, and may account for the relative paucity of Spanish language-learning texts in English in early modern print.[55] In the early eighteenth century, with England embroiled in the War of the Spanish Succession, there were two texts published for Spanish, one by Captain John Stevens, whose military credentials are made clear on the title page, and the other by Pasqual Joseph Anton, a teacher of Spanish in London, who described himself as '[d]irecting my Labour in this little Work to the Service of the Nobility and Gentry of England, that upon the Occasion of the War go to Spain'.[56] It seems competence in Spanish was mainly considered an acceptable accomplishment at times of Anglo-Spanish détente or heightened conflict.

Provision of bilingual conversation manuals teaching Dutch or German was patchy at first, with the first bilingual English-Dutch manual, Marten Le Mayre's *Dutch Schoole Master*, only appearing in London in 1606. Dutch would only become a relatively regular feature on the bilingual manual scene after 1630, with

[51] Christopher Highley, *Catholics Writing the Nation in Early Modern Britain and Ireland* (Oxford: Oxford University Press, 2008), p. 157.

[52] Stepney, *Spanish Schoole-master* (1591), title page.   [53] ibid., sig. A3v.

[54] Louis Wright argues that in spite of political antipathy, it was the increased trade with Spain that led to the boom in language-learning materials for that language at the end of the sixteenth century: Louis B. Wright, 'Language Helps for the Elizabethan Tradesman', *Journal of English and Germanic Philology* 30 (1931), pp. 343–4. The joke about the friar is Stepney, *Spanish Schoole-master* (1591), p. 66; the prayers are ibid., pp. 158–61.

[55] On Spanish print more generally, see Barry Taylor, 'Un-Spanish Practices: Spanish and Portuguese Protestants, Jews and Liberals, 1500–1900', in Taylor (ed.), *Foreign-Language Printing in London*, pp. 183–202.

[56] John Stevens, *A new Spanish and English Dictionary: Collected from the Best Spanish Authors, Both Ancient and Modern... The Whole by Captain John Stevens* (London: George Sawbridge, 1706); Pasqual Joseph Anton, *Grammatica Española/A Spanish Grammar: which is the shortest, plain, and most easy method to instruct an English man in the true Knowledge of that extensive Language... By D^n. Pasqual Joseph Anton. Master of Languages in London* (London, 1711), 'To Her Grace the Dutchess of Shrewsbury'.

at least one manual published in every decade thereafter until the 1710s; the seventeenth century would also see the publication of important Anglo-Dutch dictionaries by Henry Hexham and Willem (or William) Sewel.[57] German provision began in the 1680s with Martin Aedler's *High-Dutch Minerva*. The study of German would later be energized by the accession of the Hanoverians, while good relations between Anne's England and her German neighbours, along with the prospect of a Hanoverian succession, meant that print provision responded to a perceived increase in the desire for English competence among speakers of German.[58] Both German and Dutch conversational materials, however, were available from as early as 1525 and 1530 respectively in polyglot conversation manuals—texts that contained phrases and dialogues in more than two languages.[59]

Figure 2.3 shows the languages available in polyglot manuals during this period: we can see that Dutch and German were already well-represented in the sixteenth

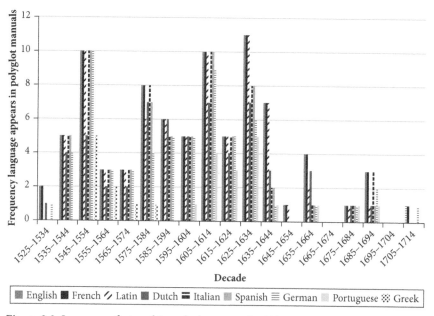

Figure 2.3 Languages featured in polyglot manuals, 1525–1714

[57] On the study of Dutch more generally, see Osselton, *Dumb Linguists*, and Christopher Joby, *The Dutch Language in Britain, 1550–1702: A Social History of the Use of Dutch in Early Modern Britain* (Leiden and Boston, MA: Brill, 2015).

[58] Fredericka van der Lubbe surveys the factors in England and in the German-speaking lands which may have motivated the appearance of the earliest English-German materials: Fredericka van der Lubbe, *Martin Aedler and the High Dutch Minerva: The First German Grammar for the English* (Frankfurt am Main: Peter Lang, 2007), pp. 33–48. See also Glück, *Deutsch als Fremdsprache*, pp. 323–37.

[59] German appeared in Anon., *Here begynneth a lytell treatyse for to lerne Englysshe and Frensshe. Sensuyt vng petit liure pour apprendre a parler Francoys, Alemant, et Ancloys* (Lyons, c.1525); Dutch in Anon., *A lytell treatyse for to lerne Englysshe and Frensshe* (Antwerp c.1530)—this latter text only survives in fragmentary form.

century, before there were any bilingual materials available for these languages. This probably reflects their status as objects of study—as foreign languages, they were more the preserve of those involved in trade, rather than prestige vernaculars like Italian or French. As such, they were probably learnt mostly as part of a programme of vocational training or apprenticeship, rather than through the formal study of a conversation manual. This was the case, for instance, for Edward Coxere, who was briefly sent to Middelburg to learn the trade of a cooper, but gave it up and became a sailor. Serving on a Dutch vessel, he had to learn Dutch quickly on the job: 'still, though I had French and English', he wrote, 'I had Dutch to learn to understand those I was withal, which I soon got'.[60] For those with less time or pedagogical opportunity, polyglot manuals could fill a niche, providing basic vocabulary and phrases appropriate to a variety of situations, many to do with travel and commerce, and often including languages less prestigious than French, Italian, and Latin (though these often featured too). They did not provide an in-depth pedagogy but acted more as cribs for travellers and merchants in multiple languages.

A sharp decline in the production of polyglot phrasebooks containing English set in around 1645. Maria Colombo Timelli notes that the last known edition of the extremely popular *Solenissimo vochabuolista* text, which appeared in a great variety of European languages and in editions published across the continent, is a Rouen edition of 1636. The production of polyglot texts based on the popular *Colloquia* initially written by Noël de Berlemont peaked around the 1590s but only really started to go into decline around 1640.[61] These two source texts had long and varied European careers: the bibliography of polyglot manuals containing English among their languages suggests that the majority were based on one or other of these source books. However, while an edition of the *Solenissimo vochabuolista* was published in Southwark in 1537, and Michael Sparke produced corrected quadrilingual editions of Berlemont in 1637 and 1639, the printing of polyglot conversation manuals containing English was not particularly common in England itself, with only sixteen published in England as against sixty-nine coming from the continent. It is difficult to pinpoint a specific reason for this, though the beginnings of the decline of the polyglot phrasebook with English provision comes at roughly the same time as the general slump in the genre seen above. Still, the market for polyglot manuals did not recover after the Interregnum. In dealing with the polyglot manuals, it is important to remember that the editions containing English among their several languages are only a subset of a

[60] E. H. W. Meyerstein (ed.), *Adventures by Sea of Edward Coxere* (Oxford: Clarendon, 1945), p. 8.
[61] Timelli, 'Dictionnaires pour voyageurs', p. 396; Stein, 'Emerging Role of English', *passim*. For more on the history of these polyglot texts, see Timelli, 'Dictionnaires pour voyageurs'; Alda Rossebastiano, 'Tradition des manuels polyglottes'; Caroline B. Bourland, '*The Spanish Schoole-master* and the Polyglot Derivatives of Noel de Berlaimont's *Vocabulare*', *Revue Hispanique* 81 (1933), pp. 283–318; Phillips, 'Schoolmasters, Seduction, and Slavery'; Stein, 'Emerging Role of English'.

broader European publishing phenomenon: there were many editions of the *Solenissimo vochabuolista* and of the Berlemont text that did not contain English material. It is also noteworthy that the rise of Dutch and German in the corpus of bilingual conversation manuals began around the time the polyglot manuals went into evident decline. Where provision for these languages had hitherto been found largely in the polyglot texts, authors were beginning to offer more complete pedagogical materials for their study, perhaps rendering the significantly cruder dialogues and extremely sparse grammatical instruction of the polyglot manuals redundant. To add another layer of complexity to this narrative, some of the bilingual English-Dutch manuals which began to appear in this period translated and adapted dialogues which had first appeared in the Berlemont text, ensuring that his dialogues (or those of the expanded editions of his original) did not disappear entirely with the decline of the polyglot phrasebook.[62] The polyglot manual did not die out altogether: in 1794, the publication of *The soldier's pocket dictionary, or friend in need: being a vocabulary of many thousand words, terms, and questions* by Captain James Willson suggested that such texts were still needed for certain polyglot milieus.[63] However, by the middle of the seventeenth century, the heyday of the pocket polyglot companion was clearly over, and the bilingual conversation manual was the standard.

Among the many bi- and multilingual texts published in early modern England, a number were not aimed—or not solely aimed—at English learners of foreign vernaculars. Some manuals addressed themselves to learners of English as a second language. The French Wars of Religion had resulted in a wave of French Protestant migrants to England in the later decades of the sixteenth century: one Frenchman, Jacques Bellot, published a text in 1586 titled *Familiar Dialogues: for the Instruction of them, that be desirous to learne to speake English, and perfectlye to pronounce the same*. Bellot's text was aimed explicitly at 'them that be refugiate in a strange countrey', offering instruction in English to refugees, emigrants, and exiles, much as would Guy Miège's *Nouvelle Methode Pour Apprendre L'Anglois* almost exactly a century later, printed at a time of renewed French migration and refuge in England (both texts are discussed at greater length in Chapter 3).[64] The *Grammaire angloise* originally published in 1625 was similarly meant for foreign learners of English, though its intended audience seems to have been mobile courtiers and members of Henrietta Maria's Francophone

---

[62] For instance, in the Dutch tradition, both Anon., *Den grooten Vocabulaer Engels ende Duyts/The Great Vocabuler, in English and Dutch* (Rotterdam, 1639) and Anon., *The Dutch-Tutor: or, a new-book of Dutch and English.* (London, 1660) borrow liberally from the Berlemont text, though the language is corrected somewhat from the corrupt state of the polyglot editions.

[63] The polyglot conversation manual has never quite died out. See, for instance, Barry McKay, *Gay Phrase Book* (London: Cassell, 1995), which teaches readers to 'Get your man in six different languages!'

[64] Jacques Bellot, *Familiar Dialogues, for the Instruction of them, that be desirous to learne to speake English, and perfectlye to pronounce the same* (London: Thomas Vautrollier, 1586), sig. A2r.

household rather than those fleeing religious or other persecution.[65] In the preface to his *Volkommener englischer Wegweiser für Hoch-Teutsche*, published in 1706, the author—Johann König, alias John King—addressed the contemporary politics of migration, writing that '[a]mong the vast Concourse of Foreigners that resort to this Flourishing Kingdom, the Germans, since their happy Alliance with the English, are not the least considerable'. Of this group, he argued, 'many of them are now particularly oblig'd, and others no less desirous, to be well acquainted with the English Tongue'.[66] Another manual published in 1710 offered English instruction to a different group of German-speaking immigrants: those who had arrived as part of the 'Palatine' migration from 1709 onwards.[67] The appetite for English study seems to have developed significantly earlier in the Low Countries than it did elsewhere, as reflected in texts like the anonymous *Den Engelschen School-Meester/The English Schole-Master* (1646), which addressed Dutch and English publics, offering '[c]ertaine rules and helpes, whereby the natives of the Netherlandes, may bee, in a short time, taught to read, understand, and speake, the English tongue', as well as parallel instruction for English learners of Dutch.[68] Even John Florio's *Firste Fruites*, a text often read as central to England's encounter with Italian, explicitly advertised its two-way usability, with Florio addressing 'all the Italian Gentlemen and Merchants who delight in the English language' alongside his English audience.[69] The prestige of English as a foreign language remained relatively low in this period, but materials nonetheless existed for the diverse groups—traders, courtiers, and migrants—who had need of English before it became an international lingua franca.

The formats in which these manuals were printed and their size became standardized during our period, with pocket-sized books (usually in octavo) gradually becoming dominant. Enormous folio volumes like John Palsgrave's *Lesclarcissement* (1530) and John Wodroephe's *True Marrowe of the French Tongue* (1623) gradually gave way to books in octavo and sextodecimo. Claudius Hollyband wrote of his *French Littelton* that 'I have caused [it] to be printed in this small volume, that it might be easier to be caried by any man about him', while the

---

[65] Stoughton, 'France's First English Textbook'.

[66] Johann König/John King, *Ein volkommener englischer Wegweiser für Hoch-Teutsche/A compleat English guide for High-Germans* (London, 1706), preface.

[67] Anon., *A Short and Easy Way For The Palatines To Learn English. Oder Eine kurze Anleitung zur Englischen Sprach, Zum Nutz der armen Pfältzer/nebst angehängten Englischen und Teutsche ABC* (London, 1710). This manual, and the linguistic aspect of the Palatine migration, are discussed in Chapter 3. For more on the printing of German manuals and German-language texts, see Graham Jefcoate, 'German Printing and Bookselling in Eighteenth-Century London: Evidence and Interpretation', in Taylor (ed.), *Foreign-Language Printing in London*, pp. 1–36.

[68] Anon., *Den Engelschen School-Meester &c. The English Schole-Master &c.* (Amsterdam, 1646), title page. Osselton, *Dumb Linguists*, contains a useful description of the study of English in the early modern Low Countries, pp. 23–33.

[69] 'A tutti i Gentilhuomini, e Mercanti Italjani, che si dilettano de la lingua Inglese': John Florio, *Florio His firste Fruites which yeelde familiar speech* (London, 1578), sig. **.i.r, **.ij.v.

author of a Spanish treatise of 1711 excused 'this small Offering, which for its Dwarfishness seems to vanish in the Hand, tho'designedly so for the greater Convenience of those that travel'.[70] Portability in travel was a concern: Addressing the readers of his *English and Nether-dutch Dictionary*, J. G. van Heldoren said that '[c]onsidering that little Books are convenient for young schollars and travellers, seeing they are easie to be carried therefore I have composed a Dictionary very brief, good and useful'.[71] A small text would be more easily consulted in an idle moment, the book's utility enhanced by its form: Pietro Paravicino boasted in 1662 of having published 'commodious Books to carry in your Pocket'.[72] Of his *Choice Phrases* he said that 'it hath been my study to make it little and good, to the end that having it in your Pocket, you may the oftner have it in your hand to read, and practise it': size and utility were directly linked.[73] Authors might struggle with the constraints of size: in 1617, William Bathe apologized for the unwieldy quarto format of his *Janua Linguarum*, saying 'I sought in adding two languages, to render the volume yet as portable as might be, and if not as a Manuall or pocket-booke, yet a Pectorall or bosome-booke, to be carried twixt jerkin and doublet'.[74] Polyglot texts often came in pocket-sized editions, their six, seven, or eight languages crammed across each opening of an octavo or sextodecimo volume. The appearance and materiality of these conversation manuals suggests a generic expectation that a speech-oriented manual would normally be of manageable size; Bathe's protestations about his 'bosome-booke' suggests that he was aware of stretching the formal expectations of the genre—as well as the jerkins of his readers—to breaking point. While folio and quarto editions were common in the sixteenth century, the octavo format had become the standard for a conversation manual by the mid-seventeenth century: affordable, portable, and useful.[75]

A book's size, among its other physical characteristics, could suggest to a reader the kind of text they were likely to encounter.[76] Some authors marketed books in different formats at readers with different needs or budgets. Two texts published by one 'A.J.' at the beginning of the eighteenth century illustrate this point: in

---

[70] Hollyband, *French Littelton*, sig. *2v; Anton, *Grammatica Española/A Spanish Grammar*, 'To Her Grace the Dutchess of Shrewsbury'.
[71] J. G. van Heldoren, *An English and Nether-dutch Dictionary* (Amsterdam, 1675), sig. A2r.
[72] Pietro Paravicino, *Choice phrases, set forth in questions and answers in Italian, rendered into English* (London, 1662), sig. A2v.
[73] Ibid., p. 1.
[74] William Bathe, *Janua Linguarum, Quadrilinguis. Or a Messe of Tongues: Latine, English, French, and Spanish. Neatly served up together, for a wholesome repast, to the worthy curiositie of the studious* (London, 1617), sig. Qr.
[75] The changes in formats over time are discussed and illustrated in John Gallagher, 'Vernacular Language-Learning in Early Modern England', unpublished PhD dissertation, University of Cambridge (2014), pp. 49–55.
[76] Paul Grendler, 'Form and Function in Italian Renaissance Popular Books', *Renaissance Quarterly* 46 (1993), p. 451.

1701, he released his *A compleat account of the Portugueze language*, a folio text containing a dictionary and rules for pronunciation, grammar, and composition. It contained no dialogues, unlike the text A.J. published in 1702, the *Grammatica Anglo-Lusitanica: or a short and compendious system of an English and Portugueze grammar*. This text—which appeared in octavo—advertised itself as containing instruction on grammar and syntax, supplemented with some '[u]seful Dialogues and Colloquies, agreeable to common Conversation', alongside 'a vocabulary of Useful Words in English and Portugueze'. The title emphasized the text's utility and even its potential use by travellers and traders, claiming to be 'Designed for, and fitted to all Capacities, and more especially such whose Chance or Business may lead them into any part of the World, where that Language is used or esteemed'.[77] A.J.'s two texts served different purposes and envisaged different kinds of usage—the folio a reference book, the octavo a socially and orally oriented utilitarian text. These usages were reflected in the shape the different texts took. Claudius Hollyband's *French Schoolemaister* appeared in octavo, while his *French Littelton* was a sextodecimo: the former was addressed more at a younger audience, and at those studying at Hollyband's school, while the *Littelton* is more of a general conversation manual aimed at the adult learner or traveller. Over two centuries, authors and publishers settled on a physical form for the manuals which became the generic standard: readers' needs, expectations, and presumably pockets, were important factors in this development.

Conversation manuals came to fit the pocket, but how did they hit the pocket? Detailed information about pricing is difficult to come by, but booksellers and book buyers have left some clues. In September 1578, John North's Italian-language diary recorded his purchase of 'Florio and another book', costing 2*s.* 9*d.* in all. In November of the same year, North paid Claudius Hollyband 14 shillings for a month's teaching, as well as 2 shillings for a book, which was probably either the *French Schoolemaister* or the *French Littelton*.[78] Printed in 1660, the front page of Pietro Paravicino's *True idioma of the Italian tongue* noted that it cost '1s. 6d. Bound'; an unbound volume would have been cheaper.[79] Early eighteenth-century advertisements show that the twentieth, twenty-first, and twenty-second editions of Claude Mauger's French grammar were all priced at two shillings.[80] Similarly, the fourth edition of Abel Boyer's *Compleat French-Master* was available for 2 shillings in 1707, and Laurentio Casotti's *New method of teaching the Italian tongue to ladies and gentlemen* was priced at 1*s.* 6*d.* in 1713.[81] All three

---

[77] A.J., *A compleat account of the Portugueze language* (London, 1701); A.J., *Grammatica Anglo-Lusitanica*. See also Kemmler, 'The *Grammatica Anglo-Lusitanica*'.

[78] Diary of John North, 1575–7, Bodleian Library, MS Add. C. 193, fols. 41r, 47r.

[79] Pietro Paravicino, *The true idioma of the Italian tongue* (London, 1660).

[80] Mauger's grammar was advertised frequently: see *Daily Courant*, issue 945 (26 April 1705); *London Gazette*, issue 4438 (20– 24 May 1708); *Daily Courant*, issue 3908 (4 May 1714).

[81] *Post Boy*, issue 1890 (24–26 June 1707); *Post Boy*, issue 2828 (23–25 June 1713).

were in octavo, though it is not clear whether or not they were sold bound. The mid-seventeenth-century travel journal of Richard Symonds refers to two French grammars as costing 8*d*. and 9*d*. apiece, when purchased at Paris.[82] There were cheaper forms of print, like ballads and newsbooks, though print that did reach a more 'popular' audience (with all the difficulties that term implies) could be more expensive: the prayer book, unbound, in quarto or duodecimo could cost between 5*d*. and 9*d*. at the end of the seventeenth century, while bound and interleaved almanacs could cost 6*d*. in the period before 1660.[83] Assuming the standard price range of manuals in this period was between 1*s*. 6*d*. and 2*s*., it suggests that manuals in octavo (the standard form by this time) were not prohibitively expensive, especially if one was content to leave them unbound—and that they were becoming cheaper in real terms across the period. Michael Sparke's 1637 edition of the Berlemont text made reference to its cheapness, particularly when compared to hiring an interpreter:

> I finding the want of these Languages, found this to bee a great helpe, with small charge. This Guide or Interpreter will not bee any wayes chargeable, more than at first buying; but shouldst thou hire another, it may cost thee some pounds.[84]

The arrival of the printed conversation manual did not render manuscript language aids obsolete. Manuscript books of phrases and dialogues continued to be prepared, sometimes by teachers, as in the case of the 'Libretto' of Italian dialogues created by Giacomo Castelvetro and discussed in Chapter 1. Peter Auger has shown that Jacques Bellot's printed French manuals had their roots in a manuscript manual Bellot had drafted for use with his students: scribal practice and pedagogical interaction fed into the creation of the printed conversation manual.[85] Other manuscript conversation aids were drafted for particular users and shaped to fit their purposes: perhaps the most famous is the trilingual primer created for Elizabeth I, which contains phrases and dialogues in Irish, Latin, and English.[86] When, in 1653, Bulstrode Whitelocke took up the post of ambassador extraordinary to Queen Christina of Sweden, he went supplied with a trilingual manuscript phrasebook (in English, French, and Latin) which contained phrases necessary for dealing with the queen and with members of the Swedish nobility, as well as for discussing and debating the finer points of the recent constitutional

---

[82]   Travel journal of Richard Symonds, British Library, Harleian MS 943, fol. 25v.

[83]   Peter Lake, 'Religion and Cheap Print', in Joad Raymond (ed.), *The Oxford Handbook of Popular Print Culture* (Oxford: Oxford University Press, 2011), pp. 219–21; Lauren Kassell, 'Almanacs and prognostications', in Raymond (ed.), *The Oxford Handbook of Popular Print Culture*, pp. 437–8.

[84]   Anon., *The English, French, Latine, Dutch, Schole-master. Or, An Introduction to teach young Gentlemen and Merchants to Travell or Trade* (London, 1637).

[85]   Peter Auger, 'Fashioned through Use: Jacques Bellot's *Rules* and its Successors', *History of European Ideas* 42 (2016), pp. 651–64. The Bellot manuscript is British Library, Sloane MS 3316.

[86]   A digitized edition of the manuscript primer has been made available online at https://www.isos.dias.ie/master.html?https://www.isos.dias.ie/libraries/MARSH/Irish_Primer/tables/2.html?, accessed 12 Mar. 2019.

upheavals in Britain. Polite utterances like '[b]e pleased to goe into this chamber, where I shall waite uppon your [Excellency]' shared space with trilingual explanations that '[t]he Parliament is the foundation of the English government, & the supreme Court & Councell of the Nation & so hath bin in all times', that '[a]ll leagues & alliances made with any Prince or State by the kinges of England before the chaunge of government have bin punctually observed afterwardes', and how '[t]he king of Denmarke was pleased to use the Commonwealth of England in such a manner as hardly could be excused of unworthines in the meanest private person'.[87] The line between print and manuscript was blurred: a 1683 manuscript Italian manual kept by John Armytage (probably of Kirklees in Yorkshire) contained phrases and dialogues transcribed from Giovanni Torriano's *The Italian Reviv'd* (1673).[88] The rise of the printed conversation manual did not mean that manuscript language aids ceased to be used.

Just as scribal practices persisted long after the coming of print, so too did some language manuals outlast the historical moment of their production and enjoy significant afterlives.[89] For instance, we might think of Claudius Hollyband as predominantly an Elizabethan author, but his *French Schoolmaster*, originally published in 1573, was reprinted throughout the seventeenth century, with the final edition appearing in 1668.[90] Hollyband is recognized as having been the most important and prolific language teacher in Elizabethan England, but his manuals—the *Schoolmaster* and the *French Littelton*—went into twenty-four editions after 1603.[91] The last edition of the *Littelton* would come in 1630, but the *French Schoolmaster* went into fifteen post-1603 editions. After Hollyband's death, revisions of the *Schoolmaster* were purportedly undertaken by Pierre Erondell—himself author of *The French Garden*, a textbook for female students of French which explicitly aimed to fill a gap in the market left by Hollyband—and subsequently by one James Giffard, a 'professor of the sayd tongue', with another edition claiming the involvement of 'divers professors' of French.[92] Beyond this, elements of Hollyband's work

[87] British Library, RP 209, fols. 5r, 25r, 28v, 49v.

[88] John Armytage, Italian manuscript phrasebook, West Yorkshire Archive Service (Calderdale), KE/8. On the vibrancy of scribal copying and manuscript culture well after the beginnings of print, see Julia Crick and Alexandra Walsham, 'Introduction: Script, Print, and History, in Crick and Walsham (eds.), *The Uses of Script and Print, 1300–1700* (Cambridge: Cambridge University Press, 2004), pp. 1–26.

[89] Lambley is good throughout on the textual histories of French-language materials: Lambley, *Teaching and Cultivation of the French Language, passim.*

[90] Claudius Hollyband, *The French school-master. Shewing the true and perfect way of pronouncing the French tongue, to the furtherance of those who desire to learn it. First collected by Mr C.H. and now truly and newly corrected and enriched with many facete proverbs and additions, for the delight and benefit of the learner. Never printed before. By James Giffard teacher of the said tongue* (London, 1668).

[91] The rights to Hollyband's *Italian Schoole-maister* were sold on in 1638, which R. C. Simonini reads as indicating a similarly long-lived popularity: R. C. Simonini, 'The Italian Pedagogy of Claudius Hollyband', *Studies in Philology* 49 (1952), p. 148.

[92] Hollyband died in 1597: Mark Eccles, 'Claudius Hollyband and the Earliest French-English Dictionaries', *Studies in Philology* 83 (1986), p. 61. After this, the 1602 edition of the *French schoole-master* claimed to have been 'newly corrected and amended by M.R.F.'. The 1606 edition advertised itself as 'now newly corrected and amended by P. Erondelle'. Erondell's name is featured on the editions

would appear in plagiarized form in the anonymous *Grammaire Angloise* and in Marten Le Mayre's *Dutch Schoole Master*, bringing his pedagogy to an audience beyond learners of French and Italian.[93] Similarly, Gabriel Meurier's *Familiare communications no leasse proppre then verrie proffytable to the Inglishe nation desirous and nedinge the Frenche language* was originally published at Antwerp in 1563, but saw the light again in a Rouen edition of 1641, as well as having its material copied by the compiler of *A plaine pathway to the French tongue* (London, 1575).[94] *The French Alphabet* by 'G.D.L.M.N.'—G. de la Mothe—went into seven editions between 1592 and 1647, and Marten le Mayre's text reused some of its material in Dutch.[95] Perhaps most strangely, elements of John Eliot's *Ortho-Epia Gallica* (1593) found their way into Peter Berault's *A New, Plain, Short, and Compleat French and English Grammar* (1688): Berault cribbed a significant proportion of his dialogues from Eliot's text, nearly a century after it was first published.[96] Guy Miège's English-French grammar, first published in 1678, looked like going out of print after the London edition of 1706, but reappeared thirty-three years later in Rotterdam, going into nine further editions printed in Rotterdam and in France, with the last recorded edition appearing in 1779.[97] These lengthy afterlives show that more popular texts were thought to have value beyond their original moment, and significantly complicate questions of the relationship between the conversation manual and its immediate temporal (and geographical) context: this suggests that some among the readers, authors, publishers, and editors of these works perceived a continuity in language-learners' needs across a long span of time.

---

of 1609, 1612, 1615, 1619, and 1623. The editions of 1628, 1631, 1636, 1641, 1649, 1655, 1660, and 1668 carry James Giffard's name, though I have been unable to discover more about him. The 1632 edition describes itself as 'First collected by Mr C.H. and since often corrected by divers professors of the sayd tongue.' Frances Yates argues that a number of Giovanni Torriano's printed dialogues were inherited in manuscript from John Florio: see Frances Yates, *John Florio: The Life of an Italian in Shakespeare's England*, pp. 322–33.

[93] Stoughton, 'France's First English Textbook', pp. 58–61; Phillips, 'Schoolmasters, Seduction, and Slavery', pp. 132–3.

[94] Anon., *A plaine pathway to the French tongue: Very profitable for Marchants, and also all other, which desire this same* (London, 1575). The changes to the Meurier text are largely superficial: the orthography is corrected and the form letters are reprinted, though not in the secretary hand of the original.

[95] Compare, for instance, 'Of Plays/Du Jeu', in G.D.L.M.N. [de la Mothe], *The French Alphabeth* (London, 1592), pp. 150–1, and 'Of Playes/Van Speulen', in Marten Le Mayre, *The Dutch Schoole Master* (London, 1606), sig. F4r–F4v; the surrounding dialogues are also lifted from de la Mothe.

[96] Compare, for instance, dialogues on 'The Barber' in John Eliot, *Ortho-Epia Gallica. Eliots Fruits for the French* (London, 1593), p. 64, and Peter Berault, *A New, Plain, Short, and Compleat French and English Grammar: Whereby the Learner may attain in few Months to Speak and Write French Correctly, as they do now in the Court of France. And Wherein all that is Dark, Superfluous, and Deficient in other Grammars, is Plain, Short, and Methodically supplied. Also very useful to Strangers, that are desirous to learn the English Tongue: for whose sake is added a Short, but very Exact English Grammar.* (London, 1688), p. 201.

[97] Guy Miège and Abel Boyer, *Grammaire angloise-françoise, par Mrs Miège & Boyer, contenant une méthode claire & facile pour acquérir en peu de temps l'usage de l'Anglois* (Lyons, 1779).

These texts did not just survive as museum pieces: some were still in use long after their original publication. Richard Symonds, travelling in France and Italy during the Interregnum, listed some 'Books brought from Paris' which included 'The French Schoole*master*', which can only be Hollyband's text.[98] At this point the text was still in print, and would be until 1668, but one traveller's journal from around 1691 shows that among books in Latin, French, English, and Spanish, he purchased a 'Dict. 8 Linguar*um*'—almost certainly a version of the polyglot Berlemont text— and a copy of Hollyband's *French Littelton*, the latest known edition of which had been published in 1630.[99] Hollyband, in choosing the title of his *Littelton*, wanted it to be as indispensable a work of reference for the student of the language as Thomas de Littleton's *Tenures* was for legal students; it seems that his hopes for posterity were at least partly justified, with travellers continuing to look to his simple but evidently effective dialogues and grammatical advice long into the next century.[100] For all that they responded to changes in fashion, politics, and peda-gogy, some conversation manuals lasted long in print and even longer in usage.

Noisy Reading: How to Use a Conversation Manual

When we talk about conversation manuals, the elephant in the room is practice. How were these texts actually used? How did print lead to speech? How did books teach linguistic competence? Users had to deal with the manuals' evident defi-ciencies, which included their inability to represent correct pronunciation with total accuracy, to teach aural comprehension, or even (in the case of many polyglot texts) to print foreign-language material free of substantial errors. The question of the manuals' usage—particularly in relation to speech—has often been sidestepped, though John Considine regards certain of the polyglot manuals as so corrupt as to be essentially unusable.[101] Generally, scholars have been reluctant to posit a model of usage in line with authors' insistence that the manuals taught speech as well as reading and writing. As a result, our understanding of these speaking books remains too silent. The conversation manual, carrying material which mimicked speech and aimed to equip its users to speak for themselves, existed between textual and oral culture: manuals' readers were urged to use the book as an aid to speech, while also using voices from outside the text to animate its materials. They practised a kind of noisy reading which capitalized on what Adam Fox has called the 'dynamic continuum' in which oral and literate cultures

---

[98] Travel journal of Richard Symonds, British Library, Harleian MS 943, fol. 111v.

[99] Journal of a gentleman's travels through Germany, Holland, Low Countries, British Library, Harleian MS 6427, fols. 55v, 55r.

[100] Claudius Hollyband, *The Frenche Littelton. A most easie, perfect, and absolute way to learne the frenche tongue* (London, [1576]), sig. *2r–*2v.

[101] Considine, 'Narrative and Persuasion'.

fed off each other in early modern England, 'a society ever more accustomed to communicating information, disseminating opinion, and enshrining ideas in text', but in which 'oral exchange remained the primary mode of receiving and transmitting cultural capital'.[102] Conversation manuals, in their pedagogies and the practices of reading they asked of their readers, model a unique relationship between early modern cultures of print, speech, writing, and hearing. These 'speaking books' are the key to understanding early modern language-learning.

Early modern materials for language pedagogy placed the study of pronunciation and speech front and centre. They made significant attempts to provide instruction in pronunciation, and suggested ways in which their readers could supplement the text with oral practice, whether in private consultation with the author or otherwise. Early modern pedagogy itself contained a substantial oral element—students at grammar schools, universities, and inns of court were familiar with the oral practices of oration and disputation, and correct, appropriate, persuasive speech was the fundamental attribute of the Ciceronian orator who was the model of humanist educational philosophy.[103] How did this orality manifest itself in vernacular language-learning? The compiler of the *Plaine pathway to the French tongue* declared that 'the learning of the French tonge consisteth on these two pointes, true pronuntiation, and proprietie of phrase': this manual, like many, began with a section on pronunciation, only giving way afterwards to dialogues.[104] De la Mothe's French manual urged pupils to begin their study of the language with three or four days spent learning the letters and their pronunciation, then proceeding to read the dialogues. Pupils were to work their way slowly through the words, applying what they had learnt of pronunciation and of orthography, and working out which letters were silent.[105] This pedagogical method—which the common placing of pronunciation materials at the beginning of manuals seems to suggest—developed reading knowledge in a way that fundamentally linked it to the acquisition of oral competence. Even the pupil who was looking to develop a reading knowledge passed through the stage of sounding out words. John Wodroephe's pedagogical programme began with pronunciation, and a practical metaphor that argued its fundamental importance:

---

[102] For 'noisy reading', see Margaret Aston, 'Epilogue', in Crick and Walsham (eds.), *The Uses of Script and Print*, pp. 278–9; John Gallagher, '"To heare it by mouth": Speech and Accent in Early Modern Language-Learning', *Huntington Library Quarterly* 82:1 (2019), pp. 63–86; Adam Fox, *Oral and Literate Culture in England 1500–1700* (Oxford: Clarendon, 2000), pp. 50, 19, 12. Compare Keith Thomas, 'The Meaning of Literacy in Early Modern England', in G. Baumann (ed.), *The Written Word: Literacy in Transition* (Oxford: Clarendon, 1986), p. 98.

[103] Jennifer Richards, *Rhetoric and Courtliness in Early Modern Literature* (Cambridge: Cambridge University Press, 2003), *passim*; Markku Peltonen, *Rhetoric, Politics, and Popularity in Pre-Revolutionary England* (Cambridge: Cambridge University Press, 2013); Clare Carroll, 'Humanism and English Literature in the Fifteenth and Sixteenth Centuries', in Jill Kraye (ed.), *The Cambridge Companion to Renaissance Humanism* (Cambridge: Cambridge University Press, 1996), p. 246; David Colclough, 'Rhetoric', in Raymond (ed.), *Oxford Handbook of Popular Print Culture*, p. 113.

[104] Anon., *Plaine pathway to the French tongue*, sig. A2r.

[105] De la Mothe, *The French Alphabet*, 'An Epistle to the Reader'.

Before wee beginne to warpe the Webbe of this thinne and shire peece of cloath,
I must go about to know if the tooles be oiled, and in good order, to the end it
may be the easier to weave by the workemen, to wit: the french Pronounciation of
the letters, comparing them with the tooles of a weaver, who can not exercise the
same unlesse they bee in good order to beginne his webbe.[106]

The system of learning described in Comenius's influential *Porta linguarum
trilinguis* urged the student to have their work corrected by a master, to read
carefully what they had to remember, and, to test their competence, to communicate what they had learnt to another student: in this way, oral practice and
classroom communication became part of the fabric of teaching and learning.[107]
Vernacular language-learning as explained in the manuals was a process which
mixed the textual encounter with oral performance: the reader who studied quietly
and learnt only to read was the exception, not the rule.

Early modern authors were divided on the place of speech in language-learning.
Writing in the early seventeenth century, the French teacher John Wodroephe
warned of the dangers of competence acquired through oral practice alone,
without the intervention of grammatical rules. To illustrate 'what Advantage hee
gaineth above him who thinketh to obtaine the said Tongue by the eare only',
Wodroephe gave the story of three sons of gentlemen who learnt more in six
months from Wodroephe's rule-based tuition than they had over four years in
Paris. He went on:

And sundry others have I helped who never saw France, and yet could talke,
reade, and write better language in one yeare, then those who have bene at Paris
two yeares, learning but the common phrase of the contrie, shaiking off a litle
paines to learne the rules.[108]

Wodroephe's insistence on rules to accompany oral experience is particularly
interesting because it betrays a concern not only with grammatically correct
speech but with the acquisition of a prestige variety. Similarly, de la Mothe warned
that those who learnt by listening to the common people of France 'cannot speake
but commonly and vulgarly, because their manner of speech and termes be
common and base, of a broken French'.[109] The kind of competence which became
increasingly valorized over the seventeenth century could only be acquired by a

[106] John Wodroephe, *The spared houres of a souldier in his travels. Or The True Marrowe of the
French Tongue, wherein is truely treated (by ordre) the Nine Parts of Speech. Together, with two rare, and
excellent Bookes of Dialogues...* (Dordrecht, 1623), p. 13.
[107] John Amos Comenius, *Porta linguarum trilinguis reserata et aperta. The gate of tongues unlocked
and opened, Or else A Seminarie or seed-plot of all Tongues and Sciences. That is, A short way of teaching
and thorowly learning within a yeare and halfe at the farthes, The Latin, English, French (and any other)
tongue, together with the ground and foundation of Arts and Sciences, comprised under an hundred
Titles, and a thousand periods*, trans. John Anchoran (London, 1631), pp. 159–60.
[108] Wodroephe, *Spared houres*, p. 7.   [109] De la Mothe, *French Alphabet*, p. 100.

combination of book and oral experience. Juan de Luna defended rules, even if they proved difficult for those who did not already have a knowledge of Latin: 'for not onely they make the way plainer and easier, but withall by their helpe, things once learned are not so easily forgotten, and things forgotten are easier remembred'. He went on to take aim at a worrying trend, writing that '[t]his erronious opinion, That it is best, to learne a language without rules, is maintained by many Teachers, who because they themselves neither know nor understand any, say, it is best learning a language by familiar discourse'.[110] For de Luna, this 'familiar discourse' had to be married with sound grammatical instruction and a good master's correct pronunciation for the student to gain adequate competence. His insistence that speech alone was not enough was not a privileging of written competence, but reflects a belief that the conversation manual should complement oral experience and practice. It was not a textual end point; instead, its pedagogical programme demanded that the words be performed orally and informed by what the pupil heard and learnt from other speakers. The exception to this rule was Giovanni Torriano, who argued that 'they who are last at speaking, speak the best and surest'.[111]

Like early modern teachers and learners, modern historians have been divided on the place of speech in early modern language pedagogy. Jason Lawrence overstates the primacy of reading and writing in early modern language pedagogy, and seems to relegate the acquisition of oral and aural competences to being a secondary accomplishment. He argues that 'The English desire to read Italian fluently in the sixteenth and early seventeenth centuries is predicated primarily on a specifically literary interest,' and sees instruction in pronunciation as only supplementary to the dialogues, arguing that

> [e]ven if the Italian character in the earlier dialogue has learnt to *speak* English by reading, the interlocutors in Florio's section on Italian grammar . . . seem to place the ability to speak the language accurately below the successful acquisition of a reading knowledge of it.[112]

Lawrence mentions Gabriel Harvey's marginalia in his copy of Florio, but does not comment on the fact that Harvey bemoans not having 'the mouth, and tongue' of an Italian, and not the hand or pen of one.[113] Harvey had noted the importance of spoken competence: reading in Scipione Lentulo's Italian grammar that 'the manner of pronouncing, cannot be shewed by writing: wherfore it is to be learned

---

[110] De Luna, *A short and compendious art*, 'An Advertisement necessary for the understanding of this Grammar'.

[111] Torriano, *Italian Reviv'd*, sig. [A4r.]

[112] Lawrence, *Who the devil*, pp. 5, 21–9 and *passim*.   [113] Ibid., p. 28.

of him that hath th'Italian tongue', Harvey scribbled the words 'viva voce' in the margin.[114] On the place of speech, Michael Wyatt comes closer to the reality suggested by conversational manuals when he argues that John Florio's inclusion of complex material from his opening chapters onwards 'reflects a pedagogical approach that values speaking above grammatical precision'.[115] While there were individuals who learnt Italian wholly or partly as a language to be read and written (Lawrence offers the example of William Drummond of Hawthornden), evidence from conversation manuals bears out the argument that speech and listening were fundamental to early modern vernacular linguistic pedagogy.[116] The *manières de langage* which were the medieval manuscript predecessors of the conversation manuals seem to have shared a preoccupation with the development of oral competence: in one text from 1396, writing was treated primarily as a means of recording spoken conversations, while appropriate speech was the main focus; in a series of fourteenth-century texts, the written material was accompanied by songs, which featured as pedagogical tools to complement a text which was focused on oral performance.[117] This was carried through into the printed conversation manual tradition.

Authors of conversation manuals worked hard to teach pronunciation, and readers worked hard to learn it. Authors employed a variety of textual strategies to recreate the sounds of words and letters on the page, from the tiny marks under letters used by Claudius Hollyband to indicate silent letters in French, to the renditions of English phrases in French phonetics attempted by Jacques Bellot, in a text aimed at French-speaking migrants arriving in Elizabethan London (see Figure 2.4).[118] John Eliot offered similar phonetic approximations in a small portion of his *Ortho-Epia Gallica*.[119] Some authors took a physiological approach, describing the physical movements of the mouth that would produce the requisite sounds—Giovanni Torriano wrote that the accented *a* in Italian would require 'a certaine jerke of the tongue' on the part of the speaker.[120] A curious section in

---

[114] Scipione Lentulo, *An Italian Grammer; written in Latin by Scipio Lentulo a Neapolitaine: and turned in Englishe: By H[enry]. G[rantham]* (London, 1575). California, Huntington Library, call number 62184, p. 17.

[115] Wyatt, *Italian Encounter*, p. 168.   [116] Lawrence, *Who the devil*, p. 11.

[117] Thérèse Bonin and Josette Wilburn, 'Teaching French Conversation: A Lesson from the Fourteenth Century', *The French Review* 51 (1977), pp. 188–96; Elizabeth Eva Leach, 'Learning French by Singing in 14th-Century England', *Early Music* 33 (2005), pp. 253–70. For editions of several *manières*, see Andres M. Kristol (ed.), *Manières de langage (1396, 1399, 1415)* (London: Anglo-Norman Text Society, 1995).

[118] For Hollyband's practice, see, for instance, Claudius Hollyband, *The French Littelton* (London, 1597); Hollyband, *A treatise for declining of verbes* (London, 1580). This seems to have become something of a trademark for Hollyband, appearing even in texts which seem unlikely to have been read aloud. See Gallagher, 'To heare it by mouth'.

[119] Eliot, *Ortho-Epia Gallica*, sig. Cr–C2v.

[120] Giovanni Torriano, *New and easie directions for attaining the Thuscan Italian tongue* (1639), p. 3.

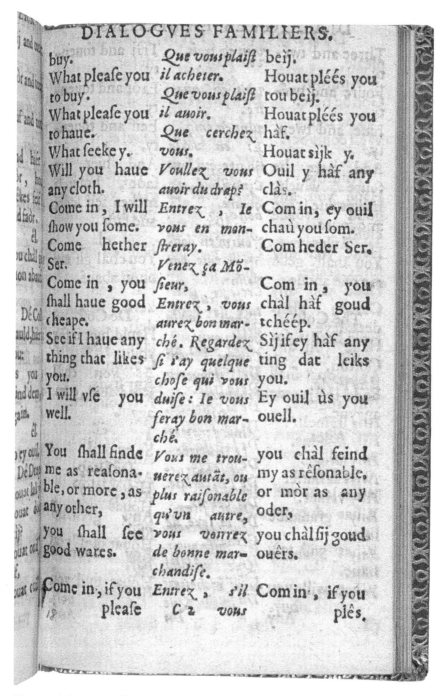

Figure 2.4 Jacques Bellot, *Familiar Dialogues* (London, 1586). Bellot printed his dialogues in parallel columns of English, French, and English in French phonetics

Torriano's *New and easie directions for attaining the Thuscan Italian tongue* (1639), borrowed and adapted from Lorenzo Franciosini, described itself as a 'Dictionarie', but was actually an attempt to offer rules for where the stress fell in Italian words depending on their endings, including an index of endings so that readers could easily look up the correct pronunciation of a new word.[121] In works like those of John Florio and César Oudin, accent marks indicated where stresses fell in words in Italian and Spanish.[122] Authors' efforts to make their printed texts more easily translatable into spoken utterance were matched by some readers' interventions in their books. One reader of John Florio's *Second Frutes* (1593) hand-marked the stresses in words like 'faréi', 'spauentéuoli', and 'leuárui' to aid with pronunciation. This reader also added their own phonetic renderings of the Italian sounds for an English reader, for instance, writing 'oo' and 'keea' above 'gucchia' or 'Lashio' in the margin next to the word 'lascio' (see Figures 2.5 and 2.6).[123] Annotations of this kind suggest a wider culture of reading for sound, and remind us that even where some conversation manuals did not make express provision for those who wished to speak their contents, readers could engage with and modify the text to serve their oral purposes.

Print was fundamentally insufficient for teaching another language, and authors often made a point of highlighting where the text's usefulness as text alone ran out. Authors of texts frequently referred to the natural deficiency of print in not being able to fully represent the sounds of spoken language, and offered compensating advice to their readers. De la Mothe warned his readers, 'do not thinke that my booke is able by it selfe to make you a good Frenchman'.[124] His remedy for this pedagogical deficit was practice with a native speaker:

> when you are pretily furthered in [the language], get you acquainted, if it be possible, with some French man, to the end you may practise with him, by daily conference together, in speech and talke, what you have learned. And if you be in place, where the Frenchmen have a Church for themselves, as they have in London, get you a French Bible, or a new Testament, and every day go both to their Lecture and Sermons. The one will confirme and strengthen your pronunciation, and the other cause you to understand when one doth speake[125]

---

[121] Torriano, *New and easie directions*, pp. 37–75.

[122] John Florio, *Queen Anna's New World of Words* (London, 1611); César Oudin, *A Grammar Spanish and English: or a briefe and compendious Method, teaching to reade, write, speake, and pronounce the Spanish Tongue* (London, 1622), for instance at pp. 216–17. A similar method is employed in the Portuguese materials published by 'A.J.' at the beginning of the eighteenth century: see Kemmler, 'The *Grammatica Anglo-Lusitanica*', p. 91.

[123] Cambridge University Library, Pet. B. 4. 35: John Florio, *Second Frutes* (London, 1593), pp. 2–4.

[124] De la Mothe, *French Alphabet*, 'An Epistle to the Reader'.   [125] Ibid.

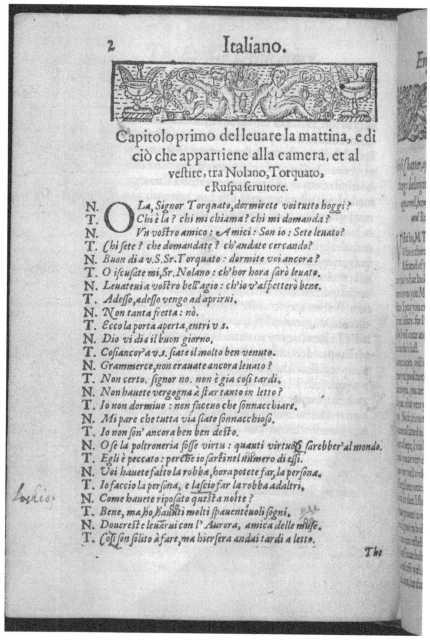

2   Italiano.

Capitolo primo del leuare la mattina, e di
ciò che appartiene alla camera, et al
veſtire, tra Nolano, Torquato,
e Ruſpa ſeruitore.

N. *O La, Signor Torquato, dormirete voi tutto hoggi?*
T.   *Chi è la? chi mi chiama? chi mi domanda?*
N.   *Vn voſtro amico: Amici: Son io: Sete leuato?*
T. *Chi ſete? che domandate? ch'andate cercando?*
N. *Buon di a v.S.Sr.Torquato: dormite voi ancora?*
T. *O iſcuſate mi, Sr. Nolano: ch'hor hora ſarò leuato.*
N. *Leuateui a voſtro bell'agio: ch'io v'aſpetterò bene.*
T. *Adeſſo, adeſſo vengo ad aprirui.*
N. *Non tanta fretta: nò.*
T. *Ecco la porta aperta, entri v s.*
N. *Dio vi dia il buon giorno,*
T. *Coſiancor'a v.s. ſiate il molto ben venuto.*
N. *Grammerce, non erauate ancora leuato?*
T. *Non certo, ſignor no. non è gia coſi tardi.*
N. *Non hauete vergogna à ſtar tanto in letto?*
T. *Io non dormiuo: non faceuo che ſonnacchiare.*
N. *Mi pare che tutta via ſiate ſonnacchioſo.*
T. *Io non ſon' ancora ben ben deſto.*
N. *O ſe la poltroneria foſſe virtu: quanti virtuoſi ſarebber'al mondo.*
T. *Egli è peccato: perche io ſarèi nel nùmero di eſſi.*
N. *Voi hauete falto la robba, hora potete far, la perſona.*
T. *Io faccio la perſona, e laſcio far la robba adaltri.*
N. *Come hauete ripoſato queſta notte?*
T. *Bene, ma ho hauùti molti ſpauenteuoli ſogni.*
N. *Doureſte leuarui con l' Aurora, amica delle muſe.*
T. *Coſi ſon ſolito à fare, ma hierſera andai tardi a letto.*

                                                        The

Figure 2.5 John Florio, *Florios second frutes* (London, 1591)

Source: Cambridge University Library, Pet.B.4.35, p. 2. Reproduced by kind permission of the Syndics of Cambridge University Library.

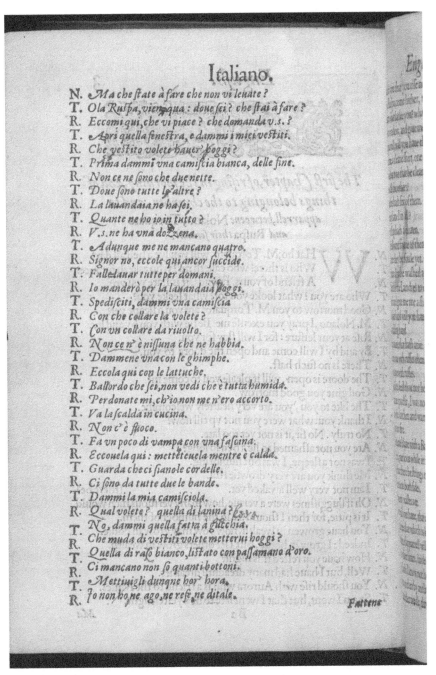

Figure 2.6 John Florio, *Florios second frutes* (London, 1591)

The anonymous compiler of *A plaine pathway to the French tongue* (London, 1575) wrote that

> for pronuntiation in this worke are contained brief rules, wherein if the learner occupieth him self, he shall nede no more to make him a perfect utterer of the speach, saving onely a little labour and leasure bestowed in the company and hearing of some Frenche man, without which no booke can throughlie instruct him[126]

Claudius Hollyband, always with one eye on commercial advantage, attempted to monetize the insufficiency of print, suggesting with regard to pronunciation that 'if those, which be in London, wil resort to Pauls churchyeard, to the signe of the golden Ball, they shall heare by mouth, to satisfie their owne minde'.[127] St. Paul's churchyard was the site of Hollyband's school. In Italian, Hollyband was just as circumspect about representing sounds in print: the sound of the letter Z, he said, could not be expressed on the page, meaning that 'it is needefull for the learner of the saide language, to heare it by mouth'.[128] Claude Mauger, the most prolific language teacher in Restoration London, admitted his own shortcomings: 'I confesse, that the Living Voice of a Master is better, then all that can be set down in writing.'[129] These author-teachers encouraged their students to go beyond the printed material and to engage with the language as spoken outside the text, though always bringing their knowledge of rules, forms, and basic language acquired from the manuals with them. The manual was meant to be used in dialogue with an oral world, and its prescriptions compared against the realities of speech.

Inside the covers of bilingual conversation manuals, the presentation of language-teaching material on the page changed over time and in dialogue with pedagogy and reading practices, with authors and printers eventually settling on a standard parallel-text format. The earliest printed language aids commonly employed interlinear rather than parallel translation—as, for instance, in Wynkyn de Worde's 1497 English-French manual (see Figure 2.7).[130] In this, they drew on the content and the presentation of their manuscript forebears, from Ælfric's *Colloquy* (a medieval text for the teaching of Latin, copies of which contain interlinear glosses in the vernacular) onwards.[131] The use of interlinear translation in language-learning materials did not disappear with the birth of print: rather, it

---

[126] Anon., *Plaine pathway*, A2r.

[127] Claudius Hollyband, *The Frenche Schoolemaister of Claudius Hollyband: Newly corrected* (London, 1582), sig. [A6v].

[128] Claudius Hollyband, *The Italian Schoole-maister* (London, 1597), sig. B3r.

[129] Claude Mauger, *True advancement of the French Tongue. Or A new Method, and more easie directions for the attaining of it, then ever yet have been published* (London, 1653), p. 6.

[130] [Wynkyn de Worde], *Here begynneth a lytell treatyse for to lerne Englysshe and frensshe* (London, 1497), sig. [A4r].

[131] Helmut Gneuss, 'The Study of Language in Anglo-Saxon England', *Bulletin of the John Rylands Library* 72 (1990), pp. 3–32. I would like to thank Kate Wiles for this reference. See also Caravolas, *La Didactique des langues*, pp. 101–2.

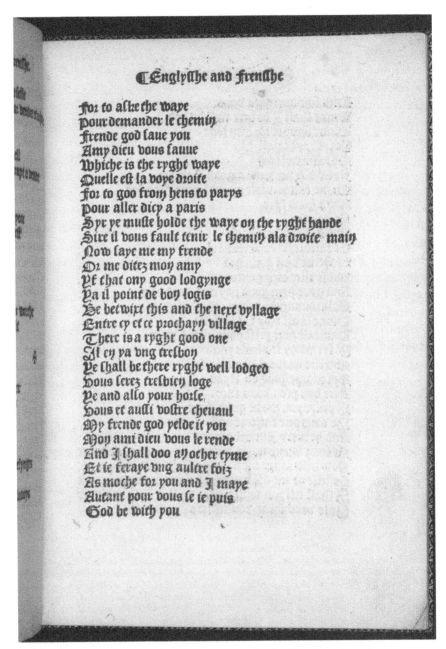

¶Englysshe and frensshe

For to aske the waye
Pour demander le chemin
Frende god saue you
Amy dieu vous sauue
Whiche is the ryght waye
Quelle est la voye droite
For to goo from hens to parys
Pour aller dicy a paris
Syr ye muste holde the waye on the ryght hande
Sire il vous fault tenir le chemin ala droite main
Now saye me my frende
Or me ditez moy amy
Yf that ony good lodgynge
Ya il point de bon logis
Be betwixt this and the next vyllage
Entre cy et ce prochayn village
There is a ryght good one
Il en ya vng tresbon
Ye shall be there ryght well lodged
Vous serez tresbien loge
Ye and also your horse
Vous et aussi vostre cheuaul
My frende god yelde it you
Mon ami dieu vous le rende
And I shall doo an other tyme
Et ie feraye vng aultre foiz
As moche for you and I maye
Autant pour vous se ie puis
God be with you

Figure 2.7 [Wynkyn de Worde], *Here begynneth a lytell treatyse for to lerne Englysshe and frensshe* (London, 1497)

Source: British Library, call number G.7570, sig. [A4r]. © The British Library Board.

remained a relatively common choice in printed conversation manuals up until around the middle of the sixteenth century. Interlinear translation can be found in mid-century manuals like *A Very necessarye boke both in Englyshce & in Frenche* (1554). It also appears in the *Boke of Englysshe, and Spanysshe* (1554), which is curious, because that text is based on the *Solenissimo vochabuolista*, a continental text whose other editions were arranged in parallel columns, suggesting there was a conscious choice made to rearrange the text for presentation in this way.[132] In the period before 1550, readers of English conversation manuals could encounter the interlinear arrangement as well its parallel-text equivalent in print. Still later, an author like John Wodroephe could employ a method that included interlinear translation and printed marginal annotation in order to try to convey information on meaning, pronunciation, and syntax all at once: the result is almost unusably confused, but it stands as a reminder that the parallel text form as a standard emerged only gradually from a combination of tradition and innovation in pedagogical print (see Figure 2.8). With the exception of rare outliers like the 1688 edition of Peter Berault's *A New, Plain, Short, and Compleat French and English Grammar*, authors of seventeenth- and eighteenth-century conversation manuals adopted the parallel-text form almost unanimously.

The triumph of the parallel-text conversation manual had its roots in Renaissance pedagogical practices. Double translation—the practice whereby a foreign language would be translated into English and then, after a period, translated back into the original, and the translations compared—was fundamental to sixteenth-century English humanist pedagogy.[133] Jason Lawrence's study of Italian language-learning and literary imitation in the period has argued convincingly for the importance of practices of translation to individuals' development of their own linguistic competence, as in the case of William Drummond of Hawthornden, who

---

[132]   The books I have found which use interlinear translation of dialogic material in whole or in part are as follows: Anon., *Here begynneth a lytell treatyse for to lerne Englysshe and Frensshe* (London, 1497), and a reissue, Anon., *Here is a good boke to lerne to speke French/Lytell treatyse for to lerne Englysshe and Frensshe* (London, 1500?); Wynkyn de Worde, *Here begynneth a lytell treatyse for to lerne Englysshe and Frensshe* (London, 1498?); Anon., *A lytell treatyse for to lerne Englysshe and Frensshe* (Antwerp, c.1530); Anon., *A Very necessarye boke both in Englyshce & in Frenche wherein ye mayst learne to speake & wryte Frenche truly in a litle space yf thou gyve thy mynde and diligence there unto* (London, 1550); Anon., *Lytell treatyse for to lerne Englysshe and Frensshe* (London, c.1553); Giles Du Wés, *An introductorie for to lerne to rede, to pronounce, and to speake Frenche trewly, compiled for the right high, excellent, and most vertuous lady, the lady Mary of Englande, doughter to our most gracious soverayn lorde kyng Henry the eight* (London, 1533?), and the editions of the same text published in 1540? and 1546?; Anon., *The boke of Englysshe, and Spanysshe* (London, 1554?). Andrew Boorde, *The fyrst boke of the introduction of knowledge* (London, 1555?), mixes parallel and interlinear translation depending on the length of the phrase; the same is true of the 1562 edition. A very late example is Peter Berault, *A New, Plain, Short, and Compleat French and English Grammar* (London, 1688).

[133]   The classic early modern English argument for double translation is found in Roger Ascham, *The Scholemaster* (London, 1570), though it was in use as a method before Ascham, being employed by John Cheke at Cambridge and by other mid-Tudor humanists. See William E. Miller, 'Double Translation in English Humanistic Education' *Studies in the Renaissance* 10 (1963), pp. 163–74; Kibbee, *For to speke Frenche trewely*, pp. 183–5; Howatt, *History of English Language Teaching*, pp. 24, 34.

The Pronounciation of the French tongue.   127

THIS small Worke of the Pronounciation (louing Countriman) will not be a litle profitable vnto thee, becaufe thou fhall find the true Nature of the french word engliſhed to thee ouer the top of it verbatim: and alſo the true phraſe thus marked(* on the lower Margen. Alſo the true Engliſh found in Syllables vpon the vpper Margent, where by thou mayeſt attaine to the right Pronounciation of the French with in the Page thus led by the Order of the [A, (B, (C, to leade thee there vnto; not omiting any Letter in the Orthographie ; but euen as the Frenches do truely write them themſelues; which ſhal be twice more Profit vnto thee, in learning it in this Manner , though tediouſly, as I confeſſe, then to follow the only doubtfull Tracke of the Phraſe, not knowing its true Nature; which ſundry [here to fore] haue taught ſparing the marrow of their famous Braines. But belieue me (if thou followeſt a generous Curioſitie for to learne to write thy Mind any where ſo wel as to ſpeake it) thou ſhalt not find thy Paines loſt. I deſire all Affable and humble Cenſurers, who haue tried both wayes (to wit Verbatim and phraſe) to tholorat this Faſhion of Doing, & conſider the Danger of thoſe who hazard to teach without Reaſon, to tell That Verbatim ſometymes muſt be had, becauſe it is requiſit, that it ſhould not be alwayes cloſed vp in a Phraſe, but ſhewed bare, as it fals very often then [nil thou wilt thou] thou muſt haue a coat to couer it, that is to ſay His true Signification, or elſe thou muſt leaue it , and run to the Dictionarie, and dazle thy eyes there a while, and be euen ſo wiſe as thou waſt before : for ſometymes they are not to be found at all in it , and ſometymes it will fall in ſome tenſe of ſome Mood which no Dictionary can yeald; yea euen thouſands. Thou haſt in this Booke all houſhold ſtuffe , and other pretty neceſſary words meete for thy dayly vſe in this Tongue. Alſo an Introduction to learne to frame all common and ordinary Phraſes pertaining to a houſe: as of Vituals dreſſing, voyaging through the land. Alſo the partes, and cloathing of a Man his body all in remarkable phraſes, where of I will ſhiew thee viuely , yea euery Member from the Crowne of the Head vnto the Foot, with either the Article, or the Pronowme for to leade the to the ſame in his right Gender: to wit [Le ſhewing thee when the Nowme is maſc. and (la when it is demonſtrated fe. with (Mon, and (Ma pronowmes in like ſorte [when they are requiſit) before the ſaid Nowmes. And as for the plurall, it is but adding this litle (s, which can alſo ſhiew thee when they are plurall ſeruing for both genders: and this [Maſc. and fem. to ſhiew thee when the Articles & Pronowmes do not preccede the Nowmes.

Our   helpe and Beginning be in the Name of God which hath made the
OSTRE aide et Commencement ſoit au Nom de Dieu qui a faict le
Heauen and the Earth, So be it.
Ciel   et la Terre, Ainſi ſoit il.
God giue me the * to him knew,   and alſo my ſelfe worthily.
Dieu me face la Grace de le B cognoiſtre [et auſſi moy meſme] dignement.   *Or God giue me the Grace (in phraſe) to
God: God the Father, God the Sone, and God the holy Ghoſt. The the   of God. know him; to wit the Lord.
Dieu: Dieu le Pere, Dieu le C Fils, et Dieu le ſaint Eſprit. La Trinté, le D Thrane de Dieu,
The   A   the   An Archangell, the   An Angell, the Lord.
Les Seraphins. Vn E Cherubins, les Cherubins. Vn Archange, les Archanges.   Vn Ange , les
A patriarke,   the
F Anges. Vn patriarche, les Patriarches.
A   the   An Apoſtle, the   An   the
Vn Prophete, les Prophetes. Vn G Apoſtre, les Apoſtres. Vn Euangiliſte, les Euangiliſtes.
A   the   The twelfe Apoſtles of our Lord,   Sauiour, and Redemtor
Vn Martyr, les Martyrs. Les Douze Apoſtres de noſtre Seigneur, H Sauueur , et Redemteur
fitting in heauen at the Right hand of God his Father.
Ieſus Chriſt   [aſſis au I Ciel) a la Dextre   de Dieu ſon Pere.
The Heauens, the   or the cope, or Scope. A   the   The Sunne, the Moone,
Les K Cieux, le Firmament, ou l' Eſtendue,   Vne Planette, les Planettes. Le Soleil, la Lune.
A Star, the The foure   The fire, the Aire, the water, and the Earth, or land, All the Earth
Vne M Eſtoile, les Eſtoiles. Lesquatre Elemës, le feu, l' Air, l'Eau, et la Terre. Toute la Terre,
or the Vniuerſall world.
ou l' Vniuers.
The world, the Sea, and the fishes. A Manthe   A woman, or wife, the.
Le Monde , la Mer, & n les Poiſſonſt Vn Homme , les Hômes. O Vne Femme, les Fêmes.
The 5. Senſes of: The ſight, the Hearing, the Smelling, the Taſt and the feeling.
Les p cinq Sens de Nature; La Veüe , l'Ouie, l'odeur , le Gouſt & le Taſte.
K 4   A or

Figure 2.8 John Wodroephe, *The spared houres of a souldier in his travels. Or the true marrowe of the French Tongue* (Dordrecht, 1623)

Source: Cambridge University Library, Bb*.2.15(C), p. 127. Reproduced by kind permission of the Syndics of Cambridge University Library.

learnt by comparing Italian books closely with their English translations.[134] The dialogues in some conversation manuals were used similarly: John Eliot, in his semi-satirical *Ortho-epia Gallica,* complained about language teachers whose 'order in teaching' was 'only to read some halfe side, and to construe it, which is no great matter'.[135] The 'construal' of a 'halfe side' refers to the blind translation of one column of text, as instructed by de la Mothe in his *French Alphabet* (first published in 1592). Once his reader had spent a good amount of time working through the sections on pronunciation and orthography, he urged them that 'when you can read truly, & pronounce perfectly, then go about to english it', checking their translation against the parallel column, and subsequently translating the same text back into French, and correcting it again. This was to be repeated several times a day and would, de la Mothe argued, lead the student to be able to read any book in French. After much practice of this kind, the student could progress to more difficult texts: de la Mothe encouraged them to buy a dictionary and use it to translate 'the hardest booke you can finde'.[136]

The parallel-text dialogues of the conversation manual brought the silent written exercise and the vocal world of the classroom together. Claudius Hollyband offered a glimpse into classroom practice (he taught both children and adults) in a dialogue from his *French Littelton*: 'Children, turne your lessons out of french into english: and then out of english into frenche: let us decline a noune and a verbe in french: how say you in french N: how do you call that in french?'[137] The teacher in his dialogues advised his pupils to '[r]ehearse after supper the lesson which you will learne to morrow morning: and read it six or seven times: then having said your prayers, sleepe upon it: you shall see that to morrow morning you will learne it easely, and soone, having repeated the same but twise'.[138] Oral practice and oral repetition of textual lessons was a useful method of memorizing and testing students' knowledge. The employment of oral translation exercises in Hollyband's noisy classroom is a reminder that, as Jennifer Richards argues in relation to Roger Ascham, double translation was 'a homosocial as well as a linguistic exercise': an activity that linked reading and writing to oral performance and social-pedagogical interaction.[139] Conversation manuals frequently feature teachers correcting their students' reading and recitation of

---

[134] Lawrence, *Who the devil*, pp. 6, 11–12.

[135] Eliot, *Ortho-Epia Gallica*, p. 5. For more on the satirical-pedagogical make-up of Eliot's text, see Frances Yates, 'The Importance of John Eliot's *Ortho-epia Gallica*', *Review of English Studies* 7 (1931), pp. 419–30; Frederic Hard, 'Notes on John Eliot and his *Ortho-epia Gallica*', *Huntington Library Quarterly* 1 (1938), pp. 169–87.

[136] I have used the edition of 1633 here: G.D.L.M.N. [G. de la Mothe], *The French Alphabet, teaching in a very short time, by a most easie way, to pronounce French naturally, to reade it perfectly, to write it truly, and to speake it accordingly. Together with The Treasure of the French tongue* (London, 1633), sig. [A7v].

[137] Claudius Hollyband, *French Littelton*, sig. [C5v].   [138] ibid. sig. [C6v].

[139] Richards, *Rhetoric and Courtliness*, p. 126. While Jason Lawrence is correct to argue that double translation 'has been almost entirely overlooked in critical accounts of sixteenth-century language-

conversation manual materials: in Edward Richardson's *Anglo-Belgica*, a governess admonishes her student, a young gentlewoman, for her oral rendition of a printed dialogue, saying 'You do not pronounce well,' 'You take no pains' (even more suggestively, the Dutch-speaking reader of one copy has annotated this section with some phonetic pronunciation notes on words in the English text (see Figure 2.9).[140] In Pierre Erondell's *French Garden*, a young female student named Fleurimond reads an exercise aloud, and is corrected on her pronunciation and delivery by her teacher, who urges her to 'speake somewhat lowder, to th'end I may heare if you pronounce well: say that worde againe'. The teacher picks up specific mistakes in pronunciation, asking 'Wherefore do you sound that s? Doe you not knowe that it must be left?'; he criticizes the speed at which the student reads, and even her physical performance of the activity of reading ('Hold your booke higher, or else set it on a cushen'). Having assessed his student's speech, the tutor proceeds to test her on questions of translation: 'Construe me, what is that? do you understand that? tell me the signification in English.'[141] The methods used by Fleurimond's teacher include reading aloud, the criticism of pronunciation, and extempore oral translation: Erondell, like Hollyband, was a working teacher, and it seems reasonable to assume that both meant their dialogues to reflect their teaching practice.[142] The dialogues of the conversation manuals written by them and by other teachers formed the foundation of a pedagogical method based on oral practice and performance.

What about less sophisticated conversation manuals, in particular those polyglot texts which offered little or no material on grammar or pronunciation, and whose texts were often seriously corrupt? These texts seem fundamentally impractical, and so their popularity in print markets throughout Europe demands an explanation. Could they actually be used as language aids? The significant historiographical problem posed by these manuals has recently been stated concisely by John Considine with regard to the *Solenissimo vochabuolista* text: '[it is] hard', writes Considine, 'to believe that anybody ever learned a language from it or made extended use of it for the purposes of communication across language barriers'. The text's lack of information on grammar and pronunciation, its limited vocabulary provision, and the corruption of the text over time—the English is frequently mangled—made it essentially impractical. Considine concedes that '[t]he numerousness of the editions of this dictionary implies that it was much read; but it must have been read just for the pleasure of seeing the world divided up by language,

---

learning techniques', it is important to note that this technique was not just a textual one: Lawrence, *Who the Devil*, p. 29.

[140]   Richardson, *Anglo-Belgica*, part II, pp. 87–8.
[141]   Peter Erondell, *The French Garden: for English Ladyes and Gentlewomen to walke in* (London, 1605), sig. [F8v].
[142]   Erondell to Elizabeth, Lady Hicks, 1 September 1613, British Library, Lansdowne MS 93, fol. 29r.

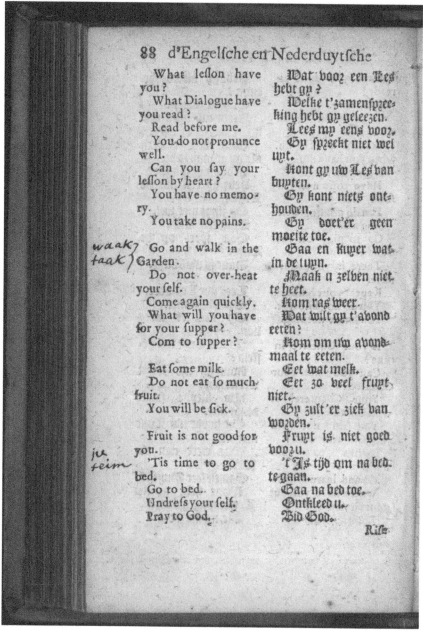

Figure 2.9 Edward Richardson, *Anglo-Belgica* (London, 1689), part II, p. 88

Source: Image courtesy of the Rare Book and Manuscript Library, University of Illinois at Urbana-Champaign.

and of being assured that the languages of Europe all divided it up alike'.[143] The *Solenissimo vochabuolista* is not the only conversation manual that presents this problem: Noël de Berlemont's *Colloquia* survives in many editions where the English text and certain other languages are corrupt—a predictable result when the type was being set by an individual who did not possess a working knowledge of six to eight languages, and was often working from an edition which was itself already corrupt. Within the polyglot manual tradition, this was recognized as problematic: Michael Sparke's 1639 edition of the Berlemont text noted proudly that previous editions had had corrupt English and Latin, and that 'I thought it a matter of good importance, to salve up this deformity, and to supply this defect.'[144] But in spite of this, Sparke (or his father) had seen the popularity of the book on the continent and was confident of its good reception in England, since he told the reader that 'I seeing the much use and good respect of it beyond the seas, thought it very fitting that it should be twice prest, to doe thee service.'[145]

Counter-intuitive though it may seem, the rudimentary layout of some of these polyglot conversation manuals need not, as Considine believes, have inhibited their usefulness, but may rather have enhanced it. To understand this, we need to look at how they were designed to be read. Crude and defective in printing though they often were, the manuals suggested and supported a utilitarian reading tied intimately to oral experience. Both the *Solenissimo vochabuolista* and the Berlemont appeared in editions which displayed six or more languages in parallel columns across two facing pages. The *Sex linguarum* (see Figure 2.10) advertised itself first and foremost as a vocabulary, with words in each language across two pages: Latin, French, and Spanish on the verso, and Italian (mislabelled as 'Vuelsch'), English, and German on the recto.[146]

The vocabulary takes up the vast majority of the book, giving way to basic phrases or elements of them, presented as in Figure 2.10. The six-column arrangement may be awkward, but actually allows for the manual to be used by a reader without any grounding in the grammar or syntax of the target language. This arrangement allows for—or, rather, insists on—the splitting up of expressions into discrete elements which can be easily compared across two pages. This leaves the reader with a toolkit of phrases which, along with the vocabulary—which is arranged not alphabetically but, like the phrases, topically—can be put together to form rudimentary sentences. In the *Solenissimo vochabuolista* text, both words and phrases alike are presented as units to be abstracted and recombined

---

[143] Considine, 'Narrative and Persuasion', p. 200.

[144] Anon., *New Dialogues or Colloquies, and A little Dictionary of eight Languages* (London: printed for E. G[riffin] for Michael Sparke junior ... 1639), sig. A4r. In the 1637 edition which preceded this, Sparke (or perhaps his father) declared that 'It spake the Latin, French, and Dutch well before, but the English too grosse, which is here refined': Anon., *English, Latine, French, Dutch, Schole-master*, 'To the Reader'.

[145] Anon., *English, Latine, French, Dutch, Schole-master*, 'To the Reader'.

[146] Here, I am working from the Venice text of 1541: *Sex linguarum, Latinae, Gallicæ, Hispanicæ, Italicæ, Anglicæ, et Teutonice, dilucidissimus dictionarius ...* (Venice, 1541).

Latinisch.	Frantzosisch.	Spanisch.	Vuelsch.	Englisch.	Teütsch.
Meo more	Selon mon acoustumance	Ami manera	A mio modo	of my facion	nach meine will
Fac secundum sensum meum	Faictez selon mon sens	Haza mi volum tad	Faa mio senno	do after mi mynde	thu nach mei nen sinne
Nolo	Ie ne vueil pas	No quiero	No voglio	Il will not	ich will nit
quare non vis	Pourquoyne voulez vous point	Por que neque tes	Perche non vol	wherfore wilte thou not?	Warumb nit
Non placet mihi	il ne me plaist pas	No me plaze	Non place	il plaseth me not	es gefelt mir nit
Bene placet mihi	il me plaist bien	Bien me plaze	Si place bene	il plaseth me well	es gefelt mir wol
Sum deceptus	Ie suis trompe	Engñado	Io so no stato in gannato	I am begiled	ich byn betro gen
A quo	Dequi	De quien	Da chi	of whom	von wem
A nebulone quodam	Duug belistre	De vn vellaco	Da vn poltrone	of a knave	von einem bu ben
Expecta	Attendez	Espera	Indugia	abyde	harrbeyth
Faciam ego	Iaulteffe mai faire	Dexa me hazer	lassa fare a me	let me doit	lass mich thum
Est homo fiu sensus	Cest ung homme de son sens	Cabecado	Egli di sua testa	It is a man of his mynde	er ist eines synns oder kopffs
Multum admiror in faciendo huj tuj modi rem	le mesmerueille en faisant telle chose	Me parece muy estraño hazer se maiantes cosas	Me pare molto strano a fare simile cosse	I marvell sore in doynge soch a thinge	es nimpt mich fast wunder ein sollich ding zu thon also thes
Ita est	il est ainsi	Assyes	Colista	It is so	wer bette das glaube
Quis hoc crede didisset	qui cutceru cela	quien lo creysse	Chi hauasse cre do quosto	who wold haue beleued it	es ist mir layd sein ding
Doleo de sua etsi spsius	Cepoyse moy de tes choses	Duelo me de sus hechos	Mi rincresce di fatti suoi	I am sory for his dedis	solt geduilt haben
Satis patientes	Ayez patience, ce nest pas vray	Ten patientia	habiate patientia	be patient	es ist nit war
Non est verum	il ne men sem blepas	No es verdad	None vero	It is not true	ich meine nit das
Non mihi videtur		Me paresce de no	Mi pare di no	methinke not	es also sey

L iij

Figure 2.10 A sample section from *Sex Linguarum* (Venice, 1541)

according to the situation. The Berlemont text faces a similar issue but a greater challenge, since where the *Sex linguarum* showed primarily small phrases and items of vocabulary, the *Colloquia* contains dialogues with sentences and phrases which frequently cross over into multiple lines. In this case, the multi-column format becomes a pedagogically useful element rather than a simple restriction. Even where the compiler attempts to show phrases too long to fit on a single line, these are frequently split up in such a way that the elements or phrases that make up a whole sentence are often presented discretely, as we see in Figures 2.11 and 2.12. The arrangement of the text may seem haphazard until it becomes clear that it has been arranged so that equivalent phrases within sentences are on the same line. The Latin has clearly been wrenched so that it fits more exactly the word orders of the surrounding European vernaculars; this can only be because the text was designed with this kind of utility in mind. The reader could read and learn the contextualized dialogues if they felt they were necessary, but they could also strip down longer sentences and phrases for parts—mouthfuls of language— to be reassembled as the situation demanded. Rather than being essentially unusable, as Considine deems the *Sex linguarum*, the form assumed by these small multi-column polyglot texts actually enhanced their usability, particularly given that they imagined a user who needed to be able to express themselves in six or more languages, and hence could not normally be expected to have a solid grasp of grammar and syntax in them all. While the competence that these texts allowed their readers to exercise had little of the refined language found in other manuals, it was utilitarian and adaptable to different situations.

Another hint as to the anticipated usage of these manuals is in the fact that their vocabularies and phrases are organized not alphabetically but topically—the 'ono- masiological' arrangement discussed in Werner Hüllen's work on dictionaries.[147] This was an arrangement found in varying forms across early modern printed conversation manuals—many texts embedded vocabulary lists into dialogues, placing all of the terms one might need to use to talk about clothing in a dialogue set at a tailor's shop, for instance. This topical arrangement reflects an ideal of situational utility which is found throughout the corpus of early modern conver- sation manuals but is at its purest in the polyglot texts. These texts are perhaps the closest to the modern phrasebook—they contained little or no significant peda- gogical programme beyond their vocabulary and phrases, and were designed to be hand-held and applicable to multiple situations by literate readers with no prior understanding of the languages they taught.

The authors of conversation manuals wanted their readers to practise a form of reading which looked outwards from the text—these were books whose information was waiting to be activated by experience in the social, oral world. In the same way

---

[147] Hüllen, *English Dictionaries, 800–1700, passim.*

Flamen.	Anglois,	Latin.
mijn moeder,	my mother/	mea mater,
ende al tghefelfchap.	and all the companie.	& vobis omnibus.
M. Ian,	M. John/	M.Ioannes,
van vvaer comdij?	from whence com pou?	vnde aduenis?
vvaer hebdij	wheare haue pou	vbi tu moratus es
foo lange ghebeyt,	tarryed fo long?	tamdiu,
vvuerom comdij fo laet?	wherfore com pou fo la-	cur ades tam ferò?
ift yvel ghedaen?	pe it well don? (te?	hoccine rectè factum eft?
ick hadde v beuolen	I bid you	iufferam tibi
te comen	to com	vt redires
te vier hueren,	at fower of the clock/	hora quarta,
het is nu	pt is now	nunc proxima eft
by den feffen:	by fir:	fexta:
feght my nu	tell mee now	dic mihi
vvaer ghy gevveeft hebt?	wheare pou haue ben?	vbi fueris?
vvant ghy hebt langhe	for pou haue ben long	nam diu iam
vvter fcholen ghevveeft,	out of the fchoole/	abfuifti à fchola,
dat vveet ick vvel:	that knowe I well:	fat fcio;

Fançois.	Espagnol.	Italien.
ma mere,	mi madre,	mia madre,
& toute la compagnie.	y a toda la compañia.	& tutta la compagnia.
M. Iean,	M. Iuan,	M. Giouanni,
d'ou venez vous?	de donde vienes?	d'onde vieni?
ou auez vous	adonde te has	doue fei
arrefté fi longuement,	detenido tanto,	reftato tanto,
pourquoy venez vous fi	Porque vienes tan tarde?	perche vieni fi tardi?
eft-ce bien faict? (tard?	es bien hecho?	è quefto ben fatto?
ie vous auois commandé	yo te auia mandado	ti haueua comandate
de venir	que veniefles	di venir
à quatre heures,	à quatro horas,	à quattro hore,
il eft maintenant	y ahora es	hor ne fono
pres de fix:	cerca de las feys:	quafi fei:
dites moy maintenant	di me ahora	dimmi hora
ou vous auez efté,	à do has eftado,	doue fei ftato?
car vous auez longuement	porque mucho ha	perche è affai
efté hors de l'efcole,	que falifte de la efcuela,	che fei fuor di fchuola,
cela fçay-ie bien:	eflo yo lo fe bien:	io'l fo bene:

C 3

Figures 2.11 & 2.12 Noel de Berlemont, *Colloquia cum dictionariolo sex linguarum : Teutonicae, Anglicae, Latinae, Gallicae, Hispanicae, & Italicae* (Antwerp, 1583), sig. C2v–C3r. –Cote : FB 926 128

Source: Tours, Bibliothèque Universitaire, Fonds Ferdinand Brunot – Bibliothèques Virtuelles Humanistes, CESR, Tours.

that Stefano Guazzo argued that civil conversation could not be taught as a set of precepts but had to be learnt through social practice in the world, so too did conversation manual authors accept their own shortcomings and insist on a reading of the world outside which would inform the reading of the text.[148] One comparable genre might be the early modern ballad: as Christopher Marsh argues, it is difficult to understand the bare printed text of a ballad without an insight into 'the sound of print': how it was performed and heard, and in what social contexts.[149] This brings us back to Ralph Thoresby, with whom this chapter began, and to his use of a 'book for the language'. By combining the study of a conversation manual with his careful observation of the realities of urban life, his lodging with a Dutch-speaking family, and some private schooling in the language, Thoresby could hope achieve a competence in Dutch that equipped him to use the language in social and professional contexts. The time he spent at the 'Verke-mart' (Varkensmarkt, or pig market) in Rotterdam was typical of this kind of learning: he noted that he had spent this period 'in the town, observing the customs, &c'. By 'observing the customs' at work in the marketplace, he could supplement the language learnt at school and in his manual with the experience of a space in which negotiation was not a formal script but a variable social performance incorporating variations in tone, gesture, and behaviour as well as the linguistic material found in a manual's dialogues. Observing it critically allowed him to supplement the linguistic and social primer of the manual with personal sensory experience, to test the knowledge of the books and of the schoolroom against the realities of the marketplace. When, in July, the family he stayed with (a foreign-language residence was another environment rich with educational potential) had praised him, it was for a competence derived not from a purely textual study, but from his usage of the conversation manual as part of a holistic pedagogy which brought experience of the social realities of language use and the sounds of the language itself to bear on the 'intent' study of the raw textual material. It was the pedagogical practice these manuals themselves demanded: the complementary reading of environment and text.

Conclusions

The conversation manual was a significant genre in early modern print, and one which underwent growth and development over the course of the sixteenth and seventeenth centuries. This chapter has charted the rise of the genre in English print, looking at provisions for different languages which were often tied to political developments as well as fashionable trends. It has sketched a typology

---

[148] On Guazzo and civil conversation, see Richards, *Rhetoric and Courtliness*, p. 24 and *passim*.
[149] Christopher Marsh, 'The Sound of Print in Early Modern England: The Broadside Ballad as Song', in Crick and Walsham (eds.), *The Uses of Script and Print*, p. 175.

of the conversation manual, and traced the ways in which developments in form drew on and influenced trends in language pedagogy. Having offered a picture of the growing trade in conversation manuals and the evolution of a genre, it has reconstructed ways of reading different kinds of conversation manual, resulting in a clearer picture than we have hitherto possessed of why these texts were produced, and what kind of usage they were meant for. The early modern conversation manual was not just a text of the scholarly and literary contexts which it has inhabited in much previous work, but existed and was used beyond, in the oral, sociable world which it drew on and was intended to feed back into. Following on from this picture of the trade in conversation manuals and the ways in which they were meant to be used, it is time to look more closely at the material they contained. In the Introduction, I argued that the early modern ideal of linguistic competence was fundamentally a social one, and that we should think less about one single ideal of competence, and more about multiple, variable, situational, social competences. Chapter 3 will look at a variety of competences with which different early modern conversation manuals attempted to equip their readers.

3

To Be 'Languaged'

Early Modern Linguistic Competences

Introduction

During his travels through Europe in the 1590s, Henry Wotton—who would later make his name as a diplomat in Venice—wrote home with a list of the 'advertisers of occurrences' he had encountered and would recommend as sources to his contacts at home. Among these was the multilingual son of the grammarian and reformed minister, Scipione Lentulo, whom he had encountered in the northern Italian town of Chiavenna. The son, who had 'been brought up most part of his life in England', was now resident in Bern, from where he could supply political information, being 'a man well travelled and languaged'.[1] In early modern English, to be 'well languaged' could mean being a skilled orator or user of one's native tongue, but it could also—as in the case of the younger Lentulo—refer to competence in multiple languages.[2] From the councillors of state who weighed the qualifications of potential intelligencers to members of trading companies who sought information about the experience of new factors, early modern people observed and interrogated each other's linguistic abilities. Those who spoke imperfectly or incorrectly could be subject to censure or ridicule: like courtesy texts, conversation manuals were deeply invested in the ideals of competent speech for a diverse group of readers.[3]

Linguistic competence has received relatively little attention as a historical category. How people spoke played into their social status, their cultural cachet, and their economic standing. Competent speech might involve a command of vernacular languages and ancient tongues, the use of slang, jargon, and dialect, the ability (or incapacity) to perform deference and superiority, and could be determined in part by the bodies from which speech emanated. We know that words had power in early modern Europe—power to determine reputation and credit, power to persuade and to rile—and it took linguistic (and often multilingual) competence to negotiate these noisy polyglot societies. Competence could be an

---

[1] Logan Pearsall Smith (ed.), *The Life and Letters of Sir Henry Wotton*, vol. 1 (Oxford: Clarendon, 1907), pp. 299–300.

[2] The *Oxford English Dictionary* has this meaning in use from the fourteenth century onwards.

[3] Thomas Hoby, *The Courtyer of Count Baldessar Castilio divided into foure bookes* (London, 1561), sig. Yy4r.

attribute, an accomplishment, and an asset: it mattered to early modern speakers and language-learners, and it should matter to us.

Linguistic competence is not—and never was—a simple binary between fluent and not: the kinds of language learnt can vary wildly from speaker to speaker, depending on their needs and the circumstances of their study. Heidi Brayman Hackel suggested the replacement of a distinction between the literate and illiterate with an understanding that there were 'multiple literacies and illiteracies' in early modern English societies.[4] Just as there were multiple literacies in early modern England, so too were there multiple linguistic competences: from the technical seagoing jargon mastered by Edward Coxere in Dutch to more refined courtly speech; and from the market talk of factors and traders to the near-native competence demanded of dissimulators and spies.[5] As Phil Withington argues, the *habitus* appropriate for speech and behaviour in one kind of company could be unusable elsewhere, with the skilled speaker requiring a range of competences in order to speak and be heard in different companies and different situations.[6] This maps onto the idea of the 'linguistic repertoire', as put forward by J. A. Fishman: a speaker's 'linguistic repertoire' is the sum of the different varieties available to them.[7] Even a 'monoglot' Englishman of the early modern period might have had a varied and complex linguistic repertoire, involving competence in the dialect of his home town, the language he used on the streets of London, the jargon of his trade or craft, the slang picked up in military service, the private and intimate languages spoken with children, a spouse, or elderly parents, and so forth. For English-speakers embedded in polyglot contexts, from Norwich to Nuremberg, their linguistic repertoire embraced yet more varieties, coloured by the worlds in which they moved.

Printed conversation manuals offered materials from which a speaker might begin to build a linguistic repertoire of their own. As such, they are a unique source for thinking about the multiple competences available to each early modern learner of languages. From their beginnings in print near the end of the fifteenth century, these multilingual primers addressed themselves to a wide and

---

[4] Heidi Brayman Hackel, *Reading Material in Early Modern England* (Cambridge: Cambridge University Press, 2005), p. 59. See also Alexandra Halasz, *The Marketplace of Print: Pamphlets and the Public Sphere in Early Modern England* (Cambridge: Cambridge University Press, 1997), p. 83. Compare Keith Thomas, 'The Meaning of Literacy in Early Modern England', in G. Baumann (ed.), *The Written Word: Literacy in Transition* (Oxford: Oxford University Press, 1986), pp. 99–100.

[5] E. H. W. Meyerstein (ed.), *Adventures by Sea of Edward Coxere* (Oxford: Clarendon, 1945), pp. 7–21. Thomas Palmer wrote that intelligencers needed '[t]o speak singularly the tongues, that may stand them in stead in that Countrey out of which they must gather intelligence, and to imitate the common gestures and behaviour of those nations, to cloke their purposes the more artificially': Thomas Palmer, *An Essay of the Meanes how to make our Travailes, into forraine Countries, the more profitable and honourable* (London, 1606), pp. 4–5.

[6] Phil Withington, *Society in Early Modern England: The Vernacular Origins of Some Powerful Ideas* (Cambridge: Polity, 2010), pp. 182–3.

[7] J. A. Fishman, 'The Sociology of Language', in Pier Paolo Giglioli (ed.), *Language and Social Context: Selected Readings* (Harmondsworth: Penguin, 1980), p. 47.

varied audience, from 'artisans and women' to merchants and princesses.[8] They promised different outcomes, from commercial success to individual transformation.[9] Conversation manuals showed speech in action: by representing a dialogue or conversation with multiple voices, the author of the conversation manual could show the codes of civility, courtliness, or politeness being followed—but also being challenged, debated, and broken. The learner who used these dialogues was not just educated to mouth phrases at particular points, but had access to codes of conversational propriety, strategies for coming out on top in bargains and arguments, and ideologies of power and repression. This chapter uses multilingual conversation manuals to explore early modern linguistic competences. What were the elements of competent speech in this period? How were different individuals and groups in society expected to speak, and how far did language pedagogies draw on or react against this? When language-learners of different social backgrounds used these books, what did they learn?

What can we say of the speech found in these manuals? It cannot be argued that they represent real speech taken down verbatim: these are always idealized and often unrealistic depictions of conversations. Even where manuals aim to reproduce the patterns of everyday speech, the printed word struggles to represent crucial elements of face-to-face conversation, like gesture, tone of voice, and accent. Linguists working in historical pragmatics, however, have argued that, in spite of their being idealized and imaginary, these dialogues paint an unusually clear picture of the language of the early modern conversational encounter.[10] Birte Bös argues that 'the aim of coursebooks is to teach spoken discourse...texts of this genre are bound to natural speech situations, and consequently the pragmatic relevance in the dialogues is probably higher than in other texts', making them the best possible sources for the language used in these encounters.[11] For Monika

---

[8] The *Solenissimo vochabuolista* text was addressed to artisans and women: Alda Rossebastiano, *Antichi vocabolari plurilingui d'uso popolare: la tradizione del 'Solenissimo Vochabuolista'* (Turin, 1984). Giovanni Torriano dedicated his early work to the Levant Company: Giovanni Torriano, *The Italian Tutor, or a new and most compleat Italian Grammer* (London, 1640). Giles du Wès's French manual was initially compiled for the use of Mary Tudor: Giles Du Wès, *An introductorie for to lerne to rede, to pronounce, and to speake Frenche trewly: compyled for the ryghte hygh, excellent, & moste vertuous lady, the lady Mary of Englande, doughter to our mooste gracious soverayne lorde kynge Henry the eight* (London, 1545?).

[9] The Berlemont polyglot manual asked 'How many are ther becom ryche, without the knoweledg of diures languages?': Anon., *Colloquia et dictionariolum septem linguarum, Belgicae, Anglicae, Teutonicae, Latinae, Italicae, Hispanicae, Gallicae* (Venice, 1606), sig. A5v. John Florio announced his intention 'of naturall Englishmen, to dye vs into artificiall Italians': John Florio, *Florio his firste Fruites* (London, 1578), fol. 106r.

[10] Jonathan Culpeper and Merja Kytö, *Early Modern English Dialogues: Spoken Interaction as Writing* (Cambridge: Cambridge University Press, 2010), pp. 3, 6, 9–17. On the relationship between manuals and spoken French and Italian, see Edgar Radtke, *Gesprochenes Französisch und Sprachgeschichte: Zur Rekonstruktion der Gesprächskonstitution in Dialogen französischer Sprachlehrbücher des 17. Jahrhunderts unter besonderer Berücksichtigung der italienischen Adaptionen* (Tübingen: Max Niemeyer Verlag, 1994).

[11] Birte Bös, '*What do you lacke? what is it you buy?* Early Modern English Service Encounters', in Susan Fitzmaurice and Irma Taavitsainen (eds.), *Methods in Historical Pragmatics* (Berlin and New York: de Gruyter, 2007), p. 224.

Becker, the fundamentally practical purpose of these books argues for the close-ness of their dialogues to actual, usable speech, since 'they contain to a high degree features of actual spoken language'.[12] This line of reasoning is followed by Jonathan Culpeper and Merja Kytö, who follow Werner Hüllen, and suggests that while these dialogues need to be approached with caution, they have some-thing to tell us about situations of oral encounter.[13] Anna Bryson's critique of Norbert Elias's reading of courtesy manuals is helpful here: she argues that while it is impossible to read an entire 'affective structure' from materials of this kind, 'it is more fruitful to approach them as more or less reliable representations of codes'.[14] Following these approaches, I would suggest that while these are not representations of actual speech, they are still useful as representations of the kinds of language deemed necessary for different speakers in different situations. They carry informa-tion about the rules and ideologies governing speech, and about what early modern writers and readers believed competence in languages could do.

Conversation manuals can offer a window into the pedagogical needs of their readers, or into what was considered necessary to be competent by a particular teacher of a particular language at a particular time. That said, the long afterlives of certain manuals discussed in Chapter 2 suggest that we need to be cautious about assuming that individual texts could only speak to their time. Evidently, there were continuities in what authors and publishers considered to be necessary in a conversation manual: bargaining dialogues may change to include new commodities, for instance, but their frameworks remain relatively static. Else-where, texts change with the times: some manuals reflect debates about ceremony, compliment, and ritual, while others respond to contemporary political events, such as the revocation of the Edict of Nantes or the accession of a foreign monarch. Common topics could be treated differently depending on the audience addressed by a particular manual. And while an understanding of and adjustment to cultural differences was a central part of early modern travel, we will see that this was not always the business of the conversation manual. Strictures on the extent to which travellers were expected to adapt to local behaviours and customs, combined with the potential for dangerous transformations—to new faiths or affected fashions—meant that some manuals flattened the differences between English and continental cultures, at least to some extent. Other manuals, particu-larly those aimed at immigrants to England, were more forthright in their presentation of cultural difference, and more forceful in their arguments for integration and assimilation.

---

[12] Monika Becker, '"Yf ye wyll bergayne wullen cloth or othir merchandise..." Bargaining in Early Modern Language Teaching Textbooks', *Journal of Historical Pragmatics* 3 (2002), p. 275.
[13] See Culpeper and Kytö's discussion of Hüllen, *Early Modern English Dialogues*, pp. 43–4.
[14] Bryson, *From Courtesy to Civility*, p. 12.

In this book's Introduction, I argued that the early modern ideal of linguistic competence was fundamentally social and oral. This chapter investigates the pedagogical materials that attempted to inculcate these aspects of competence. I look first at the question of status and deference in conversation manuals, exploring how the manuals prepared students to present themselves and to adapt their behaviour to the social status of others in an intensely hierarchized world. Turning to the kinds of competence suggested for women, I explore how strictures on female speech were reinforced or challenged by the material of conversation manuals, and argue that certain pedagogical programmes aimed at female learners were designed to restrict not only the topics they spoke on but also their freedom to move in the world. I examine the ways in which conversation manuals explored ritual language and behaviours, and also modelled their break-down. Turning to the manuals' presentation of commercial material like bargaining dialogues and lists of coins and commodities, I argue that they attempted to merge linguistic resources with the kinds of knowledge which would advantage their readers in commercial situations. Finally, I consider the materials aimed at immigrant populations in sixteenth- and seventeenth-century England, and show how these texts put forward models of immigrant speech and argued in a unique and important way for their readers' assimilation into English society. The elements of competence covered in this chapter have been selected in order to give a sense of both the changes and the continuities in the manuals' presentations of linguistic competence over nearly two centuries. The evidence shows clearly that there were some elements deemed central to being competent in a foreign language, while others changed over time as codes of behaviour and speech shifted around them.

The Prince and the Porter: Expressing Status and Deference

Early modern hierarchies of status, wealth, and gender were reflected in language. The ways an individual spoke and was spoken to helped to determine their place in society; management of one's speech and of one's place in conversation was important if one was to improve or maintain one's status. As such, a crucial element of competence was the ability to position oneself within socially varied company. Conversation manuals' provision for social interaction inculcated two separate but interdependent skills. Firstly, and obviously, they attempted to equip the speaker with the necessary language to negotiate verbally the hierarchies of early modern Europe. Secondly, the material they provided in dialogues and vocabularies was frequently presented in a way that could help a reader to view wider society critically and to understand the ways in which status, deference, and reputation were negotiated in early modern conversations. Put simply, they offered their readers the equipment to address a foreign society, but also to understand (and to harness) the forces behind it.

Speakers of early modern English were familiar with a language which distinguished between formal and informal forms (like 'vous' and 'tu' in both early modern and modern French). In English, the 'thou' form was in decline, with people more often playing it safe and using the formal 'you'.[15] A similar situation prevailed in many conversation manuals, where incidences of the 'tu' form are relatively rare, even where elite characters are dealing with social inferiors, probably in order to ensure that readers would not end up accidentally causing offence in travel. Recognizing that pronoun choice was not the only way to express superiority or deference in conversation, some manuals gave explicit instruction on how to address different sorts of people, including some description of different titles in use. In 1687, Heinrich Offelen offered an explanation of German forms of address:

> Note, That the Germans use most commonly the word *Herr*, or *Mein Herr*, answering to the Italian *Vosignoria*, and the Spanish *Vuestra Merced*, and the Third Person of the Singular Number with it . . . Sometimes they use the Second Person of the Plural Number, when they speak to Servants, or other common sort of People; as Peasants, and Tradesmen, and to a Boy, or to some body to whom they will give no Respect at all, in the Second Person of the Singular Number.

Offelen broke down his taxonomy of address with examples: a tradesman who had made his masterpiece might be asked '*Meister Henrich, wo gehet ihr hin?* Master Henry, whither are you going?'; one who was still a journeyman or a labourer would get '*Henrich, wo seid ihr gewesen?* Henry, Where have you been?'; while a 'Boy' might be bluntly addressed with '*Jung, kom her, Butz mir die Schu.* Boy, come hither, clean my Shooes.'[16] This was grammatical instruction tied closely to the social context of its usage.

Titles were important in writing, too, and a number of texts provided sample letters or sample forms of address for correspondents of differing status. In 1554, *A very profitable boke to lerne the maner of redyng, writyng, & speakyng english & Spanish* argued that '[t]hese wordes that folowe must bee used in superscripcion of letters, but you muste take heede that to every person be geven that, that is convenient'. The anonymous text offered terms of address including '[t]o the

---

[15]   Charles Barber, *Early Modern English* (Edinburgh: Edinburgh University Press, 1997), pp. 152–7; Dick Leith, *A Social History of English* (London: Routledge and Kegan Paul, 1983), pp. 82–4, 106–110; Bryson, *From Courtesy to Civility*, p. 166. For a sociolinguistic approach to early modern pronouns, see Terttu Nevalainen and Helena Raumolin-Brunberg, *Historical Sociolinguistics: Language Change in Tudor and Stuart England* (London: Longman, 2003), pp. 118–21, 141–2, 150–4, and *passim*.

[16]   Heinrich Offelen, *A Double Grammar for Germans To Learn English; and for English-Men To Learn the German-Tongue* (London, 1687), part II, p. 132. For an even more rigorous description of variations between titles, see César Oudin, *A Grammar Spanish and English: or a briefe and compendious Method, teaching to reade, write, speake, and pronounce the Spanish Tongue* (London, 1622), pp. 225–7.

honourable', '[t]o the man of singular goodnesse', and '[t]o the moste noble'.[17] The *Grooten vocabulaer* (1639), a Dutch-English text based on the Berlemont original, made the same point: 'These words following one shall use for to write without upon letters-missive: but one must looke well to it, that hee attribute to every person, such wordes as to him do belong,' warning that the English translations offered were literal translations of the Dutch and not to be used.[18] Heinrich Offelen, ever keen that his readers should address people appropriately, presented a breakdown of German-speaking society by the titles that each member was due, beginning with the emperor ('Euer keyserliche Majestaet') and an ecclesiastical elector ('Euer Churfürstliche Durchleucht', if a prince by birth; otherwise, 'Euer Churfürstliche gnaden'), and thus downwards through the ecclesiastical and secular hierarchy, as far as a doctor in law ('Euer gestrenge or Mein hoch-geehrter Herr'), a parson ('Euer Ehr-würden'), and a merchant ('Mein vielgeehrter Herr'). This was followed up with a similar, if shorter, list of titles for 'some Ladies of great Quality'.[19] Oral and scribal competences both required an understanding of social hierarchy and the acceptable language to use at various points within it.[20]

Not all conversation manuals offered such explicit instruction on register, preferring rather to show it in use in their situational dialogues. Where 'tu' forms occur in conversation manual dialogues, it is often in the context of insulting an inferior, as in this sentence (addressed to a servant) in John Minsheu's *Spanish Grammar* (1599):

Majadéro, pues el jubon me tráes, ántes que la camísa, quiéres me motejar de açotádo.

Blocke head, doest thou bring me my doublet before my shirt, wilt thou scoffe me as though I had beene whipped?[21]

---

[17] Anon., *A very profitable boke to lerne the maner of redyng, writyng, & speakyng english & Spanish. Libro muy provechoso para saber la manera de leer, y screvir, y hablar Angleis, y Español* (London, 1554), sig. [D8r].

[18] Anon., *Den grooten Vocabulaer Engels ende Duyts/The Great Vocabuler, in English and Dutch: That is to say common speaches of all sorts, also Lettres and Obligations to write. With a Dictionarie and the Conjugation* (Rotterdam, 1639), sig. F5r–F5v.

[19] Offelen, *Double Grammar*, part II, pp. 129–32. In their practice of providing lists of titles and an overview or social or political hierarchies in foreign lands, conversation manuals overlapped with some early modern travel accounts and histories of other nations (see, for instance, Paul Rycaut, *The present state of the Ottoman Empire. Containing the maxims of the the Turkish politie, the most material Points of the Mahometan religion . . . etc.* (London, 1668), pp. 28–9), and with the general principles of the *ars apodemica* or art of travel, which urged the observation and systematic recording of details of foreign societies—see Chapter 4.

[20] On the links between conversation and letter-writing, see Phil Withington, *The Politics of Commonwealth: Citizens and Freemen in Early Modern England* (Cambridge: Cambridge University Press, 2005), pp. 142–3.

[21] Richard Perceval and John Minsheu, *A Spanish Grammar, first collected and published by Richard Percivale Gent.* (London, 1599), pp. 1–2.

In the *Passenger* of Benvenuto Italiano (1613), a servant is insulted—and while the translation is as free and literary, as in the rest of the text, the use of 'tu' stands out and is mirrored in the English 'thou': '*Moccicone, e arzigogolo, che arzigoghelerie vai tu arzigogolando?* Thou slovenly lubberd, and toyish fellow, what idle toyes goest thou fantasticating'.[22] Later, servants might face fewer insults but still be referred to using the 'tu' form of the verb, as in Pietro Paravicino's *Choice Proverbs* (1660): '*Ragazzo attendi a darci a bere, non vedi che li bichiere sono vuoti* / Boy, look to give us drink, dost thou not see the glasses are empty'. The speaker's drinking companions, by contrast, are still addressed as 'voi'.[23] Claudius Holly-band's *Italian Schoole-maister* is notable as a manual in whose dialogues lower-status speakers are given more agency than is normally found in contemporary texts aimed at more courtly audiences. It was smaller, cheaper, and simpler than some of its contemporaries and may have been aiming at a wider audience than the work of someone like John Florio, who stated explicitly in his *Second Frutes* that 'my frutes will please the gentler, but offend the clayish or clownish sort, whom good things scarcely please, and I care not to displease'.[24] In the *Italian Schoole-maister*, Hollyband includes a curious dialogue under the heading '[t]o binde himselfe with a master and Marchant', in which a young man tries to persuade a merchant to take him on as an apprentice. This short dialogue shows a sensitive approach to register: the merchant is referred to using the polite 'voi' form, as would be expected, and is addressed as 'your Wor.' or 'V. S.' ('vostra Signoria'), while the young apprentice-to-be is addressed as 'tu' and as 'boy' ('garzona') by the merchant, but when the character who introduces the young man to his prospective employer addresses the young man, he uses the 'voi' form: 'Venite con me, che lo ritrovarete'; 'Come with me, that you may find him.'[25]

However it was inculcated in the reader, the ability to use correct pronouns, titles, and modes of address only scratched the surface of the social flexibility that was necessary for conversation. Even where 'vous' forms were commonly used, social distinctions could be expressed and enforced in other ways in conversation. A speaker in César Oudin's *Grammar Spanish and English* (1622) criticized the French practice:

s. Me thinks they doe better [than Spain] in France, making them all equall by this word vous.

M. That reason only sheweth their custome to be ill, seeing they equall the Prince with the Porter, and make no distinctions of persons, being fit that there were.[26]

---

[22] Benvenuto Italiano, *Il Passaggiere/The Passenger…Containing seaven exquisite Dialogues in Italian and English* (London, 1613), pp. 2–3.

[23] Pietro Paravicino, *Choice Proverbs and Dialogues, in Italian and English, Also, Delightfull Stories and Apophthegms, taken out of Famous Guicciardine* (London, 1660), pp. 104–5.

[24] John Florio, *Florios Second Frutes* (London, 1591), sig. A6r.

[25] Claudius Hollyband, *The Italian Schoole-maister* (London, 1597), sig. D2r–D3r.

[26] Oudin, *Grammar Spanish and English*, pp. 224–7.

Conversation manuals provided ways beyond the 'tu'/'vous' distinction for their readers to distinguish verbally between the prince and the porter. Where 'Monsieur', 'Vostra Signoria', etc. are frequently used to address elite males, these speakers often respond using titles which belie any parity of esteem that might be suggested by their use of 'vous'. In a conversation between a gentleman and a ploughman in Jacques Bellot's *Familiar Dialogues*, the former refers to the latter as 'my frend'/'mon amy'; the ploughman refers to his social superior as 'Syr'/'Monsieur' throughout.[27] This use of 'mon amy' is also found in Guy Miège's *Nouvelle Methode* (1685), in which a tailor is addressed as 'Mon Amy' and a coachman as 'Cocher', while the 'vous' form is still employed.[28] This condescension marks relations of status but also of gender: again in Miège, a man and a maid address each other using 'vous', but the power relation is clear from the man's use of 'ma fille'—translated as 'Sweet-heart'—as against the maid's use of 'Monsieur':

M. Monsieur, vôtre Lit est assez bassiné. *M. Sir, your Bed is warm enough.*
Aves vous quêque autre chose à me commander? *Have you any thing else to command me?*
v. Non, ma fille. *V. No, Sweet-heart.*[29]

Writing of the gradual replacement of 'degrees' by 'estates' as the means of ranking individuals in society, Keith Wrightson argues that the language of degrees was 'concerned less with universal ideas than with present realities, less with function than with place, less with vocational and occupational differentials than with the bald facts of relative wealth, status, and power'.[30] While lists of titles and rules for their application might outline universal ideas, dialogues were concerned with present realities. The use of 'you' in English was on the rise, particularly in urban environments, but these texts are a reminder that once an interlocutor's social status had been ascertained, strategies of deference and condescension remained.[31] Given the importance of communicating one's honour

[27] Jacques Bellot, *Familiar Dialogues: for the Instruction of them, that be desirous to learne to speake English, and perfectlye to pronounce the same* (London, 1586), sig. Fv.
[28] Guy Miège, *Nouvelle Methode Pour Apprendre l'Anglois* (London, 1685), p. 54.
[29] ibid., p. 58.
[30] Keith Wrightson, 'Estates, Degrees, and Sorts: Changing Perceptions of Society in Tudor and Stuart England', in Penelope Corfield (ed.), *Language, History and Class* (Oxford: Basil Blackwell, 1991), pp. 42–3. On titles and forms of address in French, with a specific focus on Parisian society, see Robert Descimon, 'Un Langage de la dignité. La qualification des personnes dans la société parisienne à l'époque moderne', in Fanny Cosandey (ed.), *Dire et vivre l'ordre social en France sous l'Ancien Régime* (Paris: École des Hautes Études en Sciences Sociales, 2005), pp. 69–124; and Laurence Croq, 'Des Titulatures à l'évaluation sociale des qualités. Hiérarchie et mobilité collective dans la société parisienne du XVIIe siècle', in Cosandey (ed.), *Dire et vivre l'ordre social en France*, pp. 125–68. Descimon and Croq's table of forms of address used among the upper ranks of Parisian male society in the period 1500–1720 is useful: Cosandey (ed.), *Dire et vivre l'ordre social en France*, pp. 66–7.
[31] Bryson, *From Courtesy to Civility*, p. 166; Terttu Nevalainen and Helena Raumolin-Brunberg, 'The Changing Role of London on the Linguistic Map of Tudor and Stuart England', in Dieter

and protecting one's reputation in travel, as well as advertising one's creditworthiness in international commerce, this was evidently knowledge which was as crucial in a second language as it was in a first.

Judicious use of condescension allowed social distance to be maintained, but it could be a risky strategy: in a French-English dialogue from 1575, a character named George interrogates a man he meets on the road, addressing him first with '[h]oula ho censier, dites moy, vay-je bien par icy, pour aller a Paris? respondes si vous voules', translated as '[h]ola ho farmer tell me goe I well here by to goe to Paris? answeare if you will'. The abrupt 'Houla ho' and the address as 'censier' (which Randle Cotgrave's 1611 dictionary gives as 'A farmer, or Fee-farmer') rather than 'monsieur' or any more respectful title may be what gets the farmer's back up: he replies with 'what meane you? are you out of your wittes'. Trying another form of address, George goes with '[n]'oyes vous goute, jardinier?' ('Heare you not gardyner?'), but is once again rebuffed with the question '[h]ow shoute you so are you out of your wittes or in rage?' The back and forth continues between the two speakers, with George ultimately staging a climbdown from his exalted rhetorical position, reframing his question as a polite one: 'Montres moy (de grace) le chemin, par ou on va à, je ne scay ou' ('Show me I pray you whether on goeth to, I can not tel whether').[32] In this conversation, George's attempt to mark the social distinction between himself and the man he asks for directions fails utterly. An English-Spanish dialogue from 1591 contained an embedded lesson (with a sting in the tail) on how to practise this kind of linguistic condescension in order to get what one wanted. Two gentlemen arrive at the gates of London at night and find the gates barred. They call the porter, who complains and refuses to open up. As the exchange descends into acrimony, the way the porter is addressed changes: from '[h]ola Señor Portero', through '[h]ola Portero', to '[h]ola, picaro' ('Ho, rascall'). The gentlemen outside the gate decide on a new strategy: one urges the other 'let us speake him faire, and after we are gotten in we will use him like a knave as he hath deserved'.[33] This prompts a deceitful change in register, as the speakers attempt to charm the porter:

Señor Portero, que assi es menester de llamarle, porque un cavallero es por lo menos por el officio que tiene: supplico que su Señoria sea servido de abrir la puerta, y le daremos un sueldo para vino.

Kastovsky and Arthur Mettinger (eds.), *The History of English in a Social Context: A Contribution to Historical Sociolinguistics* (Berlin and New York: de Gruyter, 2000), p. 326.

---

[32] Anon., *A plaine pathway to the French tongue: Very profitable for Marchants, and also all other, which desire this same* (London, 1575), sig. [D7r]–[D7v].

[33] William Stepney, *The Spanish Schoole-master. Containing Seven Dialogues* (London, 1591), pp. 36–7.

Ho maister Porter, for so he must be called, being at least a gentleman by his office: I pray you may it please you to open us the gate, and we will give you a shilling to drinke.[34]

The Spanish text is even more toadying, with its 'supplico... su Señoria' for the English 'I pray you'. When the men are grudgingly allowed in and the porter asks for the promised payment, their registers switch back with their behaviour: 'No os devo nada en verdad (que soys un vellaco) sino buenas bofetadas, y tomaldas' ('I owe thee nothing truely (for thou art a rascall) but good blowes, and hold there they are').[35] Travel writers commonly mused on the level of dissimulation which the traveller needed to practise while abroad; this dialogue offered an object lesson in switching registers in order to dissimulate for one's own benefit.[36] Bad behaviour and inappropriate speech: these dialogues portray not just successful conversations, but also the breakdown of civil and courteous behaviour.[37] They do not simply prescribe a set of behaviours: they model how codes of behaviour work, and what happens when they break down.

The vocabularies taught by conversation manuals were not politically or socially neutral: rather, by providing ways in which language-learners could speak about others, they provided a framework for viewing the world and for judging and ranking individuals. Incorporated in the topical (rather than alphabetical) form in which many texts presented vocabularies was the equipment to make value judgements, to read and critique one's environment. In William Caxton's *Dialogues in French and English*—published between 1480 and 1483, and one of the earliest printed conversation manuals to contain English—the final twenty-one of its forty-nine pages contain not dialogues but short descriptions of people. Lisa H. Cooper shows that at the heart of a text which advertised itself as useful to traders was a social-commercial taxonomy of Caxton's Bruges.[38] In cataloguing different kinds of people—most commonly in urban environments—manuals communicated hierarchies but also ways of judging others, allowing readers to sort people by their status and, crucially, their reputation. Claudius Hollyband's *French Schoolemaster* (1582) offered a list of terms to describe a man positively:

What gentilman is that? }
It is the noblest, }

---

[34] Ibid., pp. 38–9.   [35] Ibid.

[36] I discuss travel and dissimulation in Chapter 4.

[37] This argument runs counter to Niels Haastrup's claim that 'to some extent the phrase-book shows what the courtesy-book prescribes. An important difference is that the dialogues do not show what the courtesy-books forbid': Niels Haastrup, 'The Courtesy-Book and the Phrase-Book in Modern Europe', in Jacques Carré (ed.), *The Crisis of Courtesy: Studies in the Conduct-Book in Britain, 1600–1900* (London, New York, and Cologne: E. J. Brill, 1994), p. 69.

[38] Lisa H. Cooper, 'Urban Utterances: Merchants, Artisans, and the Alphabet in Caxton's *Dialogues in French and English*', *New Medieval Literatures* 7 (2005), pp. 127–62.

the hardiest,   }
the most honest,   }   of the countrie.
the wisest,   }
the richest,   }
the most humble,   }
the most courteous,   }
the most liberall.   }

To complement these, Hollyband gave derogatory terms: 'the prowdest', 'the most covetous', 'the greatest cuckold', 'the poorest'.[39] Even in the pedagogy of Claude Mauger, which helped to shift French-teaching away from the paradigm embodied in the work of Hollyband and his contemporaries, lists of this kind remained present: 'He is a man well descended, well accomplisht, of good education, very civill, courteous, merry, affable, witty, understands himselfe very well, of good repute, and estimation.'[40] Reputation, credibility, honour: these were qualities which were public as well as private, and which were susceptible to damage by the words of others.[41] The ability to describe others was powerful; one's 'common fame' was a crucial commodity. As Laura Gowing argues, '[w]ords . . . were crucially linked with reputation; and the concept of reputation held considerable sway both legally and socially'.[42] The anonymous *Plaine pathway to the French Tongue* (1575, but largely plagiarized from Gabriel Meurier's *Familiar Communications*, 1563), offers a set of terms which could be used to describe the creditworthiness of others:

A man of credite
a man payable
a man fugetif
a man of his woord
a man of honesty
a man of little estimation
a man of nothing
a man of ritches
a man of substance
a man of fayned or broken[43]

[39] Claudius Hollyband, *The French Schoole-master* (London, 1582), sig. 73v–75r. This is somewhat plagiarized by Stepney, *Spanish Schoole-master*, pp. 118–19.
[40] Claude Mauger, *The True Advancement of the French Tongue* (London, 1653), p. 169.
[41] Anthony Fletcher, *Gender, Sex and Subordination in England 1500–1800* (New Haven, CT, and London: Yale University Press, 1995), p. 126; Steven Shapin, *A Social History of Truth: Civility and Science in Seventeenth-Century England* (Chicago and London: University of Chicago Press, 1994), p. 68.
[42] Laura Gowing, *Domestic Dangers: Women, Words, and Sex in Early Modern London* (Oxford: Clarendon, 1996), p. 111. This was not only true in England: compare Elizabeth Horodowich on Venice, *Language and Statecraft in Early Modern Venice* (Cambridge: Cambridge University Press, 2008), pp. 92–124.
[43] Anon., *Plaine pathway*, sig. Fr.

The fact that these terms appear in a chapter titled 'Of the Bourse' indicate further that this vocabulary of reputation has a broader financial relevance. The importance of credit in early modern England is well known through the work of Craig Muldrew, while Laurence Fontaine has shown that comparable systems of credit existed elsewhere in early modern Europe.[44] Conversation manuals' presentation of terms of this kind allowed readers access to the criteria of judgement as well as to the vocabulary of this crucial discourse.

Europe's public squares and marketplaces were not just divided according to social or economic status: the religious ruptures of the period also gave rise to languages of their own. Some conversation manuals offered vocabulary to help their reader navigate religious difference and sort people by religious affiliation, as in the extremely popular and frequently reproduced *Sex linguarum*:

a christen
a iew
an hebrue
unfaithfull
heithen
a turch
saraiens [saracen]
an hereike
a reriagate [renegade]
a zodomite[45]

In learning this set of categories, the reader is imbibing the author's prejudices alongside vocabulary. The religious landscapes of Europe and of England had shifted significantly by 1685, when Guy Miège presented a list of different religious affiliations to his readership of French immigrants to England in the wake of Louis XIV's revocation of the Edict of Nantes. As well as the heathen, the 'Mahumetan', and the Jew, there were '[u]n Chretien, *A Christian*', '[u]n Reformé, ou Protestant, *a Protestant*', '[u]n Papiste, *a Papist*' (and not a Catholic), and '[u]n de la Religion Grecque, *one of the Greek Religion*'. Uniquely in the corpus of conversation manuals, Miège went on to give a brief list of religious factions in later seventeenth-century England:

[44] Craig Muldrew, *The Economy of Obligation: The Culture of Credit and Social Relations in Early Modern England* (Basingstoke and New York: Palgrave Macmillan, 1998), and Muldrew, 'Interpreting the Market: The Ethics of Credit and Community Relations in Early Modern England', *Social History* 18 (1993), pp. 163–83; Laurence Fontaine, *L'Économie morale: pauvreté, crédit et confiance dans l'Europe préindustrielle* (Paris: Gallimard, 2008), see especially pp. 281–98 on credit and reputation.
[45] Anon., *Sex Linguarum, Latinæ, Gallicæ, Hispanicæ, Italicæ, Anglicæ, & Teutonicæ, dilucidissimus dictionarius... A Vocabulary in six languages, Latyn, Frenche, Spanisch, Italy, Englisch, and Teutsch* (Venice, 1549), sig. [G7r].

Un Membre de l'Eglise Anglicane, *a Member of the English Church.*
Un Presbyterien, *a Presbyterian.*
Un Calviniste, *A Calvinist.*
Un Independant, *an Independant.*
Un Fanatique, ou Visionaire, *a Fanatick.*
Un Millenaire, *a Fifth-Monarchy-Man.*
Un Trembleur, *a Quaker.*
Un Anabaptiste, *an Anabaptist.*[46]

Coming as part of a topical vocabulary within a text whose main aim was to introduce English language and customs to newly arrived speakers of French, this would have allowed readers the language to deal with some of the religious heterodoxy they might have heard discussed or read about. It is no accident that 'a Member of the English Church' comes first, since this was a text which argued strongly for French immigrants' social and linguistic assimilation into urbane English society, and since Miège was of the view that the Church of England was 'the best Reformed Religion and the most agreeable to the primitive times of Christianity'.[47] More than simply descriptive, Miège's vocabulary list was loaded with value judgements about religious identity in late seventeenth-century England. Describing others in this manner was not a neutral act: it was a way of working out where they fitted into social, political, commercial, and confessional landscapes. In the oral economy of reputation, managing one's own credit required an understanding of terms like these and how they worked in the world. Socially informed vocabularies were important for understanding and making oneself understood in a strange linguistic community.

The dark side of description is insult. Insults, whether actionable or not, were words with power to damage reputation and 'common fame': 'Materially incalculable, the implications of spoken insult could still be huge'.[48] Claudius Hollyband offered a list of choice Italian insults embedded in one dialogue:

Non ho mai pensato che tu sii al ramente di quello che tu sei: ciò è, un poltrone, forfante, cattivo, buggiardo, ribaldo, ingannatore, malvagio, scavezzacolo, ragazzo, intricamondo, pazzarello, meschino, scelerato.

I never thought that thou were otherwise, or another manner of man then thou art: that is, a patch, a knave, a naughtie one, a lyar, a ruffian, a deceaver, a wild one, a rope-cracker, a scolion, troublesome, a little foole, a wretch, wicked. [49]

---

[46] Miège, *Nouvelle methode*, 'Nouvelle Nomenclature Françoise & Angloise', p. 22.
[47] Vivienne Larminie, 'Guy Miège (bap. 1644, d. in or after 1718), author and lexicographer)', in *Oxford Dictionary of National Biography* online: https://doi.org/10.1093/ref:odnb/18687.
[48] Gowing, *Domestic Dangers*, p. 138. See also Horodowich, *Language and Statecraft in Early Modern Venice*, pp. 92–124.
[49] Hollyband, *Italian Schoole-maister*, sig. [F5v]–[F6r].

Hollyband's catalogue of Italian insults contains terms like 'knave', 'liar', and 'deceiver', which could impact directly on one's credit and reputation; words like these appear among the slanderous terms recorded by Alexandra Shepard in Cambridge court cases.[50] In 1660, the anonymous *Dutch-Tutor* would offer similar terms: 'Rogue', 'traitor', 'a thief'; gendered slanders like 'buggerer', 'cuckold', 'whoremaster'; and terms of religious abuse, including 'an atheist' and 'an unbeliever'.[51] Allowing the speaker to defend his or her reputation or to assault that of others, insults—like terms of approbation—were crucial elements of the vocabulary of the socially competent linguist.

The dialogues of conversation manuals taught readers to orient themselves and their speech in a variety of social situations and in conversation with a variety of interlocutors. They did so not by setting out lists of rules to be followed in every situation, but by representing the nuanced ways in which status and deference could be expressed in multilingual and multicultural spoken interactions. They provided materials which their speakers could use to negotiate social and linguistic hierarchies, and to assert and protect their place within them. In doing so, they often carried implicit value judgements about how society should be organized. They also showed what happened when these hierarchies were challenged or broke down, and offered strategies for working through these situations of conflict. The conversation manual dialogue did not offer a one-size-fits-all approach to communicative competence, but taught its readers to comport themselves within the shifting relationships of power that underlay all early modern conversations.

'The Converse of Women'

In an exchange of letters written in the 1650s, Ralph Verney tried to talk the 10-year-old Anne Denton out of her desire to study ancient languages. Verney urged her to confine her study to the Bible and the catechism in English. In an attempt at compromise, he offered to provide her with materials for the study of French:

> In French you cannot bee too cunning for that language affords many admirable bookes fit for you as Romances, Plays, Poetry, Stories of illustrious (not learned) Woemen, receipts for preserving, makinge creames and all sorts of cookeryes, ordring your gardens and in Breif all manner of good housewifery. If you please to have a little patience with yourselfe (without Hebrew, Greeke, or Lattin) when I goe to Paris againe I will send you halfe a dozen of the french bookes to begin your Library.[52]

---

[50] Alexandra Shepard, *Meanings of Manhood in Early Modern England* (Oxford: Oxford University Press, 2003), pp. 161–64.
[51] Anon., *The Dutch-Tutor: or, a new-book of Dutch and English* (London, 1660), pp. 75–6.
[52] Cited in Hackel, *Reading Material*, pp. 201–3.

For Ralph Verney, the study of French was a permissible aspect of the education of a young gentlewoman, and the reading of secular books in that language would complement Anne Denton's upbringing as an ideal housewife and a pious bride. For at least some elite women, language-learning was seen as an acceptable occupation: Jason Lawrence argues that the study of languages in youth was 'the only means of learning available to young women in sixteenth-century England', adducing examples of women like Mary Herbert and Elizabeth Carey, who studied with private tutors.[53] Grammars and manuals by Henry Grantham, Claudius Hollyband, and Claude Mauger were dedicated to their female pupils.[54] Across the seventeenth century and into the eighteenth, some competence in modern foreign languages—particularly French—was increasingly considered a social accomplishment and a virtue among young women of relatively high status.[55]

Debates around women's study and use of foreign languages were informed by wider debates about female voices, which were considered unpredictable, suspicious, and potentially dangerous. One mid-Tudor tract said that women 'have tongue at large, voice loud and shrill...they flush and flame as hot as fire, and swell as a toad for fervent ire', while the caricatures of the 'talkative' woman—a threat to social order and to male superiority—remained current and threatening in the later seventeenth century.[56] Conversely, as Laura Gowing argues, '[w]omen's verbal restraint was one of the cornerstones of virtue', with garrulity linked in the popular imagination to harlotry.[57] Voice and speech were gendered: Michèle Cohen's work on the study of French in the eighteenth century shows

---

[53] Jason Lawrence, 'Who the devil taught thee so much Italian?' Italian Language Learning and Literary Imitation in Early Modern England (Manchester and New York: Manchester University Press, 2005), pp. 13–14.

[54] Henry Grantham, An Italian Grammer; written in Latin by Scipio Lentulo a Neapolitane: and turned in English: by H. G. (London, 1575), dedicated 'To the right vertuous mystres Mary and mysres [sic] Francys Berkeley daughters to the Right honorable Henry Lord Berkeley'; Claudius Hollyband, Campo di fior or else the flourie field of foure languages (London, 1583), dedicated 'To the yong Gentle-woman, mistris Luce Harington: daughter to the right worshipfull and right vertuous Gentle-man, Maister Jhon Harington Esquier'; Mauger's True Advancement was dedicated to named pupils at Margaret Kilvert's academy for young women: see Chapter 1.

[55] For a discussion of competence in French becoming a prized accomplishment for elite women, see Michèle Cohen, Fashioning Masculinity: National Identity and Language in the Eighteenth Century (London and New York: Routledge, 1996), pp. 30–8; Cohen, 'French Conversation or "Glittering Gibberish"? Learning French in Eighteenth-Century England', in Natasha Glaisyer and Sara Pennell (eds.), Didactic Literature in England 1500–1800: Expertise Constructed (Aldershot: Ashgate, 2003), pp. 99–102, 116–19. See also Jerome de Groot, 'Every one teacheth after thyr owne fantasie: French Language Instruction', in Kathryn M. Moncrief and Kathryn R. McPherson (eds.), Performing Pedagogy in Early Modern England: Gender, Instruction, and Performance (Farnham: Ashgate, 2011), pp. 33–51; and Vivian Salmon, 'Bathsua Makin (1600–c.1673: A Pioneer Linguist and Feminist', in Vivian Salmon, Language and Society in Early Modern England: Selected Essays 1981–1994, ed. Konrad Koerner (Amsterdam and Philadelphia, PA: John Benjamins, 1996), pp. 239–60.

[56] Amanda L. Capern, The Historical Study of Women: England 1500–1700 (Basingstoke and New York: Palgrave Macmillan, 2008), pp. 37, 50.

[57] Gowing, Domestic Dangers, p. 61. For a perspective on language and prostitution, see Horodowich, Language and Statecraft, pp. 165–206; see also Elizabeth S. Cohen, 'Back Talk: Two Prostitutes' Voices from Rome c.1600', Early Modern Women: An Interdisciplinary Journal 2 (2007), pp. 95–126.

how ideas of 'conversation' were gendered, with the topic and manner of female speech sharply restricted: after all, 'conversation' in the seventeenth century was a dangerously polyvalent term, and one which could mean sexual as well as social intercourse.[58] At the heart of the *querelle des femmes* and of popular judgements on women's voices was a fear of the influence their speech could wield and the damage it could do. As Sara Mendelson and Patricia Crawford argue, '[w]omen censored their own speech and men disparaged feminine rhetorical prowess not because it was insignificant, but because it could be powerful and dangerous'.[59] Women's voices were suspicious and always susceptible to attempts at patriarchal control.

These anxieties surrounding female speech made themselves felt in writing on language-learning, not least because even materials for the instruction of women were written entirely by men. The most famous language lesson in early modern literature, in Shakespeare's *Henry V*, is pregnant with lewdness and erotic potential: Katharine's study of English is a means to her sexual and political 'conquest' by Henry.[60] Conversation manual authors recognized the double meaning of conversation too: in a German manual from 1687, one speaker asks another whether fevers are common in England. His interlocutor replies that '[t]hey are frequent, but not mortal, as in other Country; nor do many die by excessive drinking but the converse of Women kills many more'.[61] César Oudin's 1622 Spanish-English manual showed two gentlewomen condemning their lack of discretion, by saying '[w]e women cannot keepe a secret when it is given us in charge. To this purpose I will tell you what happened in our street about a weeke a gone, if I am not troublesome.' The conversation of Oudin's female speakers is one of gossip, mockery of other women, and flirtation: commonplaces about female speech and behaviour are demonstrated, and one character says '[f]or that reason doe men say, it is ill to put trust in women; and they are not much deceived', though she concludes many men are not much better.[62] The idea of women's

---

[58] Cohen, *Fashioning Masculinity*, pp. 17–25; Richards, *Rhetoric and Courtliness*, p. 40. See also Wendy Ayres-Bennett, *Sociolinguistic Variation in Seventeenth-Century France*, pp. 111–180.

[59] Sara Mendelson and Patricia Crawford, *Women in Early Modern England 1550–1720* (Oxford: Clarendon, 1998), p. 215.

[60] Marianne Montgomery, *Europe's Languages on England's Stages, 1590–1620* (Farnham: Ashgate, 2012), pp. 36–45. Juliet Fleming compares Katharine's study of English to the French-English manual of Pierre Erondell (discussed below), arguing that each turns female speech into material for male titillation: Juliet Fleming, 'The French Garden: An Introduction to Women's French', *ELH: English Literary History* 56 (1989), pp. 19–51.

[61] Offelen, *Double Grammar*, part II, p. 221.

[62] Oudin, *A Grammar Spanish and English*, pp. 261–3. For another example of women gossiping in a language-learning dialogue, see Mauger, *True Advancement*, pp. 216–25. Mauger's dialogue, though more vicious than Oudin's, lacks the self-aware discussion by women of gossip and women's supposed nature. On gossip, see Bernard Capp, *When Gossips Meet: Women, Family, and Neighbourhood in Early Modern England* (Oxford: Oxford University Press, 2003); and Elizabeth Horodowich, 'The Gossiping Tongue: Oral Networks, Public Life and Political Culture in Early Modern Venice', *Renaissance Studies* 19 (2005), pp. 22–45.

conversation came freighted with sexual and moral suspicion, and these concerns over women's voices and their control manifested themselves in educational materials which represented women's speech or attempted to provide pedagogical programmes for female learners.

The contradictions and uncertainties surrounding women's language-learning are summed up in the edition of Giovanni Michele Bruto's *The Necessarie, fit, and convenient Education of a yong Gentlewoman* published in London in 1598. Bruto's text argued against educating women beyond some training in basic literacy: 'I know some that are of opinion, that yong gentlewomen should be taught learnings and sciences, which for my part I thinke not convenient.'[63] Female linguistic competence had for some time been feared, not least for its ability to turn women away from virtuous reading and towards writings considered immoral, like the work of Catullus or Boccaccio. As though in spite of Bruto's central argument, the 1598 edition offered the text in a parallel-text French and Italian version as well as in English, and the text which prohibited the learning of other vernaculars by women doubled as an aid to their study of them, summing up the tension between multilingualism as a prestigious accomplishment and a facilitator of vice.

The life of Bathsua Makin, one of seventeenth-century England's best-known female polyglots, helps to illuminate the continuing cultural unease about women's linguistic education throughout the seventeenth century.[64] A commonplace book of 1633 contained a story about her presentation to the king 'for an English rarity, because she could speake and rite pure Latine, Greeke and Hebrew'. James's derisive reply—'But can shee spin?'—suggests that her accomplishments were seen as derivative and even unwomanly.[65] Even if the story itself is spurious, the fact that it was in circulation during her lifetime suggests that this was considered a believable contemporary attitude. In 1673, Makin—by then in her seventies—published her *Essay to Revive the Antient Education of Gentlewomen, in Religion, Manners, Arts & Tongues* (London, 1673), but still had to include 'An Answer to the Objections against this Way of Education'. For Makin, the objections against female education were linked to wider concerns about women's tongues:

[63] Giovanni Michele Bruto, *The Necessarie, fit, and convenient Education of a yong Gentlewoman. Written both in French and Italian, and translated into English by W.P. And now printed with the three Languages together in one Volume, for the better instruction of such as are desirous to studie those Tongues* (London, 1598), sig. E4r–[E6r].

[64] On Bathsua Makin's life, see Jean R. Brink, 'Bathsua Makin: "Most Learned Matron"', *Huntington Library Quarterly* 54 (1991), pp. 313–26; Frances Teague, *Bathsua Makin, Woman of Learning* (London: Associated University Presses, 1998); Salmon, 'Bathsua Makin'.

[65] Cited in Jane Stevenson, *Women Latin Poets: Language, Gender, and Authority from Antiquity to the Eighteenth Century* (Oxford: Oxford University Press, 2005), p. 378. On Makin, see also J. Sears McGee, *An Industrious Mind: The Worlds of Sir Simonds D'Ewes* (Stanford, CA: Stanford University Press, 2015), pp. 24–5, 54.

It is objected against Women, as a reproach, that they have too much Tongue: but it's no crime that they have many Tongues...The Tongue is the only Weapon Women have to defend themselves with, and they had need to use it dextrously. Many say one tongue is enough for a Woman: it is but a quibble upon the word. Several Languages, understood by a Woman, will do our Gentleman little hurt, who have little more than their Mother-Wit, and understand only their own Mother-Tongue[66]

Makin's argument makes it clear that female multilingual competences in the period need to be understood in relation to male speech. Michèle Cohen argues that in seventeenth-century France female conversational skill was important but mainly as a foil to male *esprit* (wit) rather than as a skill in its own right. Those who could not speak within the bounds of acceptability set by patriarchy—the so-called '*précieuses*'—were considered monstrous.[67] Conversation manuals reflect this thinking about women's voices, their dialogues often restricting the subjects on which female speakers might be allowed to speak, and the spaces in which their voices might be heard.

In conversation manuals written specifically for women, the implicit argument was that the form of linguistic competence appropriate for female speakers and readers was fundamentally different from that displayed by men. Juliet Fleming argues that Erondell's *French Garden* (1605) was radical 'insofar as it assumes that [women's] interests are separate from everything already dealt with in French books and that only certain topics will be relevant to them'.[68] Erondell advertised his book as filling a gap in the market: the successful French manuals of Claudius Hollyband, argued a prefatory verse, had not provided material for female speakers.[69] The only competing text offering a pedagogical programme 'respecting or belonging properly to women' was de la Mothe's *French Alphabet*, but Erondell complained it was too short.[70] Marten le Mayre's *Dutch Schoole Master*, published the year after Erondell's text, made the same gendered distinction between linguistic competences, by providing separate chapters on '[t]he rising of men' and '[t]he rising of women'. Functionally, this kept vocabulary for men's clothing—'Helpe me to put on my Ierkin,/brush my cloake and my hatte,/helpe me to tye my points'—separate from that of women—'give me my Petticote,/lace my gowne,/where is the brush?'—but its ideological baggage was in keeping with

[66] Bathsua Makin, *An Essay to Revive the Antient Education of Gentlewomen, in Religion, Manners, Arts & Tongues* (London, 1673), p. 11.
[67] Cohen, *Fashioning Masculinity*, pp. 13–25. On the *précieuses*, see also Ayres-Bennett, *Sociolinguistic Variation*, pp. 133–43.
[68] Fleming, 'The French Garden', p. 25.
[69] Peter Erondell, *The French Garden: for English Ladyes and Gentlewomen to walke in* (London, 1605), sig. [A6r].
[70] ibid., sig. B1r.

contemporary views of linguistic competence.[71] Erondell, in trying to forge a pedagogy which was specifically aimed at a female audience, included vocabulary unlike that found in male-oriented manuals: his fifth dialogue, between '[t]he Lady' and '[t]he Nurce', used the situation of an elite woman visiting her child and his nurse as the excuse for a lesson in the kind of vocabulary and behaviour rarely found in other manuals: 'I beleeve you did leave him alone to cry and weepe: picke his nosthrils, wipe his mouth and his lips. How many teeth has he: his gummes be sore.' The baby is carefully inspected and instructions given for his care, washing, feeding, and swaddling: this is unique to this manual, and the dialogue deftly incorporates a language lesson with the edifying example of a caring mother.[72] Ralph Verney's idea of women's learning as a means to 'good housewifery' can be found in these vernacular pedagogical texts.

In Erondell's manual, women's competence did not just differ in the vocabulary it required: it was presented as qualitatively different from—and inferior to—that of men. One prefatory poem linked women and children even more closely:

> But that's not all: besides discourse with men,
> This Garden yeelds an Arbour for the Childe,
> Who with the busie Mother now and then
> May prattle of each point in phrases milde[73]

Other conversation manuals catered to children: Hollyband's *French Littleton* (first edition London, 1566), with its classroom dialogues and moral sentences, is a near-contemporary example. However, none so explicitly associated the linguistic competence of mothers with that of their children. In one sense, the verse simply reflects contemporary thought about the acquisition of linguistic competence: Thomas Elyot had expressed concerns common to humanist pedagogues about the role of the mother and the nurse in a child's education, arguing that if Latin-speaking nurses could not be found, the child should at least be surrounded by women who 'speke none englisshe but that/whiche is cleane/polite/perfectly/and articulately pronounced'. Otherwise, the child risked growing up knowing only how to speak 'lascivious and unclene wordes' with 'corrupte and foule pronunciation'.[74] Excessive maternal influence was to be avoided.[75] The grand tour was imagined by writers as a rite of passage which would separate the young man from his mother.[76] As well as recognizing the role of the mother in

---

[71] Marten le Mayre, *The Dutch Schoole Master* (London, 1606), sig. [F6v]–[F7v].

[72] Erondell, *French Garden*, sig. [G5v]–H1v.   [73] Ibid., sig. [A6r].

[74] Elizabeth Hodgson, 'Alma Mater', in Moncrief and McPherson, *Performing Pedagogy in Early Modern England*, pp. 159–76; Adam Fox, *Oral and Literate Culture in England 1500–1700* (Oxford: Clarendon, 2000), pp. 57–8; Thomas Elyot, *The boke named the Governour, devised by Thomas Elyot knight* (London, 1531), sig. 16v–17r, 18v–19v.

[75] Anthony Fletcher, *Gender, Sex and Subordination*, p. 297.

[76] Cohen, *Fashioning Masculinity*, pp. 57–8.

the child's linguistic education, Erondell's prefatory verse also drew a qualitative parallel between female speech and that of children. The book would teach the speaker to 'prattle', but little more: as the preface suggested, the competences found in Hollyband's popular works were simply unsuitable for the female reader. Erondell's *French Garden*, equating women's speech with that of children and arguing implicitly that the topics on which women's voices needed to be heard were domestic and familial as against the public, commercial language of many male-oriented manuals, constructed a pedagogy which restricted its students' capacity for expression just as it claimed to enlighten.

The conversation manuals' dialogues prepared their readers to speak and be heard in particular social situations and on specific topics, but they also located this speech in social spaces. By denying a reader the linguistic equipment necessary to get by in a market or an alehouse, a pedagogical text could implicitly deny them access to that space. Space in the early modern world was sharply gendered, and the restrictions placed on women's language in some pedagogical programmes amount to a process by which, as Juliet Fleming argues, women 'find themselves reinscribed in the traditional sphere of home and family'.[77] The 'garden' of Erondell's title prefigures the emphasis on domesticity and private space which shapes his linguistic pedagogy: the spaces in which women's language-learning can be carried on and the spaces in which female voices may be heard are sharply delineated. Erondell's manual was not the only foreign-language text to set its dialogues in England rather than in the country where the target language is spoken, but in his text the London setting is a reminder that the competence shown by his speakers is not that required of the traveller or the merchant. The competence modelled in the *French Garden* is domestic in every way: set largely in the home, and denying women's ability to go abroad, in the city or in the world.

When they venture outside the domestic sphere, Erondell's speakers require male speakers to mediate for them. Having kept his female speakers firmly within the household for the first eight of his thirteen dialogues, Erondell allows them out for 'a turne in the Exchange', a famously polyglot space.[78] In Erondell's Exchange, however, the linguistic and commercial freedoms of male speakers in conversation manuals are denied to their female counterparts: women's linguistic and financial interactions are mediated through the male voice of a chaperone. While one dialogue on the buying and selling of cloth allows a modicum of discussion of quality and price, the woman's attempts at bargaining with a shopkeeper are made to seem incompetent, with one of her friends saying of her driving down of the price that '[m]e thinketh Madame that you offer too much, as for me, I would not

---

[77] Fleming, 'The French Garden', p. 26. For a discussion of the ways in which particular spaces were gendered (and one which ties helpfully into questions of women's speech in different places and situations), see Mendelson and Crawford, *Women in Early Modern England*, pp. 205–11.

[78] Julia Gasper, 'The Literary Legend of Sir Thomas Gresham', in Ann Saunders (ed.), *The Royal Exchange* (London: London Topographical Society, 1997), p. 101.

give so much'.[79] After this rebuke—something that simply never happens to a man in the conversation manual corpus—the female customer accepts her lack of bargaining skill, and asks her male companion to intervene on her behalf: 'Master Du vault-l'amour, I pray you to buy for me yonder wastcoate that I see in that other shop, for if I cheapen it, they will over price me by the halfe, As for you, they know you have better skill in it.'[80] In the dialogue at a goldsmith's, the female speaker's participation in the bargain amounts to swapping maxims about the qualities of certain precious stones. When it comes to choosing them and setting a price, she once again leaves the bargaining—and her money—in the hands of 'Master du Vault-l'Amour'. If, as I argue below, one common feature of many conversation manuals was their embedded instruction in the techniques as well as the language of bargaining, then Erondell's omission is significant: he departs from a convention of the genre in what can only be read as part of his effort to circumscribe women's speech, by restricting its content and the spheres in which it could be employed. In doing so, he ties women's supposed unfitness for certain kinds of speech to a more general unfitness for being in the masculine worlds of commerce, exchange, and public life.

Erondell's dialogue reflects a trend in the conversation manual corpus. A thread running through a number of conversation manuals' dialogues is the incapacity of women to perform the kind of bargaining that was performed constantly by their male counterparts both in these texts and in shops and streets on an everyday basis. John Minsheu's *Spanish Grammar* (1599) contained a dialogue 'wherin is handled to buie and sell jewels and other things, between a gentleman called Thomas and his wife Margaret, and a Merchant, and a goldsmith'. The work and wordplay of a stylized bargain are undertaken by Thomas, and later Margaret's dissatisfaction with the merchandise is made the subject of a joke and linked to her sexual choice: the merchant remarks, 'I woonder how your worship married being so divers to please your fancy.' The men discuss philosophy while Margaret chooses her wares, but the bargaining is done by her husband, who accuses the merchant of trying to cheat his wife.[81] In Edward Richardson's *Anglo-Belgica* (1676/77), there is a bargaining scene which is notable for its difference from practically every other one in the corpus of conversation manuals, in that the customer's attempt at making a deal is rebuffed immediately, and that rebuff is accepted:

Madam, it is of five gilders the ell.
I can get it cheaper at another (place.)
That is the price at a word, you can not any where get it cheaper.
How many ells are there in that piece?
Just twenty five.

To how much doth that amount in all?
To an hundred and five and twenty gilders.
There is your money, send it home by the porter.[82]

Elsewhere in conversation manuals, all prices are negotiable. Here, the failure of the bargain rams home the point that this woman is in a situation for which she is thought to be essentially unsuited. In these manuals, the female voice is silenced outside the domestic sphere, unless she has a man to speak for her: the bustling commercial life of male-oriented manuals, and the competence which it entails, is denied her.

All this said, dialogues in which women are protagonists are relatively rare within the conversation manual corpus. Women, where they are represented, are overwhelmingly silent, or at least subordinate. Where they do appear, it is frequently as maids and servants, with limited linguistic agency allowed them. There is one recurring scenario, printed in multiple versions in multiple texts and in multiple languages, in which a traveller at an inn pretends to be sick before attempting to seduce the chambermaid.[83] Women appear throughout the corpus as sexual objects, silent but spoken of in relation to men: William Stepney's Spanish manual of 1591 provided no dialogues in which women were the main speakers, but offered ample ways of describing women in terms of male desire and domestic life: descriptors like 'a virgin or maid', along with 'the maidenhead' and 'she hath lost her maidenhead'; phrases like 'she will make her husband a cuckold' and 'he hath gotten her with child at the first copulation with her'. In learning to name the parts of the body, the discerning reader also learnt to say 'she is a proper woman but she hath great buttocks'.[84] Vocabularies are not neutral: they can be persuasive, and where they are organized topically, they are a potent vehicle for the statement of a world view—in this case, the reinforcement of a patriarchal view of womanhood, women's bodies, and female speech.[85] In François Hillenius's *English, and Low Dutch Instructer* (1664), a conversation between a brother and a sister about the sister's marital prospects becomes a vehicle for misogynistic cliché: not only are women 'pragmaticall, hard to be pleased, evill disposed, and very unhappy to poore men', but they are

---

[82] Edward Richardson, *Anglo-Belgica. D'Engelsche Ende Nederduytsche Academy. The English and Netherdutch Academy* (Amsterdam, 1698), part II, pp. 20–1.

[83] Some examples of variations on the seduction scene (which has its roots in the Berlemont dialogue tradition) in English: Anon., *Colloquia et dictionariolum septem linguarum*, sig. L4v–L5v; Anon., *Dutch-Tutor*, p. 48; Paul Cougneau, *A Sure Guide to The French tongue, Teaching by a most easie way, to pronounce the French naturally, to reade it perfectly, to write it truly, and to speake it readily* (London, 1635), p. 102; Hollyband, *Frenche Schoole-master*, sig. 70v–71v; there is a significantly embellished variation in John Eliot, *Ortho-Epia Gallica. Eliots Fruits for the French* (London, 1593), pp. 121–2.

[84] Stepney, *Spanish Schoole-master*, pp. 241, 242, 248.

[85] For the persuasive possibilities of vocabularies and dictionaries, see John Considine, 'Narrative and Persuasion in Early Modern English Dictionaries and Phrasebooks', *Review of English Studies* 52 (2001), pp. 195–206. See also Leith, *Social History of English*, pp. 84–7.

petulant, or lascivious, audatious (bold, stomacke full,) fonde, (false hearted) creatures, without discreation, talkatifgossips (bablers) . . . and not onely Idle, but tattlers and bussy bodies, and such immodest incivill long tongu'd pratlers that they without wit or reason will speake things they ought not.[86]

Hillenius allows the sister in this dialogue some defence of herself, but the brother concludes by suggesting she read her scriptures to see the superiority of men over women, and his resounding 'Amen' at the close of the dialogue leaves little doubt as to whose part the reader is meant to take. In a similar dialogue in Edward Richardson's *Anglo-Belgica*, the female speaker remains unconvinced by the gentleman's reasoning of male superiority.[87] It is possible to read these arguments as providing at least some materials for female defence of their sex, but their largely negative conclusions leave the status quo as before. Even where women were not the primary audience envisaged by the authors of conversation manuals, misogyny and the reinforcement of patriarchal values were the default mode in this pedagogical tradition.

With this in mind, it follows that these conversation manuals provide no sure guide to the realities of day-to-day language use. In spite of the patriarchal strictures placed on women's speech, we know that many areas outside the household—including the marketplace—were arenas where female speech was heard and respected. Mendelson and Crawford argue that '[c]ertain centres of economic activity, although technically under male jurisdiction, were apt to be colonized by female groups, including female vendors' informal control of market space'.[88] Women could be found in the marketplace and in shops and alehouses, frequently as proprietors or at least as the public face of the enterprise.[89] A manual written by François Colsoni in 1688 contained a sample letter in which '[a] Merchant gives his Wife directions how she should manage the Trade':

you must not be disturb'd if the customers talk with a more then ordinary freedom, for it is a peculiar quality they who spend their mony have, to be very pleasant with those who gain by them; answer their railleries with an aire that may engage them to give you your price for what they buy[90]

---

[86] François Hillenius, *Den Engelschen ende Ne'erduitschen Onderrichter . . . The English, and Low Dutch Instructer* (Rotterdam, 1664), p. 91.

[87] Richardson, *Anglo-Belgica*, part II, pp. 206–12.

[88] Mendelson and Crawford, *Women in Early Modern England*, p. 210. On women's voices in the marketplace, see Natasha Korda, 'Gender at Work in the Cries of London', in Karen Bamford and Mary Ellen Lamb (eds.), *Oral Traditions and Gender in Early Modern Literary Texts* (Burlington, VT: Ashgate, 2008), pp. 117–35.

[89] On the variety of employments and activities of women in London in this period, see Eleanor Hubbard, *City Women: Money, Sex, and the Social Order in Early Modern London* (Oxford: Oxford University Press, 2012).

[90] François Colsoni, *Il Nuovo Trismegiste* (London, 1688), pp. 246–8.

In 'manag[ing] the Trade', this female trader was also expected to manage her speech, and the departure from 'ordinary' speech that came with taking on a commercial role. Women's ability to move and to speak in different social situations was not always as restricted as some manuals suggest, as is suggested by the representation of female traders, particularly in Dutch-English manuals.[91] In one case, a female trader uses a reference to her gender as a bargaining tool, telling a customer that 'it is a shame that you should vex (or tempt) a woman so long for one stiver'.[92] Women worked as traders in the marketplaces of the Netherlands and of early modern Germany, but only some manuals reflected the realities of their economic roles.[93] More generally, conversation manuals tended to restrict the kinds of competence they modelled for women. Ignoring the realities of women's economic and public roles, they often forced through a prejudiced ideal of what women could say, where they could say it, and how their voices would be reckoned against those of their male counterparts.

Forms of Language: Rituals, Ceremonies, Texts

Ritual was at the heart of early modern societies: rituals defined different kinds of company and society, and the rules of ritual undergirded many early modern conversations.[94] Ritual and language-learning went together, not least in the catechism, where education in ritual went hand in hand with the development of literacy and native-language competence.[95] A. P. R. Howatt has argued that the dialogues of conversation manuals grew out of the catechetical tradition, and the practice of their rehearsal and memorization in the classroom suggests some

[91] Anon., *Dutch-Tutor*, pp. 10–15. Versions of this dialogue (from the Berlemont tradition) which contain an identifiably male and a female vendor are Hillenius, *Instructer*, pp. 13–21, and Richardson, *Anglo-Belgica*, part II, pp. 6–16. English nuns could also be energetic and opinionated language-learners: see Emilie K. M. Murphy, 'Language and Power in an English Convent in Exile, *c.*1621–*c.*1631', *Historical Journal* (forthcoming, early view available at https://doi.org/10.1017/S0018246 X17000437).

[92] Hillenius, *Instructer*, p. 19.

[93] See Danielle van den Heuvel, *Women & Entrepreneurship: Female Traders in the Northern Netherlands, c.1580–1815* (Amsterdam: Aksant, 2007), pp. 87–134, see also pp. 135–76 for women as shopkeepers; Merry E. Wiesner, *Working Women in Renaissance Germany* (Brunswick, NJ: Rutgers University Press, 1986), pp. 134–142.

[94] Withington, *Society in Early Modern England*, p. 182; on ritual more generally, see Edward Muir, *Ritual in Early Modern Europe* (Cambridge: Cambridge University Press, 1997).

[95] Mary Morrissey, 'Sermons, Primers, and Prayerbooks', in Joad Raymond (ed.), *The Oxford Handbook of Popular Print Culture* (Oxford: Oxford University Press, 2011), pp. 496–8; Ian Green, '"For children in yeeres and children in understanding": The Emergence of the English Catechism under Elizabeth and the Early Stuarts', *Journal of Ecclesiastical History* 37 (1986), p. 399; Rosemary O'Day, *Education and Society 1500–1800* (London and New York: Longman, 1982), pp. 44–6; Thomas, 'The Meaning of Literacy in Early Modern England', p. 99. Michelangelo Florio—father of John— combined his evangelical efforts with his work as a language tutor in an Italian catechism, dedicated to Robert Dudley. Frances Yates, *John Florio: The Life of an Italian in Shakespeare's England* (Cambridge: Cambridge University Press, 1934), p. 28.

overlap between the two practices, as does the inclusion of catechetical materials—as well as the Creed, and various prayers, psalms, and passages from the Bible—in many conversation manuals.[96] Conversation manuals recognized that some social interactions—such as the drinking of healths, visiting and greeting others, and the ceremonies surrounding communal dining—were governed by rituals and ceremonies, and tried to teach their readers how to navigate them. The dialogues found in manuals allowed correct and appropriate behaviour to be displayed and, where necessary, directly copied by the reader. With the dialogues' capacity for breakdown and debate, they also provided an arena for discussing, firstly, the desirability of ceremonies and compliments in English sociability and, secondly, the adaptation and adoption of ceremonies derived from continental models.

Writing about eighteenth- and nineteenth-century Germany, Angelika Linke describes the practice of calling on or visiting others as a 'communicative genre': the *Besuch* or visit was a social event 'marked by fixed linguistic patterns, whose function is to indicate the socio-cultural significance of an action'. A communicative genre is a social interaction for which there exists a pre-existing script: rather than having to work out how to deal with the situation each time it arises, participants can draw on a shared set of responses, behaviours, and phrases.[97] Anna Bryson argues for the increasing importance of ritualized visiting to seventeenth-century English social life: these visits had varying levels of formality, but 'were essentially reciprocal between equals, and a means of proffering respect to superiors'. English behaviour in the seventeenth century was codified and discussed with one eye on French manners, as the shift from an Italianate courtesy to a French-influenced civility continued throughout the century.[98]

The authors of conversation manuals taught their readers to navigate these scripted or semi-scripted social encounters: the second edition of Robert Sherwood's

---

[96] A. P. R. Howatt, *A History of English Language Teaching* (Oxford: Oxford University Press, 1984), p. 5. Prayers are very common in conversation manuals—see, for instance, Peter Berault, *A New, Plain, Short, and Compleat French and English Grammar* (London, 1688), p. 159, in which one character asks another to 'Rehearse the Lord's Prayer'; cf. Florio, *Firste Fruites*, 103v–104v, where one character asks a companion 'if you wil teache me some prayer' and is taught the Our Father, the Creed, grace before and after meals, and some prayers relating to the queen and the Church. Prayers and extracts from Scripture formed the basis of Martin Aedler's 'Pattern of the German Pronunciation': Martin Aedler, *The High Dutch Minerva A-La-Mode or A Perfect Grammar never extant before, whereby the English may both easily and exactly learne the Neatest Dialect of the German Mother-Language used throughout All Europe* (London, 1680), pp. 43–5. Catechetical materials appear explicitly in Pierre du Ploiche, *A Treatise in English and Frenche right necessary and proffitable for al young children* (London, 1551), sig. A2r–B2r; Jean de Grave, *The Path-way to the gate of tongues: being, the first instruction for little children* (London, 1633), sig. A4r–B3v, a companion volume to Comenius's *Porta Linguarum* and commonly found bound with it, contains 'The catechisme, that is to say, An Instruction to be taught, and learned of every Childe, before he be brought to be confirmed by the Bishop'; Hollyband, *Frenche Schoolemaster* contains a monolingual French catechism entitled 'La manière d'interroguer les enfans, qu'on veut recevoir à la Cene de nostre Seigneur Jesus Christ', sig. 91v–93v.
[97] Angelika Linke, 'Communicative Genres as Categories in a Socio-Cultural History of Communication', in Stephan Elspaß, Nils Langer, Joachim Scharloth, and Wim Vandenbussche (eds.), *Germanic Language Histories 'from Below'* (Berlin and New York: de Gruyter, 2007), pp. 473–93.
[98] Bryson, *From Courtesy to Civility, passim*.

The French Tutour (1634) added to the 1625 edition '[a] few French Complements, chosen out of M. L. Miche his booke of the French courtesie'.[99] Sherwood offered phrases and dialogues for particular social situations, but in a style even more rococo than that generally found in contemporary texts. His collection of complements began with '[h]ow to doe reverence to a great Lord', and included such phrases as '[m]y Lord, The honorable place you hold among the Greatest, and the exquisite Qualities wherewith you are endowed, do oblige me to offer unto your Lordship the uttermost of that little is in me, that I may be able to render unto you upon all occasions my humble service'.[100] Recalling the scripted encounters of Linke's *Besuch*, Sherwood offered language '[t]o receive a friend that comes visite us':

AL. Sir, you are welcome, you do me a thousand times more honour, than I have
     ever deserved of you.
CLO. Pardon me, Sir, it is I that receive the honour of it.
AL. Sir, it is the excesse of your good nature, that makes you speake so, together
     with the great goodnesse of your selfe, which is borne with you.
CLO. The effects shall be as so many mouths to render faithfull testimony unto you
     of the friendship I beare you.[101]

Later in the century, a Dutch text offered a similiarly ritualized visiting scene, with the addition of a formal rejection of ceremony:

Sir, according to your Commands, I come to render you my respects.
I am infinitely obliged to you for it.
Take the pains to sit down.
I do my duty.
Without ceremony.
You have prevented me.
I was resolved to go to see you the first.
Tell me what time you are at home.
You will give you self [*sic*] too much trouble.
You will do me too much honour.[102]

These delicate rituals for the preservation of the honour of both parties would have been important to the language-learner, as the diaries and records of English

---

[99] Robert Sherwood, *The French Tutour* (London, 1634), pp. 204–19. Sherwood also included form letters (and replies) appropriate to particular occasions and written in the French style, reflecting a general shift in English epistolary practice away from Ciceronian imitation and Erasmian *copia* towards the emulation of French style and compliments. See Lawrence D. Green, 'Dictamen in England, 1500–1700', in Carol Poster and Linda C. Mitchell (eds.), *Letter-Writing Manuals and Instruction from Antiquity to the Present* (Columbia, SC: University of South Carolina Press, 2007), pp. 102–26.
[100] Sherwood, *French Tutour*, pp. 204–5.   [101] ibid., pp. 210–12.
[102] Richardson, *Anglo-Belgica*, part II, p. 129.

travellers show that paying one's respects and making the acquaintance of local figures of good reputation were central to the experience of travel.[103] An ability to pay a visit in the French style was a necessary skill in building the networks of acquaintance and reputation that were one fruit of conscientious travel, while back in England the ability to perform the calculated civility of these scripted encounters in speech and in writing was important to everyday elite sociability, and to demonstrating the sophistication acquired through travel and language study.

Conversation manuals show an awareness of the differences between cultures which were described by contemporary travel writers. Some texts schooled readers in the customs of other countries. In the first dialogue of the English translation of César Oudin's *Grammar Spanish and English* (1622), on the same page as the reader learns to say '[b]eso las mános de vuésa mercéd. Sir, I kisse your hands', a learner of Spanish asks his teacher: 'I would only beseech you to relate unto me the manner of saluting used in Spaine, and such complementall words as are most commonly spoken.' The teacher replies that while there are differences in regional behaviours, the customs of the court are 'held for good' throughout the country. He begins:

> When any one goeth to visit another his equall (for thereof we speake) approaching neere unto the place where he is, hee saith unto him. I kisse your hands Sir; the party visited answereth, and I yours; he that visiteth demandeth, how doe you Sir? the other answereth, at your service Sir, and you Sir, how are you? The party visiting replieth, at your service in what estate soever. He that is visited, saith unto the other, I beseech you Sir be pleased to take a chaire.[104]

These were not idle observations: Anna Bryson argues, as did Norbert Elias, for the importance of the linguistic, gestural, and spatial elements of ceremony, down to bowing, table manners, and the doffing of hats, as all representing the symbolism of power.[105] These, like the terms of address discussed above, were the means by which hierarchies were established and confirmed in social situations, and they were keenly observed by travellers in their attempts to adapt their own behaviour to approved local custom.

Eating and drinking were occasions at which due ceremony needed to be observed, though different nations had different practices. The consideration of cultural difference fed into ongoing discussions in England about the desirability of adapting the practices—and the vocabulary—of other cultures for English use. In a dinner scene in John Minsheu's 1599 Spanish manual, a servant asks his master

---

[103] See Chapter 4.   [104] Oudin, *Grammar Spanish and English*, p. 219.
[105] Bryson, *From Courtesy to Civility*, pp. 88–94; Norbert Elias, *The Civilizing Process, Vol. 1: The History of Manners*, trans. Edmund Jephcott (Oxford: Blackwell, 1969), *passim*. See also Pierre Bourdieu, *Language and Symbolic Power*, ed. John B. Thompson (Cambridge: Polity, 1992), p. 51.

'[s]ir will your worship have your service today, after the Italian, after the French, after the English, after the Flemish, or after the Dutch manner?' The master replies:

> Of all these extremes take me out one meane, I will not have so many ceremonies as the Italian, neither will I so much curiositie as the French, neither such abundance as the English, neither will I that the meale be so long as the Flemmings, nor so moist as the Dutch, but of all these extremes, compound me a meane after the Spanish fashion.[106]

National difference was not the only prompt for negotiation of rituals. In Robert Sherwood's dialogues, the washing of hands before a meal becomes an occasion for a debate about ceremony, revolving around the honour and rank due to the diners and their host. The host urges his guests to wash their hands; they urge him to go first; he asks them not to use ceremonies, to which they reply '[s]ir, they are not ceremonies, which duty commandeth: You shall goe first if it bee your pleasure.' The host rejects this and urges a compromise—that all will wash their hands at the same time—to which the guests grudgingly oblige: 'This is a thing that ought not to be: but seeing you will have it so, we will doe it.'[107] This debate is followed by further wrangling over the places people will take at table. This, again, was of crucial social importance: Richard Lassels' manuscript account of the travels of Lady Catherine Whetenall—compiled for her husband after her death abroad—devotes significant attention to the place at the table granted to Whetenall when invited to dine with an Italian countess, showing that English travellers abroad shared the concerns about dining and status that were addressed by authors like Sherwood:

> noe body satt at the Tables end but the Countesse pressing my Lady to sitt downe on the right side of the Table neere the tables end shee placed her selfe yemediately under her on the same side of the Table and my Ladyes woman under her, The gentlemen satt over against the Ladyes according to theire qualitie and beneath them all satt the Count[108]

Similarly, one element of Fynes Moryson's disguise as a poor Dutchman while travelling in Italy was that, on reaching inns, he would habitually sit 'at the lower end of the table', the place befitting someone wearing his 'disguised poore habit'.[109] Misunderstanding could damage one's prestige or standing in a group: in Giordano

---

[106] Minsheu, *Spanish Grammar*, pp. 17–18.   [107] Sherwood, *French Tutour*, pp. 214–15.
[108] 'Account of the journey of Lady Catherine Whetenall from Brussels to Italy, and her death at Padua', British Library, Add. MS 4217, fol. 35v.
[109] Fynes Moryson, *An Itinerary written by Fynes Moryson Gent.... containing his ten yeeres travell through the twelve dominions of Germany, Bohmerland, Switzerland, Netherland, Denmarke, Poland, Italy, Turky, France, England, Scotland, and Ireland* (London, 1617), pp. 168–9.

Bruno's *Cena de le Ceneri*, Bruno and his companions (including John Florio) arrive late at a London dinner, and Florio accidentally takes the place of honour, which leads to ridicule by the company.[110] Dialogues around dining in conversation manuals equipped readers with some of the linguistic and cultural information they needed to navigate these social minefields.

English study and adaptation of foreign manners was not without its complications, and there is a residual uneasiness with the idea of ceremony which underpins much discussion and social practice. The comparison of ceremonies and social rituals across cultures provided the grounds for an English critique of ceremony itself, and an unease which manifested itself in a professed rejection of ceremonies which, over time, became itself a ritualized or commonplace stance. To return to Minsheu's dining scene, once the guests have admired the table, they go to sit down:

[G.] Everie one draw his chaire, for this is not a table of complements.
O. They ought not to be among friends.
G. I am the greatest enemie in the worlde to ceremonies.
R. None of them seeme good unto me, except it be those which the church makes.[111]

The rejection of ceremony carries interesting social overtones: it can be a means of separating the speaker's practice from an imagined courtly behaviour characterized by the stifling overuse of ceremonies, as in one Hollyband dialogue where a character asks that '*[l]asciam vi prego tale ceremonie à i cortigiani, che non ci convengono*. Let us leave I pray such ceremonies unto Courtiers, for they become us not'.[112] This critique of a rule-bound court culture can be seen in the view expressed by one of John Florio's characters, that '[at court] a man must doo everie thing by line and measure, as walke by counterpoint, speake by the pointes of the moone, and spit by doctrine'.[113] Conversely, in 1612, Benvenuto Italiano could complain that the problem with ceremonies was less their prevalence than their adoption by the lesser sort:

Ceremonies and complements are now become so common and familiar with every one, that Coblers, Taylors, Barbers, with their children, Shoomakers, Woodmongers, Sweepe-streetes, Faulkners, that every lubberly boy, with such like vulgar frie, doe teare them asunder, even as the Butcher quarters out the flesh of an olde Cow.[114]

---

[110] Giordano Bruno, *The Ash Wednesday Supper*, trans. Stanley L. Jaki (The Hague and Paris: Mouton, 1975), p. 91. Theophilus speaks:

one of us being shown to the last place, at the tail-end of the table, and thinking that it was the head of the table, out of humility wanted to go and sit where the first [dignitary] was sitting; and so there was for a little while the contrast between those who out of courtesy [propriety] wanted to seat him at the last place, and the one who out of humility wanted to sit at the first place.

[111] Minsheu, *Spanish Grammar*, p. 19.
[112] Hollyband, *Italian Schoole-maister*, sig. [C8v]–[Dr].
[113] Florio, *Second Frutes*, pp. 147–9.   [114] Italiano, *The Passenger*, p. 423.

TO BE 'LANGUAGED'   131

Paradoxically, the ostentatious rejection of ceremony often took on the character of a ceremony itself. It need not have been accompanied by much actual rejection of ceremonies: in a 1660 Italian dialogue by Pietro Paravicino, the characters go through five lines of complimentary dialogue about who shall go first to dinner before one concludes that 'I pray Sir, let's goe in, and stand no longer upon complements.'[115] By 1694, Abel Boyer's *Compleat French-Master* could list the phrases '[w]ithout complements' and '[w]ithout ceremony' alongside '[j]e vous prie' and '[j]e vous rends grace'.[116] Rather than rejecting compliments and ceremony entirely, these were phrases (little rituals themselves) that one could mouth in order to short-circuit some of the more elaborate conversational ceremonies which might otherwise have prevailed.

Drinking in company was a pastime which followed its own scripts and rituals. Maximilien Misson, in his memoirs (published in 1719), claimed that the drinking of healths remained a common custom in England, despite having fallen out of fashion among the French elite; and Misson described carefully how the ceremony would vary depending on the status and gender of the participants.[117] Earlier in the period, the rituals surrounding drinking in company were a common feature of conversation manuals. Indeed, drinking could have a language all its own: Fynes Moryson admired how drinkers in Nuremberg signalled for a new beer by leaving their glass upright, or indicated that they had drunk their fill by turning it upside down: 'they are such Masters in this Art of drinking as they are served by dumbe signes without speaking a word'.[118] In Moryson's telling, not only were German inns run according to strict cultural rules—'When you come in, you must salute the Hoste, and happy you if he salute you againe. You must drinke with him, and observe him in all things'—but they demanded the traveller's engagement in the heavy drinking for which the Germans were famous, as a good way to gain competence in German: 'he that wil be welcome in their company, or desires to learne their language, must needs practice this excesse in some measure'.[119] In a drinking dialogue, Pietro Paravicino's Italian manual provided the means for English-speakers to avoid these excesses:

Sirs, I do not see any one pledge me.
I will do it presently, but not after the German manner.
And why not after the German manner, is it not a fine thing to drink clean out?[120]

---

[115] Pietro Paravicino, *Choice Proverbs and Dialogues, in Italian and English* (London, 1660), p. 93.
[116] Abel Boyer, *The Compleat French-Master, for Ladies and Gentlemen. Being A New Method, to Learn with ease and delight the French Tongue, as it is now spoken in the Court of France* (London, 1694), p. 167.
[117] Maximilien Misson, *M. Misson's Memoirs and Observations in his travels over England* (London, 1719), pp. 69–70.
[118] Moryson, *Itinerary*, p. 87.   [119] ibid., pp. 84, 86.
[120] Paravicino, *Choice Proverbs and Dialogues*, p. 105.

These rituals were crucial in similar environments in early modern England.[121] In drinking rituals, scripts and intoxicants came together in an everyday activity in which notions of honour, mutual regard, social status, masculinity, and political identity were bound up.[122]

The cause of conviviality and conflict, health-drinking was debated throughout the period: Rebecca Lemon has mapped opinions on the practice from the later sixteenth century, when its critics saw it as an import from abroad, to the 1630s onwards, when it became the target of criticism by the godly and of celebration by Royalists who sought to paint it as an ancient, loyal custom.[123] Angela McShane has traced the development of healthing and toasting practices, and their relationship to religious and secular ritual, showing that the period from Elizabeth's accession to the end of the seventeenth century witnessed important developments in the relationship between drinking, politics, and sociability.[124] Conversation manuals show that these were concerns in polyglot contexts too. Communal drinking could seal friendships, as in the *Plaine pathway to the French tongue* (1575), where merchants renew their acquaintance after a long time apart: 'We must drinke a pinte before you depart from hence for to renew the olde amitie or frendshippe.'[125] Alehouses, and, later, coffee-houses, were 'semi-formal' commercial spaces, where contacts might be made and deals sealed.[126] These drinking rites

---

[121] Phil Withington argues that 'all company, from the ceremonial to the ephemeral, was shaped by objective factors: rituals and conventions, modes of discourse, the use of physical space, material objects... and, in many cases, intoxicants': Phil Withington, 'Company and Sociability in Early Modern England', *Social History* 32 (2007), p. 302.

[122] For an introduction to 'public houses' of various kinds in early modern Europe, see Beat Kümin and B. Ann Tlusty, 'The World of the Tavern: An Introduction', and Beat Kümin, 'Public Houses and their Patrons in Early Modern Europe', in Beat Kümin and B. Ann Tlusty (eds.), *The World of the Tavern: Public Houses in Early Modern Europe* (Aldershot: Ashgate, 2002), pp. 3–11 and 44–62. For the development of the alehouse as distinct from the inn or tavern, and for alehouse sociability, see Peter Clark, *The English Alehouse: A Social History 1200–1830* (London and New York: Longman, 1983). For drinking and masculinity, see Alexandra Shepard, 'Swil-bols and Tos-pots': Drink Culture and Male Bonding in England, *c.*1560–1640', in Laura Gowing, Michael Hunter, and Miri Rubin (eds.), *Love, Friendship and Faith in Europe, 1300–1800* (Basingstoke: Palgrave Macmillan, 2005), pp. 112–26; Shepard, *Meanings of Manhood in Early Modern England* (Oxford: Oxford University Press, 2003), pp. 100–3. On the tavern as a space where new forms of elite sociability could be developed, debated, and practised, see Michelle O'Callaghan, *The English Wits: Literature and Sociability in Early Modern England* (Cambridge: Cambridge University Press, 2007), pp. 60–79.

[123] Rebecca Lemon, 'Compulsory Conviviality in Early Modern England', *English Literary Renaissance* 43 (2013), pp. 381–414. See also Clark, *English Alehouse*, p. 156.

[124] Angela McShane, 'Material Culture and 'Political Drinking' in Seventeenth-Century England', in Phil Withington and Angela McShane (eds.), *Cultures of Intoxication* (*Past & Present*, supplement 9, 2014), pp. 247–76.

[125] *Plaine pathway* (London, 1575), sig. B2r. Compare Keith Wrightson, 'Alehouses, Order and Reformation in Rural England, 1590–1660', in Eileen Yeo and Stephen Yeo (eds.), *Popular Culture and Class Conflict 1590–1914: Explorations in the History of Labour and Leisure* (Brighton and Atlantic Highlands, NJ: The Harvester Press and Humanities Press, 1981), p. 6.

[126] For the tavern as a commercial venue, see Clark, *English Alehouse*; Kümin and Tlusty, 'World of the Tavern', p. 8. Taverns fulfilled a comparable role on the continent: compare B. Ann Tlusty, *Bacchus and Civic Order: The Culture of Drink in Early Modern Germany* (Charlottesville, VA, and London: University Press of Virginia, 2001), pp. 103–13.

were 'part of men's everyday exchange, and ideally served to oil their networks of credit and community'.[127] For those involved not just in commerce but in any form of masculine sociability it was necessary to be able to partake in this subtle everyday ritual. In Peter Berault's 1688 French manual, a section titled *Familiar Phrases* turns almost immediately to drinking, this time as an element of sociability between the sexes, and perhaps of courtship.[128] Conversation manuals' representation of drinking rituals attempted to guide their readers through a complex sociolinguistic ritual—one which could bring people together or cause conflict throughout early modern Europe.

Pledging and the drinking of healths connoted good fellowship and comradeship, but as activities which touched on male honour and political loyalty, there was room for conflict and breakdown, whose representation in dialogues acted as a lesson in itself about the norms of drinking culture and its rituals. Consider loyal healths, which, according to Gilbert Burnet, were 'set up by too many as a distinguishing mark of loyalty' at the Restoration.[129] The link between binge-drinking and loyalty had been established earlier, with the development of a Royalist healthing ideology across the previous decades in which '[l]oyal camaraderie [depended] upon participation in the drinking ritual'.[130] The social and political tensions involved in the drinking of healths—loyal and not—could spark into conflict.[131] Richardson's *Anglo-Belgica* offers one suggestion of how a loyal health could go wrong. The drinkers agree on a loyal health, and the form of words is spoken:

A.: Sir, I drink the King's Health.
B.: I accept of it with all my heart.
A.: It must go round.
B.: Sir, it is his Majesties good health, I drink it to you, Sir.

The proposer of the toast accuses his companion '[y]ou do not drink it up'. The companion protests that the glass is too full, but is given the blunt reply '[t]ruly, I drunk it so'—the importance of matching the amounts that one drinks to another is clear in these texts. As three of Richardson's characters pledge each other, a fourth is put out: 'I have drunk but one cup yet, make haste then, that I may drink at my turn.'[132] Even those drinking rituals which were not so closely

---

[127] Shepard, *Meanings of manhood*, p. 101.
[128] Berault, *French and English Grammar*, pp. 186–7.
[129] Quoted in Steve Pincus, '"Coffee Politicians Does Create": Coffeehouses and Restoration Political Culture', *Journal of Modern History* 67 (1995), p. 825.
[130] Lemon, 'Compulsory Conviviality', p. 407.
[131] John Walter, 'Gesturing at Authority: Deciphering the Gestural Code of Early Modern England', in Michael J. Braddick (ed.) *The Politics of Gesture: Historical Perspectives* (Past & Present, vol. 203, supplement 4, 2009), p. 106.
[132] Richardson, *Anglo-Belgica*, part II, pp. 228–9.

tied to national politics had the potential for this kind of breakdown: pledging may have stood for 'a symbolic equalization of status' (though persons of different rank could drink to one another, if with care), but there was room for insult if the rite was misjudged.[133] Ann Tlusty argues that, in Augsburg, 'sharing in a round of drinks was a means of establishing structural ties, whether of business, friendship, kinship, or simple camaraderie', but that social identification with others did not mean social equality: this allowed superiors and inferiors to drink together without any equalization of status.[134]

William Stepney's *Spanish Schoole-master* (1591) contains a singularly acrimonious pledging dialogue. It begins in friendly fashion, with one drinker addressing another—'Now Sir I drinke to you, and to all the companie, and first to your next neighbour, will you pledge me?'—and receiving the reply 'Yea, with as good a will as ever I came from schoole.' The pledging ritual depended on both parties drinking the same amount, a rule which was strictly enforced, and could be cause for conflict: the need to match the amount drunk could stand for an equality of esteem between the parties. Stepney's dialogue soon descends into suspicion and recrimination around this rule:

Go to, drinke, but you have not dronke all out. I will fill it you yet once full.
Wherefore should you do that? have I not drunke it out? How much lacketh it?
    I will drinke it out. Looke there, now is it emptie. Pledge me now. You seeke
    nothing but to beguile me.

Concerns of masculinity and of capacity for alcohol were at stake, too: the ability to drink more than others could be proof of manliness. Stepney's drinkers complained, variously saying 'I should not be able to drinke this out,' 'I have too much,' and asking 'What should let you? I have well dronken it out,' Next, one character accuses another of subterfuge. Underhand tactics in drinking rituals were not unknown—Fynes Moryson suggested some ruses travellers could employ in German inns to avoid drinking as much as their fellows[135]—but the suggestion of foul play spurs further conflict among Stepney's drinkers:

You had not so much as I.
Your goblet was not full.
But it was,
No it was not.
It is true, but my goblet is greater than yours.
Well let us change.
I am content, give me yours.

---

[133] Bryson, *From Courtesy to Civility*, p. 93.   [134] Tlusty, *Bacchus and Civic Order*, pp. 149–50.
[135] Moryson, *Itinerary*, part III, book II, p. 89.

I will not. I hold me by mine owne, and keepe you that which you have.
Drinke then.

To ignore another drinker and not to drink their health could be grounds for insult, while the ability to manage perceived offence and conflict in a volatile situation was important:

To whom have you dronken? Drinke to me once.
Be you angrie with me?
Wherefore should I be angrie with you?
Because you drinke not to me.
I have drunke to you.
I have not heard it.[136]

Stepney's painstaking list of faults and disagreements suggests some of the social risks of drinking and the offence that could too easily be caused.[137] He used the dialogue form to show some of the ways in which conversational harmony and ritual structures could be disrupted. Within the framework of a drinking dialogue that goes wrong, he also suggested a number of strategies for negotiating the form the practice would take. The conversation manual's capacity for showing the breakdown of ritual and conversational forms, and for negotiating the differences between national cultural practices, made them a powerful pedagogical tool.

Commercial Language: Words, Knowledge, and Behaviour in the Marketplace

William Scott's *An Essay of Drapery: or, the Compleate Citizen* (1635) offered advice for the young man hoping to make it in London trade. His essay was a conduct manual for the commercial world, sketching the ethics, behaviour, and comportment of the citizen of its title. Scott advised his would-be draper to be careful in observing necessary ceremonies, since '[t]o make no difference in the use of them, to a Lord, and a Ploughman kissing their hands, and bowing as low to a Chamber-maide, as to her Lady, is uncomely'. Control of his speech was paramount: he should speak 'with masculine and true elocution fitted to the matter and circumstances'; his words should be 'discreetly chosen, and properly applied'; and to this eloquence should be added 'a grave naturall action, wherein a man may see the visage, hands, and members of the man to speake with

---

[136] Stepney, *Spanish Schoole-master*, pp. 88–92.
[137] See McShane, 'Material Culture and "Political Drinking"', *passim*, for examples of conflict and breakdown over healths and toasts in contemporary records of communal drinking.

his mouth'. The skilled trader would be a master of speech and of bodily comportment. To trade, as Craig Muldrew shows, was to communicate: 'commerce and marketing came to be interpreted as one form of communication used to form social bonds'.[138] Scott's draper needed to possess 'communicative competence', the ability to vary his speech according to the company: 'in as much as hee is to deale with men of divers conditions, let him know that to speake according to the nature of him with whom he commerceth, is the best Rhetorick'.[139] The draper's ability to speak well, as Phil Withington argues, 'demanded psychological and social acuity'.[140] Scott's last piece of advice was that his reader should become a polyglot:

> To conclude this, that my Citizen may deale pleasingly with all men; I would have him be a good Linguist, getting so many Languages, and those so well, that if it were possible, every man he deales with, should thinke him his Countrey-man.[141]

The complete citizen would be a learner of languages, and one who displayed a competence which was inherently social: his skill in language and in the behaviour of his trade would earn him respect in the community and income from his customers.

This concern with polyglot commercial competence was shared by the authors of most conversation manuals. In the corpus of manuals, commercial material— buying and selling, bargaining, changing coin—is always to the fore. Each text deals with trade in different ways, but almost all are set in a world where every price and every payment is negotiable. Trade was an activity in which multilingual competence was crucial: as one conversation manual rhetorically asked, 'How many are ther becom ryche, without the knoweledg of divres languages?'[142] The manuals attempted to inculcate a variety of different commercial competences appropriate to their varying audiences, from haggling to buy another diner's knife at the dinner table up to complete discussions of exchange rates and international trade on the floor of a trade exchange.[143] As Phil Withington argues, 'commercial success was inextricably linked to the practice of company itself—the interlocking dynamics of purpose, power, structure, participation, culture, and *habitus* of any given instance'.[144] Knowing how to speak meant knowing how to be in company, and this was knowledge which was essential for commercial success.

---

[138] Muldrew, *Economy of Obligation*, p. 138.
[139] William Scott, *An Essay of Drapery: or, the Compleate Citizen* (London, 1635), pp. 87, 90–1.
[140] Withington, *Politics of Commonwealth*, p. 141.   [141] Ibid., p. 94.
[142] Anon., *Colloquia* (1606), sig. A5v.
[143] Anon., *Dutch-Tutor*, p. 31; Richardson, *Anglo-Belgica*, 'A Discourse concerning Bills of Exchange', part II, pp. 36–43.
[144] Withington, *Society in Early Modern England*, p. 185.

These texts show bargaining as a kind of semi-scripted ritual, a social activity whose shape appears to have been commonly accepted but which required a linguistic and social dexterity if the speaker was to come out on top. As Craig Muldrew has shown, in early modern trade, 'price was always a matter of negotiation between buyer and seller', and the bargain was recognized as having its own ethical and behavioural codes.[145] From a linguist's perspective, Monika Becker has argued that bargaining dialogues in language-learning texts are highly standardized and tend to follow a structure which is broadly uniform across the genre. She sees these dialogues as combining instruction in language with advice on the strategies necessary for success in bargaining:

> Sales talk as represented in early modern textbook dialogues tried to teach successful communication by offering different strategies and a wide range of devices which enable the learner as a client or as a salesperson to succeed in a situation with conflicting interests.[146]

Becker's analysis draws on the concepts of 'face' and 'face work', seeing the bargain as a 'conflictive game' in which the participants deploy 'face maintaining' and 'face threatening' techniques, such as the common avoidance by both parties of naming a price for as long as possible at the beginning of the dialogue; neither wishes to be the one to make the first offer. For Becker, 'sales talk' dialogues are made up of three distinct units—the opening phase, which includes the greetings, expression of interest, and presentation of the goods; the bargaining, which can be simple or complex and involve a wide variety of devices and techniques aimed at gaining the upper hand; and, after a deal has been made, the payment and handing over of goods, and the farewells. Becker argues that the shift to more conciliatory language which appears frequently once a price has been agreed on serves to re-establish friendly relations after the implicit conflict of the bargaining section.[147]

This understanding of the dialogue as a widely recognized ritual, whose twists and turns were common knowledge, is one which early modern readers would have recognized. In his 1599 *Spanish Grammar*, John Minsheu portrays a stylized commercial dialogue in which the participants repeatedly and explicitly argue that the bargain is analogous to a dance. The prospective buyer complains that '[y]ou are so deere that I know not what I may offer for it, if there bee no abatement', which is given in Spanish as '*[e]stá tan caro, que yo no sé que le ofrezca si no es una báxa*'; a marginal note explains that *báxa* refers to '[a] daunce so called. Also an

---

[145] Muldrew, *Economy of Obligation*, pp. 42–7.

[146] Becker, 'Yf ye wyll bergayne', p. 292. See also Franz Lebsanft, 'A Late Medieval French Bargain Dialogue (*Pathelin* II). Or: Further Remarks on the History of Dialogue Forms', in Andreas H. Jucker, Gerd Fritz, and Franz Lebsanft (eds.), *Historical Dialogue Analysis* (Amsterdam and Philadelphia, PA: John Benjamins, 1999), pp. 279–84; Bös, 'Early Modern English Service Encounters', pp. 219–40.

[147] Becker, 'Yf ye wyll bergayne', pp. 273–97.

abatement'. This play on words is carried on throughout the dialogue: pressing the customer to name his price first, the seller replies '[t]hat will I daunce after your worship hath strooke the trebil'. His original offer rejected, the customer asks the dealer to 'come backe and daunce againe, to see upon what you sticke'; the customer then rejects the proposed abatement with '[y]ou daunce very ill, I plaie no more'. The bargain is ultimately solved when the buyer's wife suggests a compromise.[148] Across the genre, bargaining dialogues reflect a culture in which commercial interaction was understood as ritualized and as taking an agreed form—this is why the dialogue mentioned above in which a woman's attempt at bargaining is refused and she takes her purchases at the first price named jars as it does—and in which buyers and sellers attempted to gain the upper hand by means of greater knowledge of commodities and linguistic and behavioural skills.

In these dramatized representations of market conversations, authors of conversation manuals incorporated techniques by which buyers could strengthen their position. Rhetorical references to friendship or to an ongoing relationship between buyer and seller could be used to leverage a lower price, as in Marten Le Mayre's *Dutch Schoole Master* (1606):

But I promise you that except you were my customer, you should not have it under six pounds fifteene shillings Sterlings
But seeing that it is you, I doe abate you above nine shillings in the peece assuredly.
I thinke that you desire not my losse, and truely if you do refuse it, no man in the world, shall have it for the price.
Yea, if it were mine brother,
Well you shal abate me those ten pence, for to make an even reckoning.
I will not stick at ten pence[149]

Whether the price in a case like this in fact represents one which is significantly lower than that offered to others is irrelevant: both parties have worked towards a situation in which each has saved face, with the customer being confident that they have been granted the best possible price, and the seller in a position to try to strengthen their relationship with a view to future commerce:

I hope that an other time, I shall have of your money, sooner then an other, shall I not?'
Yea indeed.
I will not forsake you for another.[150]

---

[148] Minsheu, *Spanish Grammar*, pp. 11–12.
[149] Le Mayre, *Dutch Schoole Master*, sig. [D6v]–[D7v].   [150] Ibid.

The promise of future trade was not a strategy limited to the marketplace: in *Anglo-Belgica*, an innkeeper says 'I hope you will come to see me again when you return,' while in Mayre's text, the guest tips both the maid and the ostler, '[t]o the end that thou maist remember me an other time'. Obliging, the ostler (or the host, it is unclear) replies '[y]ou shall finde me at all times ready to do you service, spare not the lodging, when you shall passe here by'.[151] The oft-copied Berlemont text showed the harmony—and pious friendship—which reigned between the participants at the end of an idealized bargain:

[D.] far Well maistris.
K. I thanze [sic] you heartelie,
my frinde,
when you have neede
of any thing,
com to mee,
I will sell it you
good chape.
d. Well maistris.
I will doo it gladlie
I commit you to god.[152]

Conversely, van Heldoren's *English and Nether-dutch Dictionary* (1675) showed a bargain which closed with an obdurate customer insisting on a low price which the seller seems only grudgingly to accept. Of interest here is the way in which the customer attempts to repair the relationship—first insisting that 'I would have you satisfied,' and then proffering a non-monetary sweetener in the form of an introduction to a friend who will in their turn provide custom to the trader:

well but are you satisfied.
Yes Sir, seeing you will give me no more.
But I would have you satisfyed.
Yes Sir, I am content.
An other time I will send for you.
Sir, command me.
Do you work for Master Tomkins?
No, Sir.
I wil recommend you to him.
You will oblidge me.

---

151 Richardson, *Anglo-Belgica*, part II, p. 179; Le Mayre, *Dutch Schoole Master*, sig. E3v–E4r.
152 Anon., *Colloquia* (1606), sig. H3v. The corruption of the English text is common in editions of Berlemont printed on the continent.

Farewel, il remember to go to him to morrow.
I have spoken to him of you.
Go there from me.[153]

Readers of these conversation manuals learnt to manage tangible assets, but also how to establish and leverage relationships to their commercial advantage.

Bargaining was a high-stakes game, and manuals showed speakers succeeding and failing in the endeavour. The 1606 seven-language edition of the Berlemont *Colloquia* showed an attempt at calling the seller's bluff by walking away. In this case, the strategy is successful:

[D.] Well,
shal I not have it?
K. Not for that price.
D. Far well then,
I go.
K. God guyde you.
Now com heere, take it,
I can not refuse myne handtsaile,
it is good chape.
D. That saye you,
but I say it is to deere,
you have begliued [sic] me.
K. I quit you therof
if you be
evell content.[154]

Here, having been called back by the seller, the buyer attempts to press his advantage, having gained the upper hand by his keen strategy. Another dialogue, recurring in several manuals, shows this strategy failing. A price cannot be reached, and the seller insists that there is not a better price to be had in London. Language to urge a customer to '[s]tay, abide', and '[g]oe where you please' is given, but ultimately the deal breaks down:

Your price is not for us.
You know what you have to doe.
Well seeing that we cannot agree of the price,
God be with you, we goe to another place.

---

[153] J. G. van Heldoren, *An English and Nether-dutch Dictionary* (Amsterdam, 1675), pp. 28–9.
[154] Anon., *Colloquia* (1606), sig. Hv.

This said, the dialogue breaks up into the views of both parties. On the side of the seller, there is '[t]hey goe away', '[t]hey are gone', '[l]et them goe', '[l]et them runne'; while the buyers discuss amongst themselves the quality of the material and realize that they have been too hasty:

We shall hardly finde such for the price.
Let us aske him if hee will abate something of it.

They return to the seller—'Here they come againe'—and a deal is made between the two, with the seller seemingly having got the upper hand, though he refuses to admit that he has won: the buyer says '[y]ou are hard to please', with the seller replying only 'I get nothing by it.'[155] His victory is not broadcast but the lesson in bargaining technique, about judging items and prices well and the loss of face (not to mention of capital) that can come with being called on one's bluff, is clear.

Conversation manuals did not just teach conversational strategies. Embedded in their vocabularies and dialogues were forms of knowledge, judgement, and discernment. When they discussed products and prices (just like when they discussed people and reputations), the dialogues instructed their readers in ways of judging quality and value. Commodity-focused dialogues were useful not just because of their linguistic material but also for the knowledge about commercial concerns which was embedded within them. Vocabularies dealing with commodities did more than teach the equivalents of English words in other languages— they organized them in hierarchies and taught the vocabulary of distinction, the language used by an insider with knowledge of the trade. John Minsheu's Spanish manual contained a dialogue discussing luxury furnishings:

From whence had you this tapestrie hangings?
Sir it came from Flaunders.
And from thence also came these pictures and portraitures?
Some of them did, others came from Italie.
Truely they are of a fine workmans doing.

When a character describes the wood in a desk: 'The red is Caóba of Havána, and this blacke is Ebonie, and the white is Ivorie,' Minsheu offers a marginal note to explain the outlandish term: 'Caóba, a fine red wood in the Indies, of which they make checker worke and other curious works in cupboords, &c'.[156] Taken

---

[155] Cougneau, *Sure Guide*, pp. 105–10. For the same dialogue in different forms, see Hollyband, *French Littelton*, p. 56 (this seems to be its first appearance); also Le Mayre, sig. Er–Ev.

[156] Minsheu, *Spanish Grammar*, p. 4. A conversation manual which is comparably concerned with naming foreign commodities (perhaps unsurprisingly, given its close links to the East India trade) is Arthus Gotthard, *Dialogues in the English and Malaiane languages* (London, 1614).

together, this offers the reader the vocabulary of an aficionado with some basic knowledge of the subject. Language and discernment are learnt together.

The same approach is at work in dialogues on cloth and clothing: this set of phrases from a 1664 English-Dutch text teaches discernment between national styles of cloth and clothing:

> Sir, have you any new fashion stuffs? have you any Hollands linnen, Chamletts, any Hollandish broad Clothes, blacke, or gray, have you any English Serges, have you any Spanish Cloth, any English broad Cloth, well drest, have you any Excester Carsies, have you any Cersies of Flanders dye, have you any Tammye, Romane Serges, Course Serges, Buckrain, Ribbands, have you any Cambricks lane, fine Holland Alkmores linnen, fine lace, or Flanders bonelace, have you any canvas, whalebone, Balleine, Castors, Bevers, hatts, (or Felts) that arevery [*sic*] good and blacke, have you any silks have you any halve Hose, and Mens stockings? &c.[157]

Other texts offered phrases with which speakers could challenge a seller's assessment of the quality or value of goods on offer. A 1575 text had a section of its vocabulary titled 'Diversitie of coulers', offering some vocabulary for describing cloth, including 'Thicke' and 'Thinne', standard colours, and more exotic (and perhaps expert-sounding) terms like 'Azure', 'Tawnie', 'Lions couler', 'Blou-dredde', 'Dyed in *the* wool', 'Bryght russet', and others.[158] The vocabularies offered elsewhere for speaking about coins—'it is short: it is of base gold: it is light: it is clipped: it is counterfait' and so forth—allowed the speaker to challenge the value of coins they were given or to defend the purity of those they used, thus extracting the maximum benefit from a transaction and avoiding being cheated.[159] Without explicit explanation of how one would judge the qualities of different kinds of cloth—or wine, or horses, or other commodities—there was naturally a limit to how much commercial knowledge could be communicated, but the ability to employ these languages of discernment had a symbolic power of its own which was of practical use in the bargain.[160] Among the 'possible symbolic functions of jargon', Peter Burke argues, is its potential to impress or to exclude those outside

---

[157] Hillenius, *Instructer*, p. 75. On cloth and vocabularies of distinction, see John Gallagher, 'The Italian London of John North: Cultural Contact and Linguistic Encounter in Early Modern England', *Renaissance Quarterly*, 70 (2017), pp. 104–6.

[158] Anon., *Plaine pathway*, sig. Br.

[159] For variations on this section, see Hollyband, *French Littelton* (1593), pp. 48–9; Hollyband, *French Schoole-master*, sig. 81v–83r; Stepney, *Spanish Schoole-master*, pp. 142–5; Le Mayre, *Dutch Schoole Master*, sig. E2r–E3r; Hillenius, *Instructer*, pp. 85–6. Hollyband seems to be the source. For discussions of coin not derived from Hollyband, see, for instance, Eliot, *Ortho-Epia Gallica*, part II, pp. 29–30; Miège, *Nouvelle methode*, pp. 114–15.

[160] Cloth and wine are discussed throughout the corpus. There is a particularly detailed and interesting horse-buying dialogue in Hollyband, *Italian Schoole-maister*, sig. C4v–[C8r].

the specialist or technical community which uses the jargon.[161] This suggests, though, that the ability to speak in the jargon of an occupational or other social group could communicate the speaker's membership of the group. To be able to use the jargon of trade could confer some authority on the speaker: knowing how to speak and how to do business were closely bound up together, and these guides attempted to give their readers a means of wielding symbolic knowledge manifested in terms of art in order to do well in a bargain.

It was not only commodities that needed to be judged. People—their credit and reputation—would be weighed by a canny tradesperson, and an understanding of the European economy was important where bills of exchange and international trade were under discussion. A 1575 French dialogue shows the credit of an international group being judged:

R. Behold a great flock of Italians
T. They be Almains & Brabenders shearmans and dressers of clothes.
R. Know you them?
T. They be verie well knowen and are honest men and of good credit
R. Call them and make them to enter[162]

In an economy in which so much trade was face-to-face, the ability to gather and weigh this kind of information was central. Commercial relationships could be turned to personal advantage: one Dutch form letter from a young merchant at the end of his apprenticeship asked an elder for help in establishing himself:

Having finished my seven years Apprentiship, am now entring into the world for imployment for my self, and knowing my Trade depends upon acquaintance, I make bold to renew former friendship with you; hoping, if it lies in your power, to do me any kindness therein, you will (for the love you bear to me) do your utmost to help me.[163]

As we have seen, conversation manuals were rich in materials for judging the credit of others and for furthering one's own reputation. When it came to credit and its relation to global trade, some authors provided detailed materials for the discussion of international commerce, whether in Richardson's detailed Exchange dialogue or in the routine exchanges of news, political and commercial, from around Europe.[164] These were all elements of the commercial competence which is an almost omnipresent concern in the corpus of conversation manuals. Prices

---

[161] Peter Burke, 'Introduction', in Peter Burke and Roy Porter (eds.), *Languages and Jargons: Contributions to a Social History of Language* (Cambridge: Polity, 1995), p. 14.
[162] Anon., *Plaine Pathway*, sig. [A7r].   [163] Richardson, *Anglo-Belgica*, p. 69.
[164] Ibid., pp. 36–43.

were almost always negotiable in early modern European societies, and, regardless of the linguist's background or occupation, they required the ability to negotiate the marketplace (locally and globally) and the conversations and interactions that sustained it. The manuals' commercial conversations helped to inculcate the mixed linguistic and commercial competence of William Scott's 'good linguist' and 'complete citizen'.

Fitting In: The Languages of Immigrants

One surprising feature of conversation manuals printed in England is that they give relatively little space to cultural differences. Manuals like John Florio's for Italian and William Stepney's for Spanish set their dialogues in London rather than abroad. Manuals in general are low on discussions, for instance, of culinary differences that travellers would encounter in other countries, while the manuals which contained more than two languages—and in particular those with up to eight parallel texts—necessarily flattened some cultural difference in attempting to provide some conversational material of near pan-European utility. This authorial decision probably has its roots in English anxieties about travel and cultural encounter: a constant note in the advice offered to travellers was that they should avoid adapting their behaviour too much while travelling abroad, lest they return like 'those fantastickes, which bring home with them, some apish ceremonies of curtesie, and strange fashions of apparell, but nothing else, to give them commendations at their returnes'.[165] A set of conversation manuals which, unlike the majority, did argue implicitly and explicitly for cultural assimilation and integration into the foreign linguistic community were those which were written for newly arrived immigrants to England. Conversation manuals for non-Anglophone audiences hoping to learn English began to appear in the later sixteenth century. Introducing his *Firste Fruites* in 1578, John Florio referred to the Italian gentlemen and merchants who had pestered him for some materials that would help their countrymen to learn the English language.[166] Florio's manual addressed Anglophone and Italian-speaking audiences, but other texts were clearer in their address to immigrant populations. A classic early example is Jacques Bellot's *Maistre d'escole Anglois* (London, 1580), which advertised itself as '[c]onteyning many profitable preceptes for the naturall borne french men, and

[165] Thomas Palmer, *An Essay of the Meanes how to make our Trauailes, into forraine Countries, the more profitable and honourable* (London, 1606), p. 61. On the figure of the returned traveller, see Sara Warneke, *Images of the Educational Traveller in Early Modern England* (London, New York, and Cologne: E. J. Brill, 1995); Hilary Larkin, *The Making of Englishmen: Debates on National Identity 1550–1650* (Leiden and Boston, MA: Brill, 2014); and Gallagher, 'The Italian London of John North'.
[166] John Florio, *Florio His firste Fruites which yeelde familiar speech* (London, 1578), sig. **.ij.r and **.ij.v, 'A tutti i Gentilhuomini, e Mercanti Italjani, che si dilettano de la lingua Inglese'.

other straungers that have their French tongue, to attayne the true pronouncing of the Englishe tongue'. Bellot followed this first book up in 1586 with *Familiar Dialogues*, 'for the Instruction of them, that be desirous to learne to speake English, and perfectlye to pronounce the same'.[167] Texts addressed to immigrant readerships tended to appear at moments when large numbers of migrants were arriving in England. Each is different, but, taken together, they give some idea of the ways in which newly arrived immigrants' language-learning and attempts at integration were coloured by the circumstances of their arrival.[168] Immigrant competences (as represented in these books) reflected wider struggles over cultural and religious identity, social status, and the place of strangers in a changing England.

Immigrant manuals, unlike those aimed at travellers and traders, were concerned with getting by but also with fitting in—with understanding and adapting to new social and cultural surroundings. Some manuals suggested the uneasy position of the non-Anglophone in England. In Pietro Paravicino's *Choice phrases*, an English-Italian manual of 1662, a character defends his position in a bargaining dialogue with the phrase '[d]o you hold me for a Poland [*Mi tenete voi per un Polacco*] that I know not what the Ware is worth', suggesting that a foreigner might be thought more easily gulled than an Englishman or a knowledgeable immigrant.[169] Heinrich Offelen's *Double Grammar for Germans To Learn English; and for English-Men To Learn the German-Tongue* (London, 1687) has a similar argument in a cloth-buying dialogue:

How! Twenty Shillings, you take me for a Stranger I see.
No Sir, we are not in France here.
We sell no dearer to a Stranger in this Countrey, than to an English-man.

Later, Offelen suggests that English antipathy towards strangers might be moderated depending on their perceived origin:

Are Strangers much esteemed in England?
Not very much of the Rabble, they take every Stranger for a French-man.[170]

---

[167] Bellot, *Familiar Dialogues*.

[168] On immigrants' integration, see Susanne Lachenicht, 'Huguenot Immigrants and the Formation of National Identities, 1548–1787', *Historical Journal* 50 (2007), pp. 309–31; Eileen Barrett, 'Huguenot Integration in late 17th- and 18th-Century London: Insights from Records of the French Church and Some Relief Agencies', in Randolph Vigne and Charles Littleton (eds.), *From Strangers to Citizens: The Integration of Immigrant Communities in Britain, Ireland and Colonial America, 1550–1750* (Brighton and Portland, OR: Sussex Academic Press, 2001), pp. 375–82.

[169] Pietro Paravicino, *Choice Phrases, set forth in questions and answers in Italian, rendered into English* (London, 1662), p. 71.

[170] Offelen, *Double Grammar*, pp. 199, 217.

Offelen's view of the 'Rabble' was essentially the same as John Florio's over a century before, when a character in his *Firste Fruites* had complained that 'the Nobilitie is very curteous but the commons are discorteous, & especially toward strangers'.[171] The implicit message of bargaining dialogues like these is that a lack of linguistic skill could lead to commercial loss. A. P. R. Howatt argues that manuals for French learners of English 'recognized the old truth that even a smattering of your client's mother tongue works wonders in business. It also helps to safeguard against sharp practice.'[172] Here, there is also the spectre of exclusion from the English-speaking linguistic community. For many immigrants, the acquisition of linguistic competence was more than just a cultural accomplishment: it was an everyday necessity.

As well as learning equivalent phrases to the ones they might have used in their native languages, learners of another language had to adapt to cultural-linguistic particularities, such as different weights, measures, and currencies. Van Heldoren's detailed '[o]f weights and measures commonly used in England' translated English ways of quantifying ale, beer, grain, fish, wool, and other commodities, as well as giving Dutch equivalents of English currency.[173] The adaptation of the Berlemont bargaining dialogue by François Hillenius in his *English and Low Dutch Instructer* (1664) performed this kind of translation between currencies in brackets:

It shall cost you a dollar, (or thirty stivers.)
How much the pound of this Cheese (supplice, the value or price.)
The pound I rate, at five groates. [i.e. 2½ stiver.][174]

A similar cultural-commercial translation was achieved silently between languages in Peter Berault's French and English grammar (1688):

How much the Yard? How much an Ell?
Combien la Verge? Combien l'Aulne?
A Crown this, and two Shillings the other.
Un Ecu cellecy, & deux Shelins l'autre.[175]

---

[171] Florio, *Firste Fruites*, sig. 9v.

[172] A. P. R. Howatt, *A History of English Language Teaching* (Oxford: Oxford University Press, 1984), p. 6.

[173] Van Heldoren, *English and Nether-dutch Dictionary*, Dialogues (the *Dictionary* is not always bound with the dialogues), pp. 39–43.

[174] Hillenius, *Instructer*, p. 15.

[175] Berault, *French and English grammar*, p. 174. See also Juan de Luna, *A short and compendious art for to learne to reade, write, pronounce and speake the Spanish Tongue* (London, 1623), sig. [M6r], which gives an in-depth explanation of the coinage of Spain; and for an example from later in the period, Boyer, *Compleat French-Master*, 'Of coins. Des Monoies', p. 155.

In Hollyband's *French Littelton*, a stranger is commended for his knowledge of English weights and measures, which are then explained in the text: 'the pint of Paris, is almost as great as the quart of London: the quart, as the pottell of England, the broc, or lot, as your gallon: the festier, as your pint: the halfe festier, as your penie pot: keepe that well, for there is a small difference'.[176]

These translations can model intercultural relationships: this is rarely more evident than in Edward Richardson's *Anglo-Belgica* (first edition published in 1677), where linguistic and sociable encounters between English- and Dutch-speakers seem to offer a model of cooperation and friendship between the two nations. One Englishman says that 'I did promise a Dutch Gentleman, who doth not understand our Language, to go along with him into the City, to help him to buy some commodities,' while a dinner between an Englishman and a Dutchman becomes an extended dialogue in which the Dutch-speaker compliments England, drinks the king's health, agrees with much of the praise his host bestows on England, and smokes together with him.[177] Richardson represents a linguistic and cultural encounter based on understanding and mutual appreciation within a text whose commercial focus is even sharper than others: the message seems to be that good relations between the two peoples and polities will underlie profitable trading relations. The language lesson—as in *Henry V*—becomes a vehicle for English policy.

Many of those who came to England did so under duress: in the years preceding the Revocation of the Edict of Nantes, England saw growing numbers of Protestant immigrants arriving from France.[178] A century before this, Jacques Bellot had described the predicament of the new immigrant, writing 'what sorow is for them that be refugiate in a strange countrey, when they can not understand the language of that place in whiche they be exiled: and when they can not make them to be understood by speach to the inhabiters of that contrey, wherein they be retired'.[179] Texts which offered instruction to immigrants in the language of their host country often carried an implicit idea of how immigrants should speak and how they should position themselves within society. The inculcation of a distinctive immigrant linguistic competence—one which prioritized certain subjects, certain kinds of speech, and a model of cultural assimilation not found elsewhere—can be seen in these texts, as early as Bellot, whose characters discuss news from France, where the Wars of Religion are still raging. One speaker asks 'What newes?'; his

---

[176] Hollyband, *French Littelton*, p. 44.

[177] Richardson, *Anglo-Belgica*, part II, pp. 246, 152–7.

[178] For an overview of the Huguenot experience in England, see Robin D. Gwynn, *Huguenot Heritage: The History and Contribution of the Huguenots in Britain* (London: Routledge and Kegan Paul, 1985); Bernard Cottret, *The Huguenots in England: Immigration and Settlement c.1550–1700*, trans. Peregrine and Adriana Stevenson (Cambridge: Cambridge University Press, 1991); Lachenicht, 'Huguenot Immigrants and the Formation of National Identities'; and the essays in Vigne and Littleton (eds.), *From Strangers to Citizens*.

[179] Bellot, *Familiar Dialogues*, sig. A2r–A2v.

neighbour responds 'There is no other newes, but the of the sickenesse and the dearth, which be now a dayes almost throughout all Fraunce.' The first speaker retorts that 'It is Gods hand which revengeth the iniurie done to his Church.'[180] Immigrants, having been forced to flee one country, were aware that their status, even in a safe haven, could change in a moment. Amid the suspicions and the general political instability of the later sixteenth century, it was politic and necessary for many of them to make their upstanding Protestant identity clear. There is some attempt in Bellot's pedagogical provision to tap into the sense of religious solidarity underlying international Protestantism, while also appealing for English sympathy for these poor refugees. One character asks about the number of refugees who have come from France, to be told that it is '[v]ery great: and there be many of them whiche doe live very hard, so great is their povertie'.[181]

This material, dating from the 1580s and the context of migrations resulting from the French Wars of Religion, finds a counterpart in a manual of the early eighteenth century. *A Short and easy way for the Palatines to learn English* was published anonymously in 1710 for the use of the German-speaking masses who had arrived in London in 1709 and 1710 under the impression that Queen Anne would grant them lands in America.[182] With the 'poor Palatines' at the heart of an immigration debate and mainly lodged in camps outside of London, it was clear that, as the manual put it, '[e]very body talks of us. *Jedermann redet von uns.*'[183] The manual written for their use carried two messages: that it was the duty of at least some of these immigrants to learn the language of their host country, and that the study of English would allow them to position themselves in society and argue for their place in the scheme of things.[184] It offered vocabularies arranged topically, basic dialogues and collections of phrases, and a set of more stylized dialogues which portray the German migrants as dutiful, honest, hard-working, and both politically and religiously unthreatening. The first of these later dialogues in the Palatine text opens with expressions of gratitude for the reception—such as it was—that they had received in England. One speaker says 'Thank God, we are at last delivered from our Enemies, and safely arrived here in

---

[180] ibid., sig. [D8r].   [181] ibid., sig. [D8v].

[182] For an overview of the Palatine migration and the issues surrounding it, see Philip Otterness, *Becoming German: The 1709 Palatine Migration to New York* (Ithaca, NY, and London: Cornell University Press, 2004), though note that Otterness pays only glancing attention to this text. For a comparative perspective on the Palatine and Huguenot migrations, see Alison Olson, 'The English Reception of the Huguenots, Palatines and Salzburgers, 1680–1734: A Comparative Analysis', in Vigne and Littleton (eds.), *From Strangers to Citizens*, pp. 481–91; see also William O'Reilly, 'The Naturalization Act of 1709 and the Settlement of Germans in Britain, Ireland and the Colonies', in Vigne and Littleton (eds.), *From Strangers to Citizens*, pp. 492–502.

[183] Anon., *A Short and Easy Way For The Palatines To Learn English. Oder Eine kurze Anleitung zur Englischen Sprach, Zum Nutz der armen Pfältzer/nebst angehängten Englischen und Teutsche ABC* (London, 1710), p. 35. For debates over immigration, naturalization, and the charity owed the 'Palatines', as well as for the problems with their identification as 'poor Palatines', see Otterness, *Becoming German*, pp. 7–66.

[184] For their duty to learn English, see Anon., *Short and Easy Way*, 'Vorrede an die Pfälzer'.

England'; his interlocutor replies 'And Thanks be to God, who has governed the Heart of the Queen of England, and some other good People, to receive us so willingly.' The first speaker responds by saying 'Let us therefore Acknowledge it, and be very thankful to God and Her Majesty for it.' The migrants' precarious situation is evident in the manual's provision of expressions of gratitude and subservience, like 'And let us likewise be Industrious in whatever Place or Station, God & Her Majesty will be pleased to put us. And to behave our selves quietly & submissively to all People, and remember that we are strangers, and here upon Charity.'[185] Even the vocabulary lists were weighted with ideologies of hard work and virtue, and their opposites. Consider this list of words:

Fool, *Narr.*
Folly, *Thorheit.*
Pity, *Mitleiden.*
pitifull, *armseelig.*
sick, *kranck.*
sickness, *Kranckheit.*
Peace, *Friede.*
War, *Krieg.*
Honest, *ehrlich.*
godly, *gottsfürchtig.*
thankful, *danckbar.*
diligent, *fleißig.*
Negligent, *nachläßig.*
Thief, *Dieb.*
Knave, *Schelm oder Betrüger.*
a Rogue, *Schelm.*[186]

Honesty, godliness, diligence, and their opposites; peace and war, gratitude, and pity—this is not a neutral thematic glossary (if such a thing exists) but a social vocabulary: a basic set of tools geared towards the social context of the Palatines' arrival, and towards positioning oneself within a society whose shifting attitudes left one's place in it constantly at risk.

The appeal to charity and Protestant solidarity was matched with a commitment in these dialogues to labour, and an engagement with the wider debates which surrounded the Palatine presence. One speaker remarks to his neighbour how 'we have had great experience already of Her Majesty's and the whole Nations great Charity, and we have still no other dependance but upon the same Charity,

---

[185] ibid., pp. 50–1. On the Palatines' industriousness and fitness for work, see Olson, 'Reception of the Huguenots, Palatines and Salzburgers', pp. 485–6.

[186] ibid., p. 32.

to put us in a way to live'; to which the neighbour responds 'Yes, I could be very glad too: that we might be soon in a way to get our living, and maintain our families, and ease the Nation of so great a charge.'[187] This hoped-for economic integration has a cultural element too: the second dialogue sees praise for England and diligence set side by side. The author attempted to communicate the link between hard work and English identity in early eighteenth-century English society, and to offer the linguistic (and proverbial) means for the German learner of the language to defend his place and ensure that his speech as well as his actions were those considered virtuous and useful:

> Very well, I think it is a very good Country, and very good encouragement for poor Men to labour; for they give good wages. And the common People enjoy more liberty in England than in any Place in the World; and they have a Proverb in England, win Gold & wear it.[188]

The praise of England contains an encoded crash course in those values held dear by English patriots, and reassured any English readers that the Palatines' religious identity was orthodox and in line with the settlement in England. A speaker notes that 'among all other things this is the best here, that there is but one Religion by Law establish'd, which is the Protestant Religion'; which, he goes on to say, 'without doubt is the best Religion in the World: tho all Sorts of People have Liberty of Conscience here'.[189] The competence deemed appropriate for German-speaking immigrants to England at the height of this immigration panic was—in the view of the *Short and Easy Way*'s author—one which allowed them to perform their gratitude and to insist on their appeal as quiet, hard-working, orthodox, and loyal subjects of Queen Anne. The conversation manual written for their use aimed to turn each language-learner into an agent of a propaganda campaign on his or her fellow migrants' behalf.

An alternative to the model of immigrant linguistic competence presented by the Palatine manual—pious, piteous, and rural—was offered by a text written in 1685, the year of the Revocation of the Edict of Nantes, and aimed at the growing community of French Protestants who had flocked to England to escape worsening persecution under Louis XIV. The Swiss-born author of this manual, the *Nouvelle methode pour apprendre l'Anglois* (1685), was Guy Miège, an author of well-regarded conversation manuals whose works went into multiple editions before 1715: he was also, as Vivienne Larminie states, 'striking as an example of

---

[187] ibid., p. 51. The use of 'neighbour' is interesting here—see Naomi Tadmor, 'Friends and Neighbours in Early Modern England: Biblical Translations and Social Norms', in Gowing et al. (eds.) *Love, Friendship and Faith in Europe*, pp. 150–76.

[188] Anon., *Short and Easy Way*, p. 53.

[189] ibid., p. 55. See Otterness, *Becoming German*, pp. 7–66 on how the Palatines' religious make-up was mischaracterized in 1709–11.

the involvement of French-speaking Protestant immigrants in apologetics for the Glorious Revolution and the Hanoverian succession'.[190] The pedagogical programme he presented to his readers was starkly different from that which would be made available to the Palatines. If, as I argue above, lists of vocabulary can communicate ideology and argument, then the lists in Miège's texts speak volumes. His list of household goods begins with lumber and furniture, followed by '[h]anging', '[t]apestry-Hanging', '[p]ictures', and '[m]aps'. These are not basic moveable goods but items for display and decoration. His lists of foods are not just about simple fare, but contain lists of expensive sweets:

Confitures seches, *dry Sweetmeats.*
Confitures liquides, *moist Sweetmeats.*
Des Biscuits, *Biskets.*
Des Macarons, *Macaroons.*
Dragées, *Sugar-plums.*
Gelée, *a Jelly.*
Oranges confites, *candy'd Oranges.*
Marmelade, *a Marmalade.*
Raisiné, *a Confection of Grapes*[191]

Miège's vocabularies imagine a life for the Huguenot refugees which is urban, urbane, and elite. For Miège, the study of language was intimately tied to integration into a new social and cultural milieu: 'I do not think that it is very necessary to show the utility of this language for strangers living in England,' he wrote. 'Those who do not speak it know well the inconvenience it causes, and the impression one makes when one is ignorant of it.'[192] His method proposed a pedagogical process by which French-speakers would find themselves transformed into English-speakers with access to sites of urban sociability which, in Miège's argument, became arenas for language-learning and for integration into English culture. Miège also shaped the dialogues of his text so that they illustrated a process of assimilation and persuasion, whereby the French-speaker forced to leave his native land was brought through London, introduced to the urban geography and the key sites of elite sociability, and gradually won over to English ways of eating, drinking, and behaving.[193] In the *Nouvelle methode*, the act of

---

[190] Vivienne Larminie, 'Immigrants in the *DNB* and British Cultural Horizons, 1550–1740: The Merchant, the Traveller, the Lexicographer and the Apologist', in Vigne and Littleton (eds.), *From Strangers to Citizens*, pp. 175–83.
[191] Miège, *Nouvelle methode*, part II, p. 9.
[192] ibid., part I, pp. 3–4. 'Je ne pense pas, qu'il soit fort necessaire de faire voir l'Usage de cette langue aux Etrangers qui resident en Angleterre... Ceux qui ne la parlent pas savent assez l'Inconvenient qu'il a, & la figure qu'on y fait, quand on l'ignore.'
[193] Another conversation manual author published a French-language guide to the city of London: François Colsoni, *Le guide de Londres, dedié aux voyageurs étrangers* (London, 1710).

language-learning is also a translation of the self, a making of anglicized gentlemen out of Huguenot arrivals.

The *Nouvelle methode* is not lacking in pedagogical apparatus, but it is fundamentally a persuasive text. At its heart is the portrayal of a new immigrant's gradual conversion to English ways of speaking, acting, and thinking. At the hatter's, he is offered a choice between an English and a French hat, and chooses 'a good English Beaver'.[194] When he queries the amount of cloth necessary to make up a coat, it comes with the understanding that as countries, languages, and measurements change, so too do fashions: 'Sir, they wear now their Coats very wide at the Pockets, and that takes up a great deal of Cloth.'[195] A '[t]able-Dialogue' functions as a useful source of vocabulary and phrases while also dramatizing the Frenchman's gradual acceptance of English practices of eating: it is explained to him that in London the done thing is to eat one big meal a day, something which initially shocks a Frenchman used to substantial suppers. At the table, he is introduced to English specialities:

V. What Dish is that, Madam?
H. This is an English Pudding.
Will you be pleased to tast on't?
V. By all means, Madam. Truly 'tis not unpleasant.
But I fear it is heavy to the Stomach.
H. Sir, I confess this is a Dish that do's not so presently agree with French Palates.
But the generality of them do in time grow in love with it.[196]

Learning to speak and learning to be in company at dinner-tables and over drinks are a common feature of all conversation manuals, but it is Miège's that makes it most explicit that these practices are interdependent and crucial for the immigrant. The dining scene ends with the Frenchman's conversion:

[Landlady.] Remember our light Suppers.
You must eat, not only to satisfy, but also to prevent hunger.
M. Madam, I am already become an Englishman.
I declare my self against Suppers from this very time.[197]

There is humour in Miège's dramatized representations of the foreigner in England, but they serve a wider argument for the importance of adaptation and assimilation. During a lengthy dialogue on a variety of subjects between 'V' (the new arrival) and 'M' (a Frenchman who has been longer in London, and a cipher

---

[194] Miège, *Nouvelle methode*, part II, pp. 72.   [195] ibid., part II, p. 69.
[196] ibid., part II, p. 81.   [197] ibid., part II, p. 82.

for Miège himself), the newly arrived immigrant is gradually convinced of the acceptability of English customs and even of the food, coming to say 'I confess there is good Bread, and good meat, and both of them even at London, at very reasonable Rates.'[198] V criticizes English beer—'You make me mad, when you talk of English Drink. Tis nothing but boiled Water'—preferring to talk of wine, but M counters this by saying 'I see I must first shake off from your mind those Prejudices you have against Beer. And so you will so much the more easily be weaned from that conceited opinion you have of Wine.'[199] Running through this text is an argument against prejudice and in favour of accommodation, constantly illustrated with information for the new arrival on custom and practice. He learns how beer is made and that the best cider comes from Hertfordshire, what wines are available in London, and that tea is 'a Liquor good for the Stomach, and they say, a great Assistant in Love Exercises'.[200] These discussions broach and debate cultural difference, with M gradually drawing V to an accommodation with English culture, as when V is amazed at the use of tobacco in England, and shocked at its use across social divides, among children, and even in the street. M's defence of tobacco culminates in a relativist argument:

[M.] Pray, don't you think the Smell of Garlick as unpleasant as that of Tobacco?'
V. They are both alike for that.
M. But, if you went to cry down Garlick in Guienne and Gascongne, don't you
      think you would be ridiculed for your pains?
V. I confess, that the Decorum of Things do's not so much ly in their Nature, as in
      the Acceptance they find in the World.[201]

The final sentence sums up Miège's approach perfectly: what was new about his *Nouvelle methode* was its status as a persuasive text which made cultural difference the engine of the dialogue form, and which had acceptance of and accommodation to a new culture—and its shibboleths, like English beer or a pipe of tobacco—as a central aim.

Miège's concern with 'the impression one makes' in company led him to offer an introduction into elite forms of sociability, and to argue that language-learning could be carried out in certain social spaces and facilitate one's entry into polite society. Literate Huguenot men were offered by Miège a means of fashioning their speech and bearing in such a way that they would be integrated not only into an

---

[198] ibid., part II, p. 97.
[199] ibid., part II, p. 99. Steve Pincus argues that in the Restoration, faced with the reputation (albeit not entirely justified) of the coffee-houses as centres of sedition, '[d]rinking English ale and English beer ... proved the ultimate litmus test for royalists': Pincus, 'Coffee Politicians Does Create', p. 825.
[200] Miège, *Nouvelle methode*, part II, p. 107.   [201] ibid., part II, pp. 108–9.

English way of life but also into a social milieu for which they judged themselves suited:

M. Will ye know, our Friend, what has been no small help to me to learn the English by? The Coffee-houses.

V. How so?

M. Because in those Houses the Companies do intermix together, so that every one has the Liberty both to speak, and to hear what others say.

M's approval of the coffee-house is about more than the supply of reading material and the freedom to smoke and talk in company: he closes his paean by saying that '[t]hey are much genteeler than Ale-houses, and yet one may come off cheaper'.[202] His recommendation of the coffee-house as a prime arena for language-learning is an argument for language-learning as a part of literate discussion in 'genteel' surroundings and company; the coffee-house's reading materials and political conversation were better places for Miège's status-hungry Frenchman to pick up the language than in the more rough-and-ready surroundings of the alehouse. Coffee houses were a prime venue for the development of civility and politeness in London. As well as key spaces in the educational economy of early modern London, as we saw in Chapter 1, they were also venues for changing forms of sociability which incorporated reading and political and literary discussion, not to mention hubs of rumour and gossip about national and international affairs—precisely the kind of social environment which would appeal to educated men of a certain standing in their own communities seeking to translate themselves into a new society.[203]

In a dialogue '[o]f Clubbs, and of the English Custom for every one to pay his Club', M explains that clubs act as the 'private Rendez-vous' of Englishmen: groups of men meet in a public house once or twice a week, where 'they have an Interview, and mutual Converse; and, to quicken the Conversation, they drink, but within bounds'.[204] Peter Clark's description of the constituents of the English club matches this: 'heavy drinking, controlled social mixing, a combination of privacy and public openness, and a predominantly masculine environment'.[205]

---

[202] ibid., part II, pp. 109–10.

[203] On coffee-houses and coffee-house culture more generally, see Lawrence E. Klein, 'Coffeehouse Civility, 1660–1714: An Aspect of Post-Courtly Culture in England', *Huntington Library Quarterly* 59 (1996), pp. 30–51; see also Brian Cowan, 'The Rise of the Coffeehouse Reconsidered', *Historical Journal* 47 (2004), pp. 21–46; Cowan, *The Social Life of Coffee: The Emergence of the British Coffeehouse* (New Haven, CT, and London: Yale University Press, 2005); Pincus, 'Coffee Politicians Does Create'. On the French presence and sociability in London, see Gesa Stedman, *Cultural Exchange in Seventeenth-Century France and England* (Aldershot: Ashgate, 2013); and Lawrence E. Klein, 'The Figure of France: The Politics of Sociability in England, 1660–1715', *Yale French Studies* 92, *Exploring the Conversible World: Text and Sociability from the Classical Age to the Enlightenment* (1997), pp. 30–45.

[204] Miège, *Nouvelle methode*, part II, p. 111.

[205] Peter Clark, *British Clubs and Societies 1580–1800: The Origins of an Associational World* (Oxford: Clarendon, 2000), p. 41.

The club, as an institution 'umbilically linked to the arrival of coffee-houses', enabled the learner to pursue learned talk and language practice in a refined environment, and guaranteed that what one learnt and the company one kept— both of which were covered by the umbrella term 'conversation'—were of impeccable quality:

M. I am sure I found it very beneficial, as for improving my self in the English Tongue.

V. But how came you to be admitted into those Clubbbs [sic], being a Stranger, and speaking but broken English?

M. Twas by the favour of one of the Members thereof, who got me in.

M goes on to convince V of the merits of the English practice whereby each person pays for their own share of the evening; V, as before, is soon converted.[206] The achievement of Miège's text was to dramatize the processes of language-learning and assimilation as part of an argument which argues for the desirability of Huguenot integration into urban, literate, largely male culture, and the practices of sociability and arenas of company which defined it. The popularity of his manual over the years that followed suggests that at least some new arrivals found its advice—and perhaps its underlying argument—useful in their own lives.

The language-learning environments Miège represents are almost entirely urban, and urbane, in contrast to those of the Palatine manual, which seem to reflect that group of immigrants' position on the edges of the city: the dialogues are largely rural in setting and in content, and the sense is of an exclusion from the urban environment and, by extension, from the urbane behaviour learnt and practised there. Urban geography was central to the *Nouvelle methode*: the characters walk through the city in a dialogue which is freighted with the political tensions of the time.[207] When the speakers view the Monument, M comments "Tis incredible, and I cannot think on't without being struck with horror'; London after the fire is described admiringly as a '[p]hoenix sprung up out of its Ashes'.[208] In London, as Offelen suggested, the 'rabble' could be unfriendly to Frenchmen, and this exchange carries the hint that it would be politic for two members of a nation which was commonly blamed for the fire to be able to bemoan its outcome and praise the contemporary city and its culture. The characters' observation of a statue of Charles I prompts the explanation that the king was 'beheaded before his Palace, January 30. 1648, by a rebellious Faction'.[209] For both Miège's French

[206] Clark, *British Clubs and Societies*, p. 40; Miège, *Nouvelle methode*, part II, pp. 112–13.

[207] On the city walk as an early modern print genre, see James S. Amelang, 'The Walk of the Town: Modeling the Early Modern City', in Kimberly Lynn and Erin Kathleen Rowe (eds.), *The Early Modern Hispanic World: Transnational and Interdisciplinary Approaches* (Cambridge: Cambridge University Press, 2017), pp. 45–61.

[208] Miège, *Nouvelle methode*, part II, p. 128.   [209] ibid., p. 123.

immigrants and the Palatines of 1709/10, linguistic competence meant being able to position oneself socially but also politically, and being able to neutralize suspicions of vice in one's behaviour or of dangerous heterodoxy in one's beliefs. Miège's text, like others aimed at immigrant audiences, focused on a process of integration into English society which also equipped the reader to defend their place in their adopted country.

Conclusion

There is no simple narrative to the history of the early modern conversation manual. For every manual that responded to the political and cultural contexts of its publication, there was a new edition of Berlemont, or Hollyband, or Mauger, still seemingly relevant long after its first appearance. There are continuities in the kind of competence they present across this period: the need to orient oneself within hierarchies of gender, rank, and wealth; the centrality of everyday rituals; the importance of sharp bargaining practice in a world of negotiable prices. And there are changes: manuals which break the mould, urging assimilation on immigrants where texts for English-speakers were more coy about cultural adaptation; or books which show rituals breaking down, revealing the conflict that lies underneath polite conversation. Fittingly, these texts give no single sense of what spoken interaction was like in early modern societies: conversation, like competence, differed depending on who was talking to whom, where, and on what topic. As with manuals of courtesy and civility, it is difficult to draw a straight line from the linguistic and behavioural ideal in print to the reality of its performance. Conversation manuals presented ideals of study and competence, but the world outside the text was rarely so simple, which is why Chapter 4 turns to travellers' experiences of acquiring and using foreign vernaculars while abroad.

Multilingual conversation manuals offer one way of getting at the question of what early modern language-learners wanted to be able to do with foreign languages. They offer one way of thinking about linguistic competence as a useful historical category. Competence shaped individuals' lives: in a native language or another vernacular, it underlay the question of who got to speak—and be heard— amid the multilingual buzz of voices that was early modern Europe. Conversation manuals show that early modern linguistic competences were many and dizzyingly varied. These competences were not abstractions: they had a social life and a social weight, and they could complement and challenge the rules of early modern conversations. Linguistic competence has for too long been a concept without a history: these polyglot dialogues are sources that can lead us to a broader, richer understanding of a multilingual England and Europe in the early modern period.

4

'A Conversable Knowledge'

Language-Learning and Educational Travel

Introduction

Writing in 1642, the traveller and author James Howell offered detailed advice to English travellers on the best way to learn foreign languages. The ideal student, he wrote, would read widely in French, from the poems of Du Bartas to the fables of Aesop, studying histories and devotional literature, reading the 'Gazets and Courants' of Paris, which are 'couched in very good Language', and practising the art of translation.[1] But in order to develop a 'praticall knowledge' of the language, the traveller needed to go beyond the pages of books, and use the oral and aural culture of early modern France as a pedagogical resource. Howell urged his traveller to spend some time in a university town in the Loire valley, away from the voices of other Englishmen. He would pick up the language quicker 'if hee repaires sometimes to the Courts of Pleading, and to the Publique Schooles; For in France they presently fall from the Latine, to dispute in the vulgar tongue'. A visit to the Académie Française, recently established by Cardinal Richelieu, would be ideal, since there 'all the Sciences are read in the French tongue, which is done of purpose to refine, and enrich the Language'. One strategy followed by travellers, wrote Howell, was to converse with French nuns at convent gates, 'for the Nunnes speake a quaint Dialect, and besides they have most commonly all the Newes that passes, and they will entertaine discours till one bee weary'; this, however, was to be avoided, since too much consorting with Catholics (and Catholic women) could be perilous for the traveller's faith and identity.[2] In spite of the dangers of conversation, Howell was clear that it was the 'most advantagious [method] for attaining a Language, the life whereof consists in societie and communication'. His term for the competence the traveller would thus acquire gives this chapter its title and its theme: 'a conversable Knowledge'.[3]

---

[1] James Howell, *Instructions for forreine travell. Shewing by what cours, and in what compasse of time, one may take an exact Survey of the Kingdomes and States of Christendome, and arrive to the practicall knowledge of the Languages, to good purpose* (London, 1642), p. 52.

[2] Ibid., pp. 32–4.   [3] Ibid., pp. 46–7.

This 'conversable knowledge' is at once the most important aspect of early modern linguistic competence and the most difficult to grasp. Most of the multilingual interactions that took place in early modern Europe are lost to us: these fleeting moments of oral (and sometimes gestural) communication went unrecorded. This poses problems for accessing much of the everyday work of language-learning and communication between languages in this period. However, one group of language-learners left a rich and unique record which allows the historian to track their interactions with polyglot oral and aural cultures, and to understand the everyday pedagogies and face-to-face practices of language-learning. These learners were the educational travellers addressed by James Howell: mostly men, and mostly young, they left England in growing numbers from the sixteenth century onwards, hoping to acquire knowledge, experience, and contacts during the course of their travels in continental Europe. This period of foreign travel became increasingly valued as the culmination of a young man's elite education, and over time it would develop into the 'grand tour'.[4] Language-learning was central to this form of travel: a typical sixteenth-century passport licensed the bearer to travel 'for the better increase in knowledg of foreyn Languages'.[5] Travellers' letters, notebooks, and diaries show them reading, listening, translating, and paraphrasing material in other vernacular

---

[4] Early modern English travel, and educational travel in particular, has received significant scholarly attention. A helpful initial overview is offered by Michael G. Brennan (ed.), *The Origins of the Grand Tour: The Travels of Robert Montagu, Lord Mandeville (1649–1654), William Hammond (1655–1658), and Banaster Maynard (1660–1663)* (London: Hakluyt Society, 2004), pp. 9–47. There is no room here for a complete bibliography, but the following works are useful and/or influential: Sara Warneke, *Images of the Educational Traveller in Early Modern England* (London, New York, and Cologne: E. J. Brill, 1995); Kenneth R. Bartlett, *The English in Italy 1525–1558: A Study in Culture and Politics* (Geneva: Centro Interuniversitario di Ricerche sul 'Viaggio in Italia', 1991); John Walter Stoye, *English Travellers Abroad 1604–1667: Their Influence in English Society and Politics* (London: Jonathan Cape, 1952); Clare Howard, *English Travellers of the Renaissance* (London: Bodley Head, 1914); Antoni Maczak, *Travel in Early Modern Europe*, trans. Ursula Phillips, (Cambridge: Polity, 1995); Timothy Raylor, 'Exiles, Expatriates and Travellers: Towards a Cultural and Intellectual History of the English Abroad, 1640–1660', in Philip Major (ed.), *Literatures of Exile in the English Revolution and its Aftermath, 1640–1690* (Farnham and Burlington, VT: Ashgate, 2010), pp. 15–43; Edward Chaney, *The Evolution of the Grand Tour: Anglo-Italian Cultural Relations since the Renaissance* (London and Portland, OR: Frank Cass, 1998); Edward Chaney, *The Grand Tour and the Great Rebellion: Richard Lassels and 'The Voyage of Italy' in the Seventeenth Century* (Geneva: Slatkine, 1985); Edward Chaney and Timothy Wilks, *The Jacobean Grand Tour: Early Stuart Travellers in Europe* (London: I. B. Tauris, 2013); Michèle Cohen, 'The Grand Tour: Constructing the English Gentleman in Eighteenth-Century France', *History of Education* 21 (1992), pp. 241–57; Rosemary Sweet, *Cities and the Grand Tour: The British in Italy, c.1690–1820* (Cambridge: Cambridge University Press, 2012); Jeremy Black, *The British Abroad: The Grand Tour in the Eighteenth Century* (Stroud: Allan Sutton, 1992); Christopher Hibbert, *The Grand Tour* (London: Weidenfeld and Nicolson, 1969). Recent work by German scholars is relevant to the English context, particularly Antje Stannek, *Telemachs Brüder: Die höfische Bildungsreise des 17. Jahrhunderts* (Frankfurt am Main and New York: Campus Verlag, 2001); Mathis Leibetseder, *Die Kavalierstour: Adlige Erziehungsreisen im 17. und 18. Jahrhundert* (Cologne, Weimar, and Vienna: Böhlau Verlag, 2004); Leibetseder, 'Across Europe: Educational Travelling of German Noblemen in a Comparative Perspective', *Journal of Early Modern History* 14 (2010), pp. 417–49.

[5] Passport granted to Anthony Mildmay by Queen Elizabeth in 1576, Northamptonshire Record Office, W(A) box 2/parcel XII/no. 1/d9.

languages: insults, street cries, proverbs, jokes, stories, ballads, and arguments. In their multilingual manuscripts, travellers record, rework, and practise real-world language. The materials they left behind allow us to go beyond textbooks and curriculums, and to understand the practices and experiences of language-learning travellers amidst the noisy and multilingual oral and aural cultures of early modern Europe.

Language-learning was fundamental to early modern educational travel. The author of a seventeenth-century manuscript of travel advice wrote that 'the tongues' were 'the keyes to open the Artes, a knowledge by *which* wee gett all knowledge'.[6] Without linguistic competence, the engagement with people and with texts demanded by educational travel curriculums could not be undertaken.[7] A strong communicative competence was necessary to engage with people abroad, argued one author (who purported to be the earl of Essex): '[the] ability to treat with men of several humours, factions, and Countries; duly to comply with them, or stand off, as occasion shall require, is not gotten onely by reading of books, but rather by studying of men'.[8] In spite of its utility, language-learning in travel was controversial: one of its more vocal critics worried that those that 'doe not carry with them, but rather goe to fetch the language of the place' would need to spend a long time abroad in doing so, 'whiles in the meane season their unthriving intermission is assailed with a thousand suggestions'.[9] Learning a language while abroad necessitated spending extended periods of time in the company of foreigners, and often necessitated the careful (and risky) negotiation of confessional,

---

[6] 'A direction for a Travailer', Bodleian Library, Perrott MS 5, fol. 10r. Anna Suranyi says this may be by William Drake, and suggests 1628 as a possible date of composition: Anna Suranyi, *The Genius of the English Nation: Travel Writing and National Identity in Early Modern England* (Cranbury, NJ: Rosemont, 2008), p. 208 n. For a similar view of linguistic competence as necessary to acquire the knowledge one was to reap from travel, see Fynes Moryson, *An Itinerary written by Fynes Moryson Gent. First in the latine Tongue, and then translated By him into English: containing his ten yeeres travell through the twelve dominions of Germany, Bohmerland, Sweitzerland, Netherland, Denmarke, Poland, Italy, Turky, France, England, Scotland, and Ireland* (London, 1617), part III, p. 14.

[7] On the traveller's 'curriculum' and the *ars apodemica*, see Justin Stagl, *A History of Curiosity: The Theory of Travel 1550–1800* (London and New York: Routledge, 1995); Joan-Pau Rubiés, 'Instructions for Travellers: Teaching the Eye to See', in Joan-Pau Rubiés, *Travellers and Cosmographers: Studies in the History of Early Modern Travel and Ethnology* (Aldershot: Ashgate, 2007), pp. 139–90; Rubiés, *Travel and Ethnology in the Renaissance: South India through European eyes, 1250–1625* (Cambridge: Cambridge University Press, 2000).

[8] Anon., *Profitable Instructions; Describing what speciall Observations are… taken by Travellers in all Nations, States and Countries; Pleasant and Profitable. By the three much admired, Robert, late Earle of Essex, Sir Philip Sidney, And, Secretary Davison* (London, 1633), 'To the Reader'. The text has been ascribed to Francis Bacon, Thomas Bodley, and Fulke Greville: for the tangled history of its attributions, see Elizabeth Williamson, 'A Letter of Travel Advice? Literary Rhetoric, Scholarly Counsel and Practical Instruction in the *ars apodemica*', *Lives and Letters* 3 (2011), pp. 1–22.

[9] Joseph Hall, *Quo vadis? A Just Censure of Travell as it is commonly undertaken by the Gentlemen of our Nation* (London, 1617), pp. 16–17. For a continental perspective on the debate over experience in educational travel, see Stannek, *Telemachs Brüder*, pp. 41–54. Those who dissented from this view included Fynes Moryson, who claimed to have travelled in order 'to enable my understanding (which I thought could not be done so well by contemplation as by experience; nor by the eare or any sence so well, as by the eies': Moryson, *Itinerary*, I, p. 197.

social, and gendered boundaries.[10] But as speakers of a marginal European vernacular practically unknown on the continent, English travellers often had no choice but to become language-learners.

Elite travel in the sixteenth and seventeenth centuries was built on an educational ideal. In 1671, Edward Leigh wrote that '[t]ravelling is the best School for life'; James Howell agreed, arguing that the practice of travel 'may be not improperly called a moving Academy, or the true Peripatetique Schoole'.[11] The early modern traveller was expected to spend time in the formal study of subjects which were deemed important to a rounded education. Latin tutors, readers in civil law, dancing masters, and even teachers of carving were engaged by English travellers to the continent in this period.[12] This formal study with dedicated teachers, however, was only the tip of the educational iceberg. Theorists, tutors, parents, and governors made it clear that every aspect of travel was to be considered as full of pedagogical potential. The traveller should translate Latin authors with a tutor, but also scan foreign-language newsbooks, guidebooks, and novels for linguistic, cultural, and political information. Godly sermons were a source of good doctrine and fine language, but they were to be complemented with the language heard at court, in the coach and the inn. The grace and poise learnt from a dancing master was to be applied not only on the dance floor, but had to be assimilated into the student's everyday bearing and conversation. This chapter is concerned with the processes by which travellers encountered, judged, recorded, and reused the information (grammatical, social, bodily) they absorbed from their surroundings. But though the educational underpinnings of early modern elite travel are hardly in doubt, they remain poorly understood. Jean Boutier says of the historiography of the grand tour that 'Paradoxically, while constantly underlining its pedagogical implications, works on the Grand Tour have very rarely attempted a systematic analysis of the processes of educational travel'.[13] It is a point which could be made more broadly for much historiography of early modern travel: while historians are

---

[10] On the confessional politics of educational travel, see Tony Claydon, *Europe and the Making of England, 1660–1760* (Cambridge: Cambridge University Press, 2007); Christopher Highley, *Catholics Writing the Nation in Early Modern Britain and Ireland* (Oxford: Oxford University Press, 2008), pp. 159–87.

[11] Edward Leigh, *Three Diatribes or Discourses. First of Travel, Or a Guide for Travellers into Forein Parts. Secondly, Of Money or Coyne. thirdly, Of Measuring of the Distance beetwixt Place and Place* (London, 1671), p. 14; Howell, *Instructions for forreine travell*, p. 8. Compare Francis Bacon, *The Essayes or Counsels, Civill and Morall, of Francis Lo. Verulam, Viscount St. Alban* (London, 1625), p. 100: 'He that travelleth into a country, before he hath some entrance into the language, goeth to school, and not to travel.'

[12] See, for instance, the sample curriculums drawn up by Theophilus Gale for the sons of Philip, Lord Wharton in 1662–4, in Bodleian Library, MS Rawlinson Letters 49, fols. 1r–3r, 11r; and Leibetseder, *Kavalierstour*, p. 108.

[13] 'Paradoxalement, tout en soulignant sans cesse ses implications pédagogiques, les travaux sur le Grand Tour ont très rarement tenté l'analyse systématique des processus d'éducation par le voyage' Jean Boutier, 'Le Grand Tour des gentilshommes et les académies d'éducation pour la noblesse: France et Italie, XVIe–XVIIIe siècle', in Rainer Babel and Werner Paravicini (eds.), *Grand Tour: Adeliges Reisen und Europäische Kultur vom 14. bis zum 18. Jahrhundert* (Ostfildern: Jan Thorbecke Verlag, 2005), p. 238. For a similar point relating to the eighteenth-century grand tour, see Keith Dent, 'Travel

agreed that education was paramount, we have very little understanding of the nature of that education, the pedagogical practices which made it up, and the success or otherwise with which it was undertaken. Put simply, the history of education is missing from the history of educational travel.

This chapter represents a critical intervention into the historiographies of travel and of language-learning. It has two overlapping aims. Firstly, where traditional historiographies have tended to privilege anecdote over analysis, it offers a history of educational travel with the education put back in. Secondly, and more broadly, this chapter uses the pedagogical experiences of these travellers to give, for the first time, a rounded picture of the practices and the processes—oral, aural, textual— that underlay early modern language-learning. These everday pedagogies were the real business of educational travel, and of language-learning more broadly. In pursuit of these aims, this chapter looks first at how travellers engaged critically with their spoken environments, seeking out the places that were known for having the best variety of language, and drawing on their oral and aural surroundings in building their competences. Next, it turns to the place of writing in educational travel, unpicking the relationship between oral and scribal cultures, and assessing travellers' letters as pieces of pedagogical performance. Lastly, it considers the importance of bodily comportment and gesture in language-learning, asking how debates about adaptation and dissimulation affected travellers abroad and on their return. This history of language-learning asks us to reconstruct sensory, social worlds of travel, and to ask how people responded to the necessity of making themselves understood. It brings to light the practices, the pedagogies, and the negotiations that helped to create a 'conversable knowledge'—and that lay behind the encounter between a marginal England and a multilingual Europe.

'Good' and 'Bad' Language: Place, Prestige, and Linguistic Variation

One early author of humanist travel advice urged the traveller to mark '[t]he speech and language of the countrie, with the manner of pronunciation, and the rules thereof'.[14] As we have seen, English language-learners were increasingly aware of 'prestige' varieties of French and Italian, and sought out teachers and books that could teach them. When they ventured abroad, travellers sought out

as Education: The English Landed Classes in the Eighteenth Century', *Educational Studies* 1 (1975), p. 171.

[14] Albrecht Meyer, *Certaine briefe, and speciall Instructions for Gentlemen, merchants, students, souldiers, marriners, &c. Employed in services abrode, or anie way occasioned to converse in the kingdomes, and governementes of forren Princes* (London, 1589), p. 14.

the 'best' and 'purest' varieties of continental vernaculars, while also giving ear to local variations, marking the difference between countries, regions, and classes. It was understood that linguistic observation could reveal deeper truths about place, culture, people, and politics. The ideas of linguistic purity and prestige which appear again and again in grammars and in travel advice were not abstract: they reflected broader debates about politics and religion, and in turn they informed itineraries and determined where travellers went, who they spoke to, and how they engaged with their oral and aural environments. Early modern educational travel was shaped by questions of place and prestige.

For much of the seventeenth century, the English were generally agreed that the best French was to be found in the cities of the Loire valley—Blois, Saumur, Angers, and Tours.[15] The author of the Perrott manuscript of travel advice felt the best language was to be found 'in France, Orléans & Blois, & there abouts as good and better cheape'.[16] Heneage Finch noted the same price differential between Paris and the towns of the Loire in 1676, writing of his hope 'to go in to the Country, either to Angiers or Somers where I may live with halfe the expence it costs me here & learn my excercises as well'.[17] Cheaper than Paris, the Loire valley towns also had the advantage of a historical association with French Protestant-ism: an important Huguenot academy was located at Saumur from 1593 until just before the Revocation of the Edict of Nantes.[18] Travelling through the region in 1609–10, William Cecil (Viscount Cranborne) noted in his French-language journal which towns contained many people 'of the religion'. Cranborne's early account was very sensitive to the Wars of Religion as a matter of the recent past: travelling in peacetime, he nonetheless marvelled at the diligence with which La Rochelle was guarded, and the ways in which Protestants could worship or assemble locally.[19] For Cranborne, this religious sympathy did not result in a longer stay, but by later in the century, the link between language, religion, and the

[15] There was also Paris, though for reasons discussed below travellers tended to prefer the Loire valley towns, at least to begin with. For debates over the best variety of French, see Peter Rickard, *A History of the French Language* (London and New York: Routledge, 1989), pp. 81–119; and Rickard, *La Langue française au seizième siècle: étude suivie de textes* (Cambridge: Cambridge University Press, 1968), pp. 18–24.

[16] Perrott MS 5, fol. 10r. Germans found the Loire valley attractive too, and Orléans in particular: Stannek, *Telemachs Brüder*, pp. 77–80.

[17] Heneage Finch the younger to Thomas Thynne, 14 August 1676, Thynne papers, Longleat House, TH/VOL/XVII, fol. 23r.

[18] J. Dumont, *Histoire de l'Académie de Saumur depuis sa fondation en 1600 par Duplessis-Mornay jusqu'à sa suppression en 1685* (Angers: Société Académique de Maine et Loire, 1862); P.-Daniel Bourchenin, *Étude sur les académies protestantes en France au XVIᵉ et au XVIIᵉ siècle* (Paris: Grassart, 1882), pp. 137–46. See also Karin Maag, 'The Huguenot Academies: Preparing for an Uncertain Future', in Raymond A. Mentzer and Andrew Spicer (eds.), *Society and Culture in the Huguenot World, 1559–1685* (Cambridge: Cambridge University Press, 2002), pp. 139–56.

[19] Travel diary of Viscount Cranborne, 29 July/8 August–20/30 October 1609, in G. Dyfnallt Owen (ed.), *HMC Salisbury*, part XXI (1609–1612) (London: Her Majesty's Stationery Office, 1970), pp. 105–8.

region's attractiveness to travellers informed English itineraries. Travelling in 1658–9, Francis Mortoft noted of Saumur that

[t]he French tongue is heere spoken with much purity and eligance, which is the reason that many strangers resort hither to inhabitt. There are also a great number of Protestants in the Towne, having their Church or Temple to resort too.[20]

Prestige and pragmatism combined to dictate the itinerary followed by English travellers, and the language they observed on the way.

From the 1630s onwards, English travellers flocked to the Loire towns to take lodgings and study the language. Thomas Abdie was in Blois in 1633–4, Lord Beauchamp in 1646, the Verney children in 1646–50; Robert Montagu went to Saumur for a year in 1649–50, as did Philip Perceval (and his mother) in the late 1670s, along with many other English travellers.[21] By the time of the Restoration, Blois at least had developed a micro-economy based on its popularity with travelling students: Jean Gailhard, an influential theorist of the early grand tour, noted that at Blois '[the] language is well spoken amongst people of some fashion, good and able Masters of Exercise are found in them, and the people thereof are very kind and civil to strangers'. As we have seen, Claude Mauger (like other Restoration London-based teachers of French) advertised himself as 'late Professor of the French Tongue at Blois', exploiting the cachet associated with the city's variety of language.[22] Overcrowding was already an issue by the mid-century: Evelyn commended Blois and Orléans for the purity of their language, but complained of the number of Germans at the latter and took up residence at Tours instead.[23] The language of Paris was prestigious too, but Gailhard argued that 'one must have learned the Language, some customs of the Nation, and gotten some experience before he be ripe for Paris': there, '[the] people of Quality have not the patience to hear a Gentleman unable to speak two words together of good

[20] Malcolm Letts (ed.), *Francis Mortoft: His Book. Being his travels through France and Italy, 1658–1659* (London: Hakluyt Society, 1925), p. 9.

[21] Travel notebook of Thomas Abdie, Bodleian Library, Rawlinson MS D1285, fols. 74r–75r, 157r. Letter from Richaud (governor to Lord Beauchamp), June 1646, Seymour MSS, Longleat House, SE/VII/2, fols. 2r–6r. For the Verneys, see Mark Motley, 'Educating the English Gentleman Abroad: The Verney Family in Seventeenth-Century France and Holland', *History of Education: Journal of the History of Education Society*, 23 (1994), pp. 243–56. For Montagu, see Brennan, *Origins of the Grand Tour*, pp. 106–20. For Perceval, see British Library, Add. MS 46953, Add. MS 46954 A, Add. MS 46954 B, Add. MS 46955 A, Add. MS 46955 B, Add. MS 46956 A. See also, for instance, S. C. Lomas (ed.), 'The Memoirs of Sir George Courthop [or Courthope]' (1616–1685), *Camden Miscellany* 11 (London, 1907), p. 105.

[22] Jean Gailhard, *The Compleat Gentleman: or Directions For the Education of Youth As to their Breeding at Home And Travelling Abroad. In Two Treatises* (London, 1678), part II, p. 35; Claude Mauger, *The True Advancement of the French Tongue* (London, 1653).

[23] E. S. de Beer (ed.), *The Diary of John Evelyn: Selected and Introduced by Roy Strong* (London: Everyman, 2006), pp. 75–80.

sense, but in other Towns it is otherwise'.[24] Paris might be better saved for the culmination of the tour, an opportunity to show off the language and conversation that the traveller had polished in the provinces.

Other nations had their own 'best' varieties. Protestant Leipzig was generally considered to have the best German: it was there that William Nicolson—later a Church of Ireland bishop, but at that point training for a diplomatic career—studied German in the winter of 1678–9.[25] Heidelberg was recommended by the author of the Perrott manuscript and by Fynes Moryson, who also suggested Strasbourg.[26] Hubert Languet bemoaned Philip Sidney's failure to get to grips with the language while in the last-mentioned city.[27] There were other issues with German: Sidney seems to have refused to learn it (at least to the standard of his French and Italian), while the tutor de Blainville and Sir William Blathwayt argued in letters over whether Blathwayt's sons should learn German while at Geneva: de Blainville was insistent that it was unnecessary.[28] As for Spanish, two Hispano-phile authors urged the study of the language, with one recommending Valladolid for its language and the other suggesting Seville, for there '[the traveller] may converse with Marchants, and their conversation is much to bee valued'.[29] However, Spain never became a regular stop on the elite seventeenth-century itinerary, in part because of a fear and mistrust of Catholicism, as well as a more general Anglophone distrust of the Spanish.[30] Indeed, Francis Cottington, English ambassador to Madrid from 1609, complained that with only one exception, 'I have never seen one honest man of them that come to see and learn the language as in other parts.'[31] Fynes Moryson's capacity in German and James Howell's in Spanish seem to have been garnered out of necessity and were not imitated by many other Protestant travellers: French and Italian remained the pre-eminent

[24] Gailhard, *Compleat Gentleman*, pp. 34–5.
[25] Nicolson's account of his travels in Germany is Queen's College, Oxford, MS 68; he wrote of Leipzig that '[a]t this day 'tis most famous for (besides the purity of the High Dutch tongue; which is thought to flourish here in a more refined strain then in any other place of Misnia, and, consequently in Germany)': fol. 28r. See also D. W. Hayton, 'Nicolson, William (1655–1727) *Oxford Dictionary of National Biography*, Oxford University Press, 2004; online edn, Jan 2008 (https://doi.org/10.1093/ref:odnb/20186).
[26] Perrott MS 5, fol. 10r; Moryson, *Itinerary*, part III, p. 14.
[27] Steuart A. Pears (ed.), *The Correspondence of Sir Philip Sidney and Hubert Languet* (London: William Pickering, 1845), p. 164.
[28] Ibid., pp. 28–9; Nora Hardwick (ed.), *The Grand Tour: Letters and Accounts Relating to the Travels through Europe of the Brothers William and John Blathwayt of Dyrham Park, 1705–1708* (Bristol: N. Hardwick, 1985), pp. 29, 67–8.
[29] Valladolid was recommended for students of Spanish by Leigh, *Three Diatribes*, p. 11; the most positive advocate for travellers to go to Spain was Howell, *Instructions for forreine travell*, p. 56 and after. See also Patricia Shaw, 'Sensual, Solemn, Sober, Slow and Secret: The English View of the Spaniard, 1590–1700', in C. C. Barfoot (ed.), *Beyond Pug's Tour: National and Ethnic Stereotyping in Theory and Literary Practice* (Amsterdam and Atlanta, GA: Rodopi, 1997), pp. 99–113.
[30] Some exceptions to this rule include men like James Howell and Endymion Porter, who spent time in Spain in the earlier seventeenth century.
[31] Chaney and Wilks, *Jacobean Grand Tour*, p. 44.

vernaculars learnt by seventeenth-century educational travellers, echoing the predominance of these languages in the corpus of manuals.

Italian presented more of a problem: each of the countries visited by travellers had its own dialect differences, but in Italy these were pronounced and more relevant because of the prestige attached to the literary Tuscan of Dante and Petrarch.[32] Robert Dallington addressed dialect differences in Italy:

> As also in Italy, the Roman hath one kinde of phrase & pronounciation; the Neapolitan another; the Venetian a third; the Bergamasco a worse; but the best of all is the Tuscan where Florence stands.[33]

Some began their study of Italian outside the country—Jean Gailhard said that, while at Lyon, the traveller should 'learn the Italian Tongue, and get the best information he can of Italy', but Tuscany was always on the horizon.[34] Thomas Roe urged Francis Fane '*that* you begin *your* language in Geneva, and perfect it in Florence', since 'in *that* good Towne, you shall have a Compendium of many, all exercises, and letters; in *the* last a Court to act, and use them in'.[35] Siena had the benefit of purity of language while being cheaper than Florence: Evelyn said that there 'the Air is incomparable … Provisions cheape, the Inhabitans Courteous, & the Italian purely spoken', an attitude echoed in the Perrott manuscript, which recommended 'Florence, but especiallie Siena, & Prato in Tuscany where is as good and better cheape the most refined speech'.[36] James Howell urged his traveller to head for Siena, 'where the prime Italian dialect is spoken, and not stirre thence till he be master of the Language in some measure'. Conversely, some places were to be avoided for the language heard there: James Howell wrote of Genoa that 'I will not wish [the traveller] to stay long there, in regard the very worst Italian dialect is spoken there.'[37] Alexandre de Rasigade, tutor to Sir Philip Perceval, was insistent that he could learn good Italian only at Rome, and certainly

---

[32] For English approaches to Italian grammar and the *questione della lingua*, see John Gallagher, '"Ungratefull Tuscans": Teaching Italian in Early Modern England', *The Italianist* 36:3 (2016), pp. 392–413. See also Helena Sanson, *Women, Language and Grammar in Italy, 1500–1900* (Oxford: Oxford University Press, 2011), pp. 8–11; Brian Richardson, 'The Concept of a *lingua comune* in Renaissance Italy', in Anna Laura Lepschy and Arturo Tosi (eds.), *Languages of Italy: Histories and Dictionaries* (Ravenna: Longo, 2007), pp. 11–28; Richardson, 'The Italian of Renaissance Elites in Italy and Europe', in Anna Laura Lepschy and Arturo Tosi (eds.), *Multilingualism in Italy Past and Present* (Oxford: European Humanities Research Centre, 2002), pp. 5–23; Peter Burke, 'Languages and Anti-Languages in Early Modern Italy', *History Workshop Journal* 11 (1981), pp. 24–32; Burke, *The Art of Conversation* (Cambridge: Polity, 1993), pp. 72–88. For German itineraries in Italy, see Stannek, *Telemachs Brüder*, pp. 73–5.

[33] Robert Dallington, *A Method for Travell* (London, 1605), sig. B3r.

[34] Gailhard, *Compleat Gentleman*, p. 141.

[35] Thomas Roe to Francis Fane, 16 August 1632, National Archives, SP 16/222, fol. 75r.

[36] De Beer, *Diary of John Evelyn*, p. 106.

[37] Howell, *Instructions for forreine travell*, pp. 102, 101.

not in Venice.[38] These were serious matters: speaking a non-prestige variety could lead to ridicule or social exclusion.

A shift towards a greater appreciation of the Italian spoken at Rome is apparent after the mid-seventeenth century: as well as Rasigade's opinion, Giovanni Torriano gave his 1657 manual the title *Della Lingua Toscana-Romana*, including a list of the ways in which Roman and Tuscan pronunciations differed.[39] By 1670, any notion of spoken Tuscan as inherently superior was undercut in Richard Lassels's highly influential *Voyage of Italy*:

> As for the Language of Florence its pure, but in their books, not in their mouths: They do so choke it in the throat, that its almost quite drownd there; nor doth it recover it self againe till it come to Rome, where Lingua Toscana in bocca Romana is a most sweet language.[40]

Lassels, whose Catholicism made him less critical of Rome than other authors, was also echoing an older belief that the ideal Italian speech was 'a Tuscan tongue in a Roman mouth'—a pleasing combination of the two varieties.[41] Travelling in 1611–12, the English Catholic Charles Somerset named Siena 'the fayrest towne next *Florence* that the Great Duke hath, and here they speake the best language of Italie, except in the Courte of *Rome*; this towne & *Florence*'.[42] Siena came to be seen by some—including the eighteenth-century travel writer Maximilien Misson—as the place where this balance between courtly Roman and Florentine could be found:

> the Florentine Pronunciation is accompanied with a Harshness that both offends the Ear, and is troublesome to the Throat; and at Rome they are confounded by the Multitudes of Strangers with whom they are daily oblig'd to converse: But at Sienna you may find what the Proverb requires; the Tuscan Language, and a Roman Mouth[43]

---

[38] Alexandre de Rasigade to Robert Southwell, 14 January 1678, BL Add. MS 46955 A, fol. 10r.

[39] Giovanni Torriano, *Della Lingua Toscana-Romana. Or, an Introduction to the Italian Tongue* (London, 1657), sig. [A8v].

[40] Richard Lassels, *The Voyage of Italy, or A Compleat Journey through Italy... With Instructions concerning Travel. By Richard Lassels, Gent. who Travelled through Italy Five times as Tutor to several of the English Nobility and Gentry* (Paris, 1670), pp. 223–4. On English views of Rome in this period and afterwards, see Rosemary Sweet, 'The Changing View of Rome in the Long Eighteenth Century', *Journal for Eighteenth-Century Studies* 33 (2010), pp. 145–64.

[41] See, for instance, Howell, *Instructions for forreine travell*, p. 139. On Lassels, see Chaney, *The Grand Tour and the Great Rebellion, passim*. Tony Claydon offers an interesting perspective on Lassels's guidebook and the confessional politics of later seventeenth-century travel: Claydon, *Europe and the Making of England*, pp. 14–66.

[42] Michael G. Brennan (ed.), *The Travel Diary (1611–1612) of an English Catholic, Sir Charles Somerset* (Leeds: Leeds Philosophical and Literary Society, 1993), p. 215.

[43] Maximilien Misson, *A New Voyage to Italy* (London, 1695), vol. 2, p. 331.

Florence was not forgotten: in 1658, William Hammond wrote to his father how he had 'made an end of the Summer in this Town, my most Visible Improvement is in the Language, of which I have enough to carry me thorowout Italy'.[44] It seems likely, though, that the growth of Rome as a site for language-learning was due to the city's becoming more hospitable to English Protestants—at the end of the sixteenth century it had to be avoided by most Protestant travellers, barring those like Henry Wotton who went in disguise.[45] As with French, the conditions under which a particular variety of language came to be seen as prestigious were intimately linked to political circumstances.

Outside these centres of prestige language, travellers encountered speech that differed (often wildly) from the elite standard. Thomas Palmer said that '[t]ravailers cannot be too good Grammarians', and many commented on the linguistic variation they encountered. Dialect, like clothing and manners, offered material for conceptualizing the difference between areas, and for thinking about local, regional, and national boundaries. Robert Bargrave, travelling in Romania, noted how 'theyr Language is now mixd, digressing from Italian, as Italian does from Latine; easy to be learnd by him that understands either'.[46] Language was one way in which differences between nations were made manifest. Travellers crossing the Alps commonly noted the ways in which French and Italian speech, manners, and clothing mixed on the way: Richard Symonds noted how in Savoy, '[t]he Inhabitants speake French, but mixt with a smack of Italian', and nearby how '[t]he language here is cheifly French but bad enough'.[47] Language could even reflect (or was thought to reflect) political realities: passing through Normandy, Robert Southwell commented that '[t]he Normans in their speech, end allwayes with a...kind of whining: which perhaps is the effect of their great taxes. as if they were complaining of their injury, and turned away at every sentence'.[48] Linguistic variation could be seen as reflecting local ethnic make-up, or a region's history: travelling through Spain in 1654–6, Robert Bargrave mused that 'the skirvy whining tone of the Jewes, is derivd from the Spanish among whom they have livd', while Thomas Raymond noted that the people of Liège 'speake French, but mixt with Low Dutch and High Dutch and a pronunciation soe uncouth that a Frenchman is often puzeld to understand them'.[49]

[44] Brennan, *Origins of the Grand Tour*, p. 194.
[45] Logan Pearsall Smith (ed.), *The Life and Letters of Sir Henry Wotton*, 2 vols (Oxford: Clarendon, 1907), vol. 1, pp. 17–21.
[46] Michael G. Brennan (ed.), *The Travel Diary of Robert Bargrave, Levant Merchant (1647–1656)* (London: Hakluyt Society, 1999), p. 134.
[47] Travel journal of Richard Symonds, British Library, Harleian MS 943, fols. 81r, 82v.
[48] Travel journal of Robert Southwell (France), British Library, Add. MS 58219, fol. 14r.
[49] Brennan, *Travel Diary of Robert Bargrave*, p. 189; G. Davies (ed.), *Autobiography of Thomas Raymond and Memoirs of the Family of Guise of Elmore, Gloucestershire* (London: Camden Society, 1917), p. 41.

The journal kept by Richard Symonds during his travels in France and Italy in the late 1640s reveals how language acquisition could equip a traveller to observe and comment on his oral environments, and to use those observations to form a broader understanding of cultural difference. Symonds had lived in Paris and paid a French master for lessons (at one point attending twice daily) before travelling southwards through France.[50] At Paris, he made notes on both elite and everyday aural and linguistic environments, describing debates at which '[e]very one has freedome to speake in the French tongue' and observing 'A Mountebancke & his boy' on the Pont Neuf, 'hanging his Crocodyle Skins & selling his medicaments *with his quack confidence*'.[51] Symonds also used social encounters as a means to access the linguistic and behavioural codes of French society, noting the ways of addressing women of differing status, and commenting on table manners and table talk:

They all Wash with bason & Eure afore they eat
Every one sayes Graces a deiu for him selfe
They talke incessantly & he that doth not is accounted sick or sad.
Este vous triste? Este vous malade?[52]

As he travelled from France to Italy, Symonds's linguistic observations reflected the confusing business of travelling through borderlands. Arriving at Chambéry, 'a good Ville *the* cheife of Savoy', he noted how '[t]he people call it Sambery': this departure from standardization was the first indication of the cultural hybridity he would encounter as he crossed the Alps.[53,54] As he made his way towards Italy, Symonds began to note the peculiarities of vocabulary he encountered, how 'for ouy. they say. way. woy.' and 'depessa. for depesche, make hast'; he remarked on how the names of trees, people, and products (they called claret wine 'Vin Ruggio') differed from those he had heard before.[55] As he approached Italy, he described the language as 'corrupted Italian'; the language of Piedmont was 'halfe French & halfe Italian corrupt'.[56] These observations on local speech were Symonds's first intimations of the political situation of the region: he would find them reflected in Turin, where public notices were posted up in both languages, and where the people were 'as much French as Italian'. Keeping his ear open for local language enabled Symonds to apprehend the cultural and political hybridity of the region: 'Here are French Clocks, & Italian dyals.'[57]

As the art of travel changed during the period, the importance of linguistic observation remained constant. Far from an abstract academic activity, it was seen as a way of getting to the heart of foreign vernacular cultures: a people's speech could be the key to understanding their character. In his continental travels,

---

[50] Harleian MS 943, fol. 27v.   [51] Ibid., fols. 44v, 49r.   [52] Ibid., fol. 47v.
[53] Ibid., fol. 80v.   [54] Ibid., fol. 81r.   [55] Ibid., fols. 82v, 83v, 84r.
[56] Ibid., fols. 84r, 85r.   [57] Ibid., fols. 85v, 87r.

the naturalist John Ray sought out information from Venetian noblemen and Neapolitan boatmen alike, and took notes on Italian habits of conversation and social interaction. Like Symonds, Ray noted how the language spoken around him changed while traversing the Alps: he wrote of the Grisons that there

> the people use a peculiar language of their own, which they call *Romansch*, that is *Lingua Romana*. It seems to be nearer Spanish than Italian, though distinct from both. Besides their own language they generally speak both Italian and Dutch: so that after we had lost Italian in the valleys we wondered to find it heer again among the hills.[58]

For Ray and others of his generation, these practices of linguistic observation translated into action after their return home. In 1691, Ray published a book documenting English words 'not generally used', in which he recalled how, while travelling through England, 'I could not but take notice of the difference of Dialect, and variety of Local words... in divers Counties, by Reason whereof in many places, especially of the North, the Language of the common people, is to a stranger very difficult to be understood.'[59] The practices of observation, recording, and analysis honed during travel were now put to the service of the proto-ethnographic project of documenting the history and the present realities of the English language, which would animate Ray and his generation of antiquarians and natural philosophers.[60] Early modern English travellers were alive to the role of language as a marker of cultural and political difference: knowledge of a prestige variety was an important attribute, but experience of variations within continental language helped the traveller to think about society, history, and cultural difference, both at home and abroad.

The Traveller's Environment as a Pedagogical Tool

James Howell's advice was clear: since 'the life [of language-learning] consists in societie and communication', the traveller in a foreign city should throw open the window of his lodging, the better to hear the language of the streets. A 'street ward' chamber would allow him 'to take in the common cry and Language, and see how

[58] John Ray, *Observations Topographical, Moral, & Physiological; Made in a Journey Through part of the Low-Countries, Germany, Italy, and France: With A Catalogue of Plants not Native of England, found Spontaneously growing in those Parts, and their Virtues... Whereunto is added A brief Account of Francis Willughby Esq; his Voyage through a great part of Spain* (London: John Martyn, 1673), p. 412.

[59] John Ray, *A Collection of English Words* (London, 1691), sig. [A5r].

[60] One collaborator of Ray's was Edward Lhuyd, the naturalist, philologist, keeper of the Ashmolean Museum, and author of the monumental and multilingual *Archaeologica Britannica*. See Brynley F. Roberts, 'Lhuyd, Edward(1659/60?–1709)',*Oxford Dictionary of National Biography*, Oxford University Press, 2004 (https://doi.org/10.1093/ref:odnb/16633).

the Town is serv'd', which would be 'no unprofitable diversion to him'.[61] Early modern language-learners were urged to treat their environment as a pedagogical tool: as a source of language in use in a variety of social (and economic) contexts, it was the ideal complement to the study of the manual or the lesson. For those who spent time in one of these cities where a prestige dialect was spoken, the urban environment was a rich source of linguistic information. John Lauder made notes on the language of the city streets while lodging at Poitiers in 1665–7, noting the audible presence of

> a fellow also that goes wt a barrel of vinegar on his back, crieng it thorow the toune; another in that same posture fresch oil, others moustard, others wt a maille to cleave wood, also poor women wt their asses loadened wt 2 barrels of water crying, *Il y a l'eau fresche*.[62]

For Lauder, coming to know the sounds of the city was a means of assimilating, linguistically and culturally, to a new urban environment: Lauder noted how the water carriers' cries of *'de l'eau'* at Paris 'seimed a litle strange to us at first, we not crying it so at home'.[63] No level of urban society was beneath the traveller's attention: in his account of continental travel (printed in 1693), William Bromley noted the variety of phrases used by beggars from place to place as one way of marking the difference between cities. Approaching Lyons, he recorded how '[b]eggars besought my Charity hereabout *pour la mort de Dieu*; others, *pour l'amour du Saint Pere & la Saincte Veirge*'; while near Piazza di Spagna in Rome he noted that '[t]he Beggars, to excite Charity, used this Phrase, to whom they addressed, *La Madonna conceda le Gratie che desideri*. The Blessed Virgin grant the Blessings you desire'.[64] Even the voices of the city's poorest could serve a pedagogical purpose. In recording the seemingly minor details of urban life, these travellers followed a pedagogy of travel which urged attention to the social life of urban speech and sound. Pedagogical processes transformed their everyday interactions.

---

[61] Howell, *Instructions for forreine travell*, pp. 46–7. Early modern urban soundscapes were a rich source of social, religious, and commercial information: see David Garrioch, 'Sounds of the City: The Soundscape of Early Modern European Towns', *Urban History* 30 (2003), pp. 5–25; Bruce R. Smith, *The Acoustic World of Early Modern England: Attending to the O-Factor* (Chicago: University of Chicago Press, 1999), pp. 49–95; Natasha Korda, *Labors Lost: Women's Work and the Early Modern English Stage* (Philadelphia, PA: University of Pennsylvania Press, 2011), pp. 144–73; Emily Cockayne, *Hubbub: Filth, Noise & Stench in England 1600–1770* (New Haven, CT, and London: Yale University Press, 2007), pp. 1–21, 106–130; Stephen J. Milner, '"Fanno bandire, notificare, et expressamente comandare": Town Criers and the Information Economy of Renaissance Florence', *I Tatti Studies in the Italian Renaissance* 16 (2013), pp. 107–51.

[62] Donald Crawford (ed.), *Journals of Sir John Lauder, Lord Fountainhall, with his Observations on Public Affairs and Other Memoranda 1665–1676* (Edinburgh: Edinburgh University Press/Scottish History Society, 1900), p. 68.

[63] Ibid.

[64] William Bromley, *Remarks made in travels through France & Italy. With many Publick Inscriptions. Lately taken by a Person of Quality* (London, 1693), pp. 12, 73–4, 195.

Moving through early modern cities, early modern travellers were keenly aware of the linguistic opportunities provided by their surroundings. English Protestants on the continent did not just cross confessional lines in order to appreciate Renaissance art: Catholic churches could also be sources of fine language.[65] For Robert Dallington, fine speech was reason enough to break the usual taboo on consorting with Jesuits: 'These men I would have my Traveller never heare, except in the Pulpit; for being eloquent, they speake excellent language.'[66] The instructions given to Mr. Snell, tutor to William Slingsby, in 1610 made it clear that 'when [Slingsby] shall well understand French it will not be impertinent to goe to the papists sermons when he cannot have meanes to goe to the protestante'.[67] James Howell may have sought to warn travellers off conversing with nuns at convent gates, seeing it as dangerous to their Protestant religion, but his remarks suggest that in contrast to the picture of sharply confessionally divided travel practices put forward in some recent work, the linguistic element of pedagogical travel commonly involved some crossing of confessional boundaries.[68]

Attendance at Protestant services while abroad allowed English travellers to hone their linguistic skills while reinforcing their religious identity. In March 1644, John Evelyn went to Charenton, outside Paris, 'to heare & see the manner of the French-Protestant Churches service'.[69] Jean Gailhard instructed his reader to attend the church there immediately after his arrival at Paris and to give thanks, 'whether or not he understands the language'.[70] Travellers' notes on sermons heard abroad were one aspect of the 'participatory listening and note-taking that were such an ingrained part of early modern pedagogy'.[71] Note-taking during sermons was not only geared towards the listener's religious education: this kind of participatory listening was also a language-learning exercise. With enough skill in language, the traveller could even critique the sermon he heard, as Thomas Raymond did of Dutch-language Calvinist sermons in the early 1630s.[72] Martin Lister, hearing a Catholic Lenten sermon in Paris in 1698, was 'not so good a

---

[65] On grand tourists and Catholic art, see Clare Haynes, 'The Culture of Judgement: Art and Anti-Catholicism in England, c.1660–c.1770', *Historical Research* 78 (2005), pp. 483–505.

[66] Dallington, *Method for Travell*, sig. B2r.

[67] Daniel Parsons (ed.), *The diary of Sir Henry Slingsby* (London: Longman, Rees, Orme, Brown, Green, and Longman, 1836), p. 261.

[68] Claydon, *Europe and the Making of England, passim*; see also Gerrit Verhoeven's characterization of the 'abrasive and quarrelsome stances' taken by Anglican travellers in Gerrit Verhoeven, 'Calvinist Pilgrimages and Popish Encounters: Religious Identity and Sacred Space on the Dutch Grand Tour', *Journal of Social History* 43:3 (2010), p. 628. On English Catholic mobility in the later seventeenth and eighteenth century, see Liesbeth Corens, 'Catholic Nuns and English Identities: English Protestant Travellers on the English Convents in the Low Countries, 1660–1730', *Recusant History* 30 (2011), pp. 441–59, and Corens, *Confessional Mobility and English Catholics in Counter-Reformation Europe* (Oxford: Oxford University Press, 2019).

[69] De Beer, *Diary of John Evelyn*, p. 64.   [70] Gailhard, *Compleat Gentleman*, part II, p. 33.

[71] Arnold Hunt, *The Art of Hearing: English Preachers and their Audiences, 1560–1640* (Cambridge: Cambridge University Press, 2010), p. 13.

[72] Davies, *Autobiography of Thomas Raymond*, p. 34.

French-Man as to understand all [the abbot] said', but nonetheless critiqued the content, the preacher's gestures, and his use of familiar language.[73] The sermon was not only a pedagogical opportunity restricted to the elite male traveller: Deborah Fowler, a woman in the entourage of Lady Katherine Perceval at Saumur in 1677, noted how 'we have a church veri neare us which my lady is early at and sum of us but we understand very littell I hope we may in good time'.[74]

The engagement with polyglot speechscapes practised by travellers bursts off the page in the travel notebooks of Edward Browne in the mid-1660s. Having arrived in France with little to no competence in spoken French, he visited Charenton for the first time to hear a sermon on 11 May 1664. The following week, he attended again and noted how 'I begin to understand the Minister.'[75] By 8 June he could note in a mixture of French and English that '[t]he text was … Si nous vivons par l'Esprit, Cheminons aussi en Esprit,' and that he had avoided a row with a bigoted Dutchman on his return trip to the city—the conversation (and the apology) were in French.[76] Browne was also attending medicine lectures in Paris, but at first regretted that 'I was much disappointed in my expectation of understanding all he [a Dr. Patin] said by reason hee used the French tongue so much.'[77] This use of the vernacular over Latin, allied with the French custom whereby students could interject with questions at any point, flummoxed Browne, but his increasingly fluent notes and descriptions of conversations suggest that he soon overcame these early difficulties. His diary for 29 April 1664 gives a sense of the activities that allowed him to progress rapidly in French:

I heard Dr. Moureau read at three of the clock, Dr. Pattin at 4 of the clock, and Dr. Dyneau at 5. I bought Charles Paiots French and latin Dictionary for un Livre, a paire of course linnen stockins for 12 solz, a map of France for cinq solz. I observe that here at Paris they aske thrice the valeu of any commodity at first, and if you chance to offer halfe you shall bee sure to have it.[78]

Hearing lectures, reading in French, mixing languages in his writing, studying the geography of France, and making notes on the manoeuvring necessary to get a bargain, Browne was a diligent but not exceptional example of a travelling language-learner.

---

[73] Martin Lister, A Journey to Paris In the Year 1698 (London, 1698), p. 174.

[74] Deborah Fowler to Helena Southwell, 10 November 1677, British Library, Add. MS 46954 B, fol. 198r. Sources like this letter by Fowler are a prompt to think more about the servants and attendants who also participated in early modern elite mobility as members of an elite traveller's entourage. For some thoughts on this, see John Gallagher, 'Language and Education on the Grand Tour of Sir Philip Perceval, 1676–9', in Helmut Glück, Mark Häberlein, and Andreas Flurschütz da Cruz (eds.), *Adel und Mehrsprachigkeit in der Frühen Neuzeit. Ziele, Formen und Praktiken des Erwerbs und Gebrauchs von Fremdsprachen* (Wolfenbüttel: Harrassowitz, forthcoming 2019).

[75] Edward Browne, A Journal of a visit to Paris in the year 1664, ed. Geoffrey Keynes (London: John Murray, 1923), pp. 10, 13.

[76] Ibid., p. 23.   [77] Ibid., p. 6.   [78] Ibid., p. 7.

The traveller's choice of lodging offered an opportunity to practise the language with native speakers. In 1678, Jean Gailhard recommended 'a convenient Lodging, of which the people be honest . . . and the Master, if possible, be a man of parts and learning, whose conversation one may have at table; which will prove pleasant and useful for the language, and other things'; he urged that the traveller choose to lodge with those 'whose conversation may be beneficial to you'.[79] For Robert Dallington, the choice to take meals in one's lodging with native speakers meant that the traveller would learn more; the choice to live at his own provision would 'hinder his profiting, and only further him with some few kitchin and market phrases'.[80] Dallington's disparaging remark about 'kitchin and market phrases' is a reminder that travellers needed to be aware about the nature of the competence they acquired, and its social uses: their attention to urban speechscapes needed to be combined with a critical management of their own speech. Many travellers chose to lodge with native speakers. Fynes Moryson recalled time spent at Leiden in 1592–3, 'where I lodged in a French-mans house, for intending to bestow all my time in the French tongue'.[81] Moryson lodged with a rich citizen of Leipzig in order to learn German, describing this experience as a kind of study distinct from and complementary to the study of the language's grammar:

> I spent this winter at Leipzig, that I might there learne to speake the Dutch toung (the Grammer wherof I had read at Witteberg,) because the Misen speech was held the purest of all other parts in Germany.[82]

Many other seventeenth-century travellers lodged with locals, with some explicitly citing language-learning as the reason. Thomas Abdie recorded lodging with a 'Monsieur Montillet' at Blois in 1633–4, and with one 'Signor Franc.' at Siena.[83] In 1656, Robert Bargrave noted how he was shown around the town of Bassano del Grappa by one 'Signor Giovanni Fresca, an Italian Priest, with whom some English have liv'd to learn the language'.[84] At Augsburg, Robert Montagu chose to lodge with his tutor's uncle 'till I had learned something of the german tongue'.[85] Edward Browne recorded his taking a room with a French-speaking landlord in a mixture of English and French: 'I went and hired a chamber in Rüe St Zacharie, for 7 livres par mois, & so je vous souhaitte le bon soir.'[86] The

---

[79] Gailhard, *Compleat Gentleman*, part II, p. 185. He goes on: 'Also, let them be Protestants, if it can be done.' Compare the anonymous 1662 'Account of my Jurny from the Citty of Burdiox to Parris Callis & London' in British Library, Add. MS 78670, which mentions finding accommodation in Paris 'at A Prodestants House', fol. 13r.

[80] Dallington, *Method for Travell*, sig. B4v.

[81] Fynes Moryson, *Itinerary*, part I, p. 46; on the practice of learning French in the Low Countries at times when a journey through France was deemed too risky, see N. E. Osselton, *The Dumb Linguists: A Study of the Earliest English and Dutch Dictionaries* (Leiden and London, 1973), p. 8.

[82] Fynes Moryson, *Itinerary*, part I, p. 12.   [83] Rawlinson MS D1285, fols. 157r–157v.

[84] Brennan, *Travel diary of Robert Bargrave*, p. 240.   [85] Ibid., p. 134.

[86] Edward Browne, travel notebook (France), British Library, Sloane MS 1906, fol. 70r.

traveller's lodging was to be seen as a classroom in its own right, and table talk a lesson.

Languages on the Page: Multilingual Practices in Travellers' Manuscripts

In 1625, Francis Bacon bemoaned a strange omission by travellers:

> It is a strange thing, that in sea voyages, where there is nothing to be seen, but sky and sea, men should make diaries; but in land-travel, wherein so much is to be observed, for the most part they omit it; as if chance were fitter to be registered, than observation. Let diaries, therefore, be brought in use.[87]

The traveller's manuscripts—notebooks, commonplace books, diaries, and letters—were where the experience of travel was recorded, reconsidered, and reworked. More prosaically and more immediately, they could also justify the time and money spent on travel to those who had underwritten it.[88] These are profoundly multilingual texts: they narrate experiences of language-learning in multiple, often macaronic ways, and abound in oral information. Edward Browne's record of his travels in France and Italy saw him practising French verbs between entries on his life in Paris, while noting alchemical symbols and their meanings in French, and giving over whole sections of his notebooks to materials culled from grammars in Italian and in French.[89] He kept lists of short phrases, occasionally with translations, in both languages—including stock expressions for use in lovers' correspondence—while also spending time doing exercises on particular verbs or forms.[90] Near the beginning of his study of French, he switched clumsily into the new language, writing ' [j]e commence parle un peu de François a vostre service et Je'esper que je parlerai mieux dans un Mois', and would go on to use it more and more (and with increasing expertise) as time went by (see Figure 4.1).[91] Notebooks

---

[87] Bacon, *Essayes*, pp. 100–1. Compare Perrott MS 5, fol. 12v on the importance of keeping 'A table booke or Noat booke'.

[88] Stagl, *History of Curiosity*, pp. 47–93. On the afterlife of these documents, see Jill Bepler, 'Travelling and Posterity: The Archive, the Library and the Cabinet', in Rainer Babel and Werner Paravicini (eds.), *Grand Tour: Adeliges Reisen und Europäische Kultur vom 14. bis zum 18. Jahrhundert* (Ostfildern: Jan Thorbecke Verlag, 2005), pp. 191–203.

[89] Sloane MS 1906, fols. 81r, 104v, 160r–173r; Edward Browne, travel notebook (France and Italy), British Library, Sloane MS 1886, fol. 14r. Sloane MS 1886 contains a lot of exercise material. Keynes's partial printed edition of MS Sloane 1906 silently omits the language exercises.

[90] Short phrases in Italian and French can be seen in Sloane MS 1906, fols. 196v–200v; verb exercises in Sloane MS 1886, fols. 12r, 26r–29v. Browne also began at least some reading in French before he left, given his notes from a French-language geometry text: BL Sloane 1906, fols. 60v–61r.

[91] 'I begin to speak a little French and I hope that I will speak it better in a month': Sloane MS 1906, fol. 85v.

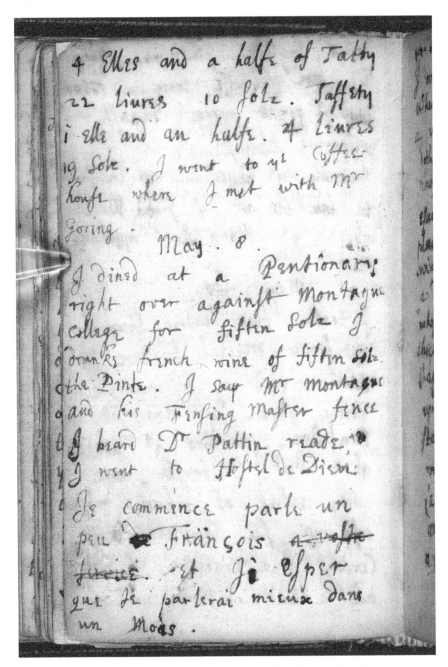

Figure 4.1 Edward Browne begins to write some of his diary in French
Source: British Library, Sloane MS 1906, fol. 85v. © The British Library Board.

like Browne's were much more than the record of a process: they were a constitutive element of the process themselves. As places to practice a new language, and spaces where oral material was recorded and reshaped for reuse in conversations, travellers' notebooks and journals offer a unique window on the interaction between the oral and scribal worlds of educational travel.

Travellers often used their notebooks to record details of polyglot reading, or simply as a place for the daily grind of language study. The notebook kept by Thomas Abdie during his travels in France in the 1630s, for instance, sheds light on one traveller's multilingual reading practice. Abdie made notes on phrases and vocabulary, often culled from his reading of Honoré d'Urfé's *L'Astrée*, published between 1607 and 1627, and popular with English travellers and those who sought to mimic French *civilité* in their conversation and writing.[92] Most of the quotations taken from the text went untranslated, while his method with individual items of vocabulary seems to have been to note them in French as he went along, and to look them up in bulk—some have no English translation, and in some places the English is in fainter ink than the French. Looking at Abdie's translations, we can even pinpoint the linguistic reference text he was using to aid his reading (see Figure 4.2). It is an edition of Randle Cotgrave's seminal *Dictionarie of the French and English Tongues* (London, 1611). Abdie translated the French 'blafard' as '[p]ale, wan, bleake of coulour', where Cotgrave offered 'Pale, wanne, lew, bleake of colour, of a decayed hue'; Abdie noted further that 'greve' can translate as 'sand or gravelle', but 'also *the* shin bone' and 'also *the* place of execution in Paris', all definitions found in Cotgrave.[93] The final proof that many of his definitions are taken from a copy of Cotgrave's *Dictionarie* is to be seen in Abdie's note on the meanings of 'roturier', defining it first as a noun, and secondly as an adjective. The first definition begins '[a] Yeoman, or Plebeyan, a Plough-man'; the second begins '[y]eomanlie, Plebeyan, ignoble'. Abdie wrote '[r]oturier. Yeomanlie. plebeian a plough ignoble', clearly beginning to copy the adjective definition but, perhaps distracted by the appearance of 'plebeyan' in both, briefly skipping to the definition of the noun before recognizing his mistake, crossing it out, and replacing it with that from the adjective definition.[94] Abdie had clearly lugged a copy of Cotgrave's bulky dictionary across the Channel with him to serve as a language-learning aid (a reminder, perhaps, that language-learning can also be a physical activity). The day-to-day work of language acquisition—conjugating verbs and memorizing vocabulary—is made visible in travellers' notebooks.

---

[92] Rawlinson MS 1285, fols. 2r–68v.

[93] Randle Cotgrave, *Dictionarie of the French and English Tongues* (London, 1611).

[94] Rawlinson MS 1285, fol. 23r. Another traveller who carried a Cotgrave was Richard Symonds, who noted among his books a 'Dictionary of English & French made by Cotgrave sometimes belonging to the Earl of Exeter': British Library, Harleian MS 943, fol. 45r.

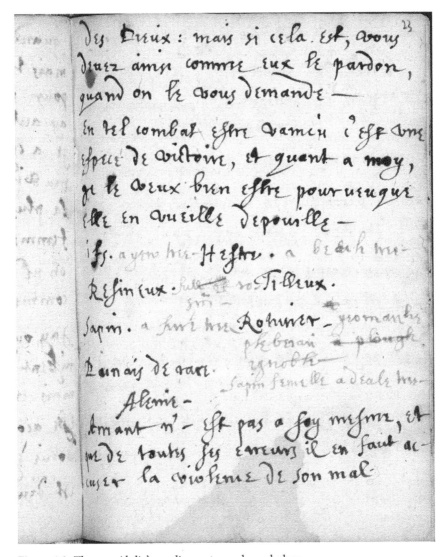

Figure 4.2 Thomas Abdie's reading notes and vocabulary

Source: Bodleian Library, Rawlinson MS D1285, fol. 23r. Image reproduced courtesy of The Bodleian Libaries, The University of Oxford.

The traveller's manuscripts were also an arena in which the new language could be practised and performed. Diaries and notebooks frequently show students switching between different languages during travel. On 9 November 1633, Abdie recorded his arrival at Blois, at which point his diary went silent until 29 April 1634. When it picks up again, the language of the text has switched to French, beginning '[j]e suis parti de Blois 29 Avrill pour commencer l'entreprise du voyage de la France' (see Figure 4.3).[95] From then on, Abdie's writing fits the model of the traveller's record, noting (in French) the features of towns he passes through, with information on fortifications, Latin inscriptions, notable sights—all the things that a good traveller was meant to observe, all noted down in his new vernacular. Other travellers switched languages too. In 1648, Richard Symonds reported a conversation he had on the road: 'Here was in *our* Company an old scholer monsi*eur* Curé ... qui m'a dit que je suis damné': this kind of casual codeswitching is common in travellers' manuscripts.[96] John North, who had travelled in Italy with Giacomo Castelvetro in the 1570s, went silent for a long period in the middle of his journal, and took it back up writing entirely in Italian—a habit which he continued even on his return to England in 1577, leaving us with an Italian-language diary of an Italianate gentleman's London life.[97] North's use of Italian is a reminder that the traveller's linguistic skill could become a performative part of his personality after his return home. For these travellers, language-learning and the record-keeping urged by the writers of travel advice merged into one, and the observation of another culture was intimately linked to learning to write about it in a new language.

A notebook was not where words went to die, but where they were recorded and reshaped in the expectation of their employment in speech as well as in writing. The notebooks kept during travel were part of a note-taking culture which prized this kind of usefulness.[98] Jean Gailhard's influential guide for grand tourists made explicit the place of note-taking in its relation to conversation:

> It must not be neglected or forgotten to write down the Histories, merry Tales, notable sentences, witty Replies, the good words, and every fine expression which every day you happen to hear in company, thereby to profit and make use of upon occasion.[99]

Daniel Woolf argues that anecdotes and oral materials like these 'became social tools, used to make points not only in private correspondence, but also in civil conversation'.[100] It was no coincidence that conversation manuals offered

---

[95] 'I left Blois on the 29th April to begin the enterprise of the tour of France': Rawlinson MS 1285, fol. 75r. Compare the French-language travel journal kept by the younger William Cecil, Lord Cranborne, during his travels in France in 1609, in Owen (ed.), *HMC Salisbury*, part XXI, pp. 105–8. Cranborne's tour has been examined in detail in Chaney and Wilks, *Jacobean Grand Tour*.

[96] 'who told me that I am damned': Harleian MS 943, fol. 73r.

[97] Travel journal of John North, 1575–7, Bodleian Library, MS Add. C. 193; John Gallagher, 'The Italian London of John North: Cultural Contact and Linguistic Encounter in Early Modern England', *Renaissance Quarterly* 70 (2017), pp. 88–131.

[98] Peter Beal, 'Notions in Garrison: The Seventeenth-Century Commonplace Book', in W. Speed Hill (ed.) *New Ways of Looking at Old Texts: Papers of the Renaissance English Text Society, 1985–1991*, (Binghamton, NY: RETS, 1993), p. 134.

[99] Gailhard, *Compleat Gentleman*, part II, p. 37.

[100] Daniel Woolf, 'Speaking of History: Conversations about the Past in Restoration and Eighteenth-Century England', in Adam Fox and Daniel Woolf (eds.), *The Spoken Word: Oral Culture in Britain 1500–1850* (Manchester and New York: Manchester University Press, 2002), p. 127.

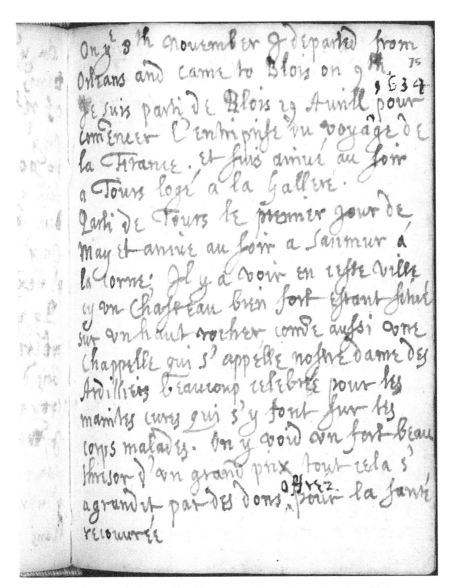

Figure 4.3 Thomas Abdie switches languages after studying French at Blois

Source: Bodleian Library, Rawlinson MS D1285, fol. 75r. Image reproduced courtesy of The Bodleian Libraries, The University of Oxford.

proverbs and, later in the period, collections of witty anecdotes in the target language for use by their readers.[101] As textual places in which knowledge was

---

[101] See, for instance, the 'Mescolanza Dolce di varie Historiette, Favole Morali & Politiche, Facetie, Motti & Burle di diversi Scrittori Italiani' appended to Giovanni Torriano, *The Italian reviv'd: or, The*

assembled and arranged, the notebook, commonplace book, and diary were not end points. Their relationship with orality was two-way: they were points of rest, repositories of knowledge to be consulted, as Ann Blair argues, as resources for future writing and conversation.[102] Notebooks are more commonly thought of as being part of a network of texts, and linked to the history of reading, though Blair recognizes their close and complex relationship with speech:

> Notes recorded from reading or experience typically contribute to one's conversation and compositions, from which others can draw in turn in their own thinking and writing, thus perpetuating a cycle of transmission and transformation of knowledge, ideas, and experiences.[103]

Heidi Brayman Hackel has shown that the Erasmian model of the commonplace book, in which 'reading begets writing begets speaking', fails to do justice to the multidirectional relationship between speech, text, and writing: 'A remark in conversation might be recorded in a commonplace book and then recopied as a formulaic phrase in a letter; a passage from a printed book might be committed to memory and then dictated later into a version of a commonplace book'.[104] Even scholars' marginalia were tied to oral usage: Jennifer Richards shows Gabriel Harvey noting jokes in the margins of his copy of the *Courtier*, with a view to using them in social situations, 'practising civility in the margins of this book'.[105] For travellers—who, as we have seen, paid more attention than most to the details of oral culture—the notebook was a fulcrum for the interlocking pedagogical processes of hearing, writing, editing, and speaking.

Notebooks were where travellers collected the material that everyday pedagogy was concerned with, such as foreign-language proverbs, jokes, songs, and riddles.[106] Authors writing about Italy commonly drew on proverbial wisdom to recall the different characters of the cities of the peninsula, as in Richard Lassels's manuscript

---

introduction to the Italian tongue (London, 1689); Giacomo Rossi, *Le Maître Aisé et Rejouissant: ou Nouvelle Methode Agreable Pour Apprendre Sans Peine La Langue Italienne* (London, 1710), pp. 221–41.

---

[102] Ann Blair, 'Note Taking as an Art of Transmission', *Critical Inquiry* 31 (2004), pp. 85–107.

[103] ibid., p. 85. See also Peter Stallybrass, Roger Chartier, J. Franklin Mowery, and Heather Wolfe, 'Hamlet's Tables and the Technologies of Writing in Renaissance England', *Shakespeare Quarterly* 55 (2004), pp. 402–3; Ann Blair, *Too Much to Know: Managing Scholarly Information before the Modern Age* (New Haven, CT, and London: Yale University Press, 2010), pp. 64–5.

[104] Heidi Brayman Hackel, *Reading Material in Early Modern England* (Cambridge: Cambridge University Press, 2005), p. 53.

[105] Jennifer Richards, *Rhetoric and Courtliness in Early Modern Literature* (Cambridge: Cambridge University Press, 2003), p. 63.

[106] On proverbs and the understanding of foreign vernacular cultures, see Michael Wyatt, *The Italian Encounter with Tudor England: A Cultural Politics of Translation* (Cambridge: Cambridge University Press, 2005), pp. 175–9. See also Walter J. Ong, *Orality and Literacy: The Technologizing of the Word* (London and New York, 1982), p. 35.

account of the travels (and death) of Catherine Whetenall in 1649-50: 'The proverbe saies of Genua that there are monte senzalegna, mare senza pesce, huominij senza fede donna senza vergogna the Last whereof is true, that few strangers passe in the streetes without being invited to naughty houses'.[107] For Robert Bargrave in Spain, proverbs offered a way of critiquing his host country and responding to its people's prejudices: 'As the Spaniards say of our Land = Buena Tierra, mala Gente = so may we of theyr Lawes = Buenas Lees, mal executadas.'[108] Oral information of this kind is common in travellers' notebooks: Richard Symonds collected stories told by fellow travellers, and jokes like the one told to him by an innkeeper in Savoy.[109] Martin Lister kept a multilingual notebook in which he recorded stories, pasquinades, and jokes, like a macaronic rendering of an imprisoned Spaniard's attempt to curry favour with his protestant captors: 'Signor Luthrano nò me matto Io credo al Diabolo come vos otros. dit le spagnuol a un soldat de la religion qui l'avoit pris.'[110] Assiduously collected oral and linguistic information like this could enliven their own future conversation, but as mnemonic devices they could help the traveller to understand better the culturally, politically, and religiously varied territories they traversed, and to show that understanding in their speech.

One traveller who was particularly committed to collecting and analysing his oral experiences was the Scotsman John Lauder of Fountainhall. In his travel account, he noted proverbs and essayed translations:

> Il faut prendre gard (saye the frenchman) d'une qui pro quo d'une Apotiquaire (as when in mistake he takes one pig for another, or out of ignorance gives a binding thing for a laxative) d'une et caetera d'un Notaire (by which is taxed the knaveries of that calling), d'une dewant une femme, d'une derriere une mule, et d'un Moin de tout costes: thats to say, diligently.[111]

Lauder also attempted to understand how these phrases were to be applied in social situations. He recorded how '[w]hen [the French] would taxe on for being much given to lying, they say, Il est un menteur comme un arracheur de dents'; explaining that these 'arracheurs de dents' ('tooth-pullers') 'wil promise that they sall not so much as touch them almost, that they sal find no peine, when in the

---

[107] 'a woodless hill, a fishless sea, faithless men and shameless women': Richard Lassels, account of Catherine Whetenall's journey from Brussels to Italy, British Library, Add. MS 4217, fol. 17r.
[108] 'Good land, evil people...good laws, badly executed': Brennan, *Travel diary of Robert Bargrave*, p. 205.
[109] British Library, Harleian MS 943, fol. 82r. On English gentlemen recording jokes they had heard, see Adam Fox, *Oral and Literate Culture in England 1500-1700* (Oxford: Clarendon, 2000), p. 39.
[110] 'Do not kill me, Signor Lutheran, I believe in the Devil like you. Said the Spaniard to a soldier of the religion who had captured him': Notebook of Martin Lister, Paris 1698, Bodleian Lister MS 26, fol. 4r.
[111] Roughly, 'One must beware...of an apothecary's quid pro quo...a lawyer's etcetera...of a woman's front, a mule's backside, and of all sides of a monk': Crawford, *Journals of Sir John Lauder*, pp. 143-4.

interim the peine wil be very sensible'.[112] Lauder's recordings of French oral culture allowed him to practise the language while gaining insight into cultural differences. In listening to his hostess telling folk tales, he was intrigued by how they shared plots and certain rhetorical flourishes with their Scottish equivalents, 'beginning wt that usually *Il y avoit un Roy et une reine*, etc.', and differing only in their vocabulary, so that 'instead of our red dracons and giants they have *lougar-ous*, or *war-woophs*'.[113] The same was true of oaths and swearing, in which Lauder showed a distinctly ethnographical interest. He compared the English and Scottish tradition of the loyal health with the near-total absence of similar drinking to the monarch in France, where he noted a common *lèse-majesté* in conversation:

> A man may live 10 years in France or he sy a French man drink their oune Kings health. Amongs on another they make not a boast to call him *bougre, coquin, frippon*, etc. I have sein them in mockery drink to the King of Frances coach-horses health.[114]

Lauder's journal is a record of language acquisition and amateur ethnography, in which his linguistic competence allowed him to access the oral cultures of France during his travels and to compare them with those that were native to him.

Travel manuscripts like those of Lauder and Symonds reveal the processes of recording, writing, and reuse that underlay the formation of a 'conversable knowledge'. Travellers' notebooks were an active element of pedagogical processes and not only a record of them. They operated not only within a network of texts, but as part of a continuum between reading, writing, speaking, and acting—at the heart of the uncertain binary between oral and textual that was central to early modern educational culture.

Performing Linguistic Competence in Letters

Travellers' letters home offered an opportunity for the practice, performance, and evaluation of the linguistic competence they acquired while abroad. They offered families and contacts a glimpse into their progress in language acquisition. They could reassure the person funding the voyage that their investment was paying off, or be circulated to siblings or relatives to show the traveller's developing prowess. Letters written home in a new language provided the basis for a pedagogical process which was dialogic and dependent on the input and opinions of those at

---

[112] 'He lies as much as a tooth-puller': ibid., p. 144.   [113] Ibid., p. 83.

[114] Ibid., p. 89. For a relevant perspective on irreverent oaths and swearing, see John Spurr, 'A Profane History of Early Modern Oaths', *Transactions of the Royal Historical Society* 11 (2001), pp. 37–63. On loyal healths, see Rebecca Lemon, 'Compulsory Conviviality in Early Modern England', *English Literary Renaissance* 43 (2013), pp. 381–414. See also the material on loyal healths and drinking in travel in Chapter 3.

home as well as the traveller and his party.[115] Travellers' multilingual letters made pedagogical processes visible: they offer insights not only into how linguistic competence was acquired, but into how it was performed for others.

During his continental tour, undertaken between December 1655 and May 1658, William Hammond laid bare the difficulties of learning French in his letters home. An early letter referred to another, which has sadly been lost, which he said 'pretended to speake nothing but French'. Hammond apologized for his broken language in that letter, but hoped that it might at least show 'my Proficiency in this Crabbed Tongue, *which* is so contrary both in Syntaxe & Pronunciation to our English, that it may well goe hand in hand with the Latine for matter of difficulty'.[116] Hammond described his pedagogical efforts and attempted to defend his lack of progress to the parents who were paying for him to be abroad:

> The Genius of the place begins to infect us with a sedentary Bookishness, which does us some good in attaining the Grounds of the French Languague; *the* Syntaxes whereof I think much harder, than that either of the latine or the Greek. I endeavour to get their History & the Country's Geophrophy together with their Languague[117]

He assured his family that he was reading histories, a life of Louis XIII, the *Gazette* for current affairs, and the letters of Guez de Balzac, 'whose Easy & Ingenuous way of writing very much resembles that of our English Dr. Donne'.[118] A fine epistolary style was one of the expected outcomes of a continental tour; it was also one of the elements of linguistic competence; hence the provision of form letters and epistolary phrases in language manuals. Letters like Hammond's recounted the practices and experiences of language-learning for an audience at home.

Others went further than simply talking *about* the language they were learning, choosing to use their new language in correspondence—the approach which Hammond had abandoned almost immediately. Letters like those written by the young Robert Bertie during his continental tour in 1598/9 give a sense of how and why languages were learnt during travel. Bertie's first surviving letter home was written on 12 September, in Latin, but by 26 January 1599, when he was at Orléans, the language of the letters had switched to French. His first French letter ends with the slightly stilted '[j]e poursuivray mes estudes en intention de vous faire paroistre de jour a autre comme je practique...les commandemens dont vous m'avez honore'—'I will pursue my studies in the hope of showing you from day to day how I practice...the commandments with which you have honoured me'.[119] These commandments he summed up in his next letter as 'to

---

[115] Hardwick, *Grand Tour*, p. 101.   [116] Brennan, *Origins of the Grand Tour*, p. 163.
[117] Ibid., p. 172.   [118] Ibid.
[119] Robert Bertie to Peregrine Bertie, 26 January 1589, Lincolnshire Archives, 8ANC7/73.

see France and to learn the language'; he promised to do more of the first, while showing his progress in the second by means of the letter.[120] The letters written by Bertie were meant to act as proof of his progress in the language and of his careful observation of French politics and affairs. They were also a means of keeping important figures at home informed about his ongoing education: a formal letter in French to the Earl of Essex is short and larded with platitudes, but its being written in French indicates that the young student was advertising himself not only as a willing correspondent and servant to the earl, but also as one with demonstrable facility in another language and experience in travel, who was already pondering 'how I may fashion myself to offer myself eternally to your commands'.[121] Similarly, a letter to the earl of Oxford written the same day lamented that he had no news to share: in fact, the 'news' of the letter was the form in which it arrived: it functioned as an announcement of a competence newly acquired and ready to be directed to the ends of those who had looked well on him before his travels.[122] A similar tactic was at work in a letter by Burghley's grandson in 1583 to Walsingham from Paris. The young William Cecil had written to other lords, and to his parents and 'friends' in French, and wrote now to Francis Walsingham, apologizing for his poor French but promising his service in future, as his education progressed.[123] The savvy traveller always had one eye on his return: the linguistic competence and the networks he developed while abroad were meant to serve him well during his future career.[124]

Where a traveller's polyglot correspondence survives, it can be possible to follow their progress in a new language. This is the case with the French-language letters written by Edward Hinchingbrooke, son to the Earl of Sandwich, during the years he spent abroad between 1660 and 1665. There are ten French letters from Hinchingbrooke to his father preserved in the Sandwich correspondence, sent at irregular intervals during and immediately following his time abroad. This first letter of late September 1662 has little of substance to report beyond the writer's continuing in good health; the deletions and superscripts (preserved in my transcription below) suggest that it might perhaps have been corrected by Hinchingbrooke himself or by his tutor:

---

[120]   Robert Bertie to Peregrine Bertie, February? 1589, Lincolnshire Archives, 8ANC7/74.

[121]   'je n'auraye autre desir n'y autre occupation que de mediter continuellement comme je pourray me façoner pour m'offrir eternellement a vos commandemens': Robert Bertie to the earl of Essex, 3 March 1589, Lincolnshire Archives, 8ANC7/75.

[122]   Robert Bertie to the earl of Oxford, 3 March 1589, Lincolnshire Archives, 8ANC7/76.

[123]   William Cecil to Walsingham, 26 October 1583, National Archives, SP 15/28/1, fol. 59r.

[124]   On the traveller's return, see Mark Williams, 'The Inner Lives of Early Modern Travel', *Historical Journal* (forthcoming, early view available at https://doi.org/10.1017/S0018246X18000237); Richard Ansell, 'Educational Travel in Protestant Families from Post-Restoration Ireland', *Historical Journal*, 58:4 (2015), pp. 931–58; Bepler, 'Travelling and Posterity'; Gallagher, 'The Italian London of John North'. On connections between travellers and England, see Corens, *Confessional Mobility*.

Mon tres Honore Pere

J ay Prit la hardiesse de vous hescrire pour vou faire a scavoir comme nous som^me segnieu de vos commands: Je vou demande excuse de se que je ne vous ay pas hescrire plutot [deletion] pource Jay eu une petite mal^adies la quelle menat enpeyche; ^{Mais [astoor?]}Je vou puis assurer que nous nou portons forbein & Je ne soit rein que vostre Benediction a

Vo^stre thres obeysant fils et Serviteur

E: Hinchinbrooke[125]

Besides its confused appearance on the page, Hinchingbrooke's French letter shows that he had yet to get to grips with elements of written French—the confusion between 'nous' and 'nou', the redundant 'a' in 'pour vou faire a scavoir', 'forbein' for 'fort bien', and 'la quelle menat enpeyche', which seems meant to be 'laquelle m'en a empêché'. It may be that he was attempting to recreate words and phrases he had heard on the page; he came close to representing some sounds without the correct orthography. Indeed, his tutor complained later about his distaste for the textual aspects of study, writing that Hinchingbrooke 'doth not like reading; which obligeth me to recurre to vocal discourse & to strive by conversation to insinuate to his soule as farre as I am able what I have learn't by bookes & meditation'.[126] But after a previous letter in Latin, this was a statement of the pupil's progress in French, and its mistakes and corrections seem to serve as an assurance that this was the pupil's work in the first instance and not that of a tutor. The pupil's progress could be judged and commented on by the recipient: one surviving letter from William Blathwayt the younger on his grand tour in 1706 has a note on the end, written by his father and correcting the son's writing: 'Will to punctuat and to begin his Perierds with great Letters and to his Christian name'.[127] Similarly, the earl of Ormond wrote to his son's tutor that 'I wish my Lord of Derby would Endeavour to mend his handwriteing & by degrees put his thoughts in Method that way,' since 'it is a thing without which neither businesse or a civill correspondence can be well done & maintained'.[128] These epistolary conversations show that the experience of language-learning in travel was dialogic: those at home were expected to observe and to comment on the process of language-learning as it happened, and not only when the traveller returned.

[125] Very roughly, 'Most honoured father, I have been so bold as to write to you to let you know how we [follow?] your commands: I ask your pardon for not having written to you earlier, because a small illness which I had kept me from doing so; I can assure you that we bear ourselves very well and I wish nothing but your blessing on Your most obedient son and servant, E. Hinchingbrooke': Edward Hinchingbrooke to the Earl of Sandwich, 29 September 1662, Bodleian Library, MS Carte 223, fol. 113r.
[126] Du Prat to Sandwich, 23 August/2 September 1664, Bodleian Library, MS Carte 223, fol. 92v.
[127] Hardwick, Grand Tour, p. 62.
[128] Ormond to Mr. Forbes, 7 August 1673, Bodleian Library, MS Carte 50, fol. 103r.

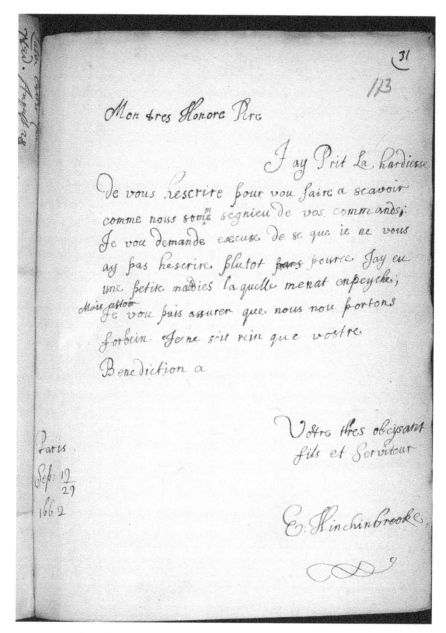

Figure 4.4 Edward Hinchingbrooke to the Earl of Sandwich, 29 September 1662

Source: Bodleian Library, MS Carte 223, fol. 113r. Image reproduced courtesy of The Bodleian Libaries, The University of Oxford.

By 31 January 1663, when Hinchingbrooke penned his next surviving letter to his father, his competence had noticeably improved, though it still displayed some idiosyncratic spellings—'Javès' for 'j'avais', and 'vaires' for 'verrez'. The expression, however, is clearer and the word order less strained than before, while the superscript corrections suggest that this was still the pupil's work. His later letters, longer and more correct, could be testament either to increased linguistic skill or to a process of drafting—or both. From Saumur in June 1664, he sent a polished French-language account of their journey from Paris and of the places they had visited along the way. The language, content, and form of this letter bear the hallmarks of the humanist pedagogy of travel: they function as testimony to its author's diligent study of his surroundings (both through direct experience and through the reading of appropriate works), and his ability to frame these observations in the language whose acquisition was one of the primary aims of his period abroad.[129] Over the years, Hinchingbrooke had used letters to perform his pedagogical process to an audience at home, narrating his experience with increasing authority over both knowledge and the language in which it was expressed. Letters like these attest to a semi-public negotiated pedagogical process involving the traveller, the tutor, and the family and 'friends' at home.

Travellers' letters mixed the personal and the public, allowing their author to fashion themselves as an assiduous language-learner on the page, practising their skills abroad while laying the ground for a triumphant return home. But polyglot letter-writing did not need to stop after the traveller's return. The languages learnt abroad could also have new usages at home, as in the case of John Talman (1677–1726), an antiquary and an expert on Italian art who spent a significant portion of his career in Italy, as a broker in the growing market for Italian artworks and antiquities in England.[130] Talman's letters show him dealing with Italian artists and artisans, as well as his clients at home, but also give some sense of the ways in which shared knowledge of a foreign language could help to forge solidarities between returned travellers. Talman wrote in Italian to the English antiquaries with whom he socialized at the Fountain inn in London: Italian seems to have functioned for them as an in-group language, a shared testimony to a shared experience. In this, Talman's group of friends—the embryo of the Society of Antiquaries—may have been one of the new kind of clubs 'for Language' mentioned by Giovanni Torriano alongside clubs 'for Musick, and for News'.[131] Little else is known of these clubs, but they seem to have been spaces where language practice and clubbable conversation went hand in hand. A community of

[129] Hinchingbrooke to Sandwich, 4 June 1664, Bodleian Library, MS Carte 223, fol. 127r.
[130] Graham Parry, 'Talman, John (1677–1726)', *Oxford Dictionary of National Biography*, Oxford University Press, 2004 (https://doi.org/10.1093/ref:odnb/26955).
[131] Giovanni Torriano, *Mescolanza dolce di varie historiette, favole morali & politiche, facetie, motti & burle di diversi scrittori Italiani; raccolta & cappata per uso, commodità & ricreatione, della Gioventù Inglese* (London,1688), p. 98.

this kind could be bonded together by language and by a shared sense of humour: Talman wrote a letter to a friend expressing his regret at the decline of the society of antiquaries which the pair frequented, beginning with a pastiche of Italianate hyperbole: 'Elà! O Sant Antonio! O Vicegerente di S. Petro! Corpo di Bacco, Corpo di Dio di legno. come sara possibile di dirne parola? che disgrazia è questa. O S: Rocco & Dio Bacco Protettori! è serrata la porta!'[132] Between friends, a shared competence in Italian was a means of making the experience of travel into an in-joke, a statement of community of interests and of humour. Language could be used after the traveller's return in ways that were social and emotional as well as pragmatic and professional.

Company and Conversation

Writing from his lodgings in Florence in 1592, Henry Wotton noted how 'my best commodity is the conversation of certain gentlemen, and their vulgar very pure and correct; so that here we have good means to speak well and do ill'.[133] Wotton's remarks showed that he understood the power of company in travel, as a source of both prestige language and political education. The question of company was one which exercised authors, tutors, and the families who funded continental travel: it was understood that speaking and hearing were central to language-learning and to educational travel more broadly—but speaking and listening to whom?[134] Central to these debates was the idea of 'conversation'—a term which encompassed the ideas of moral character, the company one kept, and the way one spoke, as well as the activity of speaking in company itself.[135] Conversation—the quality—was formed by taking part in the activity of conversation: time spent speaking and listening in company was understood to mould the individual linguistically, socially, and morally, for better or for worse.[136] In educational travel, speaking in company was crucial for the development of skill in language and of fine manners, just as it was at home. It was also in company that these social skills were practised and performed.[137]

---

[132] 'Alas! Oh Saint Anthony! Oh Vicegerent of Saint Peter! Body of Bacchus, body of Christ in wood. how is it possible to speak a word thereof? what a disgrace this is. Oh Saint Rocco and the God Bacchus protect us! the gate is closed!': John Talman to Thomas Madox, 11 September 1708. Bodleian Library, MS Eng.Lett.e.34, fol. 21r.

[133] Smith, *Life and Letters of Sir Henry Wotton*, vol. 1, p. 281.

[134] Leibetseder, *Kavalierstour*, pp. 97–103.

[135] On the changing meanings of 'conversation', see Alison Hurley, 'Peculiar Christians, Circumstantial Courtiers, and the Making of Conversation in Seventeenth-Century England', *Representations* 111 (2010), pp. 33–59. For conversation in travel in the German context, see Leibetseder, *Kavalierstour*, pp. 104–37.

[136] Richards, *Rhetoric and Courtliness*, especially pp. 21–2.

[137] Withington, *Society in Early Modern England*, p. 199.

One of the earliest English travellers to Italy to leave a detailed diary of his time abroad was Thomas Hoby, later the translator of Castiglione's *Courtier*. Having spent time studying the language at Padua and in Tuscany, he resolved to journey through Calabria and as far as Sicily, 'both to have a sight of the countrey and also to absent my self for a while owt of Englishemenne's companie for the tung's sake'.[138] He was among the earliest to recognize the disadvantage of his country-men's company when it came to his linguistic ambitions. This would become common wisdom as time went on: English-speakers abroad were expected, by and large, to leave their native language behind once they arrived on the continent. Robert Dallington, who thought speaking more important than writing in learn-ing a language, advised his traveller to beware 'the often haunting & frequenting our own countrimen' as a hindrance to learning to speak, urging his reader 'neither to dis-taste them by a too much retirednesse, nor to hinder himselfe by too much familiaritie'.[139] As the number of English travellers to the continent grew, Jacobean authors made this a ground rule of travel: Bacon said '[l]et [the traveller] sequester himself, from the company of his countrymen, and diet in such places, where there is good company of the nation where he travelleth'.[140] Fynes Moryson preached from his own experience: 'to him, that would learne the language, my counsell is, that hee shunne for the time the conversation of his owne Countrey-men'.[141] Moryson accepted the traveller's 'spending some howers of the weeke in their company to nourish acquaintance', but beyond that, he should 'bestow the rest of the time among those of the same Country wherein they live, and so better their language, and learne the state of the Countrie'.[142] As time went on and the haunts recommended to educational travellers became more and more populated with the English, it became more difficult to remove oneself entirely from one's countrymen's company. In the mid-seventeenth century, James Howell was still recommending somewhere 'unfrequented by the English' to the traveller wishing to learn good French, 'for the greatest bane of English Gentlemen abroad, is too much frequency and communication with their own Countrey-men'.[143]

Even as the art of travel took on a new form with the rise of the grand tour, this injunction remained central: the theorist of the tour, Jean Gailhard, urged travel-lers to '[s]peak your Mother Tongue as seldom as you can, and not at all if it be possible'.[144] In 1676, Heneage Finch the younger wrote that he planned to leave Paris for Angers or Saumur, 'where I may live *with* halfe the expence it costs me here & learn my excercises as well, & I am sure it will be much better for my

[138] Edgard Powell (ed.) *The Travels and Life of Sir Thomas Hoby, Knight of Bisham Abbey: Written by himself, 1547–1564* (London: Royal Historical Society, 1902), pp. 37–8.
[139] Dallington, *Method for Travell*, sig. B3v. [140] Bacon, *Essayes*, p. 103.
[141] Moryson, *Itinerary*, part III, p. 15. [142] Ibid., part III, p. 18.
[143] Howell, *Instructions for forreine travell*, pp. 32–3.
[144] Gailhard, *Compleat Gentleman*, part II, p. 186.

learning the Language for here one can never be out of English company'.[145] In 1697, Robert Clayton boasted to his father from Amsterdam that '[t]he little acquaintance I have with the English here, makes me altogether a stranger to their designs: I have travelled hitherto alone & have always industriously avoided their Company; I know none that intend for Italy or if I did would I join with them'.[146] Later in their journey, Clayton's tutor would write that his success in his travels could be seen in the company he kept: 'he keps Companij withe the best of men where wee passe and his cariage and beheavior is so prudent. that it makes his companie be courted by the most understanding men'.[147]

In spite of its utility for the traveller in terms of language-learning and local knowledge, foreign company was not without its dangers. The author of the Perrott manuscript wrote in a section titled '[w]hat companie you are to keepe' that 'For conversation. yow may contract ill manners by ill company, for ... wee are naturallie apt to imitate that which is worst'.[148] In 1649, Balthazar Gerbier argued that '[travellers] often meet with wicked persons, who does endeavour to infuse into them most pernicious principles to their native Country; but the most deplorable case of all is, the subversion of their Religion to a worse'.[149] Worries about the threats to the religion of the Protestant traveller remained potent throughout the period: in 1671, Edward Leigh warned that the traveller should 'be well grounded in the true Religion, lest he be seduced and perverted'.[150] The act of language-learning was fraught: its results were desirable, but it demanded that the learner spend a significant amount of time in the company of foreigners, at considerable risk to his identity, his morals, his faith—and his reputation. 'Conversation' was where sociability, speech, and reputation met, and the traveller who did not manage theirs—or have it carefully managed by a tutor or governor— risked irreparably damaging their credit at home.[151] This was the source of friction between tutors and their charges, as well as between travellers and their funders at home. Repingon, tutor of Lord Weymouth's son, bemoaned his charge's unwillingness to take direction and to separate himself from bad company, complaining that Venice was haunted by 'a crowd of English among whom one is not one's

[145] Heneage Finch the younger to Thomas Thynne, 14 August 1676, Thynne papers, Longleat House, TH/VOL/XVII, fol. 23r.

[146] Robert Clayton to Sir Robert Clayton, 17 August 1697, Travel correspondence of Robert Clayton, Bodleian Library, MS. Eng. lett. c. 309, fol. 25r.

[147] Francis Moll to Sir Robert Clayton, 9 April 1698: ibid., fol. 55r.

[148] Perrott MS 5, fol. 8v.

[149] Balthazar Gerbier, *A Publique Lecture On all the Languages, Arts, Sciences, and Noble Exercises, which are taught in Sr Balthazar Gerbiers Academy* (London, 1649), sig. A2r.

[150] Leigh, *Three Diatribes*, p. 5.

[151] On reputation and sociability, see Markku Peltonen, *The Duel in Early Modern England: Civility, Politeness and Honour* (Cambridge: Cambridge University Press, 2003), *passim*; Steven Shapin, *A Social History of Truth: Civility and Science in Seventeenth-Century England* (Chicago and London: University of Chicago Press, 1994), *passim*; Anna Bryson, *From Courtesy to Civility: Changing Codes of Conduct in Early Modern England* (Oxford: Clarendon, 1998), pp. 228–41.

own master'.[152] The tutor's pedagogical plans were in tension with the pupil's desire for anglophone company: he wrote from Padua that 'if I can prevaile with him wee will turn towards Florence, both places are good for *the* language but indeed tis all, there being little society'.[153] One grand tour tutor, Alexandre de Rasigade, went as far as to describe Saumur as 'an infected place' by reason of the English-language company his charge encountered there.[154]

The educational travels undertaken by the young Earl of Derby in 1673–5 were bedevilled by the problem of company. In 1673, a tutor named James Forbes was ordered by the Earl of Ormond, Derby's guardian, to ensure that his charge 'continue as much a Stranger as civilly he can to our owne Country men till he shall have attained some resonable Knowledge in the Language of the Country'.[155] Forbes assured Ormond that he had chosen lodgings 'wher ther are no inglish, but several french gentlemen of verie good qualité, I hope it will be of great advantage to him in learning of the language sooner'.[156] This proved easier said than done, however, and not ten days later Forbes worried that things were not going to plan: 'Lord Derby hath hitherto eat in his chamber but I could wish he could be persuaded to eat in Company *with* some French Gentlemen of very good Quality that live in the same house It would be a great Means to get him the French language much sooner.'[157] The servant dispatched to mend relations between Forbes and the underage earl was ordered 'to endeavour to dispose him to retire into some convenient place from Paris where he may learne the Language (which it will be a shame for him to returne without) & then find more pleasure & proffit at his returne thither': to travel without learning the language would be a waste of time; it would be necessary to attain a good reputation and advancement on his return home; and it was not to be had in a city so thronging with talkative English.[158]

The language the traveller learnt would depend on the quality of the company he kept. Whose language it was best to learn remained a hotly debated question throughout the period. At the start of the seventeenth century, Thomas Palmer could argue for a kind of language-learning that was open to multiple varieties beyond the prestige standard:

> as the Court & Citie excel in the dialect, and fine phrase; so the Countrey phrase
> & words are of no lesse esteeme and regard: in so much as no man can be

---

[152] 'une foule d'anglois au milieu desquels on n'est pas maitre de soy': P. Repingon to Lord Weymouth, late 1693, Thynne Papers, Longleat House. TH/VOL/XII, fol. 111r.

[153] Repingon to Weymouth. 16 May 1693: ibid., fol. 107r.

[154] Alexandre de Rasigade to Robert Southwell, 10 August 1677, British Library, Add. MS 46954 B, fos. 31r–31v.

[155] Ormond to Forbes, 7 August 1673, Bodleian Library, MS Carte 50, fos. 103r–103v.

[156] Forbes to Ormond, 7 August 7h 1673, Bodleian Library, MS Carte 243, fol. 87r.

[157] 'Extract of Mr Forbesses *Letter* from Paris 16. Aug. 1673': ibid., fol. 89r.

[158] 'Instructions for Mulys', Bodleian Library, MS Carte 50., fol. 111v.

accounted worthily excellent in any tongue, that wants discretion to speake Court-like and Country-like, when, and where it is requisite[159]

If this linguistic tolerance ever reflected travellers' pedagogical practices, it came under threat as the period progressed. As anxieties about the company of one's countrymen grew, so too did worries about the kinds of language the traveller would encounter. While Fynes Moryson prided himself on his ability to speak 'vulgarly' as well as in more prestigious fashion—he said of German that 'I had some skill in that Language, especially for vulgar speeches'—the idea that an ideal linguistic competence was one which would allow the speaker to communicate with people from all orders of society did not last through the seventeenth century.[160] In Richard Lassels's manuscript account of Lady Catherine Whetenall's travels, he dismissed Antwerp, saying that 'in this fine towne the best of the people are but Marchaunts; the best of theire language but Dutch and the best of theire drinke but beere'.[161] Jean Gailhard said the grand tourist needed 'to learn how to carry himself well in all kinds of company, he must see the variety of them', but 'all kinds of company' was exclusive too: the gentleman should go into company, but only that of 'persons of Quality, by whom he may well be informed of affairs and of whom he will learn a gentile, and a good behaviour'.[162] This shift in the dynamics of company in early modern travel fits with a broader transformation identified by Justin Stagl, in which 'the self-control of the mature travelling humanist was increasingly replaced by the external control of a youthful, immature traveller on his 'grand tour' by a private tutor who acted on the instructions of the traveller's family'.[163] This was part of a gradual shift from the humanist-inflected educational travel of the later sixteenth and the first half of the seventeenth century towards what would become known as the 'grand tour'. With the role of the tutor or governor in educational travel increasing in importance, the traveller's company and conversation—and the kinds of language to which he was exposed—were observed and managed yet more closely.[164]

There was one kind of cross-status communication which was unavoidable, frequently interlingual, and potentially dangerous: the relationship between

---

[159] Thomas Palmer, *An Essay of the Meanes how to make our Trauailes, into forraine Countries, the more profitable and honourable* (London, 1606), p. 58.

[160] Moryson, *Itinerary*, part I, p. 30. He paid similar attention to variation in Italian, recording how he asked directions 'to Chioza or Chioggia, or (to speake vulgarly, the better to be understood in asking the way) a Chioza': ibid., part I, p. 90.

[161] British Library, Add. MS 4217, fol. 9v.   [162] Gailhard, *Compleat Gentleman*, part II, p. 74.

[163] Stagl, *History of Curiosity*, p. 73.

[164] The role of the travelling tutor has received surprisingly little serious historical attention in English-language historiography: for three useful perspectives, see Jean Boutier, 'Compétence internationale, émergence d'une 'profession' et circulation des savoirs: le tuteur aristocratique dans l'Angleterre du XVIIe siècle', in Maria-Pia Paoli (ed.), *Saperi in movimento* (Pisa: Edizioni della Normale, 2009), pp. 149–77; Stannek, *Telemachs Brüder*, pp. 197–214; and Leibetseder, *Kavalierstour*, pp. 86–96.

travellers and their servants.[165] Thomas Abdie noted in French that '[m]y boy came to serve me on the seventh of December 1635'; that the servant was hired when Abdie had already been on the continent for some time and the language of the note suggests that the language they used between themselves may well have been French.[166] This seems to have become common practice: James Howell recommended that the young gentleman headed for Paris should take on 'a Cook, a Laquay, and some young youth for his Page, to parley and chide withall', but that of his staff 'there should be none English but his Governour'.167 Richard Lassels, guiding a generation or more of grand tourists, warned against English-speaking servants, who were often over-friendly with their charges and caused problems for the governor. Another option was to hire French servants in England and to bring them over, but their linguistic competence could pose a threat, since '[they] often, by reason of their prerogative of language, which their masters want at first, get such an ascendent over them, that they come oftentimes to be too bold, and sawcy with them' (Lassels's solution was to encourage the governor to hire new servants in each place visited).[168] John Lauder came to a similar conclusion after two months in Orléans in 1665:

> During my staying heir I have learned a lesson which may be of use to me in the rest of our travels, to wit, to beware of keiping familiar company wt gentlemens servants, for such a man sal never get respect from the Mrs.; to beware also of discoursing homly with anie servants. We sould keip both their for at a prudent distance.[169]

Anxiety about servants' linguistic 'prerogatives' needed to be balanced with their usefulness for language practice. In 1708, the tutor de Blainville wrote of an English gentleman who had taken on two French valets on his travels, 'for this Gentleman speaks French and Italian perfectly, and wishes to speak in no other language'.[170] English newspapers of the later seventeenth and eighteenth centuries frequently advertised the services of multilingual servants—male and female—who could offer foreign-language conversation even in Anglophone surroundings.[171]

---

[165] On the traveller's entourage, see Leibetseder, Kavalierstour, pp. 83–103.

[166] 'Mon garçon m'est venu servir sur le 7ᵉ Decembre 1635', Rawlinson MS D1285, fol. 157v.

[167] Howell, Instructions for forreine travell, pp. 48–9.

[168] Lassels, Voyage of Italy, sig. I4v.

[169] Crawford, Journals of Sir John Lauder, p. 14. For an account of a traveller's inappropriate relationship with a servant, see P. Repingon to Lord Weymouth, 3 April 1693, Thynne Papers, Longleat House. TH/VOL/XII, fol. 101v.

[170] Hardwick, Grand Tour, p. 117.

[171] See, for instance, the advertisement offering the services of 'a genteel Valet de Chambre, that can trim and look to a Peruke, write, cast Accompt, receive and pay money, speaks Dutch and understands French': Collection for Improvement of Husbandry and Trade, issue 186 (21 February 1696). See also, from the same year, the advertisement for '[a] Gentlewoman that has lived well, and brought up several

Servants could be educational travellers too. Travellers were often accompanied by multilingual tutors and servants, or by entourages who hoped to improve their own linguistic skills through travel. Robert Moody was a servant who wrote a retrospective account of the travels of his master, Banaster Maynard, in 1660. They entered Rome just before Christmas of that year, and Moody noted that 'I haveing live'd thre years in rome before, I knew the language and the Citty as well as if I had been borne in it.'[172] While the processes involved are harder to access for the historian, it is clear that anglophone servants could themselves become language-learners. Philip Perceval sent home one servant, an Irishman named Mr. Lugg, complaining that 'to mee hee seemd a very unnessesary moovable being master onely of as much french as would keep him from starving'.[173] During Perceval's residence in Saumur, his tutor (at this time, none other than Jean Gailhard) wrote home that Perceval was 'att the charges of having his man Thomas taught the language', along with reading and writing (presumably in French) and arithmetic.[174] The accounts kept by Gailhard record money spent on pens and ink as well as a language master for Thomas.[175] Gailhard explained that he had engaged a French servant, 'because [Thomas] for want of the language could not doe him many necessary services above his exercises and elsewhere… but now that cause [is] ceased, for Thomas understands somewhat the fashions and language'.[176]

The company of women was another arena in which pedagogical opportunity and danger were mingled. With the rise of the grand tour, female company became ever more tied to the processes of language-learning, but remained a thorny question. In a development which would cast a long shadow over English practices of sociability, Michèle Cohen argues that the development of *politesse* and *honnêteté* in elite French circles in the seventeenth-century relied on women's conversational passivity as a whetstone for the development of male conversation: '[w]omen's conversation, (as language and company), enabled men to acquire and develop the appropriate conduct of body and tongue, the *politesse* which was the soul of *honnêteté*.'[177] In the eighteenth century, Cohen argues, this model of conversation and of politeness was adopted in England too. These principles, however, are already to be seen in seventeenth-century travel advice. Jean Gailhard saw the company of women—particularly French women—as important for the development of the traveller's conversation, advising his travellers

Children, understands all kind of Works, and any thing fit for a Gentlewoman to learn: She speaks French, and desires to be Tutoress to some young Gentlewomen, or to be Housekeeper to some aged Gentleman': *Collection for Improvement of Husbandry and Trade*, issue 206 (10 July 1696).

---

[172] Brennan, *Origins of the Grand Tour*, p. 255.   [173] BL Add. MS 46954 B, fol. 168r.
[174] BL Add. MS 46953, fol. 218r.   [175] BL Add. MS 46953, fol. 220r.
[176] BL Add. MS 46954 A, fols. 282r–282v.
[177] Michèle Cohen, *Fashioning Masculinity: National Identity and Language in the Eighteenth Century* (London and New York: Routledge, 1996), p. 18.

to frequent the company of Women...because one is polished and civilized in their company and conversation, and the desire a man hath to please them, makes, he observes himself in his Cloaths, Discourses, and Actions, better than else he would do; their company gives some confidence necessary to a young man.[178]

De Blainville, tutor to the Blathwayt brothers on their grand tour at the very beginning of the eighteenth century, actively supplemented his pupils' formal language-learning with pedagogically productive periods spent in the company of multiple (unnamed) Genevan gentlewomen, writing that 'it is on these occasions there and with the Ladies, that they relax agreeably, in seeing how to play parlour games and in joining in the Conversation for politeness sake'.[179] These polite meetings were also explicitly treated by de Blainville as opportunities for language acquisition:

[a]s to the French, M. The Marquis d'Arzelliers, his three Ladies and I have never spared ourselves to inculcate in them a fair utterance, together with the best turns of our Language, as much by continuous corrections in conversation, as by the Reading of the best comments thereon.[180]

Managed conversation, company, and collaborative reading combined in this case to aid the linguistic and bodily education of these two young men. By the end of the seventeenth century, polite and feminine company, though both were increasingly managed and observed, were increasingly recognized as indispensable pedagogical tools for the traveller.

Offering advice to travellers, Fynes Moryson stressed how important it was, once the learner had some basic grammatical competence, that he 'converse with Weomen, Children, and the most talkative people', ignoring any mockery he might receive for his beginner's language, and rejecting all bashfulness about speech, since 'no Man is borne a Master in any Art'.[181] Moryson, and the travellers of this chapter, understood that competence was formed in company, in the everyday interactions between the language-learner and his equals, betters, and inferiors. Spending time in judiciously chosen company could improve the speaker's linguistic competence, but it had other impacts on his person, his manner and carriage, and his moral character. The close contact with speakers of other languages which was required in educational travel could be dangerous as well as advantageous: conversation was a double-edged sword, and bad language could have evil consequences for the traveller, his educational prospects, and his reputation.

---

[178] Gailhard, *Compleat Gentleman*, part II, p. 187.   [179] Hardwick, *Grand Tour*, pp. 55–6.
[180] Hardwick, *Grand Tour*, pp. 67–8.   [181] Moryson, *Itinerary*, III, p. 15.

Critical Imitation: Adaptation, Identity, and Dissimulation

English learners of foreign vernaculars constantly came into contact with behavioural and gestural codes foreign to their own. These could act as markers of
national difference, as well as of distinctions within nations, conveying variations
in status, gender, and political or religious affiliation. The study of these codes of
comportment was intimately linked to the acquisition of a new language. Gesture,
behaviour, and the carriage of the body interact with verbal language to 'amplify,
modify, confirm, or subvert verbal utterance'.[182] An understanding of the social
life of language required an understanding of all three codes, and of the ways in
which they interacted.[183] As such, bodily comportment is important to a study of
language-learning because how we use our bodies in company carries meaning:
gesture *is* language. The educational processes that underlay early modern travel
and language-learning were informed by discourses on civility, manners, and
politeness, and as the seventeenth century wore on and the curriculum of the
grand tour became established, the pedagogy of travel came to focus ever more
closely on a strict disciplining of the body in company.[184] The traveller's body—as
well as his tongue—was shaped by educational travel. The parallel processes of
cultural contact and of language-learning required the English traveller to inter-
pret and to perform according to new behavioural codes, at the same time as they
posed important questions about adaptation and dissimulation. The traveller's
new language represented a body of knowledge, but also a knowledge that was
written on the body.

Critical observation was at the heart of educational travel: as Justin Stagl shows
in his survey of humanist travel advice, the traveller was urged to cultivate an
unusual openness to foreign ideas and information, to seek out all and to take
all in.[185] As Henry Wotton's pride in his study of fine speech and dirty deeds
showed, the traveller was not meant to observe foreign societies and remain
entirely aloof from them. Instead, most authors of travel advice in the later
sixteenth and early seventeenth century urged some measure of adaptation to
foreign behaviours. Robert Dallington argued that '[h]e...that intends to Travell
out of his owne country, must likewise resolve to Travell out of his country
fashion, and indeed out of himselfe'.[186] Dallington's contemporary Thomas
Palmer concurred that while the traveller should do nothing immoral or irreli-
gious, 'it is the duetie of all men to fit and applie themselves...to their maners and

---

[182] Keith Thomas, 'Introduction', in Jan Bremmer and Herman Roodenburg (eds.), *A Cultural History of Gesture: From Antiquity to the Present Day* (Cambridge: Polity, 1991), p. 6.
[183] Bryson, *From Courtesy to Civility*, pp. 88–9.
[184] On travel and the discourse of civility, see Stannek, *Telemachs Brüder*, pp. 55–63.
[185] Stagl, *History of Curiosity*, pp. 47–93; Rubiés, 'Instructions for Travellers: Teaching the Eye to See', p. 172; Clare Haynes, *Pictures and Popery* (Aldershot: Ashgate, 2006), p. 44.
[186] Dallington, *Method for Travell*, sig. Br.

customes with whom they live'.[187] For the author of the Perrott manuscript of travel advice, such adaptation was politic: 'To the avoiding of singularitie from which will grow disdaine or derision, or else some publique note, conforme your self to the fashion of the place in apparell, in gesture and behaviour, yet would I not have you fantastic.'[188] Fynes Moryson was similarly pragmatic, arguing that '[i]f [the traveller] shall apply himselfe to their manners, tongue, apparrell and diet with whom he lives, hee shall catch their loves as it were with a fish-hooke'.[189] It was assumed by authors of late sixteenth- and early seventeenth-century travel advice that their readers would adapt their behaviour according to the company and the culture in which they were travelling. For English travellers abroad in a period of confessional and political conflict, a measure of adaptation was the only pragmatic choice—and the one that would enable them to reap the benefits of educational travel most effectively.

Critical observation was certainly central to early modern travel, but just as important and just as hotly debated, though little-analysed in histories of travel, was the practice of critical imitation—the assessment of foreign manners and behaviour, with a potential view to the strategic appropriation of its best elements. Fynes Moryson argued for a model whereby the traveller would imitate foreign customs critically and judiciously, saying that while 'severe and forward censors may judge it an apish vice thus to imitate other nations...this obsequiousnes of conversation, making us become all things to all men, deserves the opinion of a wise man, and one that is not subject to pride'. He placed limits on such behaviour, saying that the traveller 'must alwaies shunne extremity, lest while he affects to be affable, hee incurre the infamy of a flatterer'.[190] Moryson's traveller represents the ideal: able to observe and to imitate, while also exercising the self-control necessary to avoid becoming an apish counterfeiter of foreign fashions (the affected returned traveller was a source of comedy and anxiety in Moryson's England).[191] This controlled imitation was a central theme in early travel writing, as in a 1592 translation of the humanist author of travel advice Justus Lipsius, which argued that

> Italie (I graunt) and France, will teach us fine, and faire cariage of our body, good, & discreet deliverie of our minde, civill, and modest behaviour to others, but yet as we are to like, so wee are not straight to affect everie countrey fashion: wee are to use them seasonably, and soberly and modestly, not with thrasonicall, and presumptuous ostentation: (wherein most travailers fowly overshot themselves, by passing the bodes of decencie, and mediocritie.)[192]

---

[187] Palmer, *Essay*, p. 50.   [188] Perrott MS 5, fol. 13r.
[189] Moryson, *Itinerary*, part III, p. 23.   [190] Ibid., part III, p. 24.
[191] Warneke, *Images of the educational traveller*, *passim*.
[192] Anon., *A Direction for Travailers. Taken out of Iustus Lipsius, and enlarged for the behoofe of the right honorable Lord, the yong Earle of Bedford, being now ready to travell* (London, 1592), sig. Cv–C2r.

This was not an argument against adaptation: it made a clear distinction between the critical imitation of foreign manners and their wholesale appropriation, coming down only against 'mimicall, and miserable affecting...in the carriage of the body'.[193] Furthermore, it was blunt about the fact that late sixteenth-century England had much to learn from the elite cultures of foreign nations: the openness of the English language to ever more new terms from continental vernaculars was mirrored by a broader cultural porousness that manifested itself in changes of bodily comportment, fashion, and manners. The distinction between imitation and affectation is the governing concern of this period of travel advice. Travellers were not prohibited from imitating foreign manners, but were expected to exercise their judgement in observing and copying from the behavioural codes of foreign nations. Some argued that the stubborn maintenance of one's native customs was as much to be avoided as the overenthusiastic imitation of foreign fashions.[194] The simple rubric offered was this: 'when you see infinite variety of behavior and manners of men, you must choose and imitate the best'.[195] The critical observation which was so fundamental to early modern travel pedagogy was not an abstract skill, but one which was to be employed in the service of a critical imitation.

Critical observation and critical imitation were crucial aspects of travel because the fruits of both would be valued on the traveller's return home. By and large, histories of educational travel have been silent on the idea of return, in spite of the fact that so much of the experience was oriented towards the traveller's self-presentation at home.[196] Debates about imitation focused not only on the traveller's finding a middle way between adaptation and aloofness while abroad, but also on how the change in character and bearing would manifest themselves after the period of travel was ended. Thomas Palmer urged his traveller to display 'better judgement than those fantastickes, which bring home with them, some apish ceremonies of curtesie, and strange fashions of apparell, but nothing else, to give them commendations at their returnes'.[197] In Bacon's essay on travel, a stern warning against affectation and showiness on the part of the returned traveller sits side by side with an argument that the traveller should use what he has learnt of foreign behaviours to improve those of his home:

---

[193] Ibid.

[194] The author of the *Profitable Instructions* warned readers that

In manners, [you] must not be caught with novelties, which are pleasing to young men; nor infected with Custome, which maketh us keepe our owne ill graces, and participate of those wee see every day; nor given to affectation, which is a generall fault amongst English Travellers, which is both displeasing & ridiculous.   Anon., Profitable Instructions, pp. 48–9

[195] Anon., Profitable Instructions, p. 46.

[196] Notable exceptions to this include Bepler, 'Travelling and Posterity'; Tony Claydon on William Bromley, in Claydon, *Europe and the Making of England*, pp. 1–4; Williams, 'Inner Lives of Early Modern Travel'.

[197] Palmer, *Essay*, p. 61.

let his travel appear rather in his discourse, than his apparel or gesture; and in his discourse, let him be rather advised in his answers, than forward to tell stories; and let it appear that he doth not change his country manners, for those of foreign parts; but only prick in some flowers, of that he hath learned abroad, into the customs of his own country.[198]

The processes of travel continued on the traveller's return home, in this careful management of his self-presentation. Critical imitation lay in plucking the 'flowers' of foreign behaviour, and in applying them to one's own behaviour without affectation. It was not, however, just a question of the traveller's personal development: Bacon's suggestion that the traveller was adorning not just his own manners but 'the customs of his own country' makes it clear that he saw critical imitation as part of a wider project of improving English behaviour. The traveller's return was important both personally and politically.

It was also controversial. Critiques abounded of returned travellers and of the practice of travel itself.[199] Many of these critiques took issue with the ways in which travellers' behaviour, manners, and physical bearing had changed. A father warned his son that many young men returned home with 'crooke shoulders, unstayed countenances, mopps and maws thrusting outte the crupper, and head forward, a shaling pace, affected gestures, curchies, salutations and odd fashions of apparell, speeche [and] diet'.[200] Affectation in behaviour and affectation in speech were closely intertwined: in 1642, James Howell complained of those who went in search of an authentic French accent, saying that 'while they labour for this, they fall a lisping and mincing, and to distort and strain their mouths and voyce, so that they render themselves fantastique and ridiculous'.[201] The fear of foreign manners found in late sixteenth-century attacks on 'Italianate' Englishmen continued through the later seventeenth and eighteenth century, particularly in the figure of the Frenchified fop.[202] Travellers who brought home the behaviours and the

---

[198] Bacon, *Essayes*, p. 104.

[199] Warneke, *Images of the educational traveller*, p. 7.

[200] Ibid., p. 68. Compare Thomas Nashe, *The Unfortunate Traveller*, in J. B. Steane (ed.), *The Unfortunate Traveller and Other Works* (London: Penguin, 1985), p. 345.

[201] Howell, *Instructions for forreine travell*, p. 28.

[202] For a later expression of this critique, see Edward Leigh in 1671, who wrote that '[m]any Travellers returning to their own home, bring back only some vain Garbs and Fashions, and are leavened with the ill Customes and Manners of the Countries they passed thorough'. Leigh, *Three Diatribes*, p. 2. On Italianate Englishmen, see George B. Parks, 'The First Italianate Englishmen', *Studies in the Renaissance* 8 (1961), pp. 197–216; Bartlett, *The English in Italy 1525–1558*, pp. 77, 183–4; Lewis Einstein, *The Italian Renaissance in England* (New York: Columbia University Press, 1902), pp. 156–75; Gallagher, 'The Italian London of John North'. For attacks on Frenchified behaviour and foppishness, see Lawrence Klein, 'The Figure of France: The Politics of Sociability in England, 1660–1715', *Yale French Studies* 92, *Exploring the Conversible World: Text and Sociability from the Classical Age to the Enlightenment* (1997), pp. 30–45; Cohen, *Fashioning Masculinity*. See also Howard, *English Travellers of the Renaissance*, pp. 51–63. For an early discussion of whether it was better for the traveller to come home Italianate or Frenchified, see Dallington, *Method for travell*, sig. B4r.

manners they had learnt abroad—along with their language—were roundly mocked, and could be politically, socially, and sexually subversive. But while commentators attacked what Lipsius called '[this] mimicall, and miserable affecting' so consistently across the period, the simple historical fact is that they were largely ignored.[203] Particularly among the elite, English-speakers were open to foreign fads, whether the Italianate fashions of the later sixteenth century (and the early eighteenth), or the Francophilia of the Restoration. Manners, gestures, words, and behaviour joined ideas and goods as continental imports to England.

Dissimulation was the dark side of critical imitation. From the petty dissimulations that allowed civil conversation to run smoothly to the large-scale deceptions that enabled travellers to venture into hostile country or to avoid robbery, disguise was a key practice of early modern travel.[204] Thomas Palmer urged the traveller 'to have in journeying (if neede require) faithfull and honest guides and companions: and in speciall cases, let such change rayment with their guides'. When Fynes Moryson travelled the dangerous road to Emden, he did so as 'a poore Bohemian, [who] had long served a Merchant at Leipzig'; when he arrived at Bremen, he claimed to be a servant of Fynes Moryson rather than the man himself.[205] Robert Bargrave, travelling through Poland in 1652–3, recalled a night when 'where though Truth could not, Policie did, procure us that nights Convenience': he and the Scottish merchants with whom he was travelling were only able to get accommodation 'by pretending my Master an Ambassador, our fellow travellers his Retinue, & my selfe (still standing uncovred) his Interpreter'.[206] 'Intelligencers' and travellers who sought political information abroad were required '[t]o speak singularly the tongues, that may stand them in stead in that Countrey out of which they must gather intelligence, and to imitate the common gestures and behaviour of those nations, to cloke their purposes the more artificially'.[207] Dissimulation turned the knowledge acquired through critical observation to practical use. It is important to recognize the amount of knowledge that is necessary to carry off a successful disguise: Fynes Moryson warned his readers of 'how small a thing will make it manifest, that we are not that Country men

---

[203] Anon., *Direction for Travailers*, sig. C2r.

[204] On dissimulation and disguise in early modern Europe, see Perez Zagorin, 'The Historical Significance of Lying and Dissimulation', *Social Research* 63, *Truth-Telling, Lying and Self-Deception* (1996), pp. 863–912; Miriam Eliav-Feldon, *Renaissance Impostors and Proofs of Identity* (Basingstoke: Palgrave Macmillan, 2012), p. 1. On dissimulation, see also Jon R. Snyder, *Dissimulation and the Culture of Secrecy in Early Modern Europe* (Berkeley, Los Angeles, and London: University of California Press, 2009). On impostors, see also Stagl, *History of Curiosity*, pp. 171–208. On identity and identification, see Valentin Groebner, *Who Are You? Identification, Deception, and Surveillance in Early Modern Europe* (New York: Zone, 2007), *passim*. On dissimulation and *honestas* in civil conversation, see Richards, *Rhetoric and Courtliness*, pp. 21–42; Withington, *Society in Early Modern England*, pp. 186–9; Snyder, *Dissimulation and the Culture of Secrecy in Early Modern Europe*, pp. 28–63.

[205] Palmer, *Essay*, p. 47; Moryson, *Itinerary*, pp. 37–8.

[206] Brennan, *Travel diary of Robert Bargrave*, p. 146.   [207] Palmer, *Essay*, pp. 4–5.

whereof we speake the language'.[208] To practice dissimulation successfully, the traveller needed a deep understanding and a practical knowledge of the codes of speech and of the body through which identities were expressed.

The definitive statement in English on identity, dissimulation, and travel—and one which makes clear the centrality of linguistic and behavioural knowledge to carrying off a successful deception—is found in Fynes Moryson's vast *Itinerary*: published in 1617, it recorded Moryson's eventful peregrinations during the 1590s. Moryson, like his contemporary Henry Wotton, sought to combine the role of the gentleman traveller with that of the political informer. Each prided himself on his use of disguise to see sights that were forbidden other English travellers of the late sixteenth century: Wotton (who had disguised himself as an idiot German while travelling in Catholic Italy) boasted that '[n]o Englishman, containing himself within his allegiance to her Majesty, hath seen more concerning the points of Rome than I have done'; while Moryson breathlessly narrated his meeting (disguised as an Italian) with Cardinal Bellarmine.[209] Wotton, for his part, argued that 'he travels with mean consideration in my opinion, that is ever one countryman'.[210] For politic travellers like Moryson and Wotton, the ability to feign membership of a non-English community thanks to their mastery of language was central to pulling off the disguise and to acquiring privileged information and experience.

Fynes Moryson was the first to go beyond other writers' acceptance that adaptation to foreign customs and speeches was necessary, in order to mount a full-throated defence of dissimulation in travel. Moryson argued that for a traveller, dissimulation was no sin—in fact, '[n]o doubt simulation in fit place and time is a vertue', though, of course, a traveller ought only to employ it 'to save himselfe, not to deceive others'. He went further, arguing that dissimulation in travel was not optional or avoidable: 'He that cannot dissemble, cannot live.'[211] Disguise and dissimulation were only to be employed judiciously: 'a traveller must sometimes hide his money, change his habit, dissemble his Country, and fairely conceale his Religion, but this hee must doe onely when necessity forceth'.[212] For Moryson, dissimulation was defensible and could be to the advantage of the traveller and his nation. But for it to be successful, it required a mastery of language: a point Moryson hammered home in an anecdote about how he had inadvertently blown the disguise of a traveller who turned out to be a fellow Englishman. The story is long, but worth quoting in full:

[208] Moryson, *Itinerary*, part III, p. 16.
[209] Smith, *Life and letters of Sir Henry Wotton*, vol. 1, p. 274. On Wotton as traveller and his self-presentation on his return, see Melanie Ord, 'Returning from Venice to England: Sir Henry Wotton as Diplomat, Pedagogue and Italian Cultural Connoisseur', in Thomas Betteridge (ed.), *Borders and Travellers in Early Modern Europe* (Aldershot: Ashgate, 2007), pp. 147–66.
[210] Smith (ed.), *Life and Letters of Sir Henry Wotton*, vol. 1, p. 258.
[211] Moryson, *Itinerary*, part III, p. 29.   [212] Ibid., part III, p. 30.

> And here by chance I found an English Merchant in the Inne, who talking rashly, did voluntarily (without being examined whence he was) professe himselfe to be a Dutchman, and myself in my disguised poore habit, sitting at the lower end of the table, and speaking to him in the Dutch language, he was forced for want of the language, to say that he was a Dutch-man, but borne upon the confines of France, and knowing no other language but the French, whereupon I speaking to him in the French tongue, he had as little skill in that, as in the Dutch; so as I might perceive that he dissembled his Countrey, and being not willing to presse him, as having been myselfe often forced in like sort to dissemble my Countrey, did forbeare to speake any more to him in the Dutch or French tongue, & we began to discourse in Italian, wherin he had spoken little before he uttered these words, *Io me ne repentiva:* that is, I repented my selfe therof, whereas an Italian would have said, *Io me ne pentiva,* by which sillable added by him, I presently knew he was an English man

In Moryson's telling, the English merchant's disguise failed because he lacked the linguistic skill required to carry off the deception. The merchant, realizing his cover had been blown, feared that Moryson was a spy and went to flee, until 'I following him, and boldly speaking English to him, he was soone content to stay all night, and to take me in my homely apparell for his bedfellow'.[213] The *Itinerary* brims with anecdotes about language, identity, and disguise, through which Moryson argues implicitly for the importance of critical and strategic imitation for successful dissimulation, and for the advantage to the traveller and to the commonwealth that could come from it.[214]

Dissimulation for the purposes of espionage became less of a feature of elite travel records as the seventeenth century wore on (which is, of course, not to say that there were no more English intelligencers, just that fewer elite travellers openly combined the roles of tourist and spy), but the principle of dissimulation in travel remained contentious. Critical observation and imitation did not lose their place in the curriculum of educational travel, but discourses of dissimulation increasingly focused on how travel changed the traveller's body. Educational travel had always impacted on bodily comportment. Thomas Palmer wrote in 1606 that 'of the nobler sort it is required always, that they discover spirited bodies, and more active minds than other Gentlemen, labouring to perfect them by much industry'; he urged the traveller to learn horsemanship, music, dancing, vaulting, 'managing of all sorts of weapons', 'practising the five strengths of the arme', but he was clear that these were recreational exercises and not meant to take the place

---

[213] Ibid., part I, pp. 168–9.
[214] See, for instance, ibid., part I, pp. 37–8, 58, 154. On Moryson and 'honest dissimulation', see Mareile Pfannebecker, '"Lying by Authority": Travel Dissimulations in Fynes Moryson's *Itinerary*', *Renaissance Studies* 31:4 (2017), pp. 569–85.

of serious study.[215] Robert Southwell, long after his own continental tour, wrote to his nephew Philip Perceval in June 1676 that 'now you are about to build up your selfe a new': travel was in the service of the twofold aim, 'to enlarge your Understanding, and to adorn your behaviour'.[216] In the seventy years between Palmer's and Southwell's advice, there was a significant shift in the practices and aims of educational travel, and one that can be mapped in attitudes to the study of gesture and bodily comportment. While debates about the 'origins' or 'beginnings' of the grand tour are bound to be inconclusive, the nature of travel did shift across the seventeenth century, with the 1640s and 1650s a key period which saw increasing numbers of young elite males being sent to the continent in part to avoid the conflict and instability at home.[217] This period also saw a growing number of continental academies teaching bodily arts alongside more academic subjects, and provided an often residential environment in which manners and civility might be learnt and practised. As Jean Boutier makes clear, the expansion of the curriculum of the academies made them ideal colleges for travelling nobles, and coincided with the growth of the grand tour.[218] As this mode of touring the continent became more established, the curriculum of educational travel shifted, placing more emphasis on the body and its relation to language and sociability, and silently shifting the focus of travel away from the 'politic traveller' of the late sixteenth and early seventeenth century.

The elite 'politic traveller' was replaced, gradually, by the grand tourist. The increased emphasis placed on bodily comportment in educational travel was directly linked to the importance of the disciplined body to later seventeenth-century codes of civility.[219] When tutors enrolled their pupils with masters of dance and of fencing, as occurred during the grand tour of Philip Perceval in the 1670s, or with a teacher of carving, found by de Blainville for the Blathwayt brothers at Geneva in the first decade of the eighteenth century, it was because they recognized that these skills were central to notions of gentility, masculinity, and civility.[220] Jean Gailhard, who had been Perceval's tutor for the first part of his

[215] Palmer, *Essay*, p. 52.

[216] Robert Southwell to Philip Perceval, 5 June 1676, British Library, Additional MS 46953, fol. 102r.

[217] Raylor, 'Exiles, Expatriates and Travellers', pp. 15–43.

[218] Boutier, 'Le Grand Tour des gentilshommes et les académies d'éducation pour la noblesse'; Timothy Raylor, 'Milton, the Hartlib Circle, and the Education of the Aristocracy' in Nicholas McDowell and Nigel Smith (ed.), *The Oxford Handbook of Milton* (Oxford: Oxford University Press, 2009), pp. 382–406; see also Stannek, *Telemachs Brüder*, pp. 73.

[219] Norbert Elias, *The Civilizing Process, vol. 1: The History of Manners*, trans. Edmund Jephcott (Oxford: Blackwell, 1969); Bryson, *From Courtesy to Civility*. See also Brian Cowan, 'Public Spaces, Knowledge, And Sociability', in Frank Trentmann, *The Oxford Handbook of the History of Consumption* (Oxford: Oxford University Press, 2012), pp. 253–5.

[220] Perceval hired a fencing master at Angers in 1677: see British Library, Add. MS 46954 B, fol. 112v; Hardwick, *Grand Tour*, pp. 55–6. Hinchingbrooke and his brother attended academies while in France in the 1660s: see the letters in Bodleian MS Carte 223.

grand tour, made an explicit link between the precepts of the dancing master and the student's behaviour in polite conversation:

> coming into the place where the company is, he must remember to practise the rules he was taught by his Dancing-master, modestly, and without affectation, yet with some difference, according to the high or low quality of the persons he salutes, the carriage and gestures of his body, to be so well composed as to be far from any shew of vanity or bravery[221]

The bodily control taught by the dancing master was to be applied in company: physical education was social and communicative. This was critical imitation put to use: as Gailhard wrote, '[i]t is not enough for you to study the fashions of a Country, except you reduce them to a practice'.[222] The traveller should develop a cosmopolitan carriage which retained the traveller's fundamental Englishness, 'not forgetting himself to be an Englishman, nor with becoming a Frenchman, an Italian, or a German, but building upon the true foundation of an Englishman, and making use of the different ways of those several Nations, as Ornaments only, and not as a bottom'.[223] Richard Lassels, author of the *Voyage of Italy*—alongside Gailhard's *Compleat Gentleman*, perhaps the most important English text of travel advice in the early period of the grand tour—was similarly pivotal in the shift towards an ideal of educational travel as disciplining the body.[224] Lassels envisaged the elite traveller developing

> a free garbe or carriage; a Cavallier way of entering into a Roome; a gratefull manegeing of his mouth and smiles; a chyronomie, or decent acting with his handes, which may humour his words gravely and freely, yet not affectedly or mimically: in fine, a liberty or freedome in all his actions, which the French call liberté du corps; and it must appeare to be à la negligence, and yet must be perfectly studdyed a fore hand[225]

Lassels, conversely, modelled a bodily *sprezzatura*, one where much study and physical practice underlay an easy manner, and where the impression one made could be based on how one entered a room. By the beginning of the eighteenth century, a merchant from Frankfurt could write to Sir William Blathwayt, having met his sons on their grand tour, praising their comportment and saying that '[th]is is the greatest joy that you could have in the world to see that your children

---

[221] Gailhard, *Compleat Gentleman*, part II, p. 78.   [222] Ibid., part II, pp. 188–9.

[223] Ibid., part II, p. 4.

[224] For Lassels, see Chaney, *Grand Tour and the Great Rebellion*, and Claydon, *Europe and the Making of England*, pp. 14–18.

[225] Lassels, *Voyage of Italy*, sig. I3v. There are parallels here with Castiglione's *sprezzatura*: see Snyder, *Dissimulation and the Culture of Secrecy in Early Modern Europe*, pp. 68–103.

conduct themselves well, and this contentment surpasses anything else that you could wish to have in the world.[226] Where elite travellers of a previous generation had used competence as a means of disguise rather than display, and parlayed linguistic skill into political advantage, the grand tourist's efforts—linguistic and mimetic—were best aimed at coming off well in company. Educational travel still aimed to enhance the communicative competence of the traveller, but its results were increasingly written on the body as well as on the tongue.

Conclusion: Language and Silence in Early Modern Travel

This chapter has shown the centrality of language and the spoken word to the everyday pedagogies of early modern travel. Attention to travellers' documents as well as to the debates over travel practices reveal the extent to which early modern educational travel was based on practices of linguistic observation and imitation. They also offer the first detailed insight into the day-to-day processes of language-learning in this period. Travellers forged new linguistic identities in conversation with other European vernacular communities. But if speaking was central to early modern language-learning, so too was the decision not to speak.[227] By their nature, early modern silences seem uncommunicative, but they offer a final way of thinking about the everyday pedagogies of early modern travel. As an opportunity for active listening, or a tactic used in deception, silence was process, not passivity.

Authors of travel advice were deeply concerned with silence: the author of the Perrott MS gave instructions on how to 'avoide Arguments and too much libertie in speech', claiming that 'An over licentious tongue in travell is perilous,' and reminding the traveller that 'especiallie in wordes yow must bee silent sparing and moderate, it beeing alwaies safe to thinke, sometimes unsafe to speake'.[228] The emphasis on safety and peril is instructive here: this was not an injunction to silence merely for sociability's sake, but one which understood that to utter certain words—or to speak in certain languages—could be dangerous in a religiously and politically divided Europe. The advice of the Perrott manuscript was echoed in Henry Wotton's advice to John Milton on the latter's travelling to Italy—Wotton summed it up in the phrase 'I pensieri stretti e il viso sciolto', which he translated as keeping one's 'thoughts close' and 'countenance loose'.[229] The English translator of Lipsius attempted to balance the need for conversation and the importance of silence, arguing that '[f]or albeit wisedome and safetie, do wishe mee to counsell

---

[226] Hardwick, *Grand Tour*, p. 39.
[227] On the social history of silence, see Peter Burke, 'Notes for a Social History of Silence in Early Modern Europe', in Peter Burke, *The Art of Conversation* (Cambridge: Polity, 1993), pp. 123–42.
[228] Bodleian Library, MS Perrott 5, fol. 8v.
[229] Pears, *Correspondence of Sidney and Languet*, p. 197; Howard, *English Travellers*, p. 97.

you to silence in travelling: yet I thinke it not amisse, though you give the rains now and then to that unbrideled member, the toong'.[230] In 1642, James Howell suggested that the traveller to Italy see their manner of keeping silence as a linguistic skill in itself: there, 'one may learne not to be over prodigall of speech when there is no need, for with a nod, with a shake of the head, and shrug of the shoulder, they will answer to many questions'.[231] Thomas Palmer took the question of silence further, arguing that for the traveller to be esteemed on his return home, he would need to practice '[s]ilence; which useth few words, but fitly, and to purpose'; an injunction which chimes with Joseph Hall's criticism of those who made their travels the basis of their table talk.[232] The practice of silence was valuable, both in travel and on one's return.

Fynes Moryson's *Itinerary* is voluble in the extreme, but he recognized the importance of 'Pythagoricall silence' to language acquisition, 'to the end he may learne true pronuntiation, and the properties of each language, not to be attained by long observation and practice, that he for a time listen to others, before he adventure to speake'.[233] He also recognized the importance of silence for more politic reasons, arguing that '[n]othing doth more preserve a Traveller from falling into dangers, or sooner deliver him in any danger, then the moderate discreete use of his tongue'. The dissimulating traveller might prefer that their mind not be too well known by others; in this case, silence was their friend: 'There is great Art to shunne talkative companions, or not to seeme to heare their questions.'[234] This feigned deafness or incomprehension could help to avoid conflict, too: he recounted pretending not to have understood anti-English comments directed at him in Germany.[235] Later, travelling incognito to Rome, Moryson made an arrangement with his German companions that would stop him from being discovered by any imperfections in his own grasp of the language:

> I covenanted with these my consorts, that when any man spake Dutch to me (though I had some skill in that Language, especially for vulgar speeches), and most of all if wee were in any long discourse, one of them should take the answere out of my mouth, as being slow of speech, though it were done somewhat unmannerly.[236]

Travelling in this way, Moryson could boast that 'I had in silence, and through many dangers seene Naples subject to the King of Spaine, and was now returned to Rome.'[237] Through the *Itinerary*'s anecdotes and injunctions, he offered a

---

[230]   Anon., *Direction for Travailers*, sig. B2r.
[231]   Howell, *Instructions for forreine travell*, p. 193.
[232]   Palmer, *Essay*, p. 129; Hall, *Quo Vadis?*, pp. 37–8.   [233]   Moryson, *Itinerary*, part III, p. 15.
[234]   Ibid., part III, pp. 24, 25.   [235]   Ibid., part I, p. 3.
[236]   Ibid., part III, p. 30.   [237]   Ibid., part I, p. 121.

taxonomy of silence, showing how the decision to hold one's tongue could be an educational one.

By the Restoration, the place of silence in the pedagogy of travel had shifted. Jean Gailhard's *Compleat Gentleman*, giving advice on comportment in travel and at home, argued that 'as it is a great wisdom to hide his passions, and discover those of other men, so it is to speak little, and hear much; for whilst fools have their heart upon the tongue, wise men keep their tongue in the heart'.[238] Gailhard's praise of silence, though, was of a different character from Moryson's: where the latter had enjoined silence as a means to gather sensitive information and to keep under cover, Gailhard's concern—and that of educational travel by the time he wrote—was much more with the dangers to the speaker's reputation and social capital of an ill-considered word or an embarrassing opinion. Later, as Michèle Cohen argues in her study of language and the gendered tongue in the grand tour, silence would come to be thought of as a particularly English virtue, and travellers would have to balance a skill in verbal performance with a 'delight in Silence'.[239] Silence remained central to early modern travel, though in a gradually changing role: from an instrument used to conceal one's origin to a stamp of national identity.

Silence was social: it could help to inculcate an understanding of the rules governing others' spoken interactions, while knowing how to employ it was an element of communicative competence in itself. Silence was an educational opportunity, and one which demanded an attentiveness to one's aural environments. Silence, from facilitating information-gathering and deceit at the end of the sixteenth century, would become a prized characteristic of the English traveller of the later grand tour. And silence was the first recourse of the wise returning traveller, who had to balance the demands of educational travel and critical imitation with the ever-present injunctions against affectation in his speech and behaviour. To learn to speak, the traveller had to know how to be silent, just as he had to be competent in another language before he could learn much from travel. Linguistic skill was, as the author of the Perrott manuscript wrote, 'a knowledge by *which* wee gett all knowledge'. Language acquisition, with its interplay of speech and silence, of learning and listening, underpinned a form of educational travel which was active, interested, and often controversial. It was a sociable activity through which information and identity were negotiated in a period of conflict and change, and an activity that underpinned the cultural transmission, translation, and transformation that is at the heart of our understanding of early modern English history. Before the English could learn from the continent, they had to learn to speak its languages.

---

[238] Gailhard, *Compleat Gentleman*, part II, p. 81.
[239] Cohen, *Fashioning Masculinity*, p. 3 and *passim*.

Conclusion

On a winter's night in London in 1676, two men were drinking together when 'there arose a dispute between them concerning a Spanish word'.[1] The row quickly became heated, and when 'one affirmed that it was not properly exprest, the other gave him provoking language for saying so'. Both drinkers had to be restrained by the company from taking their dispute into the street, but gradually they settled down, until 'they seeming well reconcil'd, the company left them'. All was quiet for an hour or so, until the row erupted once again: this time, the two men went into the street and drew their swords. The scuffle that followed was soon broken up, but not before one of the men had sustained a rapier wound to the arm. The wound proved mortal, the man died, and his killer was tried for murder at the Old Bailey.

The case of a man murdered over an item of Spanish vocabulary stands for much of what is intriguing and infuriating about the study of linguistic encounters in the past. The space between English and the continental vernaculars was a source of controversy, of intemperate debate, and of anxiety. This interlingual friction was experienced in print and in person, whether in the worries about translation and the borrowing of terms from other languages, or in the mockery of foreign accents and the serious ongoing debates about immigration and assimilation. Anxieties about foreign languages rarely exploded into the kind of fatal violence seen in this case, but this did not mean that they were insignificant. Learners of vernacular languages in early modern England, whether they recognized it or not, were asking questions about the relationship between England and Europe, and about what it meant to be a speaker of English at a time of great linguistic and political change.

By the beginning of the eighteenth century, the roles of England and of English in the world were changing rapidly.[2] In 1492, Antonio de Nebrija had told Isabella of Castile that 'language always was the companion of empire'; now, in the eighteenth century, the English language would spread with English political

---

[1] *Old Bailey Proceedings Online* (www.oldbaileyonline.org, version 7.2, accessed 13 January 2018), 17 January 1676 (t16760117-3).

[2] For two recent approaches to the standardization of English in the eighteenth century, each alive to the polyglot context, see Janet Sorensen, *Strange Vernaculars: How Eighteenth-Century Slang, Cant, Provincial Languages, and Nautical Jargon Became English* (Princeton, NJ, and Oxford: Princeton University Press, 2017); Daniel DeWispelare, *Multilingual Subjects: On Standard English, its Speakers, and Others in the Long Eighteenth Century* (Philadelphia, PA: University of Pennsylvania Press, 2017).

power, and over time it would grow into the lingua franca of the modern world.[3] The hegemony of English today may go some way to explaining how little the fact of the marginality of the language and its speakers in the sixteenth and seventeenth centuries has penetrated into traditional accounts of English history. Without a sense of how little-known and little-respected the English language was outside England for most of the early modern period, the importance of language-learning does not come easily into focus. For those who ventured past Dover, however, this was not only a fact of life: it was *the* fact of life. When the author of the Perrott manuscript wrote that competence in other languages was the 'knowledge by *which* wee gett all knowledge', they were correct.[4] Language-learning underpinned cultural, economic, and political contact, enabling everything from conversations on the Antwerp Bourse to the smooth running of multilingual ships, and from the translation of religious controversy to the English encounter with the continental Renaissance.

The study of language-learning in the past requires what George Stepney in 1693 called '*the* mixt knowledge of Books & Men'.[5] In *Learning Languages in Early Modern England*, I have shown that English-speakers learning foreign languages drew on a burgeoning set of printed materials for the study of other vernaculars, but that their studies also required them to build relationships with teachers and speakers, and to engage closely with the multilingual oral cultures of early modern England and other European countries. By charting a course between the ideal competences represented by language manuals and the experiences of real-life language-learners, it has been possible to understand prevailing ideas about language competence and language acquisition, and to see how idealized curriculums and practical pedagogies interacted. Work of this kind is necessary because the history of language is more than just the history of words. Early modern languages were not abstract sign systems but social tools—people did things with them, and they shaped people's lives. In this book, I have tried to model a way of writing the history of language which is concerned with the spaces between languages, the ways in which individuals attempted to bridge them, and what that might mean for social and cultural history. In the face of a scholarship dominated by linguists and scholars of literature, whose work is often excellent but whose concerns and questions do not always overlap with those of the historian, this book has argued that language-learning matters as a subject for historical research. It stems from the belief that a polyglot history of early modern England and Europe is not only possible but necessary.

The story of the Spanish vocabulary murder is useful, too, because it reminds us of how much is lost or hidden in the study of the language of the past. The records

[3] Antonio de Nebrija, *Gramática de la lengua castellana* (Salamanca, 1492), sig. A2r.
[4] 'A direction for a Travailer', Bodleian Library, MS Perrott 5, fol. 10r.
[5] George Stepney to James Vernon, 17 November 1697, National Archives, SP 105/60, fol. 60v.

of the Old Bailey recall a violent altercation, but offer no information to indicate what the 'Spanish word' the men argued over was, how they knew each other, why they were discussing Spanish terminology, or how a foreign word could possibly have given cause to two drinkers to draw their rapiers. Similarly, in the sources for the history of language-learning, much is lost, or only approachable obliquely. Little of the language of those who were not literate or whose words were not deemed worthy of conservation has survived for us. Our picture of early modern education becomes ever more blurred the further we get from the elite individual learner: the classrooms where immigrant children or apprentices were taught vernacular languages are difficult to picture in any detail. Histories of teaching suffer similarly. We can see the letters of tutors to aristocratic travellers, or advertisements by teachers who established boarding schools and academies, but far less remains of the invisible educators who served the extracurricular economy: ushers, the wives, families, and servants of boarding school masters, the valets whose duty it was to dress the traveller or the gentleman, but also to help him practice his French or Italian. Language-learning was never the business only of the elite student: it was an activity undertaken by individuals from all social backgrounds. This book has often drawn on the records of people who led lives of privilege, but it has kept an ear open for the voices of polyglots at all levels of the social scale.

This is not to suggest that our archives have nothing to tell us about language-learning beyond the elite level. Thinking about soldiers in multilingual armies, polyglot merchants and factors, and spies for whom language was a tool of the trade (or an instrument of disguise) has the potential to transform how we think about the histories of war, trade, empire, diplomacy, and politics. Multilingual lives were lived out in the heart of the English city too: ongoing work with the records of the High Court of Admiralty is revealing a breathtaking range of linguistic abilities among the maritime communities of early modern London, showing ordinary people tied by travel and by tongues to a much wider world.[6] Urban histories, histories of gender, and histories of work can be transformed when we think about the polyglot city, the polyglot marriage, and the polyglot workshop. The archives of elite families will reveal more about education, letter-writing, and women's place in the multilingual cultures of the period. These linguistic questions can also be fruitfully applied to histories of religion and the Reformation—complicating how we think about the transmission and debate of European religious ideas outside the pages of books, and illuminating the life experiences of individuals who negotiated the fraught confessional and linguistic boundaries of early modern Europe. Beyond Europe, empire was born in polyglot contexts. The actors in *Learning Languages in Early Modern England* have

---

[6] See the ongoing research and crowdsourced document transcription by Colin Greenstreet and the Marine Lives project: http://www.marinelives.org/wiki/MarineLives, accessed 12 Mar. 2019.

mostly been European, but their histories help us to shape questions—questions of knowledge, power, and identity—which need to be asked of English, British, and European linguistic encounters in the wider world. Multilingual voices are waiting everywhere in our archives, and they will enable us to take a polyglot perspective which can transform histories from the local to the global.

This book set out to ask two questions: firstly, how early modern English-speakers went about learning vernacular European languages; and, secondly, what it meant to be competent in another language in this period, whether as a student or as a teacher. Language learning was voluble, and it was social: languages met because people did, and the grand dramas of cultural encounter were played out in face-to-face interactions. The meanings of competence varied depending on who was speaking, and in what language, but competence was never an abstract accomplishment, or a binary between fluent and not. In arguing these points, a greater truth comes into view. Early modern England was multilingual. Its encounters with the wider world, and its ideas about itself, were forged in contact with other languages—often languages which carried more power or prestige. Our present, in which English is a language which speaks with power and is understood across the globe, should not blind us to the realities of a polyglot past. To say 'This is England; we speak English' has always been historically ignorant: ideas about the past (and the present) which assume the existence of a monoglot nation are at best incomplete and at worst dangerous.

This book was completed in a time of rupture and uncertainty. Research which had at first seemed distant from the present day suddenly felt more relevant. Reading a sixteenth-century account of a brawl in which a 'stranger' was set upon in the streets after being overheard speaking a foreign language, I thought of similar attacks which followed the Brexit vote in summer 2016.[7] Cuts to funding for language teaching for migrants and dwindling provision of foreign-language teaching in schools and universities brought John Florio, with whom this book began, to mind. He was scathing in his criticism of the kind of Englishman he saw 'in company of straungers, who can neyther speake, nor understand with them, but standes as one mute'. The monoglot English-speaker was 'mocked of them, and despised of al, and none wyl make account of hym'. 'What a shame is that?' asks Florio—'what a reproche to his parentes? what a losse to him? and what harts grief to think theron?'[8] This history of a moment in England's marginal, multilingual past has no simple answers to offer to today's problems, but it was written with the ever-growing conviction that we have much to learn from a time in which a small island on the edge of Europe had to learn to speak to the world.

---

[7] See the depositions of Valentine Wood and Thomas Norton, TNA, SP 12/181, fols. 174r–174v. I discuss this brawl in Gallagher, 'Italian London of John North', pp. 119–20.

[8] John Florio, *Florio his firste fruites* (London, 1578), p. 62.

Bibliography

1. Select Bibliography of Primary Materials

(i) Manuscript Sources

Bodleian Library

MS Perrott 5: 'A direction for a Travailer'.

MS Add. C. 193: Journal of John North, 1575–80.

MS Rawlinson Letters 49: Letters to Philip, Lord Wharton about the education of his sons at Caen, 1662–4.

MS Rawlinson D1285: Travel journal of Thomas Abdie, 1633–5.

MS Lister 26: Travel notebook of Martin Lister, c.1698.

MS Bankes 6: James Howell, 'Propositions touching Forreners'.

MS Carte 50: Letters from the earl of Ormond during the grand tour of his ward, Lord Derby, 1673–5.

MS Carte 80: Correspondence and papers of Philip, 4th Lord Wharton and Thomas, 1st Marquis of Wharton.

MS Carte 223: Letters to the Earl of Sandwich, 1655–70.

MS Carte 243: Letters relating to the travels of the Earl of Derby, 1673/4.

MS Eng. lett. c.309: Travel correspondence of Robert Clayton, 1697.

British Library

Harleian MS 943: Travel journal of Richard Symonds (France), 1649–50.

Harleian MS 3344: Album amicorum and journal of Giacomo Castelvetro, late 16th and early 17th century.

Harleian MS 3492: 'Raccolta di Frasi Italiane', 1686.

Harleian MS 6427: Journal of an anonymous gentleman's travels through Germany, Holland, Low Countries, c.1691.

Egerton MS 1632: Travel journal of Robert Southwell (Italy), 1660–1.

Lansdowne MS 93: Letters, mostly to Elizabeth, Lady Hicks, c.1613–14.

Add. MS 4217: Account by Richard Lassels of Catherine Whetenall's journey from Brussels to Italy.

Add. MS 46953   }
Add. MS 46954 A }
Add. MS 46954 B } Letters relating to the grand tour of
Add. MS 46955 A } Philip Perceval, 1676–9.
Add. MS 46955 B }
Add. MS 46956 A }

Add. MS 58219: Travel journal of Robert Southwell (France), 1659–60.

Add. MS 78670: 'Account of my Jurny from *the* Citty of Burdiox to Parris Callis & London'; and copy of fragment of an Englishman's account of a trip to the Low Countries (c.1678).

Sloane MS 1886: Travel journal of Edward Browne (France and Italy), 1664–5.

Sloane MS 1906: Travel journal of Edward Browne (France), 1663–4.

RP 209: Bulstrode Whitelocke, manuscript phrasebook.

Longleat House

TH/VOL/XVII: Letters to Thomas, 1st Lord Weymouth, from members of the Finch family, 1673–1711.

SE/VII/2: General correspondence of Frances Seymour, Marchioness of Hertford, Duchess of Somerset, 1645–74.

National Archives, London

SP 11/8: Secretaries of State: State Papers Domestic, Mary I, Letters and Papers, April–May 1556.

SP 15/28/1: Secretaries of State: State Papers Domestic, Edward VI–James VI, Addenda, 1583–4.

SP 16/222: Secretaries of State: State Papers Domestic, Charles I, Letters and Papers, August 1632.

SP 16/409: Secretaries of State: State Papers Domestic, Charles I, Letters and Papers, 1–23 January 1639.

SP 18/96: State Papers Domestic, Civil War and Interregnum, Council of State, Navy Commission and related bodies, Orders and Papers, April 1655.

SP 29/51: Secretaries of State: State Papers Domestic, Charles II, Letters and Papers, 22–28 February 1662.

SP 29/95: Secretaries of State: State Papers Domestic, Charles II, Letters and Papers, 21–31 March 1664.

SP 29/251: Secretaries of State: State Papers Domestic, Charles II, Letters and Papers, 30–31 December 1668 and undated.

SP 32/7: Secretaries of State: State Papers Domestic, William and Mary, Letters and Papers, Letters and Papers, December 1696–August 1697.

SP 44/348: Secretaries of State: Entry Books, Warrants and Passes, Shrewsbury, Jersy, and Vernon, 1697–1702.

SP 70/47: Secretaries of State: State Papers Foreign, Elizabeth I, Letters and Papers, 17–31 December 1562.

SP 89/2: Secretaries of State: State Papers Foreign, Portugal, 1583–98.

SP 105/60: Letter-book of George Stepney: mission to the Holy Roman emperor and mission to Saxony, July 1693–June 1694.

C 11/715/13: Chancery pleadings in Corticelli vs Viceti, 1715.

Trinity College, Cambridge

MS R.10.6: Manuscript book of Italian dialogues, probably by Giacomo Castelvetro, with partial translation by William Woodforde, 1613.

West Yorkshire Archive Service

KE/8: Manuscript Italian phrasebook, probably belonging to John Armytage.

WYL132/257: Marriage settlement, 17 April 1652.

(ii) Online Resources

17th–18th Century Burney Collection Newspapers (http://find.galegroup.com/bncn/start.do?prodId=BBCN&userGroupName=cambuni)

Early English Books Online (www.eebo.chadwyck.com)

Eighteenth Century Collections Online (http://find.galegroup.com/ecco)

Folger Shakespeare Library, Digital Image Collection (http://luna.folger.edu)

The Gazette (www.thegazette.co.uk)

The Hartlib Papers (http://www.hrionline.ac.uk/hartlib)

National Archives, Access to Archives (www.nationalarchives.gov.uk/a2a)
Old Bailey Proceedings Online (www.oldbaileyonline.org, version 7.0)
Oxford Dictionary of National Biography (www.oxforddnb.com)
Ralph Thoresby's Diary (http://www.thoresby.org.uk/diary/diary.html)
State Papers Online 1509–1714 (http://gale.cengage.co.uk/state-papers-online-15091714.aspx)

(iii) Printed Primary Materials

Aedler, Martin, *The High Dutch Minerva A-La-Mode or A Perfect Grammar never extant before, whereby the English may both easily and exactly learne the Neatest Dialect of the German Mother-Language used throughout All Europe* (London, 1680).

A.J., *A compleat account of the Portugueze language* (London, 1701).

A.J., *Grammatica Anglo-Lusitanica: or a short and compendious system of an English and Portugueze grammar* (London, 1702).

A.J., *Grammatica Anglo-Lusitanica: or a short and compendious system of an English and Portugueze grammar* (Lisbon, 1705).

Anon., *Here begynneth a lytell treatyse for to lerne Englysshe and Frensshe* (London, 1497).

Anon., *Here is a good boke to lerne to speke French/Lytell treatyse for to lerne Englysshe and Frensshe* (London, 1500?).

Anon., *A lytell treatyse for to lerne Englysshe and Frensshe* (Antwerp, c.1530).

Anon., *Sex linguarum, Latinæ, Gallicæ, Hispanicæ, Italicæ, Anglicæ, et Teutonice* (Venice, 1541).

Anon., *A Very necessarye boke both in Englyshce & in Frenche wherein ye mayst learne to speake & wryte Frenche truly in a litle space yf thou gyve thy mynde and diligence there unto* (London, 1550).

Anon., *Lytell treatyse for to lerne Englysshe and Frensshe* (London, c.1553).

Anon., *The boke of Englysshe, and Spanysshe* (London, 1554).

Anon., *A very profitable boke to lerne the maner of redyng, writyng, & speakyng english & Spanish. Libro muy provechoso para saber la manera de leer, y screvir, y hablar Angleis, y Español* (London, 1554).

Anon., *A plaine pathway to the French tongue: Very profitable for Marchants, and also all other, which desire this same* (London, 1575).

Anon., *A Direction for Travailers. Taken out of Iustus Lipsius, and enlarged for the behoofe of the right honorable Lord, the yong Earle of Bedford, being now ready to travell* (London, 1592).

Anon., *Colloquia et dictionariolum septem linguarum* (Venice, 1606).

Anon., *Phrases Françoises fort necessaires pour ceux qui apprennent à parler françois, en forme de question* (London, 1624).

Anon., *Profitable Instructions; Describing what speciall Observations are ... taken by Travellers in all Nations, States and Countries; Pleasant and Profitable. By the three much admired, Robert, late Earle of Essex, Sir Philip Sidney, And, Secretary Davison* (London, 1633).

Anon., *The English, French, Latine, Dutch, Schole-master. Or, An Introduction to teach young Gentlemen and Merchants to Travell or Trade* (London, 1637).

Anon., *Den grooten Vocabulaer Engels ende Duyts. The Great Vocabuler, in English and Dutch* (Rotterdam, 1639).

Anon., *New Dialogues or Colloquies, and A little Dictionary of eight Languages* (London, 1639).

Anon., *Den Engelschen School-Meester &c. The English Schole-Master &c.* (Amsterdam, 1646).

Anon., *The Dutch-Tutor: or, a new-book of Dutch and English.* (London, 1660).

Anon. ['Hannah Woolley'], *The Gentlewomans Companion; or, a guide to the female sex* (London, 1683).

Anon., *The Behaviour of the Condemned Criminals in Newgate, Who were Executed On Friday the 19th of this Instant December* (London, 1684).

Anon., *A Short and Easy Way For The Palatines To Learn English. Oder Eine kurze Anleitung zur Englischen Sprach, Zum Nutz der armen Pfältzer/nebst angehängten Englischen und Teutsche ABC* (London, 1710).

Anton, Pasqual Joseph, *Grammatica Española. A Spanish Grammar: which is the shortest, plain, and most easy method to instruct an English man in the true Knowledge of that extensive Language... By D". Pasqual Joseph Anton. Master of Languages in London* (London, 1711).

Antonio, Prior of Crato, *The explanation. Of the true and lawfull right and tytle, of the most excellent prince, Anthonie the first of that name, King of Portugall... Translated into English and conferred with the French and Latine copies. By the commaundement and order of the superiors* (London, 1585).

Ascham, Roger, *The Scholemaster* (London, 1570).

Astell, Mary, *A Serious Proposal to the Ladies for the Advancement of their True and Greatest Interest. In Two parts* (London, 1697).

Bacon, Francis, *The Essayes or Counsels, Civill and Morall, of Francis Lo. Verulam, Viscount St. Alban* (London, 1625).

Barrell, Rex A., *The correspondence of Abel Boyer, Huguenot refugee 1667–1729* (Lewiston, NY, Queenston, Ont., and Lampeter: Edwin Mellen, 1992).

Bathe, William, *Janua Linguarum, Quadrilinguis. Or a Messe of Tongues: Latine, English, French, and Spanish. Neatly served up together, for a wholesome repast, to the worthy curiositie of the studious* (London, 1617).

Bekkaoui, Khalid, *White Women Captives in North Africa: Narratives of Enslavement, 1735–1830* (Basingstoke and New York: Palgrave Macmillan, 2011).

Bellot, Jacques, *Familiar dialogues, for the Instruction of them, that be desirious to learne to speake English, and perfectly to pronounce the same* (London, 1586).

Bent, J. Theodore (ed.), *Early voyages and travels in the Levant* (London: Hakluyt Society, 1893).

Berault, Peter, *A New, Plain, Short, and Compleat French and English Grammar* (London, 1688).

Berault, Peter, *A New, Plain, Short, and Compleat French and English Grammar* (London, 1700).

Berry, Herbert, *The Noble Science: A Study and Transcription of Sloane Ms. 2530, Papers of the Masters of Defence of London, Temp. Henry VIII to 1590* (Newark, NJ: University of Delaware Press, 1991).

Blount, Henry, *A Voyage into the Levant. A Breife Relation of a Journey, lately performed by Master H.B., Gentleman, from England by the way of Venice, into Dalmatia, Sclavonia, Bosnah, Hungary, Macedonia, Thessaly, Thrace, Rhodes and Egypt, unto Gran Cairo: With particular observations concerning the moderne condition of the Turkes, and other people under that Empire* (London, 1636).

Boersma, O., and A. J. Jelsma, *Unity in Multiformity: The minutes of the coetus of London, 1575 and the consistory minutes of the Italian church of London, 1570–91* (London: Huguenot Society, 1997).

Boorde, Andrew, *The fyrst boke of the introduction of knowledge* (London, 1555?).

Boyer, Abel, *The Compleat French-Master, for Ladies and Gentlemen. Being A New Method, to Learn with ease and delight the French Tongue, as it is now spoken in the Court of France* (London, 1694).

Brennan, Michael G. (ed.), *The travel diary (1611–1612) of an English Catholic, Sir Charles Somerset* (Leeds: Leeds Philosophical and Literary Society, 1993).

Brennan, Michael G. (ed.), *The travel diary of Robert Bargrave, Levant merchant (1647–1656)* (London: Hakluyt Society, 1999).

Brennan, Michael G. (ed.), *The Origins of the Grand Tour: the travels of Robert Montagu, Lord Mandeville (1649–1654), William Hammond (1655–1658), and Banaster Maynard (1660–1663)* (London: Hakluyt Society, 2004).

Bromley, William, *Remarks made in travels through France & Italy. With many Publick Inscriptions. Lately taken by a Person of Quality* (London, 1693).

Browne, Edward, *A Journal of a visit to Paris in the year 1664*, ed. Geoffrey Keynes (London: John Murray, 1923).

Bruno, Giordano, *The Ash Wednesday Supper*, trans. Stanley L. Jaki (The Hague and Paris: Mouton, 1975).

Bruto, Giovanni Michele, *The Necessarie, fit, and convenient Education of a yong Gentlewoman. Written both in French and Italian, and translated into English by W.P. And now printed with the three Languages together in one Volume, for the better instruction of such as are desirous to studie those Tongues* (London, 1598).

Buck, George, *The Third Universitie of England* (London, 1615).

Bullokar, William, *Bullokars Booke at large, for the Amendment of Orthographie for English speech* (London, 1580).

Bullokar, William, *A short Introduction or guiding to print, write, and reade Inglish speech: conferred with the old printing and writing: devised by William Bullokar* (London, 1580).

Bulwer, John, *Chirologia: or the Naturall Language of the Hand* (London, 1644).

Bulwer, John, *Philocophus: Or, The Deafe And Dumbe Mans Friend* (London, 1648).

Burnet, Gilbert, *History of His Own Time* (London, 1734).

Castelvetro, Giacomo, *The fruit, herbs and vegetables of Italy: an offering to Lucy, Countess of Bedford*, trans. Gillian Riley (Totnes: Prospect, 2012).

Castiglione, Baldassare, *The Book of the Courtier*, trans. George Bull (London: Penguin, 2003).

Cheke, John, *The Gospel according to Saint Matthew and part of the first chapter of the Gospel according to Saint Mark translated into English from the Greek, with original notes, by Sir John Cheke, Knight*, ed. James Goodwin (London: William Pickering, 1843).

Cheneau, François, *The shortest way to write and speak Latin, by numbers and rules, hereto unknown to masters* (London, 1710?).

Colsoni, François, *Il Nuovo Trismegiste* (London, 1688).

Colsoni, François, *The English Ladies New French Grammar* (London, 1699).

Colsoni, François, *Le guide de Londres, dedié aux voyageurs étrangers* (London, 1710).

Comenius, Jan Amos, *Porta Linguarum Trilinguis reserata et aperta/The Gate of Tongues unlocked or opened* (London, 1631).

Coryate, Thomas, *Coryats Crudities. Hastily gobled up in five Moneths travells in France, Savoy, Italy, Rhetia—commonly called the Grisons country, Helvetia alias Switzerland, some parts of high Germany, and the Netherlands* (London, 1611).

Coryate, Thomas, *Thomas Coriate Traveller for the English Wits: Greeting. From the Court of the Great Mogul, Resident at the Towne of Asmere, in Easterne India* (London, 1616).

Cotgrave, Randle, *Dictionarie of the French and English Tongues* (London, 1611).

Cougneau, Paul, *A Sure Guide to The French tongue, Teaching by a most easie way, to pronounce the French naturally, to reade it perfectly, to write it truly, and to speake it readily* (London, 1635).

Crawford, Donald (ed.), *Journals of Sir John Lauder, Lord Fountainhall, with his observations on public affairs and other memoranda 1665–1676* (Edinburgh: Edinburgh University Press/Scottish History Society, 1900).

d'Abbadie, Jacques, *A New French Grammar. Containing at large the Principles of that tongue* (Oxford, 1676).

Dallington, Robert, *A Method for Travell* (London, 1605).

Davies, G. (ed.), *Autobiography of Thomas Raymond and Memoirs of the family of Guise of Elmore, Gloucestershire* (London: Camden Society, 1917).

de Beaulieu, Jean, *Catalogue des livres francois italiens & espagnols* (London, 1693).

de Beer, E. S. (ed.), *The Diary of John Evelyn, selected and introduced by Roy Strong* (London: Everyman, 2006).

de'Bonarelli, Guidobaldo, *Filli di Sciro* (Paris, 1786).

Defoe, Daniel, *The Life of that incomparable princess, Mary, our late sovereign lady, of ever blessed memory* (London, 1695).

de Grave, Jean, *The Path-way to the gate of tongues: being, the first instruction for little children* (London, 1633).

Dekker, Thomas, *The Shoemaker's Holiday*, ed. R. L. Smallwood and Stanley Wells (Manchester: Manchester University Press, 1979).

de la Mothe, G., *The French Alphabeth* (London, 1592).

de la Mothe, G., *The French Alphabet, teaching in a very short time, by a most easie way, to pronounce French naturally, to reade it perfectly, to write it truly, and to speake it accordingly. Together with The Treasure of the French tongue* (London, 1633).

de Luna, Juan, *A short and compendious art for to learne to reade, write, pronounce and speake the Spanish tongue* (London, 1623).

de Nebrija, Antonio, *Gramática de la lengua castellana* (Salamanca, 1492).

de Worde, Wynkyn, *Here begynneth a lytell treatyse for to lerne Englysshe and Frensshe* (London, 1498?).

di Gregorio, Francesco, *Discepulo instrutto nelli Principij della Lingua Latina, spiegati per la Volgare & Inglese a modo di Dialogo* (London, 1643).

du Grès, Gabriel, *Dialogi Gallico-Anglico-Latini per Gabrielem Dugres linguam Gallicam in illustrissima, et famosissima, Oxoniensi Academia edocentem* (Oxford, 1639).

du Grès, Gabriel, *Dialogi Gallico-Anglico-Latini per Gabrielem Dugres linguam Gallicam in illustrissima & famosissima Oxoniensi academia haud ita pridem privatim edocentem* (Oxford, 1652).

du Grès, Gabriel, *Dialogi Gallico-Anglico-Latini. Per Gabrielem Dugres, linguæ Gallicæ in illustrissima & famosissima Oxoniensi Academia haud ita pridem privato munere præ-lectorem* (Oxford, 1660).

Dulcis, Catharinus, *Catharini Dulcis linguarum exoticarum in Academia Marpurgensi Professoris Vitae Curriculi Breviarum* (Marburg, 1622).

Dunton, John, *The parable of the top-knots* (London, 1691).

du Ploiche, Pierre, *A Treatise in English and Frenche right necessary and proffitable for al young children* (London, 1551).

du Ploiche, Pierre, *A treatise in English and Frenche, right necessarie, and profitable for all young children* (London, 1578).

D'Urfey, Thomas, *Love for Money: or, The Boarding School* (London, 1691).

Du Wès, Giles, *An introductorie for to lerne to rede, to pronounce, and to speake Frenche trewly, compiled for the right high, excellent, and most vertuous lady, the lady Mary of Englande, doughter to our most gracious soverayn lorde kyng Henry the eight* (London, 1533?).

Du Wés, Giles, *An introductorie for to lerne to rede, to pronounce, and to speake Frenche trewly, compyled for the ryghte hygh, excellent, & moste vertuous lady, the lady Mary of England, doughter to our moste gracious soverayne lorde kyng Henry the eyghte* (London, 1540?).

Du Wés, Giles, *An introductorie for to lerne to rede, to pronounce, and to speake Frenche trewly, compyled for the ryghte hygh, excellent, & moste vertuous lady, the lady Mary of*

Englande, doughter to our mooste gracious soverayne lorde kynge Henry the eight (London, 1546?).

Eliot, John, *Ortho-Epia Gallica. Eliots Fruits for the French* (London, 1593).

Eliot, John, *The Indian Grammar Begun: Or, an Essay to Bring the Indian Language into Rules* (Cambridge, 1666).

Elyot, Thomas, *The boke named the Governour, devised by Thomas Elyot knight* (London, 1531).

Elyot, Thomas, *Of the Knowledeg whiche maketh a wise man* (London, 1533).

Erondell, Peter, *The French Garden: for English Ladyes and Gentlewomen to walke in* (London, 1605).

Festeau, Paul, *New and Easie French Grammar* (London, 1667).

Festeau, Paul, *Paul Festeau's French Grammar* (London, 1671).

Festeau, Paul, *Nouvelle Grammaire Angloise, Enrichie de Dialogues curieux touchant l'Estat, & la Cour d'Angleterre* (London, 1675).

Festeau, Paul, *Paul Festeau's French Grammar* (London, 1675).

Festeau, Paul, *Nouvelle Grammaire Françoise* (London, 1679).

Florio, John, *Florio His firste Fruites which yeelde familiar speech* (London, 1578).

Florio, John, *Florios Second Frutes* (London, 1591).

Florio, John, *A Worlde of Wordes, Or Most copious, and exact Dictionarie in Italian and English* (London, 1598).

Florio, John, *Queen Anna's New World of Words, Or Dictionarie of the Italian and English tongues* (London, 1611).

Fontaine, Jacques, *Mémoires d'une famille Huguenote victime de la révocation de l'Édit de Nantes*, ed. Bernard Cottret (Montpellier: Presses du Languedoc, 1992).

Foster, William (ed.), *The Travels of John Sanderson in the Levant, 1584–1602. With his Autobiography and Selections from his Correspondence* (London: Hakluyt Society, 1931).

Gage, Thomas, *The English-American his Travail by Sea and Land: Or, A New Survey of the West-India's... With a Grammar, or some few Rudiments of the Indian Tongue, called, Poconchi, or Pocoman* (London, 1648).

Gailhard, Jean, *The Compleat Gentleman: or Directions For the Education of Youth As to their Breeding at Home And Travelling Abroad. In Two Treatises* (London, 1678).

Gerbier, Balthazar, *The Interpreter of the Academie for Forrain Languages, and all Noble Sciences, and Exercises* (London, 1649).

Gerbier, Balthazar, *A Publique Lecture On all the Languages, Arts, Sciences, and Noble Exercises, which are taught in Sr Balthazar Gerbiers Academy* (London, 1649).

Gerbier, Balthazar, *Subsidium Peregrinantibus. Or An Assistance to a Traveller in His Convers with 1. Hollanders. 2. Germans. 3. Venetians. 4. Italians. 5. Spaniards. 6. French. Directing him, after the latest Mode, to the greatest Honour, Pleasure, Security, and Advantage in his Travells. Written To a Princely Traveller for a Vade Mecum* (Oxford, 1665).

Gilbert, Humphrey, *Queene Elizabethes Achademy, A Booke of Precedence, &c., with Essays on Italian and German Books of Courtesy* (London: Early English Text Society, 1869).

Grantham, Henry, *An Italian Grammer; written in Latin by Scipio Lentulo a Neapolitane: and turned in English: by H. G.* (London, 1575).

Greg, W. W., and E. Boswell (eds.), *Records of the Court of the Stationers' Company 1576 to 1602: From Register B* (London: The Bibliographical Society, 1930).

Groto, Luigi, *La Dalida* (Venice, 1572). Online edition, ed. Dana F. Sutton (http://www.philological.bham.ac.uk/groto).

Hakluyt, Richard, *The principal navigations, voiages, traffiques and discoveries of the English nation*, 3 vols. (London, 1598–1600).

Hall, Joseph, *Quo vadis? A Just Censure of Travell as it is commonly undertaken by the Gentlemen of our Nation* (London, 1617).

Hall, Joseph, *Bishop Hall's Sayings concerning Travellers, To prevent Popish and Debauch'd Principles* (London, 1674).

Hardwick, Nora (ed.), *The Grand Tour: Letters and Accounts Relating to the Travels through Europe of the Brothers William and John Blathwayt of Dyrham Park, 1705–1708* (Bristol: Nora Hardwick, 1985).

Hart, John, *An Orthographie, conteyning the due order and reason, howe to write or paint thimage of mannes voice, most like to the life or nature* (London, 1569).

Hart, John, *A Methode or comfortable beginning for all unlearned, whereby they may bee taught to read English, in a very short time, with pleasure: So profitable as straunge, put in light, by I.H. Chester Heralt* (London, 1570).

Herbert, William, *Herberts French and English Dialogues. In a more Exact and Delightful Method then any yet Extant* (London, 1660).

Hillenius, François, *Den Engelschen ende Ne'erduitschen Onderrichter/The English, and Low Dutch Instructer* (Rotterdam, 1664).

Hoby, Thomas, *The Courtyer of Count Baldessar Castilio divided into foure bookes* (London, 1561).

Hollyband, Claudius, *The pretie and wittie historie of Arnalt & Lucenda: with certen rules and dialogues set foorth for the learner of th'Italian tong* (London, 1575).

Hollyband, Claudius, *The Frenche Littelton. A most easie, perfect, and absolute way to learne the frenche tongue* (London, 1576).

Hollyband, Claudius, *The French Littelton* (London, 1578).

Hollyband, Claudius, *Claudii a Sancto Vinculo, De pronuntiatione linguae gallicae libri duo* (London, 1580).

Hollyband, Claudius, *The French Littelton* (London, 1581).

Hollyband, Claudius, *The Frenche Schoolemaister of Claudius Hollyband: Newly corrected* (London, 1582).

Hollyband, Claudius, *Campo di fior or else the flourie field of foure languages* (London, 1583).

Hollyband, Claudius, *The French Littelton* (London, 1593).

Hollyband, Claudius, *The Italian Schoole-maister* (London, 1597).

Hollyband, Claudius, *The French school-master. Shewing the true and perfect way of pronouncing the French tongue, to the furtherance of those who desire to learn it. First collected by Mr. C.H. and now truly and newly corrected and enriched with many facete proverbs and additions, for the delight and benefit of the learner. Never printed before. By James Giffard teacher of the said tongue* (London, 1668).

Howell, James, *Instructions for forreine travell. Shewing by what cours, and in what compasse of time, one may take an exact Survey of the Kingdomes and States of Christendome, and arrive to the practicall knowledge of the Languages, to good purpose* (London, 1642).

Howell, James, *Epistolae Ho-Elianae. Familiar Letters Domestic & Forren* (London, 1645).

Howell, James, *Instructions and directions for Forren Travell. Shewing by what cours, and in what compas of time, one may take an exact Survey of the Kingdomes, and States of Christendome, and arrive to the practicall knowledg of the Languages, to good purpose. With a new Appendix for Travelling into Turkey and the Levant parts.* (London, 1650).

Howell, James, *A new English Grammar, Prescribing as certain Rules, as the Language will bear, for Forreners to learn English: Ther is also another Grammar of the Spanish or Castilian Toung. With some special remarks upon the Portugues Dialect, &c.* (London, 1662).

Italiano, Benvenuto, *Il Passaggiere. The Passenger ... Containing seaven exquisite Dialogues in Italian and English* (London, 1613).

Kirk, R. E. G., and Ernest F. Kirk (eds.) *Returns of Aliens in the City and Suburbs of London from the Reign of Henry VIII to that of James I. Part I: 1523–1571* (Aberdeen: Huguenot Society, 1900).

Kirk, R. E. G., and Ernest F. Kirk (eds.) *Returns of Aliens in the City and Suburbs of London from the Reign of Henry VIII to that of James I. Part II: 1571–1597* (Aberdeen: Huguenot Society, 1902).

König, Johann/John King, *Ein volkommener englischer Wegweiser für Hoch-Teutsche. A compleat English guide for High-Germans* (London, 1706).

Kristol, Andres M. (ed.), *Manières de langage (1396, 1399, 1415)* (London: Anglo-Norman Text Society, 1995).

Lacy, John, *Sauny the Scot. Or, the Taming of the Shrew* (London, 1698).

Lainé, Peter, *The Princely Way to the French Tongue. Or, a new and easie method to bring Her Highness, the Lady Mary, to the true and exact knowledge of that language* (London, 1667).

Lainé, Peter, *The Princely Way to the French Tongue, as it was first compiled for the use of her Highness the Lady Mary, and since taught her Royal Sister the Lady Anne* (London, 1677).

Lassels, Richard, *The Voyage of Italy, or A Compleat Journey through Italy ... With Instructions concerning Travel. By Richard Lassels, Gent. who Travelled through Italy Five times as Tutor to several of the English Nobility and Gentry* (Paris, 1670).

Latham, Robert, and William Matthews (eds.), *The diary of Samuel Pepys* (London: G. Bell and Sons, 1970).

Leigh, Edward, *Three Diatribes or Discourses. First of Travel, Or a Guide for Travellers into Forein Parts. Secondly, Of Money or Coyne. thirdly, Of Measuring of the Distance beetwixt Place and Place* (London, 1671).

Le Mayre, Marten, *The Dutch Schoole Master* (London, 1606).

Letts, Malcolm, (ed.), *Francis Mortoft: His Book. Being his Travels through France and Italy, 1658–1659* (London: Hakluyt Society, 1925).

Lister, Martin, *A Journey to Paris In the Year 1698* (London, 1698).

Lomas, S. C. (ed.), 'The Memoirs of Sir George Courthop [or Courthope]' (1616–1685), *Camden Miscellany* XI (London, 1907).

McKay, Barry, *Gay Phrase Book* (London: Cassell, 1995).

Makin, Bathsua, *An Essay to Revive the Antient Education of Gentlewomen, in Religion, Manners, Arts & Tongues* (London, 1673).

Mauger, Claude, *True advancement of the French Tongue. Or A new Method, and more easie directions for the attaining of it, then ever yet have been published* (London, 1652).

Mauger, Claude, *Mr. Mauger's French Grammar* (London, 1656).

Mauger, Claude, *Claudius Maugers French Grammar* (London, 1658).

Mauger, Claude, *Claudius Mauger's French Grammar* (London, 1662).

Mauger, Claude, *Claudius Mauger's French and English Letters, upon All Subjects, mean and sublime ... The Second Edition* (London, 1676).

Mauger, Claude, *Claudius Mauger's French Grammar* (London, 1682).

Mauger, Claude, *Claudius Mauger's French Grammar* (London, 1686).

Mauger, Claude, *Claudius Mauger's French Grammar* (London, 1688).

Mauger, Claude, *Claudius Mauger's French Grammar* (London, 1689).

Mauger, Claude, and Paul Festeau, *Nouvelle double grammaire francoise-angloise et angloise-francoise par Messrs. Claude Mauger et Paul Festeau* (The Hague, 1693).

Maupas, Charles, *A French grammar and syntaxe contayning most exact and certaine rule, for the pronunciation, orthography, construction, and use of the French language* (London, 1634).

Meurier, Gabriel, *Traicté pour apprendre a parler Françoys et Angloys* (Rouen, 1553).

Meurier, Gabriel, *Familiare communications no leasse proppre then verrie proffytable to the Inglishe nation desirous and nedinge the Frenche language* (Antwerp, 1563).

Meyer, Albrecht, *Certaine briefe, and speciall Instructions for Gentlemen, merchants, students, souldiers, marriners, &c. Employed in services abrode, or anie way occasioned to converse in the kingdomes, and governementes of forren Princes*, trans. Philip Jones (London, 1589).

Meyerstein, E. H. W. (ed.), *Adventures by Sea of Edward Coxere* (Oxford: Clarendon, 1945).

Miège, Guy, *A New French Grammar; or, a New Method for Learning of the French Tongue* (London, 1678).

Miège, Guy, *A dictionary of barbarous French. Or, a collection, by way of alphabet, of obsolete, provincial, mis-spelt, and made words in French* (London, 1679).

Miège, Guy, *A new dictionary French and English, with another English and French; According to the Present Use, and Modern Orthography of the French* (London, 1679).

Miège, Guy, *A new cosmography, or, Survey of the whole world* (London, 1682).

Miège, Guy, *A Short and Easie French Grammar, Fitted For All Sorts of Learners* (London, 1682).

Miège, Guy, *Nouvelle Methode Pour Apprendre l'Anglois* (London, 1685).

Miège, Guy, *The Great French Dictionary* (London, 1688).

Miège, Guy, *A complete history of the late revolution from the first rise of it to this present time* (London, 1691).

Miège, Guy, *Methode Abbregee pour Apprendre l'Anglois* (London, 1698).

Miège, Guy, *Miege's Last and Best French Grammar* (London, 1698).

Miège, Guy, and Abel Boyer, *Grammaire angloise-françoise, par Mrs. Miège & Boyer, contenant une méthode claire & facile pour acquérir en peu de temps l'usage de l'Anglois* (Lyons, 1779).

Misson, Maximilien, *A New Voyage to Italy*, 2 vols. (London, 1695).

Misson, Maximilien, *M. Misson's Memoirs and Observations in his travels over England* (London, 1719).

Monga, Luigi, and Chris Hassel (eds.), *Travels through France and Italy (1647–1647)* (Geneva: Slatkine, 1987).

Moryson, Fynes, *An Itinerary written by Fynes Moryson Gent. First in the latine Tongue, and then translated By him into English: containing his ten yeeres travell through the twelve dominions of Germany, Bohmerland, Sweitzerland, Netherland, Denmarke, Poland, Italy, Turky, France, England, Scotland, and Ireland* (London, 1617).

Mulcaster, Richard, *Positions wherin those primitive circumstance be examined, which are necessarie for the training up of children, either for skill in their booke, or health in their bodie* (London, 1581).

Mulcaster, Richard, *The first part of the elementarie which entreateth chefelie of the right writing of our English tung* (London, 1582).

Nashe, Thomas, *The Unfortunate Traveller*, in J. B. Steane (ed.), *The Unfortunate Traveller and Other Works* (London: Penguin, 1985).

Offelen, Heinrich, *A Double Grammar for Germans To Learn English; and for English-Men To Learn the German-Tongue* (London, 1687).

Oudin, César, *A grammar Spanish and English: or A briefe and compendious method, teaching to reade, write, speake, and pronounce the Spanish tongue* (London, 1622).

Owen, G. Dynfallt (ed.), *HMC Salisbury*, part XXI (1609–1612). (London: Her Majesty's Stationery Office, 1970), pp. 104–13.

Page, William (ed.), *Letters of Denization and Acts of Naturalization for Aliens in England, 1509–1603* (Lymington: Huguenot Society of London, 1893).

Palmer, Thomas, *An Essay of the Meanes how to make our Trauailes, into forraine Countries, the more profitable and honourable* (London, 1606).

Paravicino, Pietro, *Choice Proverbs and Dialogues, in Italian and English, Also, Delightfull Stories and Apophthegms, taken out of Famous Guicciardine* (London, 1660).

Paravicino, Pietro, *The true idioma of the Italian tongue* (London, 1660).

Paravicino, Pietro, *Choice phrases, set forth in questions and answers in Italian, rendered into English* (London, 1662).

Peacham, Henry, *The Truth of our Times: Revealed out of one Mans Experience, by way of Essay* (London, 1638).

Pears, Steuart A. (ed.), *The Correspondence of Sir Philip Sidney and Hubert Languet* (London: William Pickering, 1845).

Pellisson, Paul, *A history of the French Academy, Erected at Paris by the late Famous Cardinal de Richelieu, and consisting of the most refined Wits of that Nation* (London, 1657).

Perceval, Richard/John Minsheu, *A Spanish Grammar, first collected and published by Richard Percivale Gent.* (London, 1599).

Perceval, Richard/John Minsheu, *A dictionary in Spanish and English: first published into the English tongue by Ric. Perciuale Gent* (London, 1623).

Powell, Edgard (ed.), *The Travels and Life of Sir Thomas Hoby, Knight of Bisham Abbey: Written by himself, 1547–1564* (London: Royal Historical Society, 1902).

Ray, John, *Observations Topographical, Moral, & Physiological; Made in a Journey Through part of the Low-Countries, Germany, Italy, and France: With A Catalogue of Plants not Native of England, found Spontaneously growing in those Parts, and their Virtues... Whereunto is added A brief Account of Francis Willughby Esq; his Voyage through a great part of Spain* (London, 1673).

Raymond, John, *Il Mercurio Italico. Communicating a voyage made through Italy in the yeares 1646 & 1647* (London, 1648).

Richardson, Edward, *Anglo-Belgica. D'Engelsche Ende Nederduytsche Academy/The English and Netherdutch Academy* (Amsterdam, 1698).

Rossi, Giacomo, *Le maitre aisé & rejouissant; Ou nouvelle methode agreable pour apprendre sans peine la langue italienne* (London, 1710?).

Scott, William, *An Essay of Drapery: or, the Compleate Citizen* (London, 1635).

Sherwood, Robert, *The French Tutour* (London, 1625).

Sherwood, Robert, *The French Tutour* (London, 1634).

Smith, Logan Pearsall (ed.), *The Life and Letters of Sir Henry Wotton*, 2 vols (Oxford: Clarendon, 1907).

Spalding, Augustine, *Dialogues in the English and Malaiane languages* (London, 1614).

Sprat, Thomas, *The History of the Royal-society of London, For the Improving of Natural Knowledge* (London, 1667).

Stepney, William, *The Spanish schoole-master* (London, 1591).

Stepney, William, *The Spanish schoole-maister* (London, 1619).

Stepney, William, *The Spanish schoole-maister* (London, 1620).

Stevens, John, *A new Spanish and English Dictionary: Collected from the Best Spanish Authors, Both Ancient and Modern... The Whole by Captain John Stevens* (London, 1706).

Swift, Jonathan, 'A proposal for correcting, improving, and ascertaining the English tongue', in *The Works of Jonathan Swift* (Dublin, 1751), vol. 1, pp. 108–208.

Thomas, William, *Principal Rules of the Italian Grammar with a Dictionarie for the better understandyng of Boccace Petrarcha, and Dante, gathered into this tongue by Willyam Thomas* (London, 1550).

Torriano, Giovanni, *The Italian Tutor, or a new and most compleat Italian Grammer* (London, 1640).

Torriano, Giovanni, *Della Lingua Toscana-Romana* (London, 1657).

Torriano, Giovanni, *The Italian Reviv'd: Or, the Introduction to the Italian Tongue* (London, 1673).

van Heldoren, J. G., *An English and Nether-dutch Dictionary* (Amsterdam, 1675).

Vitkus, Daniel J. (ed.), *Piracy, Slavery, and Redemption: Barbary Captivity Narratives from Early Modern England* (New York: Columbia University Press, 2001).

Williams, Roger, *A Key into the Language of America: or, An help to the Language of the Natives in that part of America, called New-England* (London, 1643).

Wilson, Thomas, *The Arte of Rhetorique, for the use of all suche as are studious of Eloquence, sette forth in English, by Thomas Wilson* (London, 1553).

Wodroephe, John, *The spared houres of a souldier in his travels. Or The True Marrowe of the French Tongue, wherein is truely treated (by ordre) the Nine Parts of Speech. Together, with two rare, and excellent Bookes of Dialogues . . .* (Dordrecht, 1623).

Yeames, A. H. S., 'The Grand Tour of an Elizabethan', *Papers of the British School at Rome* 7 (1914), pp. 92–113.

Yonge, Nicholas, *Musica Transalpina* (London, 1588).

(iv) Newspapers and Periodicals

Athenian Gazette or Casuistical Mercury
British Mercury
Collection for Improvement of Husbandry and Trade
Daily Courant
English Post with News Foreign and Domestick
Flying Post or The Post Master
Kingdomes Intelligencer
London Gazette
Loyal Protestant and True Domestick Intelligence
New State of Europe Both As to Publick Transactions and Learning
Post Boy
Post Man and the Historical Account
Spectator
True Domestick Intelligence or News Both from City and Country

2. Select Bibliography of Secondary Works

Adair, E. R., 'William Thomas: A Forgotten Clerk of the Privy Council', in R. W. Seton-Watson (ed.), *Tudor Studies* (London: Longmans, 1924), pp. 133–60.

Alford, Stephen, *The Watchers: A Secret History of the Reign of Elizabeth I* (London: Penguin, 2013).

Alston, R. C., *A Bibliography of the English Language from the Invention of Printing to the Year 1800, vol. II: Polyglot Dictionaries and Grammars* (Ilkley: Janus, 1967).

Amato, Antonio, Francesca Maria Andreoni, Lilia Poggi Cesare, and Rita Salvi, *Teoria e pratica glottodidattica nell'opera di Claudius Holyband (alias Claude de Sainliens)*, (Rome: Bulzoni, 1983).

Amelang, James S., 'The Walk of the Town: Modeling the Early Modern City', in Kimberly Lynn and Erin Kathleen Rowe (eds.), *The Early Modern Hispanic World: Transnational and Interdisciplinary Approaches* (Cambridge: Cambridge University Press, 2017), pp. 45–61.

Ansell, Richard, 'Educational Travel in Protestant Families from Post-Restoration Ireland', *Historical Journal*, 58:4 (2015), pp. 931–58.

Ansell, Richard, 'Foubert's Academy: British and Irish Elite Formation in Seventeenth- And Eighteenth-Century Paris and London', in Rosemary Sweet, Gerrit Verhoeven, and Sarah Goldsmith (eds), *Beyond the Grand Tour: Northern Metropolises and Early Modern Travel Behaviour* (London, 2017), pp. 46–64.

Archer, Ian W., *The Pursuit of Stability: Social Relations in Elizabethan London* (Cambridge: Cambridge University Press, 1991).

Auger, Peter, 'Fashioned through Use: Jacques Bellot's *Rules* and its Successors', *History of European Ideas* 42 (2016), pp. 651–64.

Ayres-Bennett, Wendy, *A History of the French Language through Texts* (Routledge: London and New York, 1996).

Ayres-Bennett, Wendy, *Sociolinguistic Variation in Seventeenth-Century France: Methodology and Case Studies* (Cambridge: Cambridge University Press, 2004).

Barber, Charles, *Early Modern English* (Edinburgh: Edinburgh University Press, 1997).

Barker, S. K., '"Newes lately come": European News Books in English Translation', in S. K. Barker and Brenda M. Hosington (eds.), *Renaissance Cultural Crossroads: Translation, Print and Culture in Britain, 1473–1640* (Leiden and Boston, MA: Brill, 2013), pp. 227–44.

Barry, Jonathan, 'Literacy and Literature in Popular Culture: Reading and Writing in Historical Perspective', in Tim Harris (ed.) *Popular Culture in England, c.1500–1850* (Basingstoke: Macmillan, 1995), pp. 73–94.

Bartlett, Kenneth R., *The English in Italy 1525–1558: A Study in Culture and Politics* (Geneva: Centro Interuniversitario di Ricerche sul 'Viaggio in Italia', 1991).

Bartlett, Kenneth R., 'Travel and Translation: The English and Italy in the Sixteenth Century', *Annali d'Italianistica* 14 (1996), pp. 493–506.

Bartlett, Kenneth R., 'Thomas Hoby, Translator, Traveler', in Carmine G. Di Biase (ed.), *Travel and Translation in the Early Modern Period* (Amsterdam and New York: Rodopi, 2006).

Bately, Janet, 'Miège and the Development of the English Dictionary', in John Considine (ed.), *Ashgate Critical Essays on Early English Lexicographers, vol. 4: The Seventeenth century* (Aldershot: Ashgate, 2012), pp. 453–62.

Beal, Jan C., '*À la Mode de Paris*: Linguistic Patriotism and Francophobia in 18th-Century Britain', in Carol Percy and Mary Catherine Davidson (eds.), *The Languages of Nation: Attitudes and Norms* (Bristol, Buffalo, NY, and Toronto: Multilingual Matters, 2012), pp. 141–54.

Beal, Peter, 'Notions in Garrison: The Seventeenth-Century Commonplace Book', in W. Speed Hill (ed.) *New Ways of Looking at Old Texts: Papers of the Renaissance English Text Society, 1985–1991*, (Binghamton, NY: RETS, 1993), pp. 131–4.

Beck-Busse, Gabriele, 'À propos d'une histoire des 'Grammaires des Dames'. Réflexions théoriques et approches empiriques', *Documents pour l'histoire du français langue étrangère ou seconde* 47–48 (2012), online at https://dhfles.revues.org/3121.

Becker, Monika, '"Yf ye wyll bergayne wullen cloth or othir merchandise..." Bargaining in Early Modern Language Teaching Textbooks', *Journal of Historical Pragmatics* 3 (2002), pp. 273–97.

Bellorini, Mariagrazia, '"He that travelleth into a country...goeth to school": il viaggio di John North verso l'Italia e ritorno (1575-1579)', *Journal of Anglo-Italian Studies* 6 (2001), pp. 13–33.

Bennett, H. S., *English Books and Readers, 1475 to 1557: Being a Study in the History of the Book Trade from Caxton to the Incorporation of the Stationers' Company* (Cambridge: Cambridge University Press, 1952).

Bennett, H. S., *English Books and Readers, 1558 to 1603: Being a Study in the History of the Book Trade in the Reign of Elizabeth I* (Cambridge: Cambridge University Press, 1965).

Bennett, H. S., *English Books and Readers, 1603 to 1640: Being a Study in the History of the Book Trade in the Reigns of James I and Charles I* (Cambridge: Cambridge University Press, 1970).

Bepler, Jill, 'Travelling and Posterity: The Archive, the Library and the Cabinet', in Rainer Babel and Werner Paravicini (eds.), *Grand Tour: Adeliges Reisen und Europäische Kultur vom 14. bis zum 18. Jahrhundert* (Ostfildern: Jan Thorbecke Verlag, 2005), pp. 191–203.

Berec, Laurent, 'Claude de Sainliens, linguiste et pédagogue huguenot, ou le procès de la culture populaire dans l'Angleterre élisabéthaine', *Recherches anglaises et nord-américaines* 39 (2006), pp. 33–40.

Berec, Laurent, 'L'École de Claude de Sainliens', in Anne Dunan-Page and Marie-Christine Munoz-Teulié (eds.), *Les Huguenots dans les Îles britanniques de la Renaissance aux Lumières: Ecrits religieux et représentations* (Paris: Honoré Champion, 2008), pp. 89–99.

Berec, Laurent, *Claude de Sainliens: un huguenot bourbonnais au temps de Shakespeare* (Paris: Orizons, 2012).

Bergeron, David M., *Textual Patronage in English Drama, 1570–1640* (Aldershot: Ashgate, 2006).

Binns, James W., *Intellectual Culture in Elizabethan and Jacobean England: The Latin Writings of the Age* (Leeds: Francis Cairns, 1990).

Bischoff, Bernhard, 'The Study of Foreign Languages in the Middle Ages', *Speculum* 36 (1971), pp. 209–24.

Bjurman, Monica, *The Phonology of Jacques Bellot's Le Maistre d'Escole Anglois (1580)* (Stockholm: Almqvist and Wiksell, 1977).

Black, Jeremy, *The British Abroad: The Grand Tour in the Eighteenth Century* (Stroud: Allan Sutton, 1992).

Blair, Ann, 'Note Taking as an Art of Transmission', *Critical Inquiry* 31 (2004), pp. 85–107.

Blair, Ann, *Too Much to Know: Managing Scholarly Information before the Modern Age* (New Haven, CT, and London: Yale University Press, 2010).

Blank, Paula, *Broken English: Dialects and the Politics of Language in Renaissance Writings* (London and New York: Routledge, 1996).

Blayney, Peter W. M., *The Bookshops in Paul's Cross Churchyard* (London: Bibliographical Society, 1990).

Bonin, Thérèse, and Josette Wilburn, 'Teaching French Conversation: A Lesson from the Fourteenth Century', *The French Review* 51 (1977), pp. 188–96.

Bös, Birte, '*What do you lacke? what is it you buy?* Early Modern English Service Encounters', in Susan Fitzmaurice and Irma Taavitsainen (eds.), *Methods in Historical Pragmatics* (Berlin and New York: Mouton de Gruyter, 2007), pp. 219–40.

Boulton, Jeremy, 'Wage Labour in Seventeenth-Century London', *Economic History Review* 49 (1996), pp. 268–90.

Bourchenin, P.-Daniel, *Étude sur les académies protestantes en France au XVIe et au XVIIe siècle* (Paris: Grassart, 1882).

Bourdieu, Pierre, *Language and Symbolic Power*, trans. and ed. John B. Thompson (Cambridge: Polity, 1992).

Bourland, Caroline B., '*The Spanish Schoole-master* and the Polyglot Derivatives of Noel de Berlaimont's *Vocabulare*', *Revue Hispanique* 81 (1933), pp. 283–318.

Boutcher, Warren, 'Vernacular Humanism in the Sixteenth Century', in Jill Kraye (ed.), *The Cambridge Companion to Renaissance Humanism* (Cambridge: Cambridge University Press, 1996), pp. 189–202.

Boutcher, Warren, 'A French Dexterity, & an Italian Confidence: New Documents on John Florio, Learned strangers and Protestant Humanist Study of Modern Languages in Renaissance England from *c*.1547 to *c*.1625', *Reformation* 2 (1997), pp. 39–109.

Boutier, Jean, 'Le 'Grand Tour' des élites britanniques dans l'Europe des Lumières: La Réinvention permanente des traditions', in Marie-Madeleine Martinet, Francis Conte, Annie Molinié, and Jean-Marie Valentin (eds.), *Le Chemin, la route, la voie. Figures de l'imaginaire occidental à l'époque moderne* (Paris: Presses de l'Université Paris-Sorbonne, 2005), p. 225–42.

Boutier, Jean, 'Le Grand Tour des gentilshommes et les académies d'éducation pour la noblesse: France et Italie, XVIe–XVIIIe siècle', in Rainer Babel and Werner Paravicini (eds.), *Grand Tour: Adeliges Reisen und Europäische Kultur vom 14. bis zum 18. Jahrhundert* (Ostfildern: Jan Thorbecke Verlag, 2005), pp. 237–53.

Boutier, Jean, 'Compétence internationale, émergence d'une 'profession' et circulation des savoirs: le tuteur aristocratique dans l'Angleterre du XVIIe siècle', in Maria-Pia Paoli (ed.), *Saperi in movimento* (Pisa: Edizioni della Normale, 2009), pp. 149–77.

Bowden, Caroline, '"For the Glory of God": A Study of the Education of English Catholic Women in Convents in Flanders and France in the First Half of the Seventeenth Century', *Paedagogica Historica: International Journal for the History of Education* 35 (1999), pp. 77–95.

Braddick, Michael J. (ed.) *The Politics of Gesture: Historical Perspectives* (*Past & Present* 203, supplement 4, 2009).

Bremmer, Jan, and Herman Roodenburg (eds.), *A Cultural History of Gesture: From Antiquity to the Present Day* (Cambridge: Polity, 1991).

Breva-Claramonte, Manuel, 'Specialised Lexicography for Learning Spanish in Sixteenth-Century Europe', in Sylvain Auroux (ed.), *History of Linguistics 1999: Selected Papers from the Eighth International Conference on the History of the Language Sciences* (Amsterdam and Philadelphia, PA: John Benjamins, 1999), pp. 83–95.

Brink, Jean R., 'Bathsua Makin: "Most Learned Matron"', *Huntington Library Quarterly* 54 (1991), pp. 313–26.

Brundin, Abigail, and Dunstan Roberts, 'Book Buying and the Grand Tour: The Italian Books at Belton House in Lincolnshire', *The Library* 16 (2015), pp. 61–79.

Bryson, Anna, *From Courtesy to Civility: Changing Codes of Conduct in Early Modern England* (Oxford: Clarendon, 1998).

Buchtel, John A., '"To the Most High and Excellent Prince": Dedicating Books to Henry, Prince of Wales', in Timothy Wilks (ed.), *Prince Henry Revived: Image and Exemplarity in Early Modern England* (Southampton: Paul Holberton, 2007), pp. 104–33.

Burke, Peter, 'Languages and Anti-Languages in Early Modern Italy', *History Workshop Journal* 11 (1981), pp. 24–32.

Burke, Peter, *The Art of Conversation* (Cambridge: Polity, 1993).

Burke, Peter, *The Historical Anthropology of Early Modern Italy: Essays on Perception and Communication* (Cambridge: Cambridge University Press, 1987).

Burke, Peter, '"Heu Domine, Adsunt Turcae": A Sketch for a Social History of Post-Medieval Latin', in Peter Burke, *The Art of Conversation* (Cambridge: Polity, 1993), pp. 34–65.

Burke, Peter, 'A Civil Tongue: Language and Politeness in Early Modern Europe', in Peter Burke, Brian Harrison, Paul Slack (eds.), *Civil Histories: Essays presented to Sir Keith Thomas* (Oxford: Oxford University Press, 2000), pp. 31–48.

Burke, Peter, *Languages and Communities in Early Modern Europe* (Cambridge: Cambridge University Press, 2004).

Burke, Peter, 'Cultures of Translation in Early Modern Europe', in Peter Burke and R. Po-Chi Hsia (eds.), *Cultural Translation in Early Modern Europe* (Cambridge: Cambridge University Press, 2007), pp. 7–38.

Burke, Peter, and R. Po-Chi Hsia (eds.), *Cultural Translation in Early Modern Europe* (Cambridge: Cambridge University Press, 2007).

Burke, Peter, and Roy Porter (eds.), *The Social History of Language* (Cambridge: Cambridge University Press, 1987).

Burke, Peter, and Roy Porter (eds.), *Language, Self, and Society: A Social History of Language* (Cambridge: Polity, 1991).

Burke, Peter, and Roy Porter (eds.), *Languages and Jargons: Contributions to a Social History of Language* (Cambridge: Polity, 1995).

Burrows, Donald, 'George Frideric Handel, 1685-1759' in *Oxford Dictionary of National Biography*, 2007; online, http://www.oxforddnb.com/view/article/12192?docPos=1, accessed 8 July 2013.

Butler, Kathleen, 'Giacomo Castelvetro, 1546-1616', *Italian Studies* 5 (1950), pp. 1–42.

Butterfield, Ardis, *The Familiar Enemy: Chaucer, Language, and Nation in the Hundred Years War* (Oxford: Oxford University Press, 2009).

Buzard, James, 'The Grand Tour and After (1660-1840)', in Peter Hulme and Tim Youngs (eds.), *The Cambridge Companion to Travel Writing* (Cambridge: Cambridge University Press, 2002), pp. 37–52.

Capern, Amanda L., *The Historical Study of Women: England 1500-1700* (Basingstoke and New York: Palgrave Macmillan, 2008).

Capp, Bernard, *English Almanacs, 1500-1800: Astrology and the Popular Press* (Ithaca, NY: Cornell University Press, 1979).

Capp, Bernard, *When Gossips Meet: Women, Family, and Neighbourhood in Early Modern England* (Oxford: Oxford University Press, 2003).

Caravolas, Jean-Antoine, *La Didactique des langues: précis d'histoire I, 1450-1700* (Montreal: Les Presses de l'Université de Montréal, 1994).

Carey, Daniel, *Continental Travel and Journeys beyond Europe in the Early Modern Period: An Overlooked Connection* (London: Hakluyt Society, 2009).

Carroll, Clare, 'Humanism and English Literature in the Fifteenth And Sixteenth Centuries', in Jill Kraye (ed.), *The Cambridge Companion to Renaissance Humanism* (Cambridge: Cambridge University Press, 1996), pp. 246–68.

Caspari, Fritz, *Humanism and the Social Order in Tudor England* (Chicago: University of Chicago Press, 1954).

Chambrun, Clara Longworth, *Giovanni Florio: un apôtre de la Renaissance en Angleterre à l'époque de Shakespeare* (Paris: Payot, 1921).

Chaney, Edward, *The Grand Tour and the Great Rebellion: Richard Lassels and 'The Voyage of Italy' in the Seventeenth Century* (Geneva: Slatkine, 1985).

Chaney, Edward, *The Evolution of the Grand Tour: Anglo-Italian Cultural Relations since the Renaissance* (London and Portland, OR: Frank Cass, 1998).

Chaney, Edward, and Timothy Wilks, *The Jacobean Grand Tour: Early Stuart Travellers in Europe* (London: I. B. Tauris, 2013).

Charlton, Kenneth, *Education in Renaissance England* (London: Routledge and Kegan Paul, 1965).

Chartier, Roger, 'From Texts to Manners. A Concept and its Books: *Civilité* between Aristocratic Distinction and Popular Appropriation', in *The Cultural Uses of Print in Early Modern France*, trans. Lydia G. Cochrane (Princeton, NJ: Princeton University Press, 1987), pp. 71–109.

Chartier, Roger, 'Reading Matter and 'Popular' Reading: From the Renaissance to the Seventeenth Century', in *A History of Reading in the West*, trans. Lydia G. Cochrane (Cambridge: Polity, 1999), pp. 269–83.

Chartres, Richard, and David Vermont, *A Brief History of Gresham College, 1597–1997* (London: Gresham College, 1997).

Chaudhuri, K. N., *The English East India Company: The Study of an Early Joint-Stock Company, 1600–1640* (London: Frank Cass, 1965).

Chomsky, Noam, *Aspects of the Theory of Syntax* (Cambridge, MA: The MIT Press, 1965).

Clark, Peter, *The English Alehouse: A Social History 1200–1830* (London and New York: Longman, 1983).

Clark, Peter, *British Clubs and Societies 1580–1800: The Origins of an Associational World* (Oxford: Clarendon, 2000).

Claydon, Tony, *Europe and the Making of England, 1660–1760* (Cambridge: Cambridge University Press, 2007).

Cockayne, Emily, *Hubbub: Filth, Noise & Stench in England 1600–1770* (New Haven, CT, and London: Yale University Press, 2007).

Cohen, Elizabeth S., 'Back Talk: Two Prostitutes' Voices from Rome *c.*1600', *Early Modern Women: An Interdisciplinary Journal* 2 (2007), pp. 95–126.

Cohen, Michèle, 'The Grand Tour: Constructing the English Gentleman in Eighteenth-Century France', *History of Education* 21 (1992), pp. 241–157.

Cohen, Michèle, *Fashioning Masculinity: National Identity and Language in the Eighteenth Century* (London and New York: Routledge, 1996).

Cohen, Michèle, 'French Conversation or "Glittering Gibberish"? Learning French in Eighteenth-Century England', in Natasha Glaisyer and Sara Pennell (eds.), *Didactic Literature in England 1500–1800: Expertise Constructed* (Aldershot: Ashgate, 2003), pp. 99–117.

Cohen, Paul, 'Courtly French, Learned Latin, and Peasant Patois: The Making of a National Language in Early Modern France' (unpublished PhD thesis, Princeton University, 2001).

Cohen, Paul, 'Torture and Translation in the Multilingual Courtrooms of Early Modern France', *Renaissance Quarterly* 69 (2016), pp. 899–939.

Cohen, Tom, and Lesley Twomey (eds.), *Spoken Word and Social Practice: Orality (1400–1700)* (Leiden: Brill, 2015).

Coldiron, A. E. B., *Printers without Borders: Translation and Textuality in the Renaissance* (Cambridge: Cambridge University Press, 2015).

Colley, Linda, *Captives: Britain, Empire and the World, 1600–1850* (London: Jonathan Cape, 2002).

Colley, Linda, *The Ordeal of Elizabeth Marsh: A Woman in World History* (London: HarperPress, 2007).

Considine, John, 'Narrative and Persuasion in Early Modern English Dictionaries and Phrasebooks', *Review of English Studies* 52 (2001), pp. 195–206.

Considine, John, *Dictionaries in Early Modern Europe: Lexicography and the Making of Heritage* (Cambridge: Cambridge University Press, 2008).

Considine, John, *Academy Dictionaries 1600-1800* (Cambridge: Cambridge University Press, 2014).

Considine, John, *Small Dictionaries and Curiosity: Lexicography and Fieldwork in Post-Medieval Europe* (Oxford: Oxford University Press, 2017).

Cooper, Lisa H., 'Urban Utterances: Merchants, Artisans, and the Alphabet in Caxton's *Dialogues in French and English*', *New Medieval Literatures* 7 (2005), pp. 127-62.

Cooper-Rompato, Christine, 'Traveling Tongues: Foreign-Language Phrase Lists in Wynkyn de Worde and William Wey', *The Chaucer Review* 46 (2011), pp. 223-36.

Corens, Liesbeth, 'Catholic Nuns and English Identities: English Protestant Travellers on the English Convents in the Low Countries, 1660–1730', *Recusant History* 30 (2011), pp. 441–59.

Corens, Liesbeth, *Confessional Mobility and English Catholics in Counter-Reformation Europe* (Oxford: Oxford University Press, 2019).

Corfield, Penelope (ed.), *Language, History and Class* (Oxford, 1991).

Corfis, Ivy A., *Diego de San Pedro's Tractado de Amores de Arnalte y Lucenda* (London: Tamesis, 1985).

Cormier, Monique C., and Herberto Fernandez, 'A Study of the Outside Matter in 17th-Century French-English Dictionaries', in Elisa Corino, Carla Morello, Cristina Onesti (eds.), *Atti del XII Congresso Internazionale di Lessicografia*, vol. 1 (Alessandria: Edizioni dell'Orso, 2006), pp. 49–59.

Cormier, Monique C., and Herberto Fernandez, 'Standing on the Shoulders of Giants: Abel Boyer's Innovations in English-French Lexicography', in John Considine (ed.), *Ashgate Critical Essays on Early English Lexicographers, vol. 4: The Seventeenth Century* (Aldershot: Ashgate, 2012), pp. 463–93.

Cosandey, Fanny (ed.), *Dire et vivre l'ordre social en France sous l'Ancien Régime* (Paris: École des Hautes Études en Sciences Sociales, 2005).

Cottret, Bernard, *The Huguenots in England: Immigration and Settlement c.1550–1700*, trans. Peregrine and Adriana Stevenson (Cambridge: Cambridge University Press, 1991).

Coupland, Nikolas and Adam Jaworski (eds.), *Sociolinguistics: A Reader and Coursebook* (Basingstoke: Palgrave, 1997).

Cowan, Brian, 'The Rise of the Coffeehouse Reconsidered', *Historical Journal* 47 (March 2004), pp. 21–46.

Cowan, Brian, *The Social Life of Coffee: The Emergence of the British Coffeehouse* (New Haven, CT, and London: Yale University Press, 2005).

Cowan, Brian, 'Public Spaces, Knowledge, and Sociability', in Frank Trentmann (ed.), *The Oxford Handbook of the History of Consumption* (Oxford: Oxford University Press, 2012), pp. 251–66.

Cremona, Joseph, '"Accioché ognuno le possa intendere": The Use of Italian as a Lingua Franca on the Barbary Coast of the Seventeenth Century. Evidence from the English', *Journal of Anglo-Italian Studies* 5 (1997), pp. 52–69.

Cressy, David, 'Educational Opportunity in Tudor and Stuart England', *History of Education Quarterly* 16 (1976), pp. 301–20.

Cressy, David, 'A Drudgery of Schoolmasters: The Teaching Profession in Elizabethan and Stuart England', in Wilfrid Prest (ed.), *The Professions in Early Modern England* (London: Croom Helm, 1987), pp. 129–53.

Crick, Julia, and Alexandra Walsham (eds.), *The Uses of Script and Print, 1300–1700* (Cambridge: Cambridge University Press, 2004).

Crowley, Tony, *Wars of Words: The Politics of Language in Ireland 1537–2004* (Oxford: Oxford University Press, 2005).

Culpeper, Jonathan, 'Historical Sociopragmatics: An Introduction', *Journal of Historical Pragmatics* 10 (2009), pp. 179–86.

Culpeper, Jonathan, and Merja Kytö, *Early Modern English Dialogues: Spoken Interaction as Writing* (Cambridge: Cambridge University Press, 2010).

Curtin, Michael, 'A Question of Manners: Status and Gender in Etiquette and Courtesy', *Journal of Modern History* 57 (1985), pp. 395–423.

Curtis, Mark H., *Oxford and Cambridge in Transition, 1558–1642: An Essay on Changing Relations between the English Universities and English Society* (Oxford: Clarendon, 1959).

Cust, Richard, 'Charles I's Noble Academy', *The Seventeenth Century* 29:4 (2014), pp. 346–53.

Dakhlia, Jocelyne, *Lingua Franca: histoire d'une language métisse en Méditerranée* (Paris: Actes Sud, 2008).

Dall'Aglio, Stefano, Brian Richardson, and Massimo Rospocher (eds.), *Voices and Texts in Early Modern Italian Society* (London and New York: Routledge, 2017).

Davis, Natalie Zemon, *Trickster Travels: A Sixteenth-Century Muslim between Worlds* (London: Faber, 2007).

Davis, Natalie Zemon, 'Creole Languages and their Uses: The Example of Colonial Suriname', *Historical Research* 82 (2009), pp. 268–84.

Davis, Robert C., *Christian Slaves, Muslim Masters: White Slavery in the Mediterranean, the Barbary Coast, and Italy, 1500–1800* (Basingstoke and New York: Palgrave Macmillan, 2003).

Davis, Robert C., *Holy War and Human Bondage: Tales of Christian-Muslim Slavery in the Early Modern Mediterranean* (Santa Barbara, CA: Praeger, 2009).

de Clercq, Jan, Nico Lioce, and Pierre Swiggers (eds.), *Grammaire et enseignement du français, 1500–1700* (Leuven: Peeters, 2000).

de Groot, Jerome, 'Every one teacheth after thyr owne fantasie: French Language Instruction', in Kathryn M. Moncrief and Kathryn R. McPherson (eds.), *Performing Pedagogy in Early Modern England: Gender, Instruction, and Performance* (Farnham: Ashgate, 2011), pp. 33–51.

DeJongh, William F. J., *Western Language Manuals of the Renaissance* (Albuquerque, NM: University of New Mexico Press, 1949).

DeMolen, Richard L., 'Richard Mulcaster and the Profession of Teaching in Sixteenth-Century England', *Journal of the History of Ideas* 35 (1974), pp. 121–9.

Dent, Keith, 'Travel as Education: The English Landed Classes in the Eighteenth Century', *Educational Studies* 1 (1975), pp. 171–80.

de Vivo, Filippo, *Information and Communication in Venice: Rethinking Early Modern Politics* (Oxford: Oxford University Press, 2007).

DeWispelare, Daniel, *Multilingual Subjects: On Standard English, its Speakers, and Others in the Long Eighteenth Century* (Philadelphia, PA: University of Pennsylvania Press, 2017).

Di Biase, Carmine G. (ed.), *Travel and Translation in the Early Modern Period* (Amsterdam and New York: Rodopi, 2006).

Dubcovsky, Alejandra, *Informed Power: Communication in the Early American South* (Cambridge, MA: Harvard University Press, 2016).

Dumont, J., *Histoire de l'Académie de Saumur depuis sa fondation en 1600 par Duplessis-Mornay jusqu'à sa suppression en 1685* (Angers: Société Académique de Maine et Loire, 1862).

Dunn, Kevin, *Pretexts of Authority: The Rhetoric of Authorship in the Renaissance Preface* (Stanford, CA: Stanford University Press, 1994).

Duranti, Alessandro (ed.), *A Companion to Linguistic Anthropology* (Oxford, 2004).

Dursteler, Eric, *Venetians in Constantinople: Nation, Identity, and Coexistence in the Early Modern Mediterranean* (Baltimore, MD: The Johns Hopkins University Press, 2006).

Dursteler, Eric, 'Speaking in Tongues: Language and Communication in the Early Modern Mediterranean', *Past & Present* 217 (2012), pp. 47–77.

Early Modern Research Group, 'Commonwealth: The Social, Cultural, and Conceptual Contexts of an Early Modern Keyword', *Historical Journal* 54 (2011), pp. 659–87.

Eccles, Mark, 'Claudius Hollyband and the Earliest French-English Dictionaries', *Studies in Philology* 83 (1986), pp. 51–61.

Einstein, Lewis, *The Italian Renaissance in England* (New York: Columbia University Press, 1902).

Elias, Norbert, *The Civilizing Process, vol. 1: The History of Manners*, trans. Edmund Jephcott (Oxford: Blackwell, 1969).

Eliav-Feldon, Miriam, *Renaissance Impostors and Proofs of Identity* (Basingstoke: Palgrave Macmillan, 2012).

Elspaß, Stephan, 'A Twofold View "from Below": New Perspectives on Language Histories and Language Historiographies', in Stephan Elspaß, Nils Langer, Joachim Scharloth, and Wim Vandenbussche (eds.), *Germanic Language Histories 'from Below'* (Berlin and New York: de Gruyter, 2007).

Engel, William Edward, 'Knowledge that Counted: Italian Phrase-Books and Dictionaries in Elizabethan England', *Annali d'Italianistica* 14 (1996), pp. 507–22.

Escribano, Francisco Javier Sánchez, 'Portuguese in England in the Sixteenth and Seventeenth Centuries', *Sederi* 16 (2006), pp. 109–32.

Escribano, Francisco Javier Sánchez, 'Los viajes de James Howell', in *Actas del IX simposio de la Sociedad Española de Literatura General y Comparada, tomo II: La parodia/El viaje imaginario* (1994), pp. 501–508.

Eskin, Catherine R., 'The Rei(g)ning of Women's Tongues in English Books of Instruction and Rhetorics', in Barbara J. Whitehead (ed.), *Women's Education in Early Modern Europe: A History, 1500–1800* (New York and London: Garland, 1999), pp. 101–32.

Farrer, Lucy E., *La Vie et les œuvres de Claude de Sainliens alias Claudius Holyband* (Geneva: Slatkine Reprints, 1971).

Fausz, J. Frederick, 'Middlemen in Peace and War: Virginia's Earliest Indian Interpreters, 1608–1632', *The Virginia Magazine of History and Biography* 95 (1987), pp. 41–64.

Fishman, J. A., 'The Sociology of Language', in Pier Paolo Giglioli (ed.), *Language and Social Context: Selected Readings* (Harmondsworth: Penguin, 1980), pp. 45–58.

Fleck, Andy, '"Ick verstaw you niet": Performing Foreign Tongues on the Early Modern English Stage', *Medieval & Renaissance Drama in England* 20 (2007), pp. 204–21.

Fleming, Juliet, 'The French Garden: An Introduction to Women's French', *ELH: English Literary History* 56 (1989), pp. 19–51.

Fleming, Juliet, 'Dictionary English and the Female Tongue', in Richard Burt and John Michael Archer (eds.), *Enclosure Acts: Sexuality, Property, and Culture in Early Modern England* (Ithaca, NY, and London: Cornell University Press, 1994), pp. 290–309.

Fletcher, Anthony, *Gender, Sex and Subordination in England 1500–1800* (New Haven, CT, and London: Yale University Press, 1995).

Fontaine, Laurence, *L'Économie morale: pauvreté, crédit et confiance dans l'Europe préindustrielle* (Paris: Gallimard, 2008).

Fox, Adam, *Oral and Literate Culture in England 1500–1700* (Oxford: Clarendon, 2000).

Fox, Adam, and Daniel Woolf (eds.), *The Spoken Word: Oral Culture in Britain 1500–1850* (Manchester and New York: Manchester University Press, 2002).

Frantz, David O., 'Negotiating Florio's *A Worlde of Wordes*', reprinted in Roderick McConchie (ed.), *Ashgate Critical Essays On Early English Lexicographers, vol. 3: The Sixteenth Century* (Aldershot: Ashgate, 2012), pp. 317–48.

Frye, Susan, *Pens and Needles: Women's Textualities in Early Modern England* (Philadelphia, PA: University of Pennsylvania Press, 2010).

Gallagher, John, 'Encounters of Language between English and Italian, *c*.1550–1615' (unpublished MPhil dissertation, University of Cambridge, 2010).

Gallagher, John, 'Vernacular Language-Learning in Early Modern England', unpublished PhD dissertation, University of Cambridge (2014).

Gallagher, John, '"Ungratefull Tuscans": Teaching Italian in Early Modern England', *The Italianist* 36:3 (2016), pp. 392–413.

Gallagher, John, 'The Italian London of John North: Cultural Contact and Linguistic Encounter in Early Modern England', *Renaissance Quarterly*, 70 (2017), pp. 88–131.

Gallagher, John, 'Language and Education on the Grand Tour of Sir Philip Perceval, 1676–9', in Helmut Glück, Mark Häberlein, and Andreas Flurschütz da Cruz (eds.), *Adel und Mehrsprachigkeit in der Frühen Neuzeit. Ziele, Formen und Praktiken des Erwerbs und Gebrauchs von Fremdsprachen* (Wolfenbüttel, forthcoming, 2019).

Gallagher, John, 'Language-Learning, Orality, and Multilingualism in Early Modern Anglophone Narratives of Mediterranean Captivity', *Renaissance Studies* (forthcoming, 2019).

Gallagher, John, '"To heare it by mouth": Speech and Accent in Early Modern Language-Learning', *Huntington Library Quarterly* (forthcoming, 2019).

Gamberini, Spartaco, *Lo studio dell'italiano in Inghilterra nel '500 e nel '600* (Florence: G. D'Anna, 1970).

Games, Alison, *The Web of Empire: English Cosmopolitans in an Age of Expansion 1560–1660* (Oxford: Oxford University Press, 2008).

Garrioch, David, 'Sounds of the City: The Soundscape of Early Modern European Towns', *Urban History* 30 (2003), pp. 5–25.

Gasper, Julia, 'The Literary Legend of Sir Thomas Gresham', in Ann Saunders (ed.), *The Royal Exchange* (London: London Topographical Society, 1997), pp. 99–107.

Gauci, Perry, *Emporium of the World: The Merchants of London 1660–1800* (London and New York: Hambledon Continuum, 2007).

Ghobrial, John-Paul, *The Whispers of Cities: Information Flows in Istanbul, Paris, and London in the Age of William Trumbull* (Oxford: Oxford University Press, 2013).

Giglioli, Pier Paolo (ed.), *Language and Social Context: Selected Readings* (Harmondsworth: Penguin, 1980).

Glaisyer, Natasha, 'Readers, Correspondents and Communities: John Houghton's *A Collection for Improvement of Husbandry and Trade* (1692–1703)', in Alexandra Shepard and Phil Withington (eds.), *Communities in Early Modern England: Networks, Place, Rhetoric* (Manchester: Manchester University Press, 2000), pp. 235–51.

Glaisyer, Natasha, and Sara Pennell (eds.), *Didactic Literature in England, 1500–1800: Expertise Constructed* (Aldershot: Ashgate, 2003).

Glück, Helmut, *Deutsch als Fremdsprache in Europa vom Mittelalter bis zur Barockzeit* (Berlin and New York: de Gruyter, 2002).

Gneuss, Helmut, 'The Study of Language in Anglo-Saxon England', *Bulletin of the John Rylands Library* 72 (1990), pp. 3–32.

Goffman, Erving, *The Presentation of Self in Everyday Life* (Harmondsworth: Penguin, 1971).

Goffman, Erving, 'The Neglected Situation', in Pier Paolo Giglioli (ed.), *Language and Social Context: Selected Readings* (Harmondsworth: Penguin, 1980), pp. 61–6.

Goose, Nigel, and Lien Luu, *Immigrants in Tudor and Early Stuart England* (Brighton: Sussex Academic Press, 2005).

Gowing, Laura, *Domestic Dangers: Women, Words, and Sex in Early Modern London* (Oxford: Clarendon, 1996).

Grassby, Richard, *The English Gentleman in Trade: The Life and Works of Sir Dudley North, 1641–1691* (Oxford: Clarendon, 1994).

Gray, Edward, *New World Babel: Languages and Nations in early America* (Princeton, NJ: Princeton University Press, 1999).

Gray, Edward G., and Norman Fiering (eds.), *The Language Encounter in the Americas, 1492–1800* (New York and Oxford: Berghahn, 2000).

Green, Ian, '"For children in yeeres and children in understanding": The Emergence of the English Catechism under Elizabeth and the Early Stuarts', *Journal of Ecclesiastical History* 37 (1986), pp. 397–425.

Green, Ian, *The Christian's ABC: Catechisms and Catechizing in England c.1530–1740* (Oxford: Clarendon, 1996).

Green, Lawrence D., 'Dictamen in England, 1500–1700', in Carol Poster and Linda C. Mitchell (eds.), *Letter-Writing Manuals and Instruction from Antiquity to the Present* (Columbia, SC: University of South Carolina Press, 2007), pp. 102–26.

Grendler, Paul, 'Form and Function in Italian Renaissance Popular Books', *Renaissance Quarterly* 46 (1993), pp. 451–85.

Griffiths, Paul, 'Punishing Words: Insults and Injuries, 1525–1700', in Angela McShane and Garthine Walker (eds.), *The Extraordinary and the Everyday in Early Modern England: Essays in Celebration of the Work of Bernard Capp* (Basingstoke: Palgrave, 2010), pp. 66–85.

Groebner, Valentin, *Who Are You? Identification, Deception, and Surveillance in Early Modern Europe* (New York: Zone, 2007).

Gwynn, Robin D., *Huguenot Heritage: The History and Contribution of the Huguenots in Britain* (London: Routledge and Kegan Paul, 1985).

Haastrup, Niels, 'On Phrasebooks: The Phrasebook as 1) a Genre, 2) a Source, 3) a Model', in Karl Hyldgaard-Jensen and Arne Zettersten (eds.), *Symposium on Lexicography III: Proceedings of the Third International Symposium on Lexicography* (Tübingen: Max Niemeyer Verlag, 1988), pp. 389–409.

Haastrup, Niels, 'The Courtesy-Book and the Phrase-Book in Modern Europe', in Jacques Carré (ed.), *The Crisis of Courtesy: Studies in the Conduct-Book in Britain, 1600–1900* (London, New York, and Cologne: E. J. Brill, 1994), pp. 65–80.

Hackel, Heidi Brayman, *Reading Material in Early Modern England* (Cambridge: Cambridge University Press, 2005).

Hadfield, Andrew, *Literature, Travel, and Colonial Writing in the English Renaissance, 1545–1625* (Oxford: Oxford University Press, 1998).

Halasz, Alexandra, *The Marketplace of Print: Pamphlets and the Public Sphere in Early Modern England* (Cambridge: Cambridge University Press, 1997).

Hale, John, *England and the Italian Renaissance: The Growth of Interest in its History and Art* (London: Fontana, 1996).

Hard, Frederic, 'Notes on John Eliot and his *Ortho-epia Gallica*', *Huntington Library Quarterly* 1 (1938), pp. 169–87.

Haynes, Clare, 'The Culture of Judgement: Art and Anti-Catholicism in England, c.1660–c.1770', *Historical Research* 78 (2005), pp. 483–505.

Haynes, Clare, *Pictures and Popery* (Aldershot: Ashgate, 2006).

Hayton, D. W., 'Nicolson, William (1655–1727) *Oxford Dictionary of National Biography*, Oxford University Press, 2004; online edn, January 2008, https://doi.org/10.1093/ref: odnb/20186.

Heal, Felicity, 'Mediating the Word: Language and Dialects in the British and Irish Reformations', *Journal of Ecclesiastical History* 56 (2005), pp. 261–86.

Hexter, J. H., 'The Education of the Aristocracy in the Renaissance', in J. H. Hexter, *Reappraisals in History* (London: Longmans, 1961), pp. 45–70.

Hibbert, Christopher, *The Grand Tour* (London: Weidenfeld and Nicolson, 1969).

Highley, Christopher, *Catholics Writing the Nation in Early Modern Britain and Ireland* (Oxford: Oxford University Press, 2008).

Hill, Bridget, 'A Refuge from Men: The Idea of a Protestant Nunnery', *Past & Present* 117 (1987), pp. 107–30.

Hobby, Elaine, 'A Woman's Best Setting Out Is Silence: The Writings of Hannah Wolley', in Gerald Maclean (ed.), *Culture and Society in the Stuart Restoration* (Cambridge: Cambridge University Press, 1995), pp. 179–200.

Hobsbawm, Eric, 'Language, Culture, and National Identity', *Social Research* 63:4 (1996), pp. 1065–80.

Hodgson, Elizabeth, 'Alma Mater', in Kathryn M. Moncrief and Kathryn R. McPherson (eds.), *Performing Pedagogy in Early Modern England: Gender, Instruction, and Performance* (Farnham: Ashgate, 2011), pp. 159–76.

Hoenselaars, Ton, 'National Stereotypes in English Renaissance Literature', in C. C. Barfoot (ed.), *Beyond Pug's Tour: National and Ethnic Stereotyping in Theory and Literary Practice* (Amsterdam and Atlanta, GA: Rodopi, 1997), pp. 85–97.

Hoenselaars, Ton, 'In the Shadow of St. Paul's: Linguistic Confusion in English Renaissance Drama', in Ton Hoenselaars and Marius Buning (eds.), *English Literature and the Other Languages* (Amsterdam: Rodopi, 1999).

Hoftijzer, Paul, 'Henry Hexham (*c*.1585–1650), English Soldier, Author, Translator, Lexicographer, and Cultural Mediator in the Low Countries', in S. K. Barker and Brenda M. Hosington, *Renaissance Cultural Crossroads: Translation, Print and Culture in Britain, 1473–1640* (Leiden and Boston, MA: Brill, 2013), pp. 209–26.

Horodowich, Elizabeth, 'The Gossiping Tongue: Oral Networks, Public Life and Political Culture in Early Modern Venice', *Renaissance Studies* 19 (2005), pp. 22–45.

Horodowich, Elizabeth, *Language and Statecraft in Early Modern Venice* (Cambridge: Cambridge University Press, 2008).

Horodowich, Elizabeth, 'Introduction: Speech and Oral Culture in Early Modern Europe and Beyond', *Journal of Early Modern History* 16 (2012), pp. 301–13.

Houston, R. A., "Minority' Languages and Cultural Change in Early Modern Europe', in Niall Ó Ciosáin (ed.), *Explaining Change in Cultural History* (Dublin: University College Dublin Press, 2005), pp. 13–36.

Howard, Clare, *English Travellers of the Renaissance* (London: Bodley Head, 1914).

Howatt, A. P. R., *A History of English Language Teaching* (Oxford: Oxford University Press, 1984).

Hsy, Jonathan, *Trading Tongues: Merchants, Multilingualism, and Medieval Literature* (Columbus, OH: Ohio State University Press, 2013).

Hubbard, Eleanor, *City Women: Money, Sex, and the Social Order in Early Modern London* (Oxford: Oxford University Press, 2012).

Hüllen, Werner, *English Dictionaries, 800–1700: The Topical Tradition* (Oxford: Oxford University Press, 1999).

Hüllen, Werner, 'Textbook-Families for the Learning of Vernaculars between 1450 and 1700', in Sylvain Auroux (ed.), *History of Linguistics 1999: Selected Papers from the Eighth International Conference on the History of the Language Sciences* (Amsterdam and Philadelphia, PA, 1999), pp. 97–107.

Hulme, Peter, and Tim Youngs (eds.), *The Cambridge Companion to Travel Writing* (Cambridge: Cambridge University Press, 2002).

Hunt, Arnold, *The Art of Hearing: English Preachers and their Audiences, 1560–1640* (Cambridge: Cambridge University Press, 2010).

Hurley, Alison, 'Peculiar Christians, Circumstantial Courtiers, and the Making of Conversation In Seventeenth-Century England', *Representations* 111 (2010), pp. 33–59.

Hymes, Dell, *Foundations in Sociolinguistics: An Ethnographic Approach* (Philadelphia, PA: University of Pennsylvania Press, 1974).

Hymes, Dell, 'The Scope of Sociolinguistics', in Nikolas Coupland and Adam Jaworski (eds.), *Sociolinguistics: A Reader and Coursebook* (Basingstoke, 1997), pp. 12–22.

Jardine, Lisa, and Anthony Grafton, 'Studied for Action: How Gabriel Harvey Read his Livy', *Past & Present* 129 (1990), pp. 30–78.

Jefcoate, Graham, 'German Printing and Bookselling in Eighteenth-Century London: Evidence and Interpretation', in Barry Taylor (ed.), *Foreign-Language Printing in London 1500–1900* (Boston Spa and London: The British Library, 2002), pp. 1–36.

Jenner, Mark S. R and Patrick Wallis (eds.), *Medicine and the Market in England and its Colonies, c.1450–c.1850* (Basingstoke: Palgrave Macmillan, 2007).

Jewell, Helen M., *Education in Early Modern England* (Basingstoke: Macmillan, 1998).

Joby, Christopher, *The Multilingualism of Constantijn Huygens (1596–1687)* (Amsterdam: Amsterdam University Press, 2014).

Joby, Christopher, *The Dutch Language in Britain (1550–1702): A Social History of the Use of Dutch in Early Modern Britain* (Leiden and Boston, MA: Brill, 2015).

Joby, Christopher, 'Trilingualism in Early Modern Norwich', *Journal of Historical Sociolinguistics* 2:2 (2016), pp. 211–34.

Johns, Adrian, *The Nature of the Book* (Chicago: University of Chicago Press, 1998).

Jones, Richard Foster, *The Triumph of the English Language: A Survey of Opinions Concerning the Vernacular from the Introduction of Printing to the Restoration* (London: Oxford University Press, 1953).

Jucker, Andreas H., Gerd Fritz, and Franz Lebsanft, 'Historical Dialogue Analysis: Roots and Traditions in the Study of the Romance Languages, German and English', in Andreas H. Jucker, Gerd Fritz, and Franz Lebsanft (eds.), *Historical Dialogue Analysis* (Amsterdam and Philadelphia, PA, 1999), pp. 1–34.

Kaltz, Barbara, 'L'Enseignement des langues étrangères au XVIe siècle. Structure globale et typologie des textes destinés à l'apprentissage des vernaculaires', *Beiträge zur Geschichte der Sprachwissenschaft* 5:1 (1995), pp. 79–106.

Kelly, L. G., *The True Interpreter: A History of Translation Theory and Practice in the West* (Oxford: Blackwell, 1979).

Kesson, Andy, and Emma Smith (eds.), *The Elizabethan Top Ten: Defining Print Popularity in Early Modern England* (Farnham: Ashgate, 2013).

Kibbee, Douglas A., 'French Grammarians and Grammars of French in the 16th Century', in Hans-Josef Niederehe and Konrad Koerner, *History and Historiography of Linguistics: Papers from the Fourth International Conference on the History of the Language Sciences (ICHoLS IV), Trier, 24–28 August 1987*, vol. I (Amsterdam and Philadelphia, PA: John Benjamins, 1990), pp. 301–14.

Kibbee, Douglas A., *For to speke Frenche trewely: The French language in England, 1000–1600: Its Status, Description and Instruction* (Amsterdam and Philadelphia, PA: John Benjamins, 1991).

Kibbee, Douglas A., 'From Holyband to Mauger: Teaching French in 17th-Century England', in Jan de Clercq, Nico Lioce, and Pierre Swiggers (eds.), *Grammaire et enseignement du français, 1500–1700* (Leuven: Peeters, 2000), pp. 179–95.

Klein, Lawrence E., 'Coffeehouse Civility, 1660–1714: An Aspect of Post-Courtly Culture in England', *Huntington Library Quarterly* 59 (1996), pp. 30–51.

Klein, Lawrence E., 'The Figure of France: The Politics of Sociability in England, 1660–1715', *Yale French Studies* 92, *Exploring the Conversible World: Text and Sociability from the Classical Age to the Enlightenment* (1997), pp. 30–45.

Knights, Mark, 'Towards a Social and Cultural History of Keywords And Concepts. By the Early Modern Research Group', *History of Political Thought* 31 (2010), pp. 427–48.

Knowlson, James, 'The Idea of Gesture as a Universal Language in the 17th and 18th Centuries', *Journal of the History of Ideas* 26 (1965), pp. 495–508.

Knowlson, James, *Universal Language Schemes in England and France 1600–1800* (Toronto and Buffalo, NY: University of Toronto Press, 1975).

Korda, Natasha, 'Gender at Work in the Cries of London', in Karen Bamford and Mary Ellen Lamb (eds.), *Oral Traditions and Gender in Early Modern Literary Texts* (Burlington, VT: Ashgate, 2008), pp. 117–35.

Korda, Natasha, *Labors Lost: Women's Work and the Early Modern English Stage* (Philadelphia, PA: University of Pennsylvania Press, 2011).

Kümin, Beat, 'Public Houses and their Patrons in Early Modern Europe', in Beat Kümin and B. Ann Tlusty (eds.), *The World of the Tavern: Public Houses in Early Modern Europe* (Aldershot: Ashgate, 2002), pp. 44–62.

Kümin, Beat, and B. Ann Tlusty, 'The World of the Tavern: An Introduction', in Beat Kümin and B. Ann Tlusty (eds.), *The World of the Tavern: Public Houses in Early Modern Europe* (Aldershot: Ashgate, 2002), pp. 3–11.

Lachenicht, Susanne, 'Huguenot Immigrants and the Formation of National Identities, 1548–1787', *Historical Journal* 50 (2007), pp. 309–31.

Lachenicht, Susanne, 'Les Éducateurs huguenots dans les Îles britanniques (XVIe–XVIIIe siècles)', in Vladislav Rjéoutski and Alexander Tchoudinov (eds.), *Le Précepteur francophone en Europe* (Paris: L'Harmattan, 2013), pp. 53–63.

Lambley, Kathleen, *The Teaching and Cultivation of the French Language in England during Tudor and Stuart times* (Manchester: Manchester University Press, 1920).

Larkin, Hilary, *The Making of Englishmen: Debates on National Identity 1550–1650* (Leiden and Boston, MA: Brill, 2014).

Lass, Roger (ed.), *The Cambridge History of the English Language, vol. 3: 1476–1776* (Cambridge: Cambridge University Press, 1999).

Lawrence, Jason, *'Who the devil taught thee so much Italian?' Italian Language Learning and Literary Imitation in Early Modern England* (Manchester and New York: Manchester University Press, 2005).

Lawson, Philip, *The East India Company: A History* (London and New York: Longman, 1993).

Lazarus, Micha, 'Greek Literacy in Sixteenth-Century England', *Renaissance Studies* 29:3 (2015), pp. 433–58.

Leach, Elizabeth Eva, 'Learning French by Singing in 14th-Century England', *Early Music* 33 (2005), pp. 253–70.

Lebsanft, Franz, 'A Late Medieval French Bargain Dialogue (*Pathelin* II). Or: Further Remarks on the History of Dialogue Forms', in Andreas H. Jucker, Gerd Fritz, and Franz Lebsanft (eds.), *Historical Dialogue Analysis* (Amsterdam and Philadelphia, PA, 1999), pp. 279–84.

Lefevere, André (ed.), *Translation/History/Culture: A Sourcebook* (London and New York: Routledge, 1992).

Leibetseder, Mathis, *Die Kavalierstour: Adelige Erziehungsreisen im 17. und 18. Jahrhundert* (Cologne, Weimar, and Vienna: Böhlau Verlag, 2004).

Leibetseder, Mathis, 'Across Europe: Educational Travelling of German Noblemen in a Comparative Perspective', *Journal of Early Modern History* 14 (2010), pp. 417–49.

Leith, Dick, *The Social History of English* (London: Routledge and Kegan Paul, 1983).

Lemon, Rebecca, 'Compulsory Conviviality in Early Modern England', *English Literary Renaissance* 43 (2013), pp. 381–414.

Leonhardt, Jürgen, *Latin: Story of a World Language*, trans. Kenneth Kronenberg (Cambridge, MA: Harvard University Press, 2013).

Lewis, Rhodri, *Language, Mind and Nature: Artificial Languages in England from Bacon to Locke* (Cambridge: Cambridge University Press, 2012).

Linke, Angelika, 'Communicative Genres as Categories in a Socio-Cultural History of Communication', in Stephan Elspaß, Nils Langer, Joachim Scharloth, and Wim Vandenbussche (eds.), *Germanic Language Histories 'from Below'* (Berlin and New York: Walter de Gruyter, 2007), pp. 473–93.

Lockwood, Matthew, '"Love ye therefore the strangers': Immigration and the Criminal Law in Early Modern England', *Continuity and Change* 29:3 (2014), pp. 349–71.

Loewenstein, Joseph, 'Humanism and Seventeenth-Century English Literature', in Jill Kraye (ed.), *The Cambridge Companion to Renaissance Humanism* (Cambridge: Cambridge University Press, 1996), pp. 269–93.

Loonen, P. L. M., *For to learne to buye and sell: Learning English in the Low Dutch Area between 1500 and 1800. A Critical Survey* (Amsterdam and Maarssen: APA-Holland University Press, 1991).

Loonen, P. L. M., 'Edward Richardson and the Learning of English at the Time of (Prince) William and Mary', in Theo Hermans and Reinier Salverda (eds.), *From Revolt to Riches: Culture and History of the Low Countires 1500–1700: International and Interdisciplinary Persepctives* (London: Centre for Low Countries Studies, 1993), pp. 335–44.

Luu, Lien Bich, 'Les Artisans étrangers et l'économie londonienne', in Jacques Bottin and Donatella Calabi (eds.), *Les Étrangers dans la ville: Minorités et espace urbain du bas Moyen Âge à l'époque moderne* (Paris: Maison des Sciences de l'Homme, 1999).

Lyons, Mary Ann, and Thomas O'Connor (eds.), *Strangers to Citizens: The Irish in Europe, 1600–1800* (Dublin: National Library of Ireland, 2008).

Maag, Karin, 'The Huguenot Academies: Preparing for an Uncertain Future', in Raymond A. Mentzer and Andrew Spicer (eds.), *Society and Culture in the Huguenot World, 1559–1685* (Cambridge: Cambridge University Press, 2002), pp. 139–56.

McConchie, Roderick, (ed.), *Ashgate Critical Essays on Early English Lexicographers, vol. 3: The Sixteenth Century* (Aldershot: Ashgate, 2012).

McConchie, Roderick, 'Doctors and Dictionaries in Sixteenth-Century England', in Roderick McConchie (ed.), *Ashgate Critical Essays on Early English Lexicographers, vol. 3: The Sixteenth Century* (Aldershot: Ashgate, 2012), pp. 39–64.

McConica, James, 'Elizabethan Oxford: The Collegiate Society', in James McConica (ed.), *The History of the University of Oxford, vol. 3: The Collegiate University* (Oxford: Clarendon, 1986), pp. 650–722.

McConnell, Anita, 'Houghton, John (1645–1705)', *Oxford Dictionary of National Biography*, 2004, http://www.oxforddnb.com/templates/article.jsp?articleid=13868&back=, accessed 17 June 2014.

McDowell, Paula, *The Women of Grub Street* (Oxford: Clarendon, 1998).

McMullen, Norma, 'The Education of English Gentlewomen 1540–1640', *History of Education: Journal of the History of Education Society* 6 (1977), pp. 87–101.

McShane, Angela, 'Material Culture and "Political Drinking" in Seventeenth-Century England', in Phil Withington and Angela McShane (eds.), *Cultures of Intoxication* (*Past & Present* supplement 9, 2014), pp. 247–76.

Maczak, Antoni, *Travel in Early Modern Europe*, trans. Ursula Phillips, (Cambridge: Polity, 1995).

Maiden, Martin, *A Linguistic History of Italian* (London and New York: Longman, 1995).

Mallette, Karla, 'Lingua Franca', in Peregrine Horden and Sharon Kinoshita (eds.), *A Companion to Mediterranean History* (Chichester: Wiley Blackwell, 2014), pp. 330–44.

Marazzini, Claudio, 'The Teaching of Italian in 15th- and 16th-Century Europe', in Sylvain Auroux, E. F. K. Koerner, Hans-Josef Niderehe, and Kees Versteegh (eds.), *History of the Language Sciences*, vol. 1 (Berlin and New York: Walter de Gruyter, 2000), pp. 699–700.

Massarella, Derek, *A World Elsewhere: Europe's Encounter with Japan in the Sixteenth and Seventeenth Centuries* (New Haven, CT, and London: Yale University Press, 1990).

Matar, Nabil, *Turks, Moors, and Englishmen in the Age of Discovery* (New York: Columbia University Press, 1999).

Matthiessen, F. O., *Translation: An Elizabethan Art* (Cambridge, MA: Harvard University Press 1931).

Mattingly, Garrett, *Renaissance Diplomacy* (London: Jonathan Cape, 1955).

Mazzio, Carla, *The Inarticulate Renaissance: Language Trouble in an Age of Eloquence* (Philadelphia, PA: University of Pennsylvania Press, 2008).

Mendelson, Sara, and Patricia Crawford, *Women in Early Modern England 1550–1720* (Oxford: Clarendon, 1998).

Michalove, Sharon D., 'Equal in Opportunity? The Education of Aristocratic Women 1450–1540', in Barbara J. Whitehead (ed.), *Women's Education in Early Modern Europe: A History, 1500–1800* (New York and London: Garland, 1999), pp. 47–74.

Miller, William E., 'Double Translation in English Humanistic Education', *Studies in the Renaissance* 10 (1963), pp. 163–74.

Mills, Simon, 'Learning Arabic in the Overseas Factories: The Case of the English', in Jan Loop, Alastair Hamilton, and Charles Burnett (eds.), *The Teaching and Learning of Arabic in Early Modern Europe* (Leiden: Brill, 2017), pp. 272–93.

Milner, Stephen J., '"Fanno bandire, notificare, et expressamente comandare": Town Criers and the Information Economy of Renaissance Florence', *I Tatti Studies in the Italian Renaissance* 16 (2013), pp. 107–51.

Mitchell, Linda C., 'Language and National Identity in 17th- and 18th-century England', in Carol Percy and Mary Catherine Davidson (eds.), *The Languages of Nation: Attitudes and Norms* (Bristol, Buffalo, NY, and Toronto: Multilingual Matters, 2012), pp. 123–40.

Moncrief, Kathryn M., and Kathryn R. McPherson, *Performing Pedagogy in Early Modern England: Gender, Instruction, and Performance* (Farnham: Ashgate, 2011).

Montgomery, Marianne, *Europe's Languages on England's Stages, 1590–1620* (Farnham: Ashgate, 2012).

Morgan, Victor, and Christopher Brooke (eds.), *A History of the University of Cambridge*, vol. 2 (Cambridge: Cambridge University Press, 2004).

Morini, Massimiliano, *Tudor Translation in Theory and Practice* (Aldershot: Ashgate, 2006).

Motley, Mark, 'Educating the English Gentleman Abroad: The Verney Family in Seventeenth-Century France and Holland', *History of Education: Journal of the History of Education Society*, 23 (1994), pp. 243–56.

Muir, Edward, *Ritual in Early Modern Europe* (Cambridge: Cambridge University Press, 1997).

Muldrew, Craig, 'Interpreting the Market: The Ethics of Credit and Community Relations in Early Modern England', *Social History* 18 (1993), pp. 163–83.

Muldrew, Craig, *The Economy of Obligation: The Culture of Credit and Social Relations in Early Modern England* (Basingstoke and New York: Palgrave Macmillan, 1998).

Murphy, Emilie K. M., 'Language and Power in an English Convent in Exile, *c*.1621–*c*.1631', *Historical Journal* (forthcoming, early view available at https://doi.org/10.1017/S0018246X17000437).

Nagy, Andrea R., 'Authenticity and Standardization in Seventeenth-Century Dictionaries', *Studies in Philology* 96 (1999), pp. 439–56.

Nevalainen, Terttu, 'Early Modern English Lexis and Semantics', in Roger Lass (ed.), *The Cambridge History of the English Language, vol. III: 1476–1776* (Cambridge: Cambridge University Press, 1999), pp. 332–458.

Nevalainen, Terttu, *An Introduction to Early Modern English* (Oxford: Oxford University Press, 2006).

Nevalainen, Terttu and Helena Raumolin-Brunberg (eds.), *Sociolinguistics and Language History: Studies Based on the Corpus of Early English Correspondence* (Amsterdam and Atlanta: Rodopi, 1996).

Nevalainen, Terttu, and Helena Raumolin-Brunberg, 'The Changing Role of London on the Linguistic Map of Tudor and Stuart England', in Dieter Kastovsky and Arthur Mettinger (eds.), *The History of English in a Social Context: A Contribution to Historical Sociolinguistics* (Berlin and New York: de Gruyter, 2000), pp. 279–337.

Nevalainen, Terttu and Helena Raumolin-Brunberg, *Historical Sociolinguistics: Language Change in Tudor and Stuart England* (Harlow: Longman, 2003).

Niederehe, Hans-Josef, 'Die Geschichte des Spanischunterrichts von den Anfängen bis zum Ausgang des 17. Jahrhunderts', in Konrad Schröder, *Fremdsprachenunterricht 1500–1800* (Wiesbaden: Harrassowitz, 1992), pp. 135–55.

Nocera Avila, Carmela, *Studi sulla traduzione nell'Inghilterra del seicento e del settecento* (Caltanissetta and Rome: Sciascia Editore, 1990).

O'Callaghan, Michelle, *The English Wits: Literature and Sociability in Early Modern England* (Cambridge: Cambridge University Press, 2007).

O'Connor, Desmond J., 'John Florio's Contribution to Italian-English Lexicography', *Italica* 49 (1972), pp. 49–67.

O'Connor, Desmond J., 'Florio, John (1553–1625), Author and Teacher of Languages', in *Oxford Dictionary of National Biography*, 2008, http://www.oxforddnb.com/view/article/50429, accessed 12 July 2014.

O'Day, Rosemary, *Education and Society 1500–1800* (London and New York: Longman, 1982).

O'Day, Rosemary, *Women's Agency in Early Modern Britain and the American Colonies: Patriarchy, Partnership and Patronage* (Harlow: Pearson Longman, 2007).

Ong, Walter J., *Orality and Literacy: The Technologizing of the Word* (London and New York: Methuen, 1982).

Ord, Melanie, 'Returning from Venice to England: Sir Henry Wotton as Diplomat, Pedagogue and Italian Cultural Connoisseur', in Thomas Betteridge (ed.), *Borders and Travellers in Early Modern Europe* (Aldershot: Ashgate, 2007).

Osselton, N. E., *The Dumb Linguists: A Study of the Earliest English and Dutch Dictionaries* (Leiden: Leiden University Press, 1973).

Ostler, Nicholas, *Empires of the Word: A Language History of the World* (London: HarperCollins, 2005).

Otterness, Philip, *Becoming German: The 1709 Palatine Migration to New York* (Ithaca, NY, and London: Cornell University Press, 2004).

Ottolenghi, Paola, *Giacopo Castelvetro: esule modenese nell'Inghilterra di Shakespeare: spiritualità riformata e orientamenti di cultura nella sua opera* (Pisa: ETS, 1982).

Parkin, Stephen, 'Italian Printing in London, 1553–1900', in Barry Taylor (ed.), *Foreign-Language Printing in London 1500–1900* (Boston Spa and London: British Library, 2002), pp. 133–74.

Parks, George B., 'The First Italianate Englishmen', *Studies in the Renaissance* 8 (1961), pp. 197–216.

Payne, Helen, 'Russell [Née Harington], Lucy, Countess of Bedford (bap. 1581, d. 1627)', *Oxford Dictionary of National Biography*, Oxford University Press, 2004; online edn, May 2014, https://doi.org/10.1093/ref:odnb/24330.

Peck, Linda Levy, 'Hobbes on the Grand Tour: Paris, Venice, or London?', *Journal of the History of Ideas* 57 (1996), pp. 177–83.

Pellegrini, Giuliano, 'Michelangelo Florio e le sue regole de la lingua thoscana', *Studi di filologia italiana* 12 (1954), pp. 72–201.

Peltonen, Markku, *The Duel in Early Modern England: Civility, Politeness and Honour* (Cambridge: Cambridge University Press, 2003).

Peltonen, Markku, *Rhetoric, Politics and Popularity in Pre-Revolutionary England* (Cambridge: Cambridge University Press, 2013).

Pettegree, Andrew, *Foreign Protestant Communities in Sixteenth-Century London* (Oxford: Clarendon, 1986).

Pettegree, Andrew, 'Translation and the Migration of Texts', in Thomas Betteridge (ed.), *Borders and Travellers in Early Modern Europe* (Aldershot: Ashgate, 2007), pp. 113–25.

Pfannebecker, Mareile, '"Lying by Authority": Travel Dissimulation in Fynes Moryson's *Itinerary*', *Renaissance Studies* 31:4 (2017), pp. 569–85.

Pfister, Manfred, and Ralf Hertel, *Performing National Identity: Anglo-Italian Cultural Transactions* (Amsterdam and New York: Rodopi, 2008).

Phillips, Susan E., 'Schoolmasters, Seduction, and Slavery: Polyglot Dictionaries in Pre-Modern England', *Medievalia et Humanistica* 34 (2008), pp. 129–58.

Pincus, Steve, '"Coffee Politicians Does Create": Coffeehouses and Restoration Political Culture', *Journal of Modern History* 67 (1995), pp. 807–34.

Pizzoli, Lucilla, *Le grammatiche di italiano per inglesi (1550–1776): un'analisi linguistica* (Florence: Accademia della Crusca, 2004).

Pocock, J. G. A., 'The Concept of Language and the *métier d'historien*: Some Considerations on Practice', in Anthony Pagden (ed.), *The Languages of Political Theory in Early Modern Europe* (Cambridge: Cambridge University Press, 1987), pp. 21–5.

Pollard, A. W., 'Claudius Hollyband and his French Schoolmaster and French Littelton,' *The Library* 21:6 (1915) pp. 77–93.

Pollnitz, Aysha, 'Princely Education in Sixteenth-Century Britain' (Unpublished PhD dissertation, University of Cambridge, 2005).

Pollnitz, Aysha, 'Humanism and the Education of Henry, Prince of Wales', in Timothy Wilks (ed.), *Prince Henry Revived: Image and Exemplarity in Early Modern England* (Southampton: Paul Holberton, 2007), pp. 22–64.

Quadflieg, Helga, 'Approved Civilities and the Fruits of Peregrination: Elizabethan and Jacobean Travellers and the Making of Englishness', in Hartmut Berghoff, Barbara Korte, Ralf Schneider, and Christopher Harvie (eds.), *The Making of Modern Tourism: The Cultural History of the British Experience, 1600–2000* (Basingstoke: Palgrave, 2002), pp. 21–46.

Radtke, Edgar, *Gesprochenes Französisch und Sprachgeschichte: Zur Rekonstruktion der Gesprächskonstitution in Dialogen französischer Sprachlehrbücher des 17. Jahrhunderts unter besonderer Berücksichtigung der italienischen Adaptionen* (Tübingen: Max Niemeyer Verlag, 1994).

Randall, Dale B. J., and Jackson C. Boswell, *Cervantes in Seventeenth-Century England* (Oxford: Oxford University Press, 2009).

Rappaport, Steve, *Worlds within Worlds: Structures of Life in Sixteenth-Century London* (Cambridge: Cambridge University Press, 1989).

Raylor, Timothy, 'Milton, the Hartlib Circle, and the Education of the Aristocracy', in Nicholas McDowell and Nigel Smith (ed.), *The Oxford Handbook of Milton* (Oxford: Oxford University Press, 2009), pp. 382–406.

Raylor, Timothy, 'Exiles, Expatriates and Travellers: Towards a Cultural and Intellectual History of the English Abroad, 1640–1660', in Philip Major (ed.), *Literatures of Exile in the English Revolution and its Aftermath, 1640–1690* (Farnham and Burlington, VT: Ashgate, 2010), pp. 15–43.

Raymond, Joad, *The Invention of the Newspaper: English Newsbooks 1641–1649* (Oxford: Clarendon, 1996).

Raymond, Joad, *Pamphlets and Pamphleteering in Early Modern Britain* (Cambridge: Cambridge University Press, 2003).

Raymond, Joad, *The Oxford Handbook of Popular Print Culture* (Oxford: Oxford University Press, 2011).

Reinburg, Virginia, *Books of Hours: Making an Archive of Prayer* (Cambridge: Cambridge University Press, 2012).

Rhodes, Neil, 'Status Anxiety and English Renaissance Translation', in Helen Smith and Louise Wilson (eds.), *Renaissance Paratexts* (Cambridge: Cambridge University Press, 2011), pp. 107–20.

Richards, Jennifer, *Rhetoric and Courtliness in Early Modern Literature* (Cambridge: Cambridge University Press, 2003).

Richards, Jennifer, *Voices and Books in the English Renaissance: A New History of Reading* (Oxford: Oxford University Press, forthcoming).

Richardson, Brian, 'The Italian of Renaissance Elites in Italy and Europe', in Anna Laura Lepschy and Arturo Tosi (eds.), *Multilingualism in Italy Past and Present* (Oxford: European Humanities Research Centre, 2002), pp. 5–23.

Richardson, Brian, 'The Concept of a *lingua comune* in Renaissance Italy', in Anna Laura Lepschy and Arturo Tosi (eds.), *Languages of Italy: Histories and Dictionaries* (Ravenna: Longo, 2007), pp. 11–28.

Rickard, Peter, *La Langue française au seizième siècle: étude suivie de textes* (Cambridge: Cambridge University Press, 1968).

Rickard, Peter, *A History of the French Language* (London and New York: Routledge, 1989).

Rjéoutski, Vladislav, and Alexander Tchoudinov (eds.), *Le Précepteur francophone en Europe* (Paris: L'Harmattan, 2013).

Roberts, Brynley F., 'Lhuyd, Edward (1659/60?–1709)', *Oxford Dictionary of National Biography*, Oxford University Press, 2004, https://doi.org/10.1093/ref:odnb/16633.

Robins, R. H., *A Short History of Linguistics* (London and New York: Longman, 1997).

Rollison, David, 'Conceit and Capacities of the Vulgar Sort: The Social History of English as a Language of Politics', *Cultural and Social History* 2 (2005) pp. 141–63.

Romaine, Suzanne, *Socio-Historical Linguistics: Its Status and Methodology* (Cambridge: Cambridge University Press, 1982).

Romaine, Suzanne, *Language in Society: An Introduction to Sociolinguistics* (Oxford: Oxford University Press, 2000).

Rosenberg, Eleanor, 'Giacopo Castelvetro: Italian Publisher in Elizabethan London and his Patrons', *Huntington Library Quarterly* 6 (1943), pp. 119–48.

Rossebastiano, Alda, *'Introito e Porta': vocabolario italiano-tedesco compiuto per Meistro Adamo de Roduila, 1477 adi 12 Augusto* (Turin: Edizioni dell'Orso, 1971).

Rossebastiano, Alda, *Antichi vocabolari plurilingui d'uso popolare: la tradizione del 'Solenissimo Vochabuolista'* (Turin: Edizioni dell'Orso, 1984).

Rossebastiano, Alda, 'La Tradition des manuels polyglottes dans l'enseignement des langues', in Sylvain Auroux, E. F. K. Koerner, Hans-Josef Niderehe, and Kees Versteegh (eds.), *History of the Language Sciences*, vol. 1 (Berlin and New York: Walter de Gruyter, 2000), pp. 688–95.

Rossi, Sergio, 'Note sugli italiani in Inghilterra nell'età del Rinascimento', in Sergio Rossi (ed.), *Saggi sul Rinascimento* (Milan: Unicopli, 1984), pp. 55–115.

Rossi, Sergio, 'Italy and the English Renaissance: An Introduction', in Sergio Rossi and Daniella Savoia (eds.), *Italy and the English Renaissance* (Milano: Unicopli, 1989).

Rothman, E. Natalie, 'Interpreting Dragomans: Boundaries and Crossings in the Early Modern Mediterranean', *Comparative Studies in Society and History* 51 (2009), pp. 771–800.

Rothman, E. Natalie, *Brokering Empire: Trans-Imperial Subjects between Venice and Istanbul* (Ithaca, NY: Cornell University Press, 2012).

Rubiés, Joan-Pau, *Travel and Ethnology in the Renaissance: South India through European eyes, 1250–1625* (Cambridge: Cambridge University Press, 2000).

Rubiés, Joan-Pau, 'Instructions for Travellers: Teaching the Eye to See', in Joan-Pau Rubiés, *Travellers and Cosmographers: Studies in the History of Early Modern Travel and Ethnology* (Aldershot: Ashgate, 2007), pp. 139–90.

Ruddock, Alwyn A., *Italian Merchants and Shipping in Southampton 1270–1600* (Southampton: University College, 1951).

Saenger, Michael, *The Commodification of Textual Engagements in the English Renaissance* (Aldershot: Ashgate, 2006).

Salmon, Vivian, 'Arabists and Linguists in Seventeenth-Century England', in G. A. Russell (ed.), *The 'Arabick' Interest of the Natural Philosophers in Seventeenth-Century England* (Leiden: Brill, 1994), pp. 54–69.

Salmon, Vivian, *Language and Society in Early Modern England: Selected Essays, 1981–1994* (Amsterdam and Philadelphia, PA: Rodopi, 1996).

Sanders, Julie, 'Lacy, John (c.1615–1681)', *Oxford Dictionary of National Biography*, Oxford University Press, 2004, https://doi.org/10.1093/ref:odnb/15856.

Sanson, Helena, *Women, Language and Grammar in Italy, 1500–1900* (Oxford: Oxford University Press, 2011).

Scammell, Geoffrey Vaughan, *The World Encompassed: The First European Maritime Empires, c.800–1650* (London and New York: Methuen, 1981).

Schoeck, R. J., 'The Italian Colony in Early Tudor London', in Renzo S. Crivelle and Luigi Sampietro (eds.), *Il passaggiere italiano: Saggi sulle letterature di lingua inglese in onore di Sergio Rossi* (Rome: Bulzoni, 1994).

Schroeder, Konrad (ed.), *Fremdsprachenunterricht 1500–1800* (Wiesbaden: Harrassowitz, 1992).

Schuchardt, Hugo, *Pidgin and Creole Languages: Selected Essays*, ed. trans. Glenn G. Gilbert (Cambridge: Cambridge University Press, 1980).

Scott, M. A., *Elizabethan Translations from the Italian* (Boston, MA, and New York: Houghton Mifflin, 1916).

Scott-Warren, Jason, *Sir John Harington and the Book as Gift* (Oxford: Oxford University Press, 2001).

Selbach, Rachel, 'On a Famous Lacuna: Lingua Franca the Mediterranean Trade Pidgin?', in Esther-Miriam Wagner, Bettina Beinhoff, and Ben Outhwaite (eds.), *Merchants of Innovation: The Languages of Traders* (Berlin: De Gruyter Mouton, 2017), pp. 252–71.

Shapin, Steven, *A Social History of Truth: Civility and Science in Seventeenth-Century England* (Chicago and London: University of Chicago Press, 1994).

Sharpe, J. A., *Defamation and Sexual Slander in Early Modern England: The Church Courts at York* (York: Borthwick, 1980).

Shaw, David J., 'French-Language Publishing in London to 1900', in Barry Taylor (ed.), *Foreign-Language Printing in London 1500–1900* (Boston Spa and London: British Library, 2002), pp. 101–22.

Shaw, Patricia, 'Sensual, Solemn, Sober, Slow and Secret: The English View of the Spaniard, 1590–1700', in C. C. Barfoot (ed.), *Beyond Pug's Tour: National and Ethnic Stereotyping in Theory and Literary Practice* (Amsterdam and Atlanta, Georgia: Rodopi, 1997), pp. 99–113.

Shepard, Alexandra, *Meanings of Manhood in Early Modern England* (Oxford: Oxford University Press, 2003).

Shepard, Alexandra, 'Swil-bols and Tos-pots': Drink Culture and Male Bonding in England, c.1560–1640', in Laura Gowing, Michael Hunter, and Miri Rubin (eds.), *Love, Friendship and Faith in Europe, 1300–1800* (Basingstoke: Palgrave Macmillan, 2005), pp. 112–26.

Sheridan, Geraldine, and Viviane Prest (eds.), *Les Huguenots éducateurs dans l'espace européen à l'époque moderne* (Paris: Honoré Champion, 2011).

Shrank, Cathy, 'Rhetorical Constructions of a National Community: The Role of the King's English in Mid-Tudor Writing', in Phil Withington and Alex Shepard (eds.), *Communities in Early Modern England* (Manchester: Manchester University Press, 2000), pp. 180–98.

Simonini, R. C., 'The Genesis of Modern Foreign Language Teaching', *The Modern Language Journal* 35 (1951), pp. 179–86.

Simonini, R. C., 'The Italian Pedagogy of Claudius Hollyband', *Studies in Philology* 49 (1952), pp. 144–54.

Simonini, R. C., *Italian Scholarship in Renaissance England* (Chapel Hill, NC: The University of North Carolina Studies in Comparative Literature, 1952).

Skinner, Quentin, *Visions of Politics, vol. 1: Regarding Method* (Cambridge: Cambridge University Press, 2002).

Slack, Paul, 'Mirrors of Health and Treasures of Poor Men: The Uses of the Vernacular Medical Literature of Tudor England', in Charles Webster (ed.), *Health, Medicine and Mortality in the Sixteenth Century* (Cambridge: Cambridge University Press, 1979), pp. 237–73.

Smith, Bruce R., *The Acoustic World of Early Modern England: Attending to the O-Factor* (Chicago: University of Chicago Press, 1999).

Smith, Bruce R., 'The Soundscapes of Early Modern England', in Mark M. Smith (ed.), *Hearing History: A Reader* (Athens, GA: University of Georgia Press, 2004), pp. 85–96.

Smith, Helen, and Louise Wilson (eds.), *Renaissance Paratexts* (Cambridge: Cambridge University Press, 2011).

Smith, Nigel, 'Exile in Europe during the English Revolution and its Literary Impact', in Philip Major (ed.), *Literatures of Exile in the English Revolution and its Aftermath, 1640–1690* (Farnham and Burlington, VT: Ashgate, 2010), pp. 105–18.

Smyth, Adam, *Autobiography in Early Modern England* (Cambridge: Cambridge University Press, 2010).

Snyder, Jon R., *Dissimulation and the Culture of Secrecy in Early Modern Europe* (Berkeley, Los Angeles, and London: University of California Press, 2009).

Sorensen, Janet, *Strange Vernaculars: How Eighteenth-Century Slang, Cant, Provincial Languages, and Nautical Jargon Became English* (Princeton, NJ, and Oxford: Princeton University Press, 2017).

Spufford, Margaret, *Contrasting Communities: English Villagers in the Sixteenth and Seventeenth Centuries* (London: Cambridge University Press, 1974).

Spufford, Margaret, *Small Books and Pleasant Histories: Popular Fiction and its Readership in Seventeenth-Century England* (London: Methuen, 1981).

Spurr, John, 'A Profane History of Early Modern Oaths', *Transactions of the Royal Historical Society* 11 (2001), pp. 37–63.

Stagl, Justin, *A History of Curiosity: The Theory of Travel 1550–1800* (London and New York: Routledge, 1995).

Stallybrass, Peter, Roger Chartier, J. Franklin Mowery, and Heather Wolfe, 'Hamlet's Tables and the Technologies of Writing in Renaissance England', *Shakespeare Quarterly*, 55:4 (Winter, 2004), pp. 379–419.

Stannek, Antje, *Telemachs Brüder: Die höfische Bildungsreise des 17. Jahrhunderts* (Frankfurt am Main and New York: Campus Verlag, 2001).

Stedman, Gesa, *Cultural Exchange in Seventeenth-Century France and England* (Aldershot: Ashgate, 2013).

Stein, Gabriele, *John Palsgrave as Renaissance Linguist: A Pioneer in Vernacular Language Description* (Oxford: Oxford University Press, 1997).

Stein, Gabriele, 'The Emerging Role of English in the Dictionaries of Renaissance Europe', reprinted in Roderick McConchie (ed.), *Ashgate Critical Essays on Early English Lexicographers, vol. 3: The Sixteenth Century* (Aldershot: Ashgate, 2012), pp. 87–120.

Stein, Gabriele, 'Palsgrave, John (d. 1554), Teacher and Scholar of Languages', in *Oxford Dictionary of National Biography*, 2004, http://www.oxforddnb.com/view/article/21227.

Steiner, George, *After Babel: Aspects of Language and Translation* (Oxford: Oxford University Press, 1975).

Stern, Virginia F., *Gabriel Harvey: His Life, Marginalia and Library* (Oxford: Clarendon, 1979).

Stevenson, Jane, *Women Latin Poets: Language, Gender, and Authority from Antiquity to the Eighteenth Century* (Oxford: Oxford University Press, 2005).

Stone, Lawrence, 'The Educational Revolution in England, 1560–1640', *Past & Present* 28 (1964), pp. 41–80.

Stoughton, Nigel, "His hatband is made of diamondes': France's First English Textbook', *The Book Collector* 60 (2011), pp. 57–66.

Stoye, John Walter, *English Travellers Abroad 1604–1667: Their Influence in English Society and Politics* (London: Jonathan Cape, 1952).

Suranyi, Anna, *The Genius of the English Nation: Travel Writing and National Identity in Early Modern England* (Cranbury, NJ: Rosemont, 2008).

Sweet, Rosemary, 'The Changing View of Rome in the Long Eighteenth Century', *Journal for Eighteenth-Century Studies* 33 (2010), pp. 145–64.

Sweet, Rosemary, *Cities and the Grand Tour: The British in Italy, c.1690–1820* (Cambridge: Cambridge University Press, 2012).

Taavitsainen, Irma, and Susan Fitzmaurice, 'Historical Pragmatics: What It Is and How to Do It', in Susan Fitzmaurice and Irma Taavitsainen (eds.), *Methods in Historical Pragmatics* (Berlin and New York: de Gruyter, 2007), pp. 11–36.

Tadmor, Naomi, 'Friends and Neighbours in Early Modern England: Biblical Translations and Social Norms', in Laura Gowing, Michael Hunter, and Miri Rubin (eds.), *Love, Friendship and Faith in Europe, 1300–1800* (Basingstoke: Palgrave Macmillan, 2005), pp. 150–76.

Tate, W. E., 'The Episcopal Licensing of Schoolmasters in England', *Church Quarterly Review* 157 (1956), pp. 426–32.

Taylor, Barry, 'Un-Spanish Practices: Spanish and Portuguese Protestants, Jews and Liberals, 1500–1900', in Barry Taylor (ed.), *Foreign-Language Printing in London 1500–1900* (Boston Spa and London: British Library, 2002), pp. 183–202.

Taylor, Hillary, '"Branded on the Tongue": Rethinking Plebeian Inarticulacy in Early Modern England', *Radical History Review* 121 (2015), pp. 91–105.

Teague, Frances, *Bathsua Makin, Woman of Learning* (London: Associated University Presses, 1998).

Thomas, Keith, 'The Meaning of Literacy in Early Modern England', in Gerd Baumann (ed.), *The Written Word: Literacy in Transition* (Oxford: Clarendon, 1986), pp. 97–131.

Thomas, Keith, 'Introduction', in Jan Bremmer and Herman Roodenburg (eds.), *A Cultural History of Gesture: From Antiquity to the Present Day* (Cambridge: Polity, 1991), pp. 1–14.

Timelli, Maria Colombo, 'Dictionnaires pour voyageurs, dictionnaires pour marchands ou la polyglossie au quotidien aux XVIe et XVIIe siècles', *Linguisticae Investigationes* 16 (1992), pp. 395–421.

Tlusty, B. Ann, *Bacchus and Civic Order: The Culture of Drink in Early Modern Germany* (Charlottesville,VA, and London: University Press of Virginia, 2001).

Toomer, G. J., *Eastern Wisedome and Learning: The Study of Arabic in Seventeenth-Century England* (Oxford: Clarendon, 1996).

Trotter, D. A. (ed.), *Multilingualism in Later Medieval Britain* (Cambridge: D. S. Brewer, 2000).

Trudgill, Peter, 'East Anglia and the Spanish Inquisition', in Peter Trudgill, *Investigations in Sociohistorical Linguistics: Stories of Colonisation and Contact* (Cambridge: Cambridge University Press, 2010), pp. 36–60.

Trudgill, Peter, *Investigations in Sociohistorical Linguistics: Stories of Colonisation and Contact* (Cambridge: Cambridge University Press, 2010).

Ungerer, Gustav, 'The Printing of Spanish Books in Elizabethan England', *The Library* 20 (1965), pp. 177–229.

van den Heuvel, Danielle, *Women & Entrepreneurship: Female Traders in the Northern Netherlands, c.1580–1815* (Amsterdam: Aksant, 2007).

van der Lubbe, Fredericka, *Martin Aedler and the High-Dutch Minerva: The First German Grammar for the English* (Oxford: Peter Lang, 2007).

van der Lubbe, Fredericka, 'One Hundred Years of German Teaching', *AUMLA: Journal of the Australasian Universities Language and Literature Association. Special issue: Refereed Proceedings of the 2007 AULLA Conference: Cultural Interactions in the Old and New Worlds* (December 2007), pp. 143–52.

Vander Motten, J. P., 'James Howell's *Instructions for forreine travell* (1642): The Politics of Seventeenth-Century Continental Travel', in C. C. Barfoot (ed.), *Beyond Pug's Tour: National and Ethnic Stereotyping in Theory and Literary Practice* (Amsterdam and Atlanta, GA: Rodopi, 1997), pp. 115–24.

Verhoeven, Gerrit, 'Calvinist Pilgrimages and Popish Encounters: Religious Identity and Sacred Space on the Dutch Grand Tour', *Journal of Social History* 43:3 (2010).

Vigne, Randolph, and Charles Littleton (eds.), *From Strangers to Citizens: The Integration of Immigrant Communities in Britain, Ireland and Colonial America, 1550–1750* (Brighton and Portland, OR: Sussex Academic Press, 2001).

Voss, Paul J., 'Books for Sale: Advertising and Patronage in Late Elizabethan England', *Sixteenth Century Journal* 29 (1998), pp. 733–56.

Walter, John, 'Gesturing at Authority: Deciphering the Gestural Code of Early Modern England', in Michael J. Braddick (ed.) *The Politics of Gesture: Historical Perspectives* (*Past & Present* 203, supplement 4, 2009), pp. 96–127.

Waquet, Françoise, *Latin, or the Empire of a Sign*, trans. John Howe (London: Verso, 2001).

Warneke, Sara, *Images of the Educational Traveller in Early Modern England* (London, New York, and Cologne: E. J. Brill, 1995).

Watkin, David, 'The Architectural Context of the Grand Tour: The British as Honorary Italians', in Clare Hornsby (ed.), *The Impact of Italy: The Grand Tour and Beyond* (London: The British School at Rome, 2000), pp. 49–62.

Watson, Foster, *The Beginnings of the Teaching of Modern Subjects in England* (London: Sir Isaac Pitman and Sons, 1909).

Watt, Tessa, *Cheap Print and Popular Piety, 1550–1640* (Cambridge: Cambridge University Press, 1991).

Watts, Richard J., '*Refugiate in a Strange Countrey*: Learning English through Dialogues in the 16th Century', in Andreas H. Jucker, Gerd Fritz, and Franz Lebsanft (eds.), *Historical Dialogue Analysis* (Amsterdam and Philadelphia, PA: John Benjamins, 1999), pp. 215–41.

Webster, Charles, *The Great Instauration: Science, Medicine and Reform, 1626–1660* (London: Duckworth, 1975).

Wells, C. J., *German: A Linguistic History to 1945* (Oxford: Clarendon, 1985).

Whitehead, Barbara J. (ed.), *Women's Education in Early Modern Europe: A History, 1500–1800* (New York and London: Garland, 1999).

Wierzbicka, Anna, *Understanding Cultures through their Key Words* (New York and Oxford: Oxford University Press, 1997).

Wiesner, Merry E., *Working Women in Renaissance Germany* (Brunswick, NJ: Rutgers University Press, 1986).

Williams, Mark, 'The Inner Lives of Early Modern Travel', *Historical Journal* (forthcoming, early view available at https://doi.org/10.1017/S0018246X18000237).

Williams, Raymond, *Keywords: A Vocabulary of Culture and Society* (London: Fontana, 1976).

Williamson, Elizabeth, 'A Letter of Travel Advice? Literary Rhetoric, Scholarly Counsel and Practical Instruction in the *ars apodemica*', *Lives and Letters* 3 (2011), pp. 1–22.

Winny, James (ed.), *Elizabethan Prose Translation* (Cambridge: Cambridge University Press, 1960).

Withington, Phil, *The Politics of Commonwealth: Citizens and Freemen in Early Modern England* (Cambridge: Cambridge University Press, 2005).

Withington, Phil, 'Company and Sociability in Early Modern England', *Social History* 32 (2007), pp. 291–307.

Withington, Phil, *Society in Early Modern England: The Vernacular Origins of Some Powerful Ideas* (Cambridge: Polity, 2010).

Withington, Phil, 'The Semantics of 'Peace' in Early Modern England', *Transactions of the Royal Historical Society* 23 (2013), pp. 127–53.

Withington, Phil, and Alexandra Shepard, *Communities in Early Modern England: Networks, Place, Rhetoric* (Manchester: Manchester University Press, 2000).

Wogan-Browne, Jocelyn (ed.), *Language and Culture in Medieval Britain: The French of England c.1100—c.1500* (York: York Medieval Press, 2009).

Wood, Alfred C., *A History of the Levant Company* (London: Frank Cass, 1964).

Woolf, Daniel, 'Conscience, Constancy, and Ambition in the Career and Writings of James Howell', in John Morrill, Paul Slack, and Daniel Woolf (eds.), *Public Duty and Private Conscience in Seventeenth-Century England: Essays Presented to G. E. Aylmer* (Oxford: Clarendon, 1993), pp. 243–78.

Woolf, Daniel, 'Speaking of History: Conversations about the Past in Restoration and Eighteenth-Century England', in Adam Fox and Daniel Woolf (eds.), *The Spoken Word: Oral Culture in Britain 1500-1850* (Manchester and New York: Manchester University Press, 2002), pp. 119–37.

Woolf, Daniel, 'Howell, James (1594?-1666), Historian and Political Writer', in *Oxford Dictionary of National Biography*, 2008, http://www.oxforddnb.com/view/article/13974?docPos=1, accessed 12 June 2014.

Woolfson, Jonathan, *Padua and the Tudors: English Students in Italy, 1485-1603* (Cambridge: James Clarke, 1998).

Woolfson, Jonathan, 'Padua and English students Revisited', *Renaissance Studies* 27 (2013), pp. 572–87.

Wright, Laura, 'Early Modern London Business English', in Dieter Kastovsky (ed.), *Studies in Early Modern English* (Berlin and New York: de Gruyter, 1994), pp. 449–66.

Wright, Laura, 'Speaking and Listening in Early Modern London', in A. Cowan and J. Steward (eds.), *The City and the Senses: Urban Culture since 1500* (Aldershot: Ashgate, 2006), pp. 60–74.

Wright, Louis B., 'Language Helps for the Elizabethan Tradesman', *Journal of English and Germanic Philology* 30 (1931), pp. 335–47.

Wrightson, Keith, 'Alehouses, Order and Reformation in Rural England, 1590-1660', in Eileen Yeo and Stephen Yeo (eds.), *Popular Culture and Class Conflict 1590-1914: Explorations in the History of Labour and Leisure* (Brighton and Atlantic Highlands, NJ: The Harvester Press and Humanities Press, 1981) pp. 1–27.

Wrightson, Keith, *English Society 1580-1680* (Routledge: London and New York, 1982).

Wrightson, Keith, 'Estates, Degrees, and Sorts: Changing Perceptions of Society in Tudor and Stuart England', in Penelope Corfield (ed.), *Language, History and Class* (Oxford: Basil Blackwell, 1991), pp. 30–52.

Wyatt, Michael, *The Italian Encounter with Tudor England: A Cultural Politics of Translation* (Cambridge: Cambridge University Press, 2005).

Yates, Frances, 'The Importance of John Eliot's *Ortho-epia Gallica*', *Review of English Studies* 7 (1931), pp. 419–30.

Yates, Frances, *John Florio: The Life of an Italian in Shakespeare's England* (Cambridge: Cambridge University Press, 1934).

Yates, Frances, 'Italian Teachers in Elizabethan England', *Journal of the Warburg Institute* 1 (1937), pp. 103–16.

Yates, Frances, 'An Italian in Restoration England', *Journal of the Warburg and Courtauld Institutes* 6 (1943), pp. 216–20.

Yates, Frances, 'Italian Teachers in England', in Frances Yates, *Renaissance and Reform: The Italian Contribution* (London: Routledge and Kegan Paul, 1983), pp. 161–79.

Zagorin, Perez, 'The Historical Significance of Lying and Dissimulation', *Social Research* 63, *Truth-Telling, Lying and Self-Deception* (1996), pp. 863–912.

3. Supplementary Bibliography

(i) Conversation manuals containing English and at least one other European language, printed in the period 1480–1715

This bibliography follows the definition of 'conversation manual' offered in Chapter 2. It only contains texts which include English and at least one other language, and which contain dialogues, conversational phrases, or similarly speech-directed material. Hence, grammars and dictionaries are included only where they contain a clearly speech-directed component.

Polyglot (Containing English and more than one Other Language)

Anon., *Here begynneth a lytell treatyse for to lerne Englysshe and Frensshe. Sensuyt vng petit liure pour apprendre a parler Francoys, Alemant, et Ancloys* (Lyons, c.1525).

Anon., *A lytell treatyse for to lerne Englysshe and Frensshe* (Antwerp c.1530).

Anon., *Sex linguaru[m], Latine, Teuthonice, Gallice, Hispanice, Italice, Anglice, dilucidissimus dictionarius, mirum q[uam] vtilis, ne dicam necessarius omnibus linguarum studiosis. A vocabulary in six languages, Latyn, Dutch, Frenche, Spanish, Italy, and Englysh* (London, 1537).

Anon., *Septem Linguarum Latinae, Teutonicae, Gallicae, Hispanicae, Italicae, Anglicae, Almanicae, dilucidissimus dictionarius, mirum quam utilis, nec dicam necessarius, omnibus linguarum studiosis. A vocabulary in seven languages: Latyn, Deutch, frenche, Spantsh, Italy, English, and Hye Aleman* (Antwerp, 1540).

Anon., *Septem linguarum Latinæ Teutonicae Gallicae Hispanicae Italicae Anglicae Almanicæ dilucidissimus dictionarius mirum quam utilis, nec dicam necessarius, omnibus linguarum studiosis* (Antwerp, 1540).

Anon., *Sex linguarum, Latinae, Gallicæ, Hispanicæ, Italicæ, Anglicæ, et Teutonice, dilucidissimus dictionarius miru[m] quam vtilis, nec dicam necessarius omnibus linguarum studiosis* (Venice, 1541).

Anon., *Septem linguarum, Latinæ, Teutonicæ, Gallicæ, Hispanicæ, Italicæ, Anglicæ, Almanicæ, dilucidissimus dictionarius, mirum quâm vtilis, nec dicam necessarius, omnibus linguarum studiosis. A vocabulary in seuen languages, Latyn, Deutch, Frenche, Spanish, Italy, Englisch, and Hye Alman* (Paris, 1542).

Anon., *Le dictionaire des huict languages: c'est à sçauoir Grec, Latin, Flamen, Francois, Espagnol, Italien, Anglois, & Aleman: fort vtile & necessaire pour tous studieux & amateurs des lettres* (Paris, 1548).

Anon., *Sex linguarum, Latinæ, Gallicæ, Hispanicæ, Italicæ, Anglicæ, & Teutonice, dilucidissimus dictionarius mirum quam vtilis, nec dicam necessarius omnibus linguarum studiosis* (Nuremberg, 1548).

Anon., *Sex linguarum, Latinæ, Gallicæ, Hispanicæ, Italicæ, Anglicæ, & Teutonicæ, dilucidissimus dictionarius mirum quam utilis, nec dicam necessarius omnibus linguarum studiosis* (Venice, 1549).

Anon., *Sex linguarum, Latinæ, Gallicæ, Hispanicæ, Italicæ, Anglicæ, & Teutonice, dilucidissimus dictionarius mirum quam vtilis, nec dicam necessarius omnibus linguarum studiosis* (Nuremberg, 1549).

Anon., *Sex linguarum Latinae, Gallicae, Hispanicæ, Italicæ, Anglicæ, & Teutonice, diluci-dissimus dictionarius, mirum quam utilis, nec dicam necessarius omnibus linguarum studiosis. A vocabulary in six languages, Latyn, Frenche, Spanisch, Italy, Englisch, and Teutsch* (Venice, 1550?).

Anon., *Le dictionaire des huict langaiges: c'est à sçavoir Grec, Latin, Flameng, François, Espagnol, Italien, Anglois & Aleman: fort utile & necessaire pour tous studieux & amateurs des lettres* (Paris, 1552).

Anon., *Le dictionaire des huict langaiges* (Paris, 1552).

Anon., *Le dictionaire des huict langaiges* (Paris, 1552).

Anon., *Sex lingvarvm, Latinae, Gallicae, Hispanicæ, Italicæ, Anglicæ & Teutonicæ* (Zürich, 1553).

Boorde, Andrew, *The fyrst boke of the introduction of knowledge. The whych dothe teache a man to speake parte of all maner of languages, and to knowe the vsage and fashion of al maner of countreys. And for to know the moste parte of all maner of coynes of money, the whych is currant in euery region* (London, 1555?).

Anon., *A boke intituled Italion, Frynsshe, Englysshe and Laten* (London, 1557).

Boorde, Andrew, *The fyrst boke of the introduction of knowledge* (London, 1562?).

Anon., *Sex linguarum, Latinæ, Gallicæ, Hispanicæ, Italicæ, Anglicæ, & Teutonicæ* (Venice, 1563).

Anon., *A Boke intituled Ffrynsshe Englysshe and Duche* (London, 1569). [not in STC]

Anon., *Septem lingvarvm Latinae, Tevtonicae Gallicae Hispanicae, Italicae, Anglicæ, alma-nicæ* (Antwerp, 1569).

Anon., *Sex lingvarvm Latinæ, Gallicæ, Hispanicæ, Italicæ, Anglicæ & Teutonicæ* (Zürich, 1570).

Anon., *Le dictionaire des huict langages* (Lyons, 1573).

Anon., *Colloques ou dialogues avec un dictionaire en six langues: Flamen, Anglois, Alleman, François, Espaignol, & Italien* (Antwerp, 1576).

Anon., *Colloques ou Dialogues en Quattre langues, Flamen Françoys, Espaignel et Italien, with the Englishe to be added thereto* (London, 1578).

Anon., *Colloques ou dialogues, avec un dictionaire en six langues, flamen, anglois, alleman, françois, espagnol, & italien: tres-vtil à tous marchands, ou autres de quelque estat qu'ils soyent. Nouuellement reueus, corrigez & augmentez de deux dialogues, tres profitables & vtils tant pour s'en ayder aux champs qu'en l'hostellerie* (Antwerp, 1579).

Anon., *Sex linguarum Latinæ, Gallicæ, Hispanicæ, Italicæ, Anglicæ & Teutonicae* (Zürich, 1579).

Anon., *Le dictionaire des huict langages: C'est à scauoir Grec, Latin, Flamen, François, Espagnol, Italian, Anglois, & Aleman* (Paris, 1580).

Hollyband, Claudius, *Campo di Fior, or else the Flourie Field of Foure Languages* (London, 1583).

Anon., *Colloquia cum dictionariolo sex linguarum: teutonicæ, anglicæ, latinæ, gallicæ, hispanicæ, & italicæ* (Antwerp, 1583).

Anon., *Familiaria colloquia cum dictionariolo sex linguarum: Latinæ, Teutonicæ, Gallicæ, Hispanicæ, Italicæ & Anglicæ* (Antwerp, 1584).

Anon., *Colloques ou dialogues, auec vn dictionaire en quatre langues: flamen, anglois, françois, & latin.* (Leiden, 1585).

Anon., *Colloquia et dictionariolum septem linguarum, Belgicæ, Anglicæ, Teutonicæ, Latinæ, Italicæ, Hispanicæ, Gallicæ* (Antwerp, 1586).

Anon., *Colloquia et dictionariolum septem linguarum, Belgigicæ [sic], Anglicæ, Teutonicæ; Latinæ, Italicæ, Hispanicæ, Gallicæ. Liber omnibus linguarum studiosis domi ac foris apprime necessarius* (Liège, 1589).

Anon., *Colloquia et dictionariolum septem linguarum, Belgicæ, Anglicæ, Teutonicæ; Latinæ, Italicæ, Hispanicæ, Gallicæ. Liber omnibus linguarum studiosis domi ac foris apprime necessarius.* (Liège, 1591).

Anon., *Colloquia et dictionariolum septem linguarum, Belgicæ, Anglicæ, Teutonicæ; Latinæ, Italicæ, Hispanicæ, Gallicæ. Liber omnibus linguarum studiosis domi ac foris apprime necessarius* (Padua, 1592).

Anon., *Colloquia et dictionariolum septem linguarum, Belgicæ, Anglicæ, Teutonicæ, Latinæ, Italicæ, Hispanicæ, Gallicæ* (Leiden, 1593).

Anon., *Colloquia et dictionariolum septem linguarum, Belgicæ, Anglicæ, Teutonicæ, Latinæ, Italicæ, Hispanicæ, Gallicæ.* (Liège, 1595).

Anon., *Colloquia et dictionariolum septem linguarum, Belgicæ, Anglicæ, Teutonicæ, Latinae, Italicae, Hispanicae, Gallicae* (Liège, 1597).

Anon., *Colloquia et dictionariolum octo linguarum, Latinæ, Gallicæ, Belgicæ, Teutonicæ, Hispanicæ, Italicæ, Anglicæ, et Portugallicæ* (Delft, 1598).

Anon., *Colloquia et dictionariolum septem linguarum, Belgicæ, Anglicæ, Teutonicæ, Latinæ, Italicæ, Hispanicæ, Gallicæ. Liber omnibus linguarum studiosis domi ac foris apprime necessarius* (Liège, 1600).

Anon., *Colloquia et dictionariolum septem linguarum, Belgicæ, Anglicæ, Teutonicæ, Latinæ, Italicæ, Hispanicæ, Gallicæ* (Liège, 1604).

Anon., *Colloquia et dictionariolum octo linguarum, Latinæ, Gallicæ, Belgicæ, Teutonicæ, Hispanicæ, Italicæ, Anglicæ, et Portugallicæ* (Delft, 1605).

Anon., *Colloquia et dictionariolum septem linguarum, Belgicæ, Anglicæ, Teutonicæ, Latinæ, Italicæ, Hispanicæ, Gallicæ* (Venice, 1606).

Anon., *Colloquia et dictionariolum sex linguarum, Latinæ, Gallicæ, Teutonicæ, Hispanicæ, Italicæ, et Anglicæ* (Geneva, 1608?).

Anon., *Colloquia et dictionariolum septem linguarum, Belgicæ, Anglicæ, Teutonicæ, Latinæ, Italicæ, Hispanicæ, Gallicæ* (Liège, 1610).

Anon., *Colloquia et dictionariolum sex linguarum, Latinae, Gallicae, Teutonicae, Hispanicae, Italicae, et Anglicae* (Cologne, 1610).

Anon., *Le dictionaire des six langues. C'est à sçavoir latin, flamen, françois, espagnol, italien, & anglois* (Rouen, 1611).

Anon., *Colloquia et dictionariolum octo linguarum, Latinæ, Gallicæ, Belgicæ, Teutonicæ, Hispanicæ, Italicæ, Anglicæ, et Portugallicæ* (The Hague, 1613).

Anon., *Colloquia et dictionariolum octo linguarum, Latinæ, Gallicæ, Belgicæ, Teutonicæ, Hispanicae, Italicae, Anglicae et Portugallicae* (Flushing, 1613).

Anon., *Colloquia et dictionariolum octo linguarum, Latinæ, Gallicæ, Belgicæ, Teutonicæ, Hispanicæ, Italicæ, Anglicæ, et Portugallicæ* (Delft, 1613).

Anon., *Colloques ou dialogues avec un dictionaire en six langues* (Heidelberg, 1614).

Anon., *Colloquia et dictionariolum septem linguarum, Belgicae, Teutonicae, Anglicae, Gallicae, Latinae, Hispanicae, et Italicae* (Antwerp, 1616).

Anon., *Colloquia et dictionariolum octo linguarum; Latinæ, Gallicæ, Belgicæ, Teutonicæ, Hispanicæ, Italicæ, Anglicæ, et Portugallicæ* (Amsterdam, 1622).

Anon., *Colloques ou dialogues avec un dictionaire en six langues* (Geneva, 1622).

Anon., *Colloquia et dictionariolum octo linguarum; Latinæ, Gallicæ, Belgicæ, Teutonicæ, Hispanicæ, Italicæ, Anglicæ, et Portugallicæ* (Amsterdam, 1623).

Anon., *Colloques ou dialogues avec un dictionaire en six langues* (Amsterdam, 1624).

Anon., *Le dictionnaire des six langages. C'est à sçavoir Latin, Flamen, François, Espagnol, Italien, & Anglois* (Rouen, 1625).

Anon., *Colloquia, et dictionariolum octo linguarum; Latinæ, Gallicæ, Belgicæ, Teutonicæ, Hispanicæ, Italicæ, Anglicæ, et Portugallicæ* (Venice, 1627).

Anon., *Colloquia et dictionariolum octo linguarum, Latinæ, Gallicæ, Belgicæ, Teutonicæ, Hispanicæ, Italicæ, Anglicæ, et Portugallicæ* (Antwerp, 1630).

Anon., *Colloquia et dictionariolum octo linguarum, Latinæ, Gallicæ, Belgicæ, Teutonicæ, Hispanicæ, Italicæ, Anglicæ, et Portugallicæ* (Delft, 1631).

Anon., *Colloquia et dictionariolum octo linguarum, Latinæ, Gallicæ, Belgicæ, Teutonicæ, Hispanicæ, Italicæ, Anglicæ, et Portugallicæ* (Amsterdam, 1631).

Anon., *Colloquia et dictionariolum octo linguarum; Latinæ, Gallicæ, Belgicæ, Teutonicæ, Hispanicæ, Italicæ, Anglice, et Portugallicæ* (Middelburg, 1631).

Comenius, Jan Amos, *Porta Linguarum Trilinguis reserata et aperta. The Gate of Tongues unlocked or opened* (London, 1631).

Comenius, Jan Amos, *Porta linguarum trilinguis reserata et aperta. The gate of tongues unlocked and opened* (London, 1633).

de Grave, Jean, *The path-vvay to the gate of tongues: being, the first instruction for little children. With a short manner to conjugue the French verbes* (Oxford, 1633).

Anon., *Colloquia . . . sex linguarum* (Geneva, 1634).

Anon., *Le dictionnaire des six langages. C'est à sçavoir Latin. Flamen, François, Espagnol, Italien, & Anglois* (Paris, 1634).

Anon., *Le dictionnaire des six langages. C'est à sçavoir, Latin, Flamen, François, Espagnol, Italien & Anglois* (Rouen, 1636).

Anon., *The English, Latine, French, Dutch, Schole-master. Or, An introduction to teach young gentlemen and merchants to travell or trade. Being the onely helpe to attaine to those languages. Printed in the Netherlands 25 times; and this being the first edition in London.* (London, 1637).

Comenius, Jan Amos, *Porta linguarum, trilinguis reserata & aperta, sive Seminarium linguarum & scientiarum omnium* (London, 1637).

Anon., *New Dialogues or Colloquies and a little Dictionary of eight Languages. A Booke very necessary for all those that sutdy these tongues either at home or abroad, now perfected and made fit for travellers, young merchants and seamen, especially those that desire to attain to the use of the tongues* (London, 1639).

Comenius, Jan Amos, *Porta linguarum, trilinguis reserata & aperta. Gate of tongues unlocked and opened* (London, 1639).

Comenius, Jan Amos, *Porta linguarum trilinguis reserata & aperta* (London, 1640).

Anon., *Dictionariolum et colloquia octo linguarum, Latinæ, Gallicæ, Belgicæ, Teutonicæ, Hispanicæ, Italicæ, Anglicæ, et Portugallicæ* (Antwerp, 1662).

Anon., *Colloquia, et dictionariolum octo linguarum, Latinæ, Gallicæ, Belgicæ, Teutonicæ, Hispanicæ, Italicæ, Anglicæ, et Portugallicæ* (Venice, 1677).

Anon., *Colloquia, et dictionariolum octo linguarum, Latinæ, Gallicæ, Belgicæ, Teutonicæ, Hispanicæ, Italicæ, Anglicæ, & Portugallicæ* (Bologna, 1692).

Beyer, Guillaume, *Vraye instruction des trois langues la Francoise, l'Angloise, & la Flamende* (Dordrecht?, 1660).

Beyer, Guillaume, *La vraye Instruction des trois langues La Francoise, l'Angloise, & la Flamende. The right Instruction of three languages, French, English and Dutch. De rechte Onderwysinge van de Fransche, Engelsche en Nederduitsche Talen* (Dordrecht, 1661).

Colsoni, Francesco Casparo, *Il Nuovo Trismegiste, overo Il maestro di tre lingue dal quale l'Italiano, il Francese e l'Inglese, imparano vincedevolmente a discorrere Frà se stessi. The New Trismageister or the New Teacher of three Languages by whom an Italian, an English* and a French Gentelman, may Learn mutually to Discourse together each in their several Languages (London, 1688).

Du Grès, Gabriel, Dialogi Gallico-Anglico-Latini per Gabrielem Dugres linguam Gallicam in illustrissima, et famosissima, Oxoniensi Academia edocentem (Oxford, 1639).

Du Grès, Gabriel, Dialogi Gallico-Anglico-Latini per Gabrielem Dugres linguam Gallicam in illustrissima & famosissima Oxoniensi academia haud ita pridem privatim edocentem (Oxford, 1652).

Du Grès, Gabriel, Dialogi Gallico-Anglico-Latini. Per Gabrielem Dugres, linguæ Gallicæ in illustrissima & famosissima Oxoniensi Academia haud ita pridem privato munere præ-lectorem (Oxford, 1660).

Gonzaga, Luigi, The eloquent master of languages, that is a short but fundamental direction to the four principal languages, to witt: French, English, and Italien, High-Dutch. Which are so placed together that every one may see the difference in each, & so easily learn both to read, pronounce & understand them without much trouble. To which are added the Rodomontades, of the invincible Spanish captain Rodomond (Hamburg, 1693).

Ludovici, Christian, A dictionary English, German and French, containing not only the English words...but also their proper accent, phrases, figurative speeches, idioms, & proverbs, taken from the best new English dictionaries (Leipzig, 1706).

English-Dutch

Le Mayre, Marten, The Dutch Schoole Master. Wherein is shewed the true and perfect way to learne the Dutch tongue, to the fartherance of all those which would gladlie learne it. Collected by Marten le Mayre, professor of the said tongue, dwelling in Abchurch lane (London, 1606).

Anon., Den grooten Vocabulaer Engels ende Duyts. The Great Vocabuler, in English and Dutch: That is to say common speaches of all sorts, also Lettres and Obligations to write. With a Dictionarie and the Conjugation (Rotterdam, 1639).

Anon., Den grooten vocabulaer, Engels ende Duyts (Rotterdam, 1644).

Anon., The English Schole-Master or Certaine rules and helpes, whereby the natives of the Netherlandes, may bee, in a short time, taught to read, understand, and speake, the English tongue (Amsterdam, 1646).

Anon., The English schole-master (Amsterdam, 1658).

Anon., The Dutch-tutor: or, A new-book of Dutch and English. Containing plain and easie rules for the ready pronouncing, writing, speaking, and understanding the Dutch-tongue. Compiled for the benefit and furtherance of all that would easily and speedily learn the same (London, 1660).

Anon., The English schole-master (Amsterdam, 1663).

Hillenius, François, Den Engelschen ende Ne'erduitschen Onderrichter. The English, and Low Dutch Instructer, Disposed, in to Two Parts; The First, whereof containeth, Brief, and Necessary Rules, for the Instructing of the Dutch Tongue. The Second, Common dialogues, Communications, Discourses, Letters, and Sentences readily for to come thereby to the knowledge and liking of the same (Rotterdam, 1664).

Anon., The Dutch-tutor (London, 1669).

Hillenius, François, Den Engelschen ende Ne'erduitschen Onderricter. The English, and Low-dutch instructer (Rotterdam, 1671).

van Heldoren, Jan Gosens, A new and easy English grammar, containing brief fundamental rules, usual phrases pleasant and choise dialogues concerning the present state and court of England (Amsterdam, 1675).

Hillenius, François, Den Engelschen ende Ne'erduitschen Onderrichter (Rotterdam, 1677).

Richardson, Edward, *Anglo-Belgica. The English and Netherdutch Academy* (Amsterdam, 1677).

Hillenius, François, *Den Engelsen ende Ne'erduitschen onderrichter* (Rotterdam, 1678).

Richardson, Edward, *Anglo-Belgica* (Amsterdam, 1689).

van Heldoren, Jan Gosens, *Een nieuwe en gemakkelijke Engelsche spraak-konst/A new and easie English grammar* (London, 1690).

Richardson, Edward, *Anglo-Belgica* (Amsterdam, 1698).

Sewel, William, *A compendious guide to the Low Dutch language* (Amsterdam, 1700).

Sewel, William, *Korte Wegwyzer der Engelsche Taale. A Compendious Guide To the English Language* (Amsterdam, 1705).

Sewel, William, *A compendious guide to the Low-Dutch language* (Amsterdam, 1706).

English-French

Anon., *Here endeth this doctrine at Westmestre by london in fourmes enprinted. In the whiche one everich may shortly lerne. Frenssh and englissh* (London, 1480).

Anon., *Tres bonne doctrine pour aprendre briefment francoys et engloys* (London, 1483?).

Anon., *Here begynneth a lytell treatyse for to lerne Englysshe and Frensshe* (London, 1497).

Anon., *Here is a good boke to lerne to speke French* (London, 1500?).

Valence, Pierre, *Introductions in Frensshe, for Henry ye yonge erle of Lyncoln* (London, 1528?).

Palsgrave, John, *Lesclarcissement de la langue francoyse compose par maistre Iehan Palsgraue Angloyse natyf de Londres, et gradue de Paris* (London, 1530).

Anon., *A lytell treatyse for to lerne Englysshe and Frensshe* (Antwerp, 1530?).

Du Wés, Giles, *An introductorie for to lerne to rede, to pronounce, and to speake Frenche trewly, compiled for the right high, excellent, and most vertuous lady, the lady Mary of Englande, doughter to our most gracious soverayn lorde kyng Henry the eight* (London, 1533?).

Du Wés, Giles, *An introductorie for to lerne to rede, to pronounce, and to speake Frenche trewly, compyled for the ryghte hygh, excellent, & moste vertuous lady, the lady Mary of England, doughter to our moste gracious souerayne lorde kyng Henry the eyghte* (London, 1540?).

Du Wés, Giles, *An introductorie for to lerne to rede, to pronounce, and to speake Frenche trewly, compyled for the ryghte hygh, excellent, & moste vertuous lady, the lady Mary of Englande, doughter to our mooste gracious souerayne lorde kynge Henry the eight* (London, 1546?).

Du Wés, Giles, *An introductorie for to lerne to rede to pronounce, and to speke Frenche trewly* (London, 1546?).

Anon., *A Very necessarye boke both in Englyshce & in Frenche* (London, 1550?).

Du Ploiche, Pierre, *A treatise in English and Frenche right necessary and proffitable for al young children* (London, 1551).

Du Ploiche, Pierre, *A treatise in Englishe and Frenche righte necessarie and profitable for al yonge children (the contentes wherof appeare in a table in the ende of this booke) made by Peter du Ploiche teacher of the same, dwelling in Oxforde* (London, 1553).

Meurier, Gabriel, *Traicté pour apprendre a parler Françoys et Angloys* (Rouen, 1553).

Anon., *Lytell treatyse for to lerne Englysshe and Frensshe* (London, c.1553).

Meurier, Gabriel, *Communications familieres non moins propres que tres utiles à la nation Angloise desireuse & diseteuse du langage François par Gabriel Meurier/Familiare communications no lease proppre then verrie proffytable to the Inglishe nation desirous and nedinge the Ffrenche language* (Antwerp, 1563).

Hollyband, Claudius, *The French schoolemaister, wherin is most plainlie shewed, the true and most perfect way of pronouncinge of the Frenche tongue, without any helpe of maister or teacher: set foorthe for the furtherance of all those whiche doo studie privatly in their owne study or houses: unto the which is annexed a vocabularie for al such woordes as bee used in common talkes: by M. Claudius Hollybande, professor of the Latin, Frenche, and Englishe tongues* (London, 1573).

Anon., *A plaine pathway to the French Tongue, very profitable for Marchants and also all other which desire the same, aptly divided into nineteen chapters* (London, 1575).

Hollyband, Claudius, *The Frenche Littelton. A most easie, perfect, and absolute way to learne the frenche tongue: newly set forth by Claudius Holliband, teaching in Paules Churchyarde by the signe of the Lucrece* (London, 1576).

Du Ploiche, Pierre, *A treatise in Englishe and Frenche, right necesarie, and profitable for all young children (the contentes whereof appeare in a table in the ende of this booke) made by Peter du Ploiche, teacher of the same: and newly reuised by the saied authour, and the ortographie corrected, as it must bee pronounced* (London, 1578).

Hollyband, Claudius, *The French Littelton. A most easie, perfect and absolute way to learne the frenche tongue: newly set forth by Claudius Holliband, teaching in Paules Churchyarde by the signe of the Lucrece* (London, 1578).

Hollyband, Claudius, *The Frenche Littelton. A most easie, perfect, and absolute way to learne the frenche tongue: newly set forth by Claudius Hollyband, teaching in Paules Church-yarde by the signe of the Lucrece. Let the reader peruse the epistle to his owne instruction* (London, 1579).

Anon., *A plaine pathwaie to the French tongue: verie profitable for merchants, and also all other which desire the same* (London, 1580?).

Bellot, Jacques, *Le maistre d'escole Anglois. Contenant plusieurs profitables preceptes pour les naturelz francois, et autres estrangers qui ont la langue francoise pour paruenir a la vraye prononciation de la langue Angloise. The Englishe Scholemaister. Conteyning many profitable preceptes for the naturall borne french men, and other straungers that haue their French tongue, to attayne the true pronouncing of the Englishe tongue* (London, 1580).

Hollyband, Claudius, *The Frenche Littelton* (London, 1581).

Hollyband, Claudius, *The Frenche schoolemaister of Claudius Hollyband: newly corrected. Wherein is most playnely shewed, the true and most perfect way of pronouncing of the Frenche tongue, to the furtherance of all those which doo studye privately in their owne study or houses* (London, 1582).

Hollyband, Claudius, *The Frenche Littelton: a most easie, perfect, and absolute way to learne the Frenche tongue* (London, 1583).

Bellot, Jacques, *Familiar Dialogues, for the instruction of them, that be desirous to learne to speake English, and perfectlye to pronounce the same* (London, 1586).

Hollyband, Claudius, *The French Littelton* (London, 1591).

de la Mothe, G. [G.D.L.M.N], *The French alphabeth teaching in a very short tyme, by a most easie way, to pronounce French naturally, to reade it perfectly, to write it truely, and to speake it accordingly* (London, 1592).

Eliot, John, *Ortho-epia Gallica. Eliots fruits for the French: enterlaced with a double new invention, which teacheth to speake truely, speedily and volubly the French-tongue* (London, 1593).

Hollyband, Claudius, *The French Littelton* (London, 1593).

de la Mothe, G. [G.D.L.M.N]., *The French alphabet* (London, 1595).

Hollyband, Claudius, *The French schoolmaster* (London, 1596).

Hollyband, Claudius, *The French Littelton* (London, 1597).

Hollyband, Claudius, *The French Littelton* (London, 1602).

Hollyband, Claudius, *The French schoole-master wherein is most plainly shewed the true and perfect way of pronouncing the French tongue, to the furtherance of all those which would gladly learne it first collected by C.H.; and now newly corrected and amended by M.R.F.* (London, 1602).

Erondell, Peter, *The French Garden: for English Ladyes and Gentlewomen to Walke in* (London, 1605).

Hollyband, Claudius, and Pierre Erondell, *The French schoole-maister wherein is most plainely shewed the true and perfect way of pronouncing the French tongue, to the furtherance of all those which would gladly learne it first collected by Mr. C.H.; and now newly corrected and amended by P. Erondelle* (London, 1606).

Hollyband, Claudius, *The French Littelton* (London, 1609).

Hollyband, Claudius, and Pierre Erondell. *French schoole-maister* (London, 1609).

Hollyband, Claudius, and Pierre Erondell, *The French schoole-maister* (London, 1612).

de la Mothe, G. [G.D.L.M.N], *The French alphabet* (London, 1615).

Hollyband, Claudius, and Pierre Erondell, *The French schoole-maister* (London, 1615).

Hollyband, Claudius, *The French Littelton* (London, 1616).

Hollyband, Claudius, and Peter Erondell, *The French schoolemaister* (London, 1619).

Erondell, Pierre, *The French Garden... Newly corrected and augmented with necessary rules, by the author Peter Erondell, professor of the same language: and John Fabre his adjoint* (London, 1621).

Anon., *Grammaire Angloise. Contenant reigles bien exactes. Fr. a. Eng.* (London, 1622).

Bellot, Jacques, *Familiar Dialogues* (London, 1622).

Hollyband, Claudius, and Peter Erondell, *The French schoole-maister* (London, 1623).

Wodroephe, John, *The spared houres of a souldier in his travels. Or The true marrowe of the French tongue, where in is truely treated (by ordre) the nine parts of speech: Together, with two rare, and excellent bookes of dialogues* (Dordrecht, 1623).

Anon., *Grammaire angloise. Pour facilement et promptement apprendre la langue angloise. Qui peut aussi aider aux anglois pour apprendre la langue françoise.* (Paris, 1625).

Hollyband, Claudius, *The French Littelton* (London, 1625).

Wodroephe, John, *The marrow of the French tongue* (London, 1625).

Sherwood, Robert, *The French Tutour* (London, 1625).

Hollyband, Claudius, *The French Littelton* (London, 1626).

Hollyband, Claudius, and James Giffard, *The French schoole-maister. Wherein is most plainely shewed the true and perfect way of pronouncing the French tongue, to the furtherance of all those which would gladly learne it. First collected by Mr. C. H. and now newly corrected and amended by Iames Giffard, professor of the sayd tongue* (London, 1628).

Hollyband, Claudius, *The French Littelton* (London, 1630).

de la Mothe, G. [G.D.L.M.N.], *The French alphabet* (London, 1631).

Hollyband, Claudius, and James Giffard, *The French schoole maister* (London, 1631).

Hollyband, Claudius, *The French schoole maister. Wherin is most plainely shewed the true and perfect way of pronouncing the French tongue, to the furtherance of all those which would gladly learne it. First collected by Mr. C.H. and since often corrected by divers professors of the sayd tongue* (London, 1632).

de la Mothe, G. [G.D.L.M.N.], *The French alphabet* (London, 1633).

Mason, George, *Grammaire angloise contenant certaines reigles bien exactes pour la pro-nonciation, orthographie, & construction de nostre langue: en faveur des estrangers qui en sont desireux par George Mason, marchand de Londres* (London, 1633).

Sherwood, Robert, *The French Tutour* (London, 1634).

Cougneau, Paul, *A sure guide to the French tongue, teaching by a most easie way, to pronounce the French naturally, to read it perfectly, to write it truly, and to speake it readily. Together with the verbes personall and impersonall, and usefull sentences added to everyone of them, most profitable for all sorts of people to learne. Painfully gathered, and set in order after the alphabeticall way, for the better benefit of those that are desirous to learne the French* (London, 1635).

Hollyband, Claudius, and James Giffard, *The French schoole-master* (London, 1636).

Anon., *Grammere angloise* (Rouen, 1639).

de la Mothe, G. [G.D.L.M.N.], *The French alphabet* (London, 1639).

Hollyband, Claudius, and James Giffard, *The French schoole-master* (London, 1641).

Meurier, Gabriel, *Communications familieres* (Rouen, 1641).

Gostlin, Edward, *Aurifodina linguæ Gallicæ or The gold mine of the French language opened. In a more accurate method, and more exact and certaine rules, and more complying with the most common capacity, then hitherto have ever beene printed in any tongue. By Edmund Gostlin, gent.* (London, 1646).

de la Mothe, G. [G.D.L.M.N.], *The French alphabet* (London, 1647).

Hollyband, Claudius, and James Giffard, *The French schoole-master* (London, 1649).

Cougneau, Paul, *A sure guide to the French tongue* (London, 1651).

Mauger, Claude, *The true advancement of the French tongue. Or a new method, and more easie directions for the attaining of it, then ever yet have been published. Whereunto are added many choise and select dialogues, containing not onely familiar discourses, but most exact instructions for travell, in a most elegant stile and phrase, very useful and necessary for all gentlemen that intend to travell into France. Also a chapter of Anglicismes, wherein those errors which the English usually commit in speaking French, are demonstrated, and corrected* (London, 1653).

Hollyband, Claudius, and James Giffard, *The French schoole-master* (London, 1655).

Lainé, Pierre de, *A compendious introduction to the French tongue ... Illustrated by several elegant expressions, and choice dialogues, useful for persons of quality that intend to travel into France, leading them, as by the hand, to the most noted and principal places of that kingdom* (London, 1655).

Mauger, Claude, *Mr. Mauger's French grammar enriched with severall choise dialogues, containing an exact account of the state of France, ecclesiasticall, civil, and military, as it flourisheth at present under King Louis the fourteenth. Also a chapter of Anglicismes; vvith instructions for travellers into France* (London, 1656).

Cougneau, Paul, *A sure guide to the French tongue* (London, 1658).

Mauger, Claude, *Claudius Maugers French grammar* (London, 1658).

Herbert, William, *Herberts French and English dialogues. In a more exact and delightful method than any yet extant* (London, 1660).

Hollyband, Claudius, and James Giffard, *The French schoolemaster* (London, 1660).

Mauger, Claude, *Claudius Mauger's French grammar* (London, 1662).

Festeau, Paul, *A new and easie French grammar, or, A compendious way how to read, speak, and write French exactly very necessary for all persons whatsoever: with variety of dialogues, whereunto is added a nomenclature English and French* (London, 1667).

Lainé, Pierre de, *The princely way to the French tongue: as it was first compiled for the use of Her Highness, the Lady Mary, and since taught her royal sister, the Lady Anne: to which is added a chronological abridgment of the Sacred Scripture by way of dialogue: together with a larger explication of the French grammar, choice fables of Æsop in burlesque French, and lastly some models of letters French and English by P.D.L., Tutor for the French to both Their Highnesses* (London, 1667).

Mauger, Claude, *Claudius Mauger's French grammar* (London, 1667).

Hollyband, Claudius, and James Giffard, *The French school-master* (London, 1668).

Anon., *Grammaire angloise, et françoise* (Rouen, 1670).

Mauger, Claude, *Claudius Mauger's French grammar* (London, 1670).

Festeau, Paul, *Paul Festeau's French grammar* (London, 1671).

Festeau, Paul, *Nouvelle grammaire angloise, enrichie de dialogues curieux touchant l'estat, et la cour d'Angleterre, et d'une nomenclature. angloise et francoise* (London, 1672).

Mauger, Claude, *Claudius Mauger's French grammar* (London, 1673).

Anon., *Grammaire angloise, et françoise* (Rouen, 1674).

Festeau, Paul, *Nouvelle grammaire Angloise* (London, 1675).

Festeau, Paul, *Paul Festeau's French grammar* (London, 1675).

d'Abbadie, J. G., *Nouvelle grammaire françoise contenant au long les principes de la langue, ou, les regles exactes, les observations critiques, & les exemples convenables, pour montrer & pour âprendre methodiquement le françois, tel que les esprits, ou messieurs de l'Academie françoise, le parlent & le prononcent aujourd'huy, composée pour l'usage de messieurs les anglois par J. G. d'Abadie Ec.* (Oxford, 1676).

Mauger, Claude, *Claudius Mauger's French grammar* (London, 1676).

Miège, Guy, *A new French grammar, or, A new method for learning of the French tongue: to which are added, for a help to young beginners, a large vocabulary and a store of familiar dialogues. Besides four curious discourses of cosmography, in French, for proficient learners to turn into English. By Guy Miege, author of the New French dictionary, professor of the French tongue, and of geography.* (London, 1678).

Festeau, Paul, *Nouvelle grammaire francoise* (London, 1679).

Mauger, Claude, *Claudius Mauger's French grammar* (London, 1679).

Mauger, Claude, *Claudius Mauger's French grammar* (London, 1682).

Vairasse d'Allais, Denys, *A short and methodical introduction to the French tongue. Composed for the particular use and benefit of the English, by D. V. d'Allais a teacher of the French, and English tongues in Paris* (Paris, 1683).

Mauger, Claude, *Claudius Mauger's French grammar* (London, 1684).

Vairasse, Denis, *A short and methodical introduction to the French tongue* (Paris, 1684).

Festeau, Paul, *Nouvelle grammaire françoise* (London, 1685).

Miège, Guy, *Nouvelle methode pour apprendre l'anglois. Avec une nomenclature, francoise & angloise; un recueil d'expressions familieres; et des dialogues, familiers, & choisis* (London, 1685).

Mauger, Claude, *Claudius Mauger's French grammar* (London, 1686).

Miège, Guy, *The grounds of the French tongue, or, A new French grammar: according to the present use, and modern orthography, digested into a short, easy, and accurate method: with a vocabulary, and dialogues* (London, 1687).

Berault, Peter, *A new, plain, short, and compleat French and English grammar: whereby the learner may attain in few months to speak and write French correctly, as they do now in the court of France. And wherein all that is dark, superfluous, and deficient in other grammars, is plain, short, and methodically supplied. Also very useful to strangers, that are desirous to learn the English tongue: for whose sake is added a short, but very exact English grammar* (London, 1688).

Mauger, Claude, *Claudius Mauger's French grammar* (London, 1688).

Mauger, Claude, *Claudius Mauger's French grammar* (London, 1689).

Mauger, Claude, *Grammaire angloise de Claude Mauger succincte & methodique, expliquée en françois pour l'utilité de ceux qui souhaitent d'apprendre cette langue. Où l'on voit un bon ordre & de bonnes raisons pour tout ce qu'elle contient, sans revoyer à l'usage. Exactement corrigée par l'auteur professeur des langues à Paris, & presentement à Londres* (London, 1689).

Mauger, Claude, and Paul Festeau, *New Double Grammar French-English And English-French By M. Claudius Mauger And Mr. Paul Festeau, Professors of these Languages* (Leiden, 1690).

Pujolas, Jean, *The key of the French tongue; or, A new method for learning it well, easily, in short time and almost without a master* (Glasgow, 1690).

Berault, Peter, *New, plain, short, and compleat French and English grammar* (London, 1691).

Berault, Peter, *A new, plain, short, and compleat French and English grammar* (London, 1693).

Festeau, Paul, *Paul Festeau's French grammar* (London, 1693).

Mauger, Claude, *Claudius Mauger's French grammar* (London, 1693).

Mauger, Claude, and Paul Festeau, *Nouvelle double grammmaire francoise-angloise et angloise-francoise par Messrs. Claude Mauger et Paul Festeau* (The Hague, 1693).

Boyer, Abel, *The compleat French-master, for ladies and gentlemen. Being a new method, to learn with ease and delight the French tongue, as it is now spoken in the court of France* (London, 1694).

Mauger, Claude, *Claudius Mauger's French grammar* (London, 1694).

Mauger, Claude, *Claudius Mauger's French grammar* (London, 1696).

Mauger, Claude, and Paul Festeau, *Nouvelle double grammaire francoise-angloise et angloise-francoise* (Brussels, 1696).

Mauger, Claude, *Claudius Mauger's French grammar* (London, 1698).

Miège, Guy, *Méthode Abbregée pour apprendre l'anglois avec une nomenclature & un corps de dialogues un recueil de plaisans contes, & bons mots, de lettres galantes, & caracteres bien tournez par le sieur Guy Miege auteur du dictionaire anglois* (London, 1698).

Miège, Guy, *Miege's last and best French grammar: or, a new method to learn French. Containing the quintessence of all other grammars; with such plain and easy rules, as will make one speedily perfect in that famous language* (London, 1698).

Boyer, Abel, *The compleat French-master* (London, 1699).

Colsoni, François, *The English ladies new French grammar, fitted to the meanest capacity; enrich'd with new words, a new method, and all the improvements of that famous language, as it is now spoken at the court of France, and new dialogues. To which is added, the golden key of the English tongue, very useful and fit for foreigners. As also, the chronological history of the kings of England, since William the Conqueror, to the present King William III* (London, 1699).

Mauger, Claude, *Grammaire angloise, expliquée par regles generales* ('London' [France], 1699).

Berault, Peter, *A new, plain, short, and compleat French and English grammar* (London, 1700).

Festeau, Paul, *Nouvelle grammaire francoise* (London, 1701).

Roussier, Abraham, *A new and compendious French grammar: wherein all the rules necessary for the attaining of that language are comprised in a shorter and more exact method than in any other* (Oxford, 1701).

Mauger, Claude, *Claudius Mauger's French grammar* (London, 1702).

Boyer, Abel, *The compleat French-master* (London, 1703).

Mauger, Claude, and Paul Festeau, *Nouvelle double grammaire francoise-angloise et angloise-francoise* (The Hague, 1703).

Mauger, Claude, *Claudius Mauger's French grammar* (London, 1705).

Boyer, Abel, *The compleat French-Master* (London, 1706).

Berault, Peter, *Nouvelle & complete grammaire françoise & angloise* (London, 1706).

Miège, Guy, *Miege's last and best French grammar* (London, 1706) .

Berault, Peter, *A New and Compleat French and English Grammar* (London, 1707).

Bérault, Peter, *Nouvelle & complete grammaire françoise & angloise* (London, 1708).

Mauger, Claude, *Claudius Mauger's French grammar with additions* (London, 1708).

Boyer, Abel, *The compleat French-Master* (London, 1710).

Mauger, Claude, *Grammaire angloise, expliquée par regles generales* (Rouen, 1712).

Anon., *Certain phrases, or idioms, of the French tongue. Collected for the use of Mr. Caverley's school* (London, 1713).

Boyer, Abel, *The compleat French-master* (London, 1714).

Mauger, Claude, *Claudius Mauger's French grammar* (London, 1714).

Mauger, Claude, *Nouvelle grammaire angloise* (Bordeaux, 1714).

English-German

Aedler, Martin, *The high Dutch Minerva a-la-mode* (London, 1680).

Aedler, Martin, *Minerva. The High-Dutch grammer, teaching the English-man perfectly, easily and exactly the neatest dialect of the High-German language* (London, 1685).

Offelen, Heinrich, *A double grammar for Germans to learn English, and for English-men to learn the German-tongue* (London, 1687).

Scheibner, Johann David, *Upright Guide for the Instruction of the English Tongue* (London, 1688).

F.K., *A little grammar, or short guide to learn the Englisch tongue. Kleine Grammatica, oder Kurtzer Wegweiser* (Hamburg, 1699).

F.K., *A little grammar, or Short guide to learn the Englisch tongue together with some few selected dialogues, and a mean alphabeticall, nomenclator, out of joyned morning and evening prayers. Kleine Grammatica, oder kurtzer Wegweiser, zur Erlernung der englischen Sprache, sampt wenigen auserlesenen Gesprachen, und ein klein alphabetisch Nomenclator, aus hinten angefügten Morgen- und Abend-Gebeten* (Hamburg, 1699).

Ludwig/Ludovico, Christian, *Choice English and High-Dutch Dialogues and Letters, together with a Vocabulary. Auserlesene englische und deutsche Gespräche* (Leipzig, 1705).

König, Johann/John King, *A compleat English guide for High-Germans/Ein volkommener Englischer Wegweiser für Hoch-Teutsche* (London, 1706).

Anon., *A short and easy way for the Palatines to learn English. Oder eine kurze Anleitung zur englischen Sprach, zum Nutz der armen Pfälzer* (London, 1710).

König, Johann/John King, *A royal compleat grammar, English and High-German. Das ist: eine Königliche vollkommene Grammatica* (London, 1715).

König, Johann/John King, *Der vollkommene englische Weg-weiser für die Teutschen/The compleat English guide for the Germans* (Leipzig, 1715).

English-Italian

Hollyband, Claudius, *The pretie and wittie historie of Arnalt & Lucenda: with certen rules and dialogues set foorth for the learner of th'Italian tong: and dedicated vnto the Worshipfull, Sir Hierom Bowes Knight* (London, 1575).

Florio, John, *Florio His firste Fruites which yeelde familiar speech, merie Prouerbes, wittie Sentences, and golden sayings. Also a perfect Induction to the Italian, and English tongues,* as in the Table appeareth. The like heretofore, neuer by any man published (London, 1578).

Florio, John, *Florios second frutes, to be gathered of twelue trees, of diuers but delightsome tastes to the tongues of Italians and Englishmen. To which is annexed his Gardine of recreation yeelding six thousand Italian prouerbs* (London, 1591).

Hollyband, Claudius, *The Italian schoole-maister: contayning rules for the perfect pronouncing of th'italian tongue: with familiar speeches: and certaine phrases taken out of the best Italian authors. And a fine Tuscan historie called Arnalt & Lucenda. A verie easie way to learne th'italian tongue. Set forth by Clau: Holliband. Gentl. of Bourbonnois* (London, 1597).

Hollyband, Claudius, *The Italian schoole-maister: contayning rules for the perfect pronouncing of th'italian tongue: with familiar speeches: and certaine phrases taken out of the best Italian authors. With a historie called Arnalt and Lucenda. Set forth by Clau: Hollyband Gent: and now reuised and corrected by F.P. an Italian, professor and teacher of the Italian tongue* (London, 1608).

Italiano, Benvenuto, *Il Passaggiere. The Passenger: Of Benvenuto Italian, Professour of his Natiue Tongue, for these nine yeeres in london. Diuided into two Parts, Containing seauen exquisite Dialogues in Italian and English* (London, 1612).

Torriano, Giovanni, *The Italian Tutor, or a new and most compleat Italian Grammer. Containing above others a most compendious way to learne the Verbs, and rules of Syntax. To which is annexed a display of the monasillable particles of the Language, with the English to them* (London, 1640).

Paravicino, Pietro, *Choice phrases in Italian rendred into English; wherein all the chief difficulties about the particles, in the said language, are made easie by example; each line being a sentence, to the end that the learner may the better retain them in his memory. To which are added, al the most usual Italian proverbs. Lately published by Peter Paravicino, master of the Italian tongue, and approved of by two other masters of the said tongue, to be a work very useful, not only for those who begin to learn; but also those who desire to attain to the perfection thereof* (London, 1656).

Torriano, Giovanni, *Della Lingua Toscana-Romana. Or, an Introduction to the Italian Tongue. Containing Such grounds as are most immediately useful, and necessary for the speedy and easie attaining of the same. As also A new Store House of proper and choice Dialogues Most Useful for such as desire the speaking part, and intend to travel into Italy, or the Levant. Together with The Modern way of addressing Letters, and stiling of persons, as well in actual Discourse, as in Writing* (London, 1657).

Paravicino, Pietro, *A short and safe guide to lead all such scholars as are lovers of the Italian tongue, to the gaining thereof, wherein is contained a short dialogue to incite them to be diligent, and willing to profit themselves by it, and immediately follow rules of pronunciation, as also the principall grounds of the said tongue, with the greatest brevity possible, to the end I may fit my self to the genius and disposition of those that learn of me. It is fitting every one do prepare such tools as are useful for his trade, which are here furnished by Peter Paravicino master oF the italian tongue, for the benefit and use of his scholars* (London, 1658).

Paravicino, Pietro, *The true idioma of the Italian tongue wherein is contained many choice sentences and dialogues in Italian and English. Also, delightful dialects and apophthegms taken out of a famous author: and other necessary things mentioned in the table. Very pleasant and profitable for the lover of the Italian tong[ue.] Never printed before. Published by P.P. an Italian, and teacher of the Italian tongue, dwelling in the Old-Jury, at the Wind-mill* (London, 1660).

Paravicino, Pietro, *Choice phrases, set forth in questions and answers in Italian, rendered into English; wherein all the chief difficulties about the particles, in the said language, are made easie by examples; each line being a sentence, to the end that the learner may the better retain the in his memory: to which are added in this second impression, many other choice phrases, short dialogues; and a pretty discourse of commerce: he that shall read this little book twice may easily understand any Italian author in prose. Lately published and well corrected by P.P. Master of the Italia tongue, and approved of by other masters of the said tongue, to be a work very useful, not only for those who begin to learn; but also for those who desire to attain to the perfection thereof; the only way to learn a language is to learn it in its proper phrases.* (London, 1662).

Paravicino, Pietro, *True idioma of the Italian tongue/Choice proverbs and dialogues, in Italian and English* (London, 1666).

Torriano, Giovanni, *Piazza universale di proverbi Italiani: or, A common place of Italian proverbs and proverbial phrases. Digested in alphabetical order by way of dictionary. Interpreted, and occasionally illustrated with notes. Together with a supplement of Italian dialogues. Composed by Gio: Torriano, an Italian, and professor of that tongue* (London, 1666).

Torriano, Giovanni, *The Italian reviv'd: or, The introduction to the Italian tongue. Containing such grounds as are most immediately useful, and necessary for the speedy and easie attaining of the same. As also a new store-house of proper and choice dialogues, most useful for such as desire the speaking part, and intend to travel into Italy, or the Levant. Together with the modern way of addressing letters, and stiling of persons, as well in actual discourse, as in writing. With alterations and additions. By Gio. Torriano, an Italian, and professor of the Italian tongue, &c. in London* (London, 1673).

Torriano, Giovanni, *Mescolanza dolce di varie historiette, favole morali & politiche, facetie, motti & burle di diversi scrittori Italiani; raccolta & cappata per uso, commodità & ricreatione, della Gioventù Inglese, in particolare de' Gioveni di Banco, dell Honoratissima compagnia di turchia in Londra, vaghi di lingua Italiana. Da Gio. Torriano. Mastro de lingue. Con gionta di dialoghi novi, non più stampati, & tradotti in lingua Inglese dal medesimo* (London, 1688).

Torriano, Giovanni, *The Italian reviv'd: or, The introduction to the Italian tongue. Containing such grounds as are most immediately useful and necessary for the speedy and easie attaining of the same. As also a new store-house of proper and choice dialogues, most useful for such as desire the speaking part, and intend to travel into Italy, or the Levant. Together with the modern way of addressing letters and styling of persons, as well in actual discourse as in writing. With alterations and additions. By Gio. Torriano, an Italian, and professor of the Italian tongue, &c. in London.* (London, 1689).

Pleunus, Arrigo/Plenus, Henry, *Nuova, e perfetta grammatica inglese* (Livorno, 1701).

Pleunus, Arrigo/Plenus, Henry, *A new, plain, methodical and compleat Italian grammar vvhereby you may very soon attain to the perfection of the Italian Tongue, dedicated Alphabetically to the worthy English gentlemen, merchants at Legorne Viz to Mr. Cristopher Michel. M. Daniel Gould. M. Edvvard Nelthorpe. M. Fisher Jackson. M. Francis Arundel. M. George Colling. S.r George Davies Bar.t M. George Lambe. M. George Rivers. M. Gilbert Serle. M. Humphry Chetham. Mr. James Harriman. M. James Paitfield. M. John Horsey. M. Jonathan Basket. M. Richard Frome. M. Samuel Lambert. M. Samuel Thorold. M. Thomas Balle. Thomas Châberlayne Esquire. M. Thomas Dorman. M. Vvilliam Bury. By Henry Pleunus Master of the Latin, French, Italian, German, and English Tongue* (Livorno, 1702).

Casotti, Laurentio, *A new method of teaching the Italian tongue to ladies and gentlemen. Wherein all the difficulties are explain'd in such a manner, that every one, by it, may attain the Italian tongue to perfection* (London, 1709).

Pleunus, Arrigo/Plenus, Henry, *A new, plan, methodical and compleat Italian grammar* (Livorno 1710).

Rossi, Giacomo/Jacques, *Le maitre aisé & rejouissant; Ou nouvelle methode agreable pour apprendre sans peine la langue italienne. Divisée en deux parties. La premiere contient des regles faciles, & à chaque regle des phrases sur toutes fortes de sujets familiers. La seconde contient des dialogues de complimens & d' Amour: des dialogues familiers & burlesques: des lettres d' Amour avec leurs reflexions: des contes divertissans: des proverbes: & de la poesie italienne claire & facile. Dedie'e a son excellence monseigneur le Comte de Berkeley, Vicomte de Dursley, Baron du Chateau de Berkeley, & du Conseil Privé de S Majeste, &c. &c. Par Jacques Rossi, Maitre Langue Italienne.* (London, 1710).

English-Spanish

Anon., *The boke of Englysshe, and Spanysshe* (London, 1554).

Anon., *A very profitable boke to lerne the maner of redyng, writyng, & speakyng English & Spanish. Libro muy pronechoso para saber la manera de leer, y screuir, y hablar Angleis, y Espanol* (London, 1554).

Stepney, William, *The Spanish schoole-master* (London, 1591).

Perceval, Richard, and John Minsheu, *A Spanish grammar, first collected and published by Richard Percivale Gent. Now augmented and increased with the declining of all the irregular and hard verbes in that toong, with diuers other especiall rules and necessarie notes for all such as shall be desirous to attaine the perfection of the Spanish tongue. Done by Iohn Minsheu professor of languages in London* (London, 1599).

Stepney, William, *The Spanish schoole-maister* (London, 1619).

Stepney, William, *The Spanish schoole-maister* (London, 1620).

Oudin, César, *A grammar Spanish and English: or A briefe and compendious method, teaching to reade, write, speake, and pronounce the Spanish tongue. Composed in French by Cæsar Oudin, and by him the third time corrected and augmented. Englished, and of many wants supplied, by I.W. Who hath also translated out of Spanish the fiue dialogues of Iuan de Luna, Cast. which are annexed to the grammar* (London, 1622).

Luna, Juan de la, *A short and compendious art for to learne to reade, write, pronounce and speake the Spanish tongue. Composed by Iohn de Luna of Castile, interpreter of the Spanish tongue in London. Arte breve, y conpendiossa para aprender a leer, escreuir, pronunciar, y hablar la lengua Española* (London, 1623).

Perceval, Richard, and John Minsheu, *A dictionary in Spanish and English: first published into the English tongue by Ric. Percivale Gent.* (London, 1623).

James Howell, *A new English grammar, prescribing as certain rules as the language will bear, for forreners to learn English: ther is also another grammar of the Spanish or Castilian toung, with som special remarks upon the Portugues dialect, &c. Whereunto is annexed a discourse or dialog containing a perambulation of Spain and Portugall, which may serve for a direction how to travell through both countreys, &c.* (London, 1662).

Stevens, John, *A new Spanish and English dictionary* (London, 1706).

Index

Huguenots, *see* immigrants
Hüllen, Werner 97, 103–4
humanism 18–19, 80, 90–2, 161–2, 192,
    196–8
Hymes, Dell 7–8

immigrants 8–9, 72–3
    assimilation 12, 104–5, 113–14, 141,
        153, 208
    as language-learners 1–2, 12, 83–5, 104–5,
        113, 141
    as teachers 1–2, 14–16, 19–20, 30, 34–5, 37,
        53–4, 63–5, 72–3, 141
    language of 2–3, 141
India 24–5
inkhorn debate, *see* language debates
inns of court 80
inns, *see* alehouses
insult 114–15, 134, 158–9, 182
integration, *see* assimilation
intelligencers, *see* spying
interpreters 2–3, 9–11, 75–6, 200–1
Interregnum 63–5, 71–2, 79, 202–3
invisible educators 34–5
Irish 2–3, 76–7
Isabella of Castile 208–9
Islam 113
Istanbul 66–7
Italian 118
    in conversation manuals 5–6, 56, 60–2,
        65–8, 72–3, 95, 108, 114–15, 130–1,
        141–3
    in English manuscripts 21–3, 66–7, 75–7,
        174–8, 187–8
    pronunciation and accent 83–5, 88
    spoken in England 2–3, 23–4, 31n.78, 40–1,
        65–6
    taught in England 14–16, 18–21, 23–9,
        34–5, 40–3, 65–6, 75–6, 82–3, 90–2,
        161–2
    trading language 9–11, 40, 66–7, 108
    travellers encountering 1–2, 164–5, 174–8,
        193, 202, 209–10
    varieties of 165–8, 192n.160
Italianate Englishmen 199–200
Italiano, Benvenuto 108, 130
Italy 1–2, 51–2, 66–7, 79, 128–9, 165–8,
    174–8, 180–1, 187–90, 197, 201,
    204–6
Izmir 66–7

James VI and I 23–4, 118
jargon 101–2, 140
Jenner, Mark 36

Jesuits 170
jokes 5–6, 68–9, 122, 158–9, 178–81, 187–8
Judaism 113, 167

Kilvert, Margaret 31–6
Kinaston sisters (pupils at Margaret Kilvert's
    academy) 33–4
King, John, *see* König, Johann
King's College, Cambridge 21n.30
König, Johann 72–3
Kynaston, Francis 14–15
Kytö, Merja 58–9, 103–4

l'Amy, Hugh 14–15
La Rochelle 162–3
Lacy, John 35–6
Lainé, Pierre (de) 24–5
Lambley, Kathleen 3–5, 46–7
language debates 11
    in English 51–2
    in French 38n.104, 50n.160
    in German 52n.169
    inkhorn debate 8–9
    questione della lingua 165n.32
Languet, Hubert 164–5
Larminie, Vivienne 148
Lassels, Richard 128–9, 166, 180–1, 192–3, 204–5
Latin 8–11, 14–23, 26–9, 39–45, 51–4, 63–5,
    68n.47, 70–1, 76–7, 79, 81–2, 88–90, 93–7,
    115, 118, 120–1, 157, 160–1, 167, 172,
    177–8, 183–5
Lauder, John 169–70, 181–2, 192–3
Lawrence, Jason 82–3, 90–2, 93n.140, 116
le Doux, Catherin 16–18
le Mayre, Marten 26–7, 69–70, 77–8, 119–20,
    137–8, 142n.159
le Pruvost, Peter 14–15
Leeds 55–6
Leiden, as site for learning French 173
Leigh, Edward 160–1, 190–1, 199n.202
Leipzig 164–5, 173, 200–1
Lemon, Rebecca 131–2
Lentulo, Scipione 40–1, 65–6, 82–3, 101
letter-writing and language-learning 55–6,
    106–7, 127n.99, 141, 174–6, 180, 182,
    209–10
Levant Company 9–11, 40, 66–7, 103n.8
Lhuyd, Edward 169
licensing of teachers 44–5
Liège 167
'lingua toscana in bocca romana' 166
linguistic competence 30–1, 38, 46–8, 99–100,
    209, 211
    as a historical category 3–8, 12

Printed and bound by CPI Group (UK) Ltd, Croydon, CR0 4YY